# Maritime Cabotage Law

This is the most comprehensive review of maritime cabotage law. It introduces the new theory of developmental sovereignty to jurisprudence. The maritime cabotage law provisions and approaches as adopted in many states and jurisdictions have been extensively scrutinised. This book challenges the established and accepted wisdom surrounding maritime cabotage by presenting new reasoning on the underpinning principles of the concept of maritime cabotage law. The book offers a vibrant discussion on the adjustment in the regulatory approaches of maritime cabotage, from one that was intrinsically premised on the idea of national sovereignty to one that now embraces the broader ideology of development. It investigates what the common understanding of the law of maritime cabotage should be and on what intellectual basis it can be justified. It reduces the inconsistencies and confusion that surround the concept and application of maritime cabotage law, to provide a more certain and more robust concept of maritime cabotage.

**Dr Aniekan Akpan** is a lecturer in law at City, University of London. He is also a specialist maritime law consultant in the city of London and overseas.

# Maritime Cabotage Law

Aniekan Akpan

Routledge
Taylor & Francis Group

LONDON AND NEW YORK

First published 2019
by Routledge
2 Park Square, Milton Park, Abingdon, Oxon OX14 4RN

and by Routledge
605 Third Avenue, New York, NY 10017

First issued in paperback 2021

*Routledge is an imprint of the Taylor & Francis Group, an informa business*

*British Library Cataloguing in Publication Data*
A catalogue record for this book is available from the British Library

*Library of Congress Cataloging-in-Publication Data*
Names: Akpan, Aniekan, author.
Title: Maritime cabotage law / by Aniekan Akpan.
Description: New York, NY : Routlege, 2019. | Includes index.
Identifiers: LCCN 2018035396 | ISBN 9781138300668 (hbk)
Subjects: LCSH: Cabotage. | Maritime law. | Jurisdiction.
Classification: LCC K1155 .A47 2019 | DDC 343.09/6--dc23
LC record available at https://lccn.loc.gov/2018035396

Typeset in Galliard
by Taylor & Francis Books

ISBN 13: 978-1-03-224156-2 (pbk)
ISBN 13: 978-1-138-30066-8 (hbk)

DOI: 10.4324/9780203733240

This book is dedicated to my parents, Sylvester and Theresa; and my siblings: Mfonobong, Rosemary, Anthony, Helen and Regina.

# Contents

# Illustrations

**Figure**

**Tables**

# Preface

There is no gain in shying away from the fact that the law of maritime cabotage is confusing and complicated on many levels of jurisprudence. Maritime cabotage law is steeped in history and its reputation for being a complex subject matter even for the most sophisticated legal system is not without merit. The basis for this is the lack of certainty as to what can correctly be understood as falling within the context of maritime cabotage law. Furthermore, the concept of state sovereignty under international law means that the three primary approaches in which maritime cabotage law applies, vary uncontrollably from one jurisdiction to another. Therefore, it is not disingenuous to posit that the lack of a common understanding of the concept of maritime cabotage law has facilitated its use as a 'special purpose vehicle' to advance alleged national interests even if that requires disregarding the rule of law.

Nevertheless, all of these should not prevent us from attempting to distil some of the complexities that surround the subject into a manageable scholarly work that is less daunting to comprehend. It is in considering this that this book sets out to unravel the misunderstanding and misrepresentation of maritime cabotage law, by pursuing relentlessly its systematic transition from a sovereignty-based concept to an economic development-based ideology.

Some commentators have gone so far as to invite us to accept the viewpoint that because of the complex nature of maritime cabotage law, there is no purpose in developing a harmonised international maritime cabotage law framework. If we accept such invitation, we would at the very least be contributing to the continued mystification of maritime cabotage law. By doing so, we would miss the opportunity to tackle an issue that is slowly becoming an international concern. I agree that maritime cabotage law is complex, but I do not accept that there are no solutions to the challenges that arise from this area of law – even if it means going at it piecemeal.

This book is a comprehensive review of maritime cabotage law and it presents new reasoning on the underpinning principles of the concept of maritime cabotage. It is written to be a one-stop knowledge bank for the academia and industry professionals involved with maritime cabotage. It features deep and critical analyses of many judicial rulings on maritime cabotage in several jurisdictions.

There are also several novel concepts that are introduced in this book. I am especially proud to develop the theory of 'developmental sovereignty', which explains what factors should drive every nation's strategic maritime cabotage approach agenda. This theory, which is applied throughout this book can also be applied in many other areas outside of maritime cabotage law. Furthermore, this book challenges the established but incorrect understanding that traditionally describes the requirements of domestic shipbuilding, indigenous ship ownership, indigenous crew and domestic ship registration under various maritime cabotage regimes as the four pillars of maritime cabotage. Rather, it explains why these requirements can only correctly be described as features of maritime cabotage, and goes further to introduce what is considered new features of maritime cabotage law. These would compulsorily require all cabotage vessels to undergo classification by an indigenous classification society and for those ships to be recycled in a domestic ship recycling facility in the host maritime cabotage country. Also, the shipowner is clearly defined in the context of maritime cabotage law, thus avoiding the confusion that surrounds the identity of a shipowner in other areas of maritime law.

It is my hope that I have succeeded in doing two things with this book. First, that I have succeeded in bringing the law of maritime cabotage into the mainstream of legal discourse. Second, that I have succeeded in my own unique style to distil the intricate legal complexities that surround maritime cabotage law into a manageable scholarly discourse. The strategy has been to rein in the inconsistencies that surround the concept and application of maritime cabotage law and to replace the confusing patchwork of ideologies with a certain and more robust concept of maritime cabotage.

I have wrestled unsuccessfully with the great temptation to resist mentioning names – for I know I will forever be in debt to those who contributed in some way to the success of this book – but whose names are not mentioned here. For those people, I apologise in advance. However, it is with genuine rather than conventional sincerity that I wish to show appreciation to some people whose support has been direct and instrumental to the success of this work. I would like to thank Chris Atwell for recommending this work after only reading the first draft proposal. I would also like to express my gratitude to the editorial and production team at Routledge for doing an excellent job of turning this work into a comprehensible readable text. Thank you to Gill for ensuring that this work followed a consistent approach. I am grateful to James Kelleher for always reassuring me that all will be well. Many thanks to Chinedu and Jacque for helping with the proof reading. I am grateful to Victor Udoh for the opportunity to witness the workings or lack thereof of the Nigerian maritime cabotage law in reality. Telcy and Olutomi, thank you so very much for your unwavering support. Many thanks to Jordan and Michael for being my gentle reminders for when the book will be out – albeit in hope that you would get complimentary copies instead of purchasing it. Thank you to Eric and Laurel for raising two separate issues (without meaning to) that sharpened my thinking as I thought and wrote chapter 9 of this book.

I cannot thank Comfort, Victor and Ogechukwu enough for often pulling me away from the pressure that I can sometimes immense myself in.

In writing this book, I have drawn on my experience as an academic and consultant to ensure that the readers will find it informative, reflective and reformative of their view of maritime cabotage. If I have managed to do that, then a major aim of this work will have been accomplished. Friends and family who have witnessed me labouring day and night with this work have asked if the satisfaction of completing this book surpasses the difficulties of the many challenging days and nights of researching and writing. Some have gone further to ask with childlike curiosity whether I will attempt to write another book. To these questions, my answer is: have your guess!

Aniekan Akpan
Southampton
Autumn 2018

# Table of cases

# Table of legislation

## Australia

## Brazil

## Canada

## Chile

## China

## England

## Great Britain

## Greece

# Italy

# Japan

# Malaysia

# Mexico

# New Zealand

## South African Development Community

# Table of international treaties
# and conventions

# 1 Introduction to the law of maritime cabotage

Maritime cabotage is an area of maritime and shipping law that is traditionally concerned with the controlling powers of a sovereign state over her territorial waters. This is normally 12 nautical miles from the country's baseline, although we shall see in later chapters that some countries have extended their cabotage laws beyond the scope of the territorial sea. As a result, many coastal states opt to reserve maritime activities in their territorial seas to their national instrumentalities of commerce. The autonomy of states to determine how they wish to control maritime activities in their territorial waters means that the law of maritime cabotage is applied disparately in various maritime jurisdictions.

Maritime cabotage has various identities in different jurisdictions, which include: coasting trade, coastwise trade, colonial trade, and short sea shipping. All of them signify the freedom, or lack thereof, to perform maritime activities within the maritime territory of a country or group of countries. The operative maritime cabotage law of a sovereign state can be found in legislations such as acts of parliaments, customs law, national constitutions, immigration acts, shipping laws and company law. Alternatively, the law may in fact result from combined legislations in various sectors of a country. It is because of this complexity and its sometimes controversial nature that there is real uncertainty on the appropriate approach to maritime cabotage.

However, one can argue that the concept of maritime cabotage has now developed beyond its traditional basis of sovereignty. This is due to the evolved nature of maritime activities occurring in coastal waters, which has expanded beyond the basic act of navigating the seas and now includes exploratory and hydrographical maritime activities. This has further driven the desire of sovereign states to benefit from maritime activities in their territorial waters. Therefore, it is fair to say that the traditional premise of sovereignty is now challenged by a new conceptualization of maritime cabotage that embraces a wider spectrum of commercial activities. This raises fundamental questions about what the common understanding of the law of maritime cabotage should be and how this law should then apply at the national, regional and international domains. Therefore, the underlying argument in this book is that because of the lack of a common understanding of a maritime cabotage concept and the disparate application of the law in various jurisdictions, the scene is set for a new conceptualization of maritime cabotage in legal theory to be developed.

The earliest documentation of maritime cabotage legislation dates to the four-teenth century when, under the reign of Richard II, a law was promulgated in 1382 prohibiting the import or export of merchandise at any port in England except in ships belonging to the king's ligeance.[1] There are suggestions that documented legislation on maritime cabotage existed long before then, although there is no intelligible account of any enactment at so distant an epoch.[2]

Maritime cabotage has since undergone such transformation that as a legal concept it is devoid of consistency and legal certainty. In that regard, this book reinforces the need to rein in the inconsistencies that make it difficult to under-stand what, as a matter of law, is considered maritime cabotage. Therefore, we will attempt to investigate the adjustment in the regulatory approaches to the law of maritime cabotage from one that was intrinsically premised on the idea of national sovereignty to one that embraces the economic development ideology of maritime cabotage law. Furthermore, we will scrutinize the degree to which a compromise can be reached between a sovereignty-directed concept and the broader economic development concept of maritime cabotage.

Three main approaches may be discerned in how maritime cabotage law is applied in different jurisdictions. First, the protectionist approach attempts to reserve all activities in a country's territorial waters and how those activities are performed to their domestic resources. Second, the liberal approach allows all or most of the activities in its territorial waters to be performed by all who are eligible regardless of whether they are domestic or foreign. Third, the flexible approach simply alternates between the protectionist and the liberal approaches. It should be noted that, regardless of the maritime cabotage approach adopted, there is usually an element of protectionism embedded in it. Hence, the concept of maritime cabotage has proven to be a venerable rule of law that is developed with the preconceived mercantilist objective of reserving domestic maritime services based on indigeneity.

A cabotage right normally reserves national maritime commerce for national car-riers and indigenous persons within the territorial state. In that sense, it serves as a national sovereignty agenda, with coastal states ensuring that the maritime resources and opportunities within their sovereign entity are protected and preserved. A classic protectionist maritime cabotage regime requires vessels to be owned and crewed by citizens of the host country, and for those vessels to be built and registered in the host country. However, globalization and the emergence of robust regional blocs mean that maritime cabotage law has taken on a broader character. The regional agenda of maritime cabotage is developing fast, with the ASEAN region, African Union, NAFTA (now USMCA) region and European Union setting up regional maritime cabotage frameworks. However, the absence of a harmonized interna-tional legal framework to regulate maritime cabotage is conspicuous. This is peculiar because the maritime sector is saturated with a plethora of international regulations.

---

1  5 Richard II. Stat. i, c. 3.
2  See: A. Smith (1828), 'An Inquiry into the Nature and Causes of the Wealth of Nations', in J. McCulloch (ed.), *With a Life of the Author: An Introductory Discourse, Notes, and Supplemental Dissertations*, vol. IV, 378 (Longman).

It is unfortunate that the idea of a harmonized legal framework for maritime cabotage is often seen as an anomalous subject best treated under a 'sui generis' regime. This has led, in turn, to an unfortunate though avoidable situation in which the concept of maritime cabotage law is generally abused under national, regional and international jurisdictions.

Despite the absence of a universally accepted legal framework, the concept of maritime cabotage has been used for many centuries. For instance, maritime cabotage was practised commonly in England as far back as 1382 under the reign of King Richard II. Similarly, in the Middle Ages, the ancient maritime nations of Venice, Phoenicia, Genoa, Carthage and Rhodes exercised rigid control over their territorial seas as they competed for sea and mercantile supremacy. This was done to stifle the competition and threat posed by other competitors by preventing foreign vessels from accessing their coastal waters. Indeed, it was the argument over how much controlling power a state should have over her territorial seas that was central to the debate over open or closed seas, as epitomized in the 'battle of the books'. The debate over the 'freedom of the seas' is represented by Hugo Grotius's *Mare Liberum (1609)*, John Selden's *Mare Clausum (1635)*, Jan Pontanus' *dominium maris adjacentes (1637)* and Cornelius Van Bynkershoek's *De Dominio Maris (1702)*. Apart from the argument over what the most appropriate maritime cabotage approach for a sovereign country should be, there is always a risk that maritime cabotage is understood incorrectly as a means of barring foreign vessels from entering the territorial waters of a sovereign state. This would contrast with the 'one port in-country stop' concept, which is the more appropriate representation of the modern maritime cabotage concept. Even the most stringent maritime cabotage approach does not prescribe its use as a mechanism for prohibiting ineligible vessels from entering the territorial waters of a sovereign state. Such a task falls better (and rightly so) on the shoulders of the 'sister legal framework' of Port State Control (PSC).

Over the years, the law of maritime cabotage has taken on a more complex character. One only need look at the number of debatable judicial decisions in the United States, Europe and other jurisdictions to appreciate the degree of this complexity. Moreover, there are two principal misconceptions that further complicate issues and facilitate the use of maritime cabotage as a 'special purpose vehicle' to advance alleged national interests even if that requires disregarding the rule of law. The first misconception concerns the idea that maritime cabotage revolves around the concept of protectionism and liberalization of trade. The second misconception asserts that maritime cabotage law is strictly a national concern without any international character. The latter misconception has been disproved by recent events surrounding the disputes in the South China Sea that resulted in the cardinal ruling of the Permanent Court of Arbitration in *The Republic of the Philippines v The People's Republic of China*.[3] With regard to the first misconception and without prejudice to the serious debate on trade, it will be shown during the course of this book that maritime cabotage law is diverse and

[3] (2016) PCA Case No. 2013–19.

goes beyond the theories of protectionism and liberalization of trade. The reason why one should take care not to be misled by these misconceptions about maritime cabotage is twofold. First, it is reasonable to suggest that the thinking on trade liberalization and protectionism will always be subject to debate. Second, it is submitted that the premise underlining the adoption of a maritime cabotage law is transitioning from national sovereignty to economic development.

At the forefront of this subject matter lies a fundamental problem regarding what the law relating to maritime cabotage is and how this law should be applied in the national, regional and international domains. This is significant because of the regularity with which the law of maritime cabotage is applied disparately in different maritime jurisdictions. It is perhaps no surprise that, as with other things, the concept of maritime cabotage has developed beyond its traditional premise of sovereignty. This is due to the evolved nature of maritime activities in coastal waters, which now extend beyond simply navigating the seas to include exploratory and hydrographical maritime activities. There is no doubt that the varied nature of maritime activities that occur within the territorial waters of a country has contributed to the complicated nature of maritime cabotage. This broader scope of maritime activities is a driving factor behind the proactive approach by sovereign states looking to take advantage of the opportunities that arise from the use of their territorial waters. Within the framework of maritime cabotage, maritime activities can be categorized broadly as follows:

a  Maritime transport involving the carriage of goods and or passengers from a domestic port of origin to another domestic port in the same country or group of countries.
b  Maritime auxiliary services concerned with cargo manipulation in ports and on ships. This includes cargo handling, storage and warehousing, customs clearance and maritime agency.
c  Port services concerned with the management of vessels in port. This includes pilotage, towing and tug assistance, and shore-based operational services.

Perhaps it is useful at this point to consider briefly how the concept of cabotage operates in other transport sectors. The law of cabotage has transcended its maritime origins and now applies in land (road and rail) and international air law. The varying degrees of application and the different tolerance levels for the concept of cabotage in the different transport sectors is indicative of the polarizing nature of the law of cabotage. In aviation law, the concept of cabotage does not appear to generate the kind of contentious debate that has become common in the maritime sector. This is significant, considering that the objective of a cabotage law is the same regardless of the sector. Article 7 of the Convention on International Civil Aviation 1944 (Chicago Convention) stipulates that:

> Each contracting State shall have the right to refuse permission to the aircraft of other contracting States to take on in its territory passengers, mail and

cargo carried for remuneration or hire and destined for another point within its territory.

The intended effect of the above provision is not different from that contemplated under a maritime cabotage law concept. Furthermore, land cabotage is focused on reserving the rights of carriage on domestic road and rail to indigenous transport operators. Naturally, this includes reserving the part of multimodal transportation of cargo that requires domestic transport operators to perform by road or rail. Land cabotage is less controversial because the national road and rail system is generally accepted as reserved for domestic transport operators. This acceptance forms the basis for those advocating for a protectionist maritime cabotage regime. The protectionist agenda advocates an inflexible stance that maritime cabotage should enjoy the same domestic protection and privileges as land cabotage. However, if the 'Rotterdam Rules' (formally, the United Nations Convention on Contracts for the International Carriage of Goods Wholly or Partly by Sea) comes into force, land cabotage will likely be subjected to more scrutiny. The Rotterdam Rules was designed to be the legal framework providing for performance through the combined carriage of goods by sea and land. However, it is unclear how cabotage might function within the different transport modes under the Rules. The idea of cabotage was considered during the preparatory work for the Rotterdam Rules, although exactly how much thought was given to it is unclear. A major challenge with including maritime cabotage within the Rules would be how often the sea leg of the carriage would occur between two points of the same state within the context of the Rotterdam Rules.

The challenge of incorporating maritime cabotage into any form of international law is a long-standing issue and there appears to be a well-rehearsed strategy for avoiding the subject at international forums. If the idea behind this strategy is that it is somehow an alternative way of bringing about a harmonized framework for maritime cabotage, then it is unclear how successful it has been. For instance, the discussions on maritime cabotage at the 1994 Uruguay Round were suspended and rescheduled for the Doha Round in 2001. However, maritime cabotage was not even on the agenda for discussion at the Doha Round. The reasoning behind this strategy seems to be that it is pointless, even if desirable, to deliberate issues of maritime cabotage if it has no chance of universal acceptance. This is based on the fear that including maritime cabotage in the debate could scuttle chances for a broader agreement to limit protectionism in the provision of maritime transport services. It is observable that since then, neither the WTO nor any other international institution has taken any active steps to focus on the important issues of maritime cabotage.

The tendency to avoid dealing with these issues appears to come from the thinking that there is no need to consider any aspect of the subject until all the issues that arise from maritime cabotage can be resolved together under one framework. This would appear to be ambitious given the complicated nature of maritime cabotage. A more logical approach might be to divide the contentious issues arising from maritime cabotage into segments, enabling the different interests to reach satisfactory compromises, be it at national, regional or international level. Working in this way would allow the inconsistencies to be reconciled through a harmonized maritime cabotage framework.

Furthermore, the disparity in policy positions on maritime cabotage taken by different nations has raised important questions in the courts, academia and the maritime sector. It is suggested that maritime cabotage cannot remain under the sole regulatory mechanism of sovereign nations and be expected to be devoid of polarization. A harmonized legal framework can help combat the inconsistencies surrounding the concept of maritime cabotage. This would require setting up regional legal instruments to follow the format of the WTO legal framework instruments. Alternatively, it could be modelled after the United Nations Convention on the Law of the Sea (UNCLOS) 1982. This should allow the negotiations on a harmonized maritime cabotage concept to focus on important areas where there is common agreement.

Finally, the hope is that this book will succeed in forging an understanding of how the different facets of maritime cabotage apply within the legal context. The idea is to distil the complexity of the concept of maritime cabotage and the intricate legal issues it raises into a manageable set of discussions so that a more certain concept of maritime cabotage can be established.

## Definition and scope of maritime cabotage

Maritime cabotage law is a legal instrument that allows a sovereign state to reserve all or some of the maritime activities taking place between two or more geographical points of its territorial waters to its national instrumentalities of commerce. By national instrumentalities of commerce, we are referring to indigenous sea and shore personnel, institutions such as ship registers, and maritime infrastructures such as ships and shipyards.

However, maritime cabotage undertakes an expanded scope in commercial treaties. Lassa Oppenheim[4] commented that in this context it means sea trade between two ports of the same country on either the same coast (petit cabotage) or different coasts (grand cabotage), provided that the different coasts are the coasts of one and the same country as a political and geographical unit, in contradistinction to the coasts of colonial dependencies of such country. Oppenheim argued in his treatise that the confusion surrounding the meaning of maritime cabotage under international law and commercial treaties is twofold. First, he contended that some nations have more than one stretch of coast, which result in 'petit' and 'grand' cabotage. Second, he asserted that other nations have dismembered territories (islands) under one sovereign control. However, he stopped short of putting forward an argument that tackles the concerns that arise from applying the concept of maritime cabotage in international law and commercial treaties. Nonetheless, within the context of the modern practice of maritime

---

4  L. Oppenheim (1908), 'The Meaning of Coasting-trade in Commercial Treaties', *Law Quarterly Review*, 24(1), 328–330.

cabotage, Oppenheim's argument is now only partly valid, and only to the extent that the principle of sovereignty remains pivotal to the law of maritime cabotage. Moreover, the reasoning as opined by Oppenheim regarding the confusion surrounding maritime cabotage has shifted considerably. It is now based largely on which maritime cabotage approach a country adopts and the rationale behind their choice.

It is obvious that the original meaning of maritime cabotage under international law has been stretched under commercial treaties. However, there is scant commentary on the impact that such expansion in meaning has on maritime trade and services in coastal waters. On the other hand, according to Article 2 of the United Nations Convention on the Law of the Sea 1982, a littoral state can restrict foreign competition from the maritime cabotage trade and services between ports of the same coast or sea of the same country. Therefore, the disparity in the scope of the concept of maritime cabotage between commercial treaties and international law deserves consideration, with the hope of restoring some form of legal certainty.

The fact that the meaning and scope of maritime cabotage varies depending on the context in which it is applied offers some explanation for the confusion that surrounds the subject. This is despite efforts at the international level to establish a common meaning of maritime cabotage or restrict maritime cabotage to its original meaning under international law. At the Barcelona Convention in 1921, the League of Nations (now the United Nations) concluded that a sovereign nation shall have the right to reserve, to its own flag vessels, the transport of goods and passengers from one port to another. This right is subject to the proviso that the two ports in question are under the sovereignty of the same nation as a political and geographical unit.[5] Similarly, the Geneva Convention on Maritime Ports 1923 echoed the same position by asserting that the scope of maritime cabotage should be restricted to navigation between two ports of the same nation.[6] It was also accepted that a littoral nation had sovereign authority over its territorial sea to reserve maritime activities to its nationals.

The customary practice is that the breadth of the territorial sea is 12 nautical miles from the baseline of the state. Furthermore, according to Article 2 of the Convention on the Law of the Sea 1982, the sovereignty of the coastal state extends to the air space over the territorial sea as well as to its bed and subsoil. However, it is not unusual for states to apply maritime cabotage law up to 200 nautical miles from the baseline of the state. From a simplistic perspective therefore, maritime cabotage law requires the use of national flag vessels for carriage of goods and or passengers by sea between two geographical points in a country.

---

5 Article 5 of the Statue on the Regime of Navigable Waterways of International Concern 1921.

6 Article 9 of the Convention and Statute of the International Regime of Maritime Ports 1923.

It is generally accepted that every coastal nation is entitled to have sovereignty over the belt of sea adjacent to its coast known generally as the territorial sea.[7] In the Anglo-Norwegian Fisheries case,[8] Sir Arnold McNair in his dissenting opinion stated that the possession of a territorial sea by a coastal nation is a compulsory responsibility. Therefore, it is neither optional nor dependent upon the will of that state. He went on to posit that to every nation whose land territory is washed by sea, international law attaches a corresponding portion of maritime territory consisting of territorial waters. Since international law does not offer any maritime nation a choice to decide whether they wish to claim their territorial waters, no maritime nation can refuse to claim. Rather, every maritime state must perform the obligation and exercise the rights conferred upon it by sovereignty, which it must exert over its maritime territory.

However, the complexity begins where the law is applied to a broader spectrum of activities within a country's maritime sector. In many countries, maritime cabotage law is applied to activities in the areas of construction, immigration, corporation, economic development, and national security. For instance, shipbuilding and repair would be better regulated in the construction sector; similarly, the issues relating to employment of foreign crew would be better regulated under the employment and immigration laws of a country. Indeed, this has been shown to work in New Zealand and Brazil. The ownership and establishment of principal places of business in foreign countries would be better regulated under the company laws of the host country. Finally, there is no reason why economic development and national security issues would not be more appropriately regulated under the respective relevant parastatals and agencies of government, rather than under a maritime cabotage law framework.

## Distinguishing between maritime cabotage and maritime delimitation

We have dealt with the general overview of maritime cabotage, its meaning, scope, and application. Here, it is important to distinguish between maritime cabotage and maritime delimitation. Issues that arise out of maritime delimitation are sometimes confused with maritime cabotage and vice versa. The idea in this subchapter is not to provide a comprehensive discussion on maritime delimitation. Rather, it is to draw attention to the use of the concept of sovereignty that is an underlying theme for cabotage and delimitation. It is useful to mention here that international law (UNCLOS 1982) recognizes four maritime zones that sovereign states have varying sovereign control or rights over. They are: territorial sea (12 nm), contiguous zone (24 nm), exclusive economic zone (200 nm), and continental shelf (usually 200 nm but can extend up to 350 nm). The distances of these various maritime zones are measured from the baseline of the coastal state.

Many sections of the sea will fall under one of the maritime zones controlled by a sovereign state. Nevertheless, as with land, there are sections of the sea that will

7  Article 2(1) of the Convention on the Law of the Sea 1982.
8  *United Kingdom v. Norway* (1951) I.C.J. Rep. 116.

overlap the maritime zones of more than one state. Where this happens, states need to agree on how to delimitate the section of the sea in question. Alternatively, in the absence of an agreement, disputes may be submitted to the International Court of Justice or an arbitral tribunal. This two-step process to delimitation is captured by the provisions of Article 15 of UNCLOS 1982. Delimitation may be carried out between two adjacent coasts or between two opposite coasts depending on the location of the overlapping zones. In essence, a maritime delimitation is not different from a land border indicating where one country's territory stops and where the territory belonging to another country begins.

All maritime zones may be subject to maritime delimitation. In this section we are only concerned with the delimitation of the territorial sea. This is because the territorial sea entitles the coastal state to full sovereign control as opposed to sovereign rights entitlements in the other maritime zones. The challenges associated with maritime delimitation have raised many questions of international law before the courts. In this regard, a useful case to follow is the decision of the International Court of Justice (ICJ) in *Qatar v. Bahrain*.[9] Although there are more recent judicial decisions on maritime delimitation, this case highlights the variety of issues that require consideration when dealing with maritime delimitation. Furthermore, the ICJ adopted an approach on maritime delimitation line that appears to have become the standard approach to delimitation.

A useful example is the Anglo-Norwegian Fisheries[10] case, which originated in 1933, and was a dispute between Norway and the United Kingdom. This case was concerned with first, what extent of the body of water surrounding Norway was Norwegian waters, thereby giving her exclusive fishing rights, and second, what area of the sea was classified as the high seas, thus entitling the United Kingdom to carry out fishing activities. The United Kingdom challenged the baseline system employed by Norway in measuring her territorial sea. The argument presented by the United Kingdom was that the baseline system (rather than the low water mark system) extended unfairly the limit of the Norwegian territorial sea into the high sea, thus breaching international law. The International Court of Justice upheld Norway's claims that the limit of her waters was consistent with international laws with regard to the ownership of local sea-space because it was imperative to give cognizance to the geographical realities of the region.

## Historical review of maritime cabotage from the fourteenth to twenty-first century

The origin of maritime cabotage is uncertain, although it appears to have come out of either Spanish or French culture. The general understanding is that it comes from the French verb *caboter*, which derives from the Spanish word *cabotaje*, and means to navigate along the coast without losing sight of it. However, this narrow meaning has never really been adopted in practice. Some countries

---

9 (1994) I.C.J. 112.
10 *United Kingdom v. Norway* (1951) I.C.J. Rep. 116.

were simply not content with restricting their sea exploration and navigation to the coast. The United States, England, and Portugal are examples of countries that extended the concept of cabotage to include restricting to ships and personnel of the mother nation, sea trade and carriage of goods or persons by sea between mother nation and their colonies. Hence, between 1898 and 1899, the United States classified trade between her and the Philippines, Hawaiian Islands and Island of Puerto Rico as cabotage trade. This meant that even the external trade of the colony was carried by vessels flying the United States flag with her national crew. This kind of maritime cabotage practice is now uncommon, due largely to the abolition of active colonialism. The closest remnants of extended maritime cabotage policy now only exist in two instances. First, where the concept of grand cabotage is used to reserve maritime cabotage activities between a port in the mainland state and a port in one of her overseas territories. This is perhaps appropriately represented by the one country, two systems principle adopted by the People's Republic of China, which allows her to retain influence over territories such as Hong Kong and Macau. The second situation arises when a developing country is annexed and depends on an industrialized country to sustain its national economy. It is reasonable to expect that the developing country may avoid enacting cabotage legislations that are contrary to the counterpart legislations of the industrialized country. This is certainly the case with many African states that are yet to emancipate their national policies from their colonial past.

Generally, coastal states are protective of their maritime sector because of the strategic importance of trade, navigation and other maritime activities in coastal waters. For centuries, many maritime nations with a coastal shipping trade implemented a protectionist maritime cabotage law. However, it is now increasingly difficult to sustain this protectionist approach because:

a   more states are open to experimenting with liberal policies in trade and services;
b   the fierce competition between traditional shipping nations appears to have waned;
c   there has been a drastic depletion in the national fleets of traditional maritime nations.

The adventure and exploration of the sea was pursued by maritime powers such as Egypt, Carthage, Rhodes, Phoenicia and Rome, which exercised control and sovereignty over their adjacent waters (territorial sea). The aim was to restrict the foreign vessels of rival nations from trading or pursuing other maritime activities in their ports and sea areas. Accordingly, it can be argued that the concept of maritime cabotage at that time was likely to have been facilitated by political and commercial needs rather than legal reasoning. The earliest known documentation of maritime cabotage legislation was adopted in 1382 under the reign of Richard II, and it stipulated that 'No person shall import or export merchandise in any port within the realm of England but in ships of the King's liegance.'[11]

---

11 5 Richard II. Stat. i, c. 3.

Similar legislations were maintained consistently, and at times made more stringent, by successors to Richard II. Edward IV (1461–1483), Henry VII (1485–1509) and Elizabeth 1 (1558–1603) all sought to protect the coastal waters of England and prevent foreign vessels from engaging in her coastal trade and services.[12] England pursued a stringent maritime cabotage policy for more than two and a half centuries (1382–1650) before the enactment of the Navigation Act of 1651 by Oliver Cromwell. This act prohibited third party foreign vessels from trading in English waters. It stipulated that trade to and from British colonies was exclusively reserved for British vessels, or vessels of the country from which the goods were imported.[13] This was aimed at controlling the overwhelmingly growing influence of the Dutch merchant marine. The Navigation Act of 1660 came after the Restoration, when the English, Scottish and Irish monarchies were re-established under Charles II, allowing him to amend the earlier act. It became more stringent due to the geographical expansion in scope and a tightened crew requirement. It stipulated that:

> No Goods shall be imported to or exported from Asia, Africa or America but in English ships, in the command of an English Master with Three-fourths of the Mariners English men. No Goods to be carried from one port of England to another in the vessel of any Alien.[14]

The Scottish Navigation Act was enacted in 1661, as neither Cromwell's 1651 nor Charles II's 1660 navigation act covered Scotland. At that time, Scotland was considered alien and remained so until the Act of Union took effect in 1707. The Navigation Act was repealed in 1849 in the United Kingdom. However, maritime cabotage trade was still protected for British ships carrying British seamen until 1854. It was at that point that the last relic of the protectionist act, which had spanned over four and a half centuries (1382–1854), was finally repealed.[15]

Similarly, other maritime powers enacted protectionist maritime cabotage legislation around the same time. In 1670, trade between France and her colonies was reserved for French ships only. This protectionist maritime policy became law in 1740, when maritime cabotage was legislated in the French Royal Decree. The legislation specified two types of cabotage, namely grand cabotage and petit cabotage. In France, grand cabotage relates to trade and the provision of maritime services between the ports of Mediterranean France and ports in France's overseas territories such as Martinique and Guadeloupe. The important point here is that the two ports should be on different coasts. A voyage between Bordeaux and Marseille would also be classed as 'grand' cabotage as the two points are on different coasts. Petit cabotage relates to the trade and the provision of maritime

---

12  See: 3 Edward IV, c. 1; 4 Henry VII, c. 10 s i and ii; 5 Elizabeth, c. 5.
13  See: The Navigation Act 1651 (Cap. 22) Goods from Foreign Ports by Whom to be imported. Enacted 9 October 1651. In force 1 December 1651.
14  12 Charles II. c. 18, i, iii and vi.
15  See: Coasting Trade Bill. House of Common Bill (1853–1854) (131).

services between two or more French ports on the same coast. A voyage between Calais and Marseille, which are both on the same coast, would be categorized as 'petit' cabotage. About half a century later, the level of protectionism was increased further in the French maritime cabotage sector and led to the 1791 publication of a ban on foreign ships.

In 1789, The United States Congress imposed added duties on goods transported by foreign vessels. In addition, a prohibitive tax was placed on foreign-built and foreign-owned ships.[16] In a move similar to that of the French nearly a century before, the United States Congress enacted the Navigation Act of 1817. This barred foreign vessels from domestic commerce and coastwise competition in the coastal waters of the United States.[17] The Passenger Vessel Services Act of 1886 further extended the United States maritime cabotage law to cover passenger vessels.[18] Together, the 1817 and 1886 acts reserved marine transportation of freight and passengers to United States-built, registered, owned and crewed vessels. At present, several protectionist laws exist to cover dredging, towing and salvage operations in the coastal waters of the United States.[19] The Merchant Marine Act 1920, or Jones Act, is the maritime cabotage law that currently applies in the United States of America. In essence, it is a more stringent form of the 1789 act.[20] Protectionist policies with regard to territorial waters continued to spread in northern America. In 1869, Canada enacted its first independent legislation, which restricted maritime trade in Canadian waters to British vessels. The restriction to British vessels was because Canada was a British colony at the time. Following the signing of the British Commonwealth Merchant Shipping Agreement in 1931, vessels from Commonwealth countries had the same status as British ships and could thus take part in the Canadian coasting trade. It should be noted that similar protectionist legislations had already been abolished in the United Kingdom, first through the repeal of the Navigation Act in 1849 and then by the subsequent removal of restrictions in the coasting trade between ports in the United Kingdom in 1854. It is clear from this evidence that although the British government had ended the protectionist maritime cabotage regime in the United Kingdom, it was happy to export and retain those same protectionist policies in her various colonies around the world. Nevertheless, the origins of a strict Canadian maritime cabotage trade policy predates her independence and could be traced back to the Paris Treaty of 1763. This treaty contributed to Britain's undisputed control of the sea and maritime commerce. Although the British North America Act 1867 gave authority to the Parliament of Canada over navigation and shipping, Canadian legislation was still required to be consistent with

16  1 Stat. 24: An Act for laying a Duty on Goods, Wares and Merchandises Imported into the United States [4 July 1789].
17  Section 4 of an Act Concerning the Navigation of the United States. Approved 1 March 1817.
18  Section 8 of the Passengers Vessels Services Act of 19 June 1886. 24 Stat. 81. 46 U.S. C. 55103.
19  See: The Dredging Act of 1906 and Towing Statute of 1940.
20  See: 46 U.S.C. 81; 46 U.S.C. 121; 46 U.S.C. 551.

the laws of the United Kingdom. This remained the case until the Canada Shipping Act 1934 put shipping under the full jurisdiction of Canada. The Coasting Trade Act 1992 now regulates a continued protectionist maritime cabotage policy in Canada.

The need to reserve maritime activities in national coastal waters was not only centered on Britain and North America. In Eurasia, the Russian empire's first attempt at restricting coasting trade to Russian vessels in 1830 was unsuccessful because at that time Russia viewed coasting trade as insignificant and hence it was unprotected from foreign competition.[21] The important city of Vladivostok was not part of Russia at the time. It was part of many nations before it was acquired by Russia through the 1860 Treaty of Beijing. However, in 1897 Russia enacted a *ukase*, which is a decree in imperial Russia that had the force of law. The *ukase* became law in 1900 and established that 'any trade between any of Russia's ports and the port of Vladivostok would be classified as cabotage trade and therefore reserved exclusively for Russian vessels'. Since then Russia has paid more attention to the concept of maritime cabotage and taken advantage of its large geographical mass. It now uses important sections of its coastal waters as strategic security posts. This is demonstrated by Russia's annexation of Crimea from Ukraine. It has also developed modern maritime legislation and the 1999 Merchant Shipping Code of the Russian Federation currently regulates its maritime cabotage.[22] Also, the Treaty of Lausanne opened the doors for the Turkish Maritime Cabotage Act to come into effect in 1926. From that period, any maritime cabotage privilege that was previously granted to foreign vessels in Turkey was withdrawn. It has been suggested that this decision played an important part in facilitating Turkey's efforts to develop its maritime sector.

It is perhaps appropriate to provide a cursory overview of how the protectionists' maritime cabotage policies were enforced before the modern laws of maritime cabotage came into being in the twentieth century. It is essential to remember that at that time, many countries fighting for maritime and sea supremacy reserved maritime activities in their coastal waters to vessels and crew of their nationality. Furthermore, many of these countries operated a monarchical system of governance. Hence, the monarch had special advisers who were representatives of the throne in different sectors of the kingdom. Those representatives were tasked with monitoring the coastal waters for foreign vessels and enforcing the protectionist maritime cabotage laws on behalf of the monarch. Therefore, any foreign vessels that violated these laws were arrested with their crew and subjected to various levels of punishment such as fines, cargo seizure, forfeiture of vessels and imprisonment of crew.[23] However, after prolonged discussions spanning many years, some countries in Europe came together and agreed to liberalize maritime cabotage. This was achieved through Council Regulation (EEC) No.

21  See: J. Karel (1897), 'Consular Report: Reports from the consuls of the United States on the commerce, manufactures, etc., of their consular districts', vol. LV, no. 204.
22  See: Article 4 of the Merchant Shipping Code of the Russian Federation 1999.
23  See: 3 Edward IV, c. 1; 4 Henry VII, c. 10 s i and ii; and 5 Elizabeth, c. 5.

3577/92, which came into force in January 1993 under the auspices of the European Union (which was then known as the European Community; the European Union came into official being with the 1993 Maastricht Treaty). Council Regulation 3577/92 regulates the freedom to provide maritime services between member states of the European Union without restrictions.[24] Prior to this regulation, independent countries in Europe had maritime cabotage legislation that suited their national purposes. The northern European countries such as Denmark, Norway, the United Kingdom and the Netherlands had already implemented liberal maritime cabotage policies. On the other hand, southern European countries, including Greece, Spain and Italy, pursued protectionist maritime cabotage policies. It is useful to note here that one of the likely consequences of Brexit (the United Kingdom voting in 2016 to leave the European Union by 2019, with a further transition period, when the post-Brexit rules will apply, extending to 2021 or beyond) is that the United Kingdom will cease to be a beneficiary of the liberal EU maritime cabotage policy reserved exclusively for member states. In what may appear to be the direction in which the law of maritime cabotage is going, several countries have resorted to enacting a protectionist maritime cabotage law since the turn of the twenty-first century. They include China, Brazil, India, Nigeria and Malaysia.

## Introducing the theory of developmental sovereignty

The lack of a common understanding of the concept of maritime cabotage warrants a new conceptualization of maritime cabotage in legal theory. Legal theory is understood here to reflect assessment of domestic and international law and the institutions whose workings benefit from the theories of development, economics and sovereignty. In this book we will from time to time apply the normative and analytic jurisprudence forms of legal theory to present a clearer understanding of the issues. Normative jurisprudence will be applied to investigate the purpose of the law of maritime cabotage, while analytic jurisprudence will be used to explain the legal concept of maritime cabotage. A detailed discussion of the theory is scheduled for chapter 3 of this book, but it is useful to give a preview into the theory.

The theory of developmental sovereignty states that:

> The authority bestowed on a sovereign state under international law to enact legislations that regulate the performance of maritime activities between any two points of its littoral territory, should be governed by the impact that such laws have on the economic development of the country.

The theory of developmental sovereignty is an original concept not seen in existing literature. This theory will be posited against other theories, particularly those from a sovereignty perspective, with the hope of advancing a clearer understanding of

---

24 See: Council Regulation (EEC) No. 3577/92 of 7 December 1992; applying the Principle of Freedom to Provide Services to Maritime Transport Within Member States (Maritime Cabotage); O.J. L 364.

maritime cabotage law. The important benefit of this theory is that it reduces the rationales for the choice of maritime cabotage approach to the simple question of whether the host country has the necessary pre-requisites to implement their choice of maritime cabotage approach effectively. This is achieved by replacing the confusing patchwork of ideologies with a certain and more robust concept of maritime cabotage.

Generally, sovereign states put forward various rationales for adopting a protectionist, liberal, or flexible maritime cabotage approach. In modern times, these rationales now usually revolve around national economic development of the sovereign state. The theory of developmental sovereignty argues that these rationales for the choice of a maritime cabotage approach should be justified by the degree to which it promotes the economic development of a country. This will allow the coastal state to concentrate on the areas of maritime cabotage that they can effectively regulate within the indigenous framework. Hence, the other areas of the domestic maritime sector would be opened to free competition, even if this may result in the unintended consequence of foreigners dominating the domestic maritime sector. For instance, one can argue that it is difficult for Nigeria to justify adopting a protectionist maritime cabotage approach that stipulates that vessels engaged in maritime cabotage should be constructed in Nigeria. It is obvious that at present, Nigeria does not possess the capacity to build vessels at a commercial level.[25] Similarly, how is it that the United States can continue to stipulate that coastwise vessels must be constructed in the United States under their maritime cabotage law,[26] when it is five times cheaper to build similar vessels in Asia. These are clear examples of how the choice of maritime cabotage approach may negatively impact on rather than promote economic development of the coastal state, regardless of the country's sovereign autonomy. It is the impact that these various maritime cabotage law approaches have on national economic development that the theory of developmental sovereignty addresses. We should hasten to add that the theory of developmental sovereignty incorporates completely the themes surrounding the notion of sustainable development. The Brundtland Report defines sustainable development as development that meets the needs of the present without compromising the ability of future generations to meet their own needs.[27] Moreover, the theory of developmental sovereignty challenges the established and accepted wisdom surrounding maritime cabotage by presenting new reasoning on the underpinning principles of the concept of maritime cabotage law. The theory questions the established rationale behind the adoption of maritime cabotage approaches. It argues that rationales such as sovereignty and national security are not by themselves enough to justify the adoption of a specific approach of maritime cabotage law. The theory of developmental sovereignty is presented as new

25 See: Sections 3 and 6 of The Coastal and Inland Shipping (Cabotage) Act, No. 5 of 2003.
26 See: Section 27 of the Merchant Marine Act, 1920. 46 U.S.C. App. § 833, 46 U.S.C. 50101 and 46 U.S.C. 55102.
27 See the 1987 Report of the World Commission on Environment and Development: Our Common Future. Transmitted to the General Assembly as an Annex to document A/42/427.

thinking and argues that this should be the underpinning principle that guides the adoption of a maritime cabotage approach by any sovereign state.

## Overview of the fundamental themes of maritime cabotage law

We have stated above that the law of maritime cabotage is complex. It is therefore imperative to have a clear understanding of its underlying themes. The objective here is to provide a quick overview of some of the themes that inform its development and application. We have scheduled a comprehensive discussion of these themes and the role they play in the development and application of maritime cabotage law for subsequent chapters. In this section, we will provide a clear and succinct investigation of the themes that surround maritime cabotage law. We should emphasize that the two themes of sovereignty and sovereign rights are also the legal principles that traditional maritime cabotage law is based upon.

### Sovereignty

This is the primary basis without which no coastal state can exercise maritime cabotage control. It must be distinguished from 'sovereign right', which we shall deal with shortly. Sovereignty is the right of every coastal state to control, without interference from third party states, all maritime activities in its territorial waters. The only exemption to this absolute control is the right of innocent passage by a foreign vessel,[28] where such passage is indeed innocent and poses no harm or risk to the coastal state.[29] It should be noted that the controlling power arising from sovereignty is traditionally restricted to the breadth of the territorial sea, which is normally 12 nautical miles from the baseline of the coastal state.[30] In *Anglo-Norwegian Fisheries*,[31] Sir Arnold McNair stated that for every nation whose land territory is washed by sea, international law attaches a corresponding portion of maritime territory consisting of territorial waters. The possession of a territorial sea by a coastal nation is a compulsory responsibility that is neither optional nor dependent upon the will of that state. Therefore, every maritime state must perform the obligation and exercise the rights conferred upon it by sovereignty, which it must exert over its maritime territory. Sovereignty has traditionally been the primary basis for pursuing a maritime cabotage concept and remains pivotal to its development.

### Sovereign rights

If sovereignty bestows absolute control of a section of the sea as reward for every nation whose land territory is washed by sea, then the next in the order of importance are the privileges enjoyed from sovereign rights. Every coastal state has

28 Article 17 of the United Nations Convention on the Law of the Sea 1982.
29 Articles 18 and 19 of the United Nations Convention on the Law of the Sea 1982.
30 Article 3 of the United Nations Convention on the Law of the Sea 1982.
31 United Kingdom v Norway (1951) I.C.J. Rep. 116.

the right to use and explore the section of the seas classified as the contiguous zones and Exclusive Economic Zones. These are usually 24 and 200 nautical miles respectively from the baseline of the coastal state.[32] The important point here to note is that sovereign rights do not bestow absolute control of these sea sections. Rather, they allow for the common usage and exploration of the sea section by all neighbouring coastal states.

## National economic development

The choice of a maritime cabotage approach by many states is informed by the desire to stimulate and sustain the economic development of the sovereign state. In the context of this book, the term 'economic development' is understood as the scope for capacity building as facilitated by the maritime cabotage approach adopted in a country. In essence, this is focused on promoting domestic and indigenous growth. It requires improving the human, infrastructural and institutional resources of the country. For instance, human resource development will require equipping people with the training and access to information that enables them to perform efficiently. One way of achieving this is to implement a dedicated programme of maritime education, training and continuous professional development to ensure that personnel competency skills are updated on a regular basis. This will serve as a strategic response to the problem of skills deficiency that many countries face in their maritime sector. It was once possible to remain sufficiently employed in the maritime sector by possessing a basic entry-level qualification. However, this is no longer the case. This is because maritime organizations are now focused on continual professional development (CPD) training programmes. These training frameworks can be integrated into management development programmes to produce skilled and efficient personnel that are ready to tackle the challenges of the maritime sector. Similar strategic frameworks will need to be developed to build maritime infrastructural capacity and robust institutional support. This is important as the basis for adopting a maritime cabotage law is transitioning towards economic development.

## National security

Many states have developed a stringent maritime cabotage law on the basis that it is imperative to their national security. The idea seems to be that if foreigners are forbidden from operating within the coastal waters of the country, then the threat to their national security is avoided. It is suggested that this argument is based on two false premises. First, foreign vessels that are not eligible to engage in activities within the coastal waters are not necessarily prohibited from traversing the coastal waters while they are undertaking international voyages. Therefore, if there is an intention to threaten the national security of a coastal state, that risk is not

32 Articles 33 and 57 respectively of the United Nations Convention on the Law of the Sea.

eliminated since there is still an opportunity. Moreover, the coastal states that operate a liberal maritime cabotage policy have no issue with threats to their national security. Second, it is disingenuous to suggest that threats to national security from the coastal waters can only be carried out by foreign entities. For example, during the Niger Delta crisis in Nigeria, the main threats posed to national security from the coastal waters came from indigenous activists, not foreign vessels.

### *Protectionism and liberalization*

The concept of maritime cabotage has often been seen from a trade protectionism and liberalization perspective, even though maritime cabotage has a deeper context, one that goes beyond the debate on trade policies. Nevertheless, this is still an important theme, particularly considering the different approaches to maritime cabotage (protectionist, liberal and flexible) adopted by states. With the evolved concept of maritime cabotage, this theme perhaps relates better to the provision of maritime services than to trade. For example, a classic protectionist maritime cabotage approach stipulates that vessels used for coastwise trade and services should be built domestically, owned by an indigene, employ indigenous crew and registered in the host maritime cabotage country. Effectively, this prevents foreign entities from engaging in maritime activities in coastal waters. The United States is an example of a country that has adopted and implemented this type of protectionist maritime cabotage approach. On the other hand, a classic liberal maritime cabotage approach allows free competition between domestic and foreign entities in coastal waters. This is often subject to the proviso that they meet specific requirements usually relating inter alia to health and safety of persons and the environment. South Africa and New Zealand operate a liberal maritime cabotage policy. However, the European Union is perhaps the best example of how a liberal maritime cabotage policy functions. Member states can provide maritime services in the coastal waters of other member states if they are eligible to do the same in their home state. Two things should be noted however. First, the concept of maritime cabotage in the European Union operates from a regional perspective rather than what is obtainable in a sovereign state. Second, the liberal maritime cabotage policy applies to member states only. Therefore, there is scope to argue that the European Union maritime cabotage framework is somewhat protectionist against non-member states.

## Conclusion

In summarising this introductory chapter, a pertinent question for consideration is what the central underlying objective that drives a national maritime cabotage policy in the various sovereign nations is? For one, the rationale for adopting a mainly protectionist maritime cabotage approach has shifted from the desire to acquire sea supremacy in war- and peace-time to the need to promote national economic development. Hence, the justification for promoting a national maritime cabotage policy appears to be crafted with the overriding question in the form of: how does adopting a specific maritime cabotage approach impact the national economic interest of the sovereign state? However, there is bound to be criticism regardless of which maritime cabotage approach a country adopts. For instance, where a protectionist approach is adopted, the complaint is that the protectionist policies benefit a few (indigenous shipowners) at the expense of more general members of society. These complaints generally come from indigenous shippers and consumers who are forced to pay higher freights for domestic shipments and who pay a higher price for goods respectively. A good example of this is the effect that the protectionist maritime cabotage law of Malaysia had on the states of Sabah and Sarawak before some temporary liberal measures were introduced in 2009 to ease the impact. On the other hand, where a liberal approach is adopted, indigenous shipowners are often quick to indicate the failure to accord them the privilege of operating in the domestic sector free from foreign competition and interference. The American Maritime Partnership (AMP), described as the voice of the United States domestic maritime industry, has consistently put forward fierce argument that the protectionist Jones Act sustains the United States domestic maritime industry by supporting nearly 500,000 American jobs and almost $100 billion in annual economic impact, in addition to more than $20 billion in domestic investments through shipbuilding.[33]

Finally, there will be frequent reminders of the issues identified in this chapter in the subsequent chapters of this book. Some of the issues introduced in this chapter have been scheduled consciously for comprehensive treatment in more appropriate chapters.

33 Comments of the American Maritime Partnership before the United States Customs and Border Protection on the Proposed Modification and Revocation of Ruling Letters Relating to Customs Application of the Jones Act to the Transportation of Certain Merchandise and Equipment Between Coastwise Points dated 18 April 2017, in: *Customs Bulletin & Decisions*, 51(3), 1; and *Customs Bulletin & Decisions*, 51(6), 22.

# 2 The evolutionary synthesis in the development of maritime cabotage law and public international law

Maritime cabotage law and public international law share some commonalities in their development and how they influence the commercial conduct of sovereign nations. In this chapter we will assess how maritime cabotage law and public international law have developed concurrently. We will also identify the important junctions and elucidate the salient commonalities of both areas of the law. To do this, we will assess the theoretical paradigm of the evolution of the law of maritime cabotage with public international law serving as the benchmark.

The foremost point to note here is that the sound understanding of the concept of maritime cabotage relies on comprehending how its various approaches are applied in the national and regional domains without infringing international law. Such understanding allows for an objective review of the sequence of events that have been instrumental in the development of both maritime cabotage law and public international law.

The increased importance of public international law, particularly in the twentieth century, can be largely attributed to the increase in international trade, 90 per cent of which (in volume) is transported by sea.[1] This brings us to the law of maritime cabotage which, when narrowly construed, defines where international transport of goods by sea stops and domestic transport of goods by sea begins.

While the first documented legislation on maritime cabotage can be traced back to the fourteenth century,[2] public international law dates from the Middle Ages.[3] However, it was not until the middle of the nineteenth century that much of the modern corpus of public international law began to develop.[4] The first international

---

1 See: UNEP, ITC and ICTSD, 'Trade and Environment Briefings: International Transport; ICTSD Programme on Global Economic Policy and Institutions' [2012], Policy Brief No. 5, International Centre for Trade and Sustainable Development.

2 5 Richard II. Stat. i, c. 3 – the 1382 promulgation by King Richard II.

3 W. Preiser (1984), 'History of The Law of Nations: Ancient Times To 1648', in R. Bernhardt (ed.), *Encyclopedia of Public International Law*, (7(1), pp. 132–159.

4 See: B. Fassbender and A. Peters, 'Introduction: Towards A Global History of International Law', in B. Fassbender and A. Peters (eds), *The Oxford Handbook of the History of International Law* (Oxford University Press 2012), pp. 3–24.

law conference was held in The Hague in 1930.[5] This was followed by the 1958 Conference on the Law of the Sea.[6] It was at the 1958 conference, held under the auspices of the United Nations, that conventions on the territorial sea, contiguous zone and high seas were all adopted.[7]

It is useful to provide a brief overview of the early relationship in the development of maritime cabotage law and public international law. From the records of the Codification Division of the United Nations Office of Legal Affairs, the International Law Commission selected the regimes of both territorial waters and the high seas as topics for codification at its first session, which was held in 1949. These topics were considered by the Commission starting from its second session in 1950 to her eighth session in 1956. Contributions to the discussions were made by various stakeholders including state governments and international organizations.

The final report on the territorial sea was adopted by the Commission in 1956. Meanwhile, the final drafts on the continental shelf, fisheries and the contiguous zone were submitted by the Commission to the General Assembly at its fifth session in 1953. Hence, at the eighth session in 1956, the draft articles on the contiguous zone, continental shelf, fisheries and high seas were included in a single bundle designed to constitute a final draft on the law of the sea. Following the discussion of the International Law Commission's report on the work of its eighth session,[8] the General Assembly adopted resolution 1105 (XI) of 21 February 1957. It was decided in that resolution to convene the United Nations Conference on the Law of the Sea in Geneva from 24 February to 27 April of 1958. The mandate of the conference was to review the law of the sea, taking account of not only the legal but also the technical, biological, economic and political aspects of the various issues. Eighty-six sovereign nations participated in the Conference and the result of its work was to be embodied in one or more conventions or other appropriate instruments. Accordingly, four separate conventions were adopted by the Conference on 29 April 1958 and were open for signature until 31 October 1958. It was thereafter open for accession by all member states of the United Nations, as well as other states and specialized agencies invited by the General Assembly to become party to the four conventions. They include: the convention on the territorial sea and the contiguous zone (entered into force on 10 September 1964); the Convention on the High Seas (entered into force on 30 September 1962); the Convention on Fishing and Conservation of the Living Resources of the High Seas (entered into force on 20 March 1966), and the Convention on the Continental Shelf (entered into force on 10 June 1964). In addition, an optional protocol of signature concerning the compulsory settlement of disputes was adopted and entered into force on 30 September 1962. The Conference also

5  See: Convention on Certain Questions Relating to The Conflict Of Nationality Laws. Held from 13 March 1930 to 12 April 1930, in The Hague.
6  The United Nations Conference on the Law of the Sea concluded on 29 April 1958, as recorded in the Final Act (A/CONF.13/L.58, 1958, UNCLOS, Off. Rec. vol. 2, 146).
7  J. Veon, *The United Nations Global Straightjacket* (Hearthstone 1999).
8  (A/CN.4/104).

adopted the following resolutions: Nuclear tests on the high seas, Pollution of the high seas by radio-active materials, International fishery conservation conventions, Co-operation in conservation measures, Humane killing of marine life, Special situations relating to coastal fisheries, Régime of historic waters, Convening of a second United Nations Conference on the Law of the Sea, and Tribute to the International Law Commission. A second conference was held in 1960 to reconsider the topics not agreed upon at the 1958 Conference. Finally, a third conference was held from 1973 to 1982 and resulted in the adoption of the United Nations Convention on the Law of the Sea (UNCLOS 1982), which has superseded, for those states party to it, the four conventions adopted in 1958. UNCLOS 1982 is now the principal international law dealing with issues relating to the law of the sea.

## International law

Since the definition of maritime cabotage has already received sufficient attention, it is now imperative to define international law within the context of this book. There are several variations in the definition of international law. It depends on whether the definition stems from a sovereignty, religious, nature, political or moral perspective. Here we will focus on the sovereignty and political perspectives. The objective of this section is not to provide a comprehensive survey of the development of international law. However, the problem is that the discourse that follows may be trapped unintentionally in the Eurocentric and Euro-American ideologies of the development of international law.

Basically, international law may be defined as the law of the political system of nation-states. It is a distinct and self-contained system of law that is independent of the national systems with which it interacts. It deals with relations that it does not effectively govern.[9] International law is generally described as the law of nations since nation-states are still the most important subjects of international law.[10]

However, new developments suggest that to continue to define international law narrowly as a law regulating relationship between sovereign states is no longer entirely correct. This is because international organizations (often referred to as legal persons) and, in some circumstances, natural persons may be subjected to the rules and principles of international law.[11] Therefore, the absence of an overall legislative body in the international system dictates that the principles of international law should be identified through a variety of mechanisms. This lack of an overriding legislative authority can encourage a misconception that international law is difficult to comprehend.[12]

---

9 K. McKeever, *Researching Public International Law* (Columbia University 2006).
10 See: J. Bentham, *Introduction to the Principles of Morals and Legislation* (London 1780).
11 See the *Rome Statute of the International Criminal Court*.
12 H. Koh, 'Why Do Nations Obey International Law?' [1997], Yale Law School Legal Scholarship Repository Faculty Scholarship Series, Paper 2101, 1–62.

International law is widely perceived as the product of a slow historical evolution. It experienced a steady rise from around the seventeenth century, and by the twentieth century was generally accepted as the authority governing relations between nations. Presently, the scope of international law includes the rights and duties pertaining to international organizations, companies and human persons. International law was Eurocentric for many generations. It only began to expand beyond Europe to cover those nations that became independent of European colonization at the back end of the eighteenth century and start of the nineteenth century. Turkey became the first non-Christian nation to be subjected to international law by the mid-nineteenth century.[13] The start of the twentieth century witnessed further expansion, with Asian countries including China, Persia and Japan embracing international law. The establishment of the League of Nations in 1920 opened membership to any nation.[14] This marked the advent of the automatic application of international law to all nations irrespective of character or location.[15]

The origin of international law is often tied to events that took place many thousands of years ago. Frequent reference is usually made to the alleged solemn treaty between the rulers of Lagash and Umma around 2550 BC.[16] This treaty is

13 G. Oduntan, 'International Laws and the Discontented: Westernisation, the Development and the Underdevelopment of International Laws', in A. Dhanda and A. Parashar (eds), *Decolonisation of Legal Knowledge* (Taylor & Francis 2009).

14 Article 1 of the Covenant of the League of Nations.

15 D. Harris, *Cases and Materials on International Law* (7th edn, Thomson Reuters 2010).

16 Lagash and Umma, were adjacent Sumerian kingdoms only 20 miles apart. They fought constantly over the stretch of the *Gu'edena* valley that ran between their two cities. According to the treaty of Mesilim or peace treaty, dated 2550 BC, the kingdoms of Lagash and Umma agreed to a set border between their two limitrophe territories, to be marked by a *stele* (in those days, a land border was marked by a large stone marker, a small stone pillar, called a *stele*). It is suggested that this treaty is more appropriately a treaty of delimitation, establishing territorial boundary and sovereignty between the two warring kingdoms. The best record of the world's oldest international law treaty is now in the Louvre Museum in Paris, inscribed on the sides of a large clay peg. In the style of the time, the inscription sets out the formal pronouncement of the historical record of the Lagash ruler, circa 2400 BC, Entemena. The inscription on the sides of the clay peg refers to the original border treaty between Umma and Lagash as having been set by Mesilim around 2550, although the accuracy of this date has been questioned and other dates cited. The document suggests that soon after the stele was put in place, Umma gained the upper hand and began routinely ignoring the border. In 2400 BC, according to another archaeological document known as the Stele of Vultures, the king of Lagash, Eannatum, went to war with Umma and won. He forced the Umma king to take an oath that his inhabitants would stick to their side of the canal. The Stele of Vultures was discovered at Telloh, on the site of what used to be Girsu, but there were only fragments. The reference to the treaty of 2550 BC is hidden in the statements of religious celebration and pronouncements of the victory of Eannatum in 2450 BC. Eventually, the historic border became moot when a group known as the Akkads defeated most of the Sumerian cities and brought them into a new kingdom called the Babylonian Empire, after their capital city of Babylon. Still, the two ancient neighbours fought intermittently for hundreds

said to have established a defined boundary between both communities. In addition, more than a thousand years later, the treaty between Rameses II of Egypt and the king of the Hittites established peace and respect for territorial integrity.[17] However, one must stop to ponder how an agreement between two ancient communities came to be characterized as the origin of a law that binds the nations of the world today. Nevertheless, it is such references that give credence to the difficulty of establishing the exact origin of international law.

This difficulty leads to the separate but related and important issue of prejudiced literature. This is because the formative period of international law is often discussed from a Eurocentric angle. This ignores equally important contributions to the development of this area of law from other regions of the world.[18] On the other hand, the acknowledgement of non-Eurocentric contributions to the development of international law is generally consigned to the post-colonial era.[19] However, this perception, as created by the available literature, is not correct. From the medieval period, the Asian continent has contributed to the development of certain principles of modern international law.[20] Some of these principles were already developed and practised in the ancient empires of Carthage, Rhodes, Egypt and the Phoenicians.[21] The Mughal Empire in India, the Maratha state in India, the Indonesian states, the kingdoms of

---

of years and the border moved with the fortunes of war. This relative success of legal documents formed the background of legal codes between ruler and citizen and citizen and citizen, including Urukagina's Code and, six hundred years later, Hammurabi's glorious code of law. For a broader and more instructive read on ancient international law treaties, see: C. Phillips and A. Axelrod, *Encyclopedia of Historical Treaties And Alliance: From Ancient Times to the 1930s* (vol. 1, 2nd edn, Facts on File Library of World History, 2006).

17   See the peace treaty between Ramses II and Hattusili III – which had both Hittite and Egyptian versions. This treaty, considered the world's first peace treaty, was signed in 1258 BCE and read in part: 'Reamasesa, the great king, the king of the country of Egypt, shall never attack the country of Hatti to take possession of a part (of this country). And Hattusili, the great king, the king of the country of Hatti, shall never attack the country of Egypt to take possession of a part (of that country).' For an expanded read, see: S. Langdon, and A. Gardiner, 'The Treaty of Alliance between Ḫattušili, King of the Hittites, and the Pharaoh Ramesses II of Egypt' [1920], *Journal of Egyptian Archaeology*, 6(3), 179–205. See also: R. Wallace and O. Martin-Ortega, *International Law* (7th edn, Sweet & Maxwell 2013). See further: J. Mark, 'The Battle of Kadesh and the First Peace Treaty' [2012], *Ancient History Encyclopedia*, 18 January.

18   A. Lorca, 'Eurocentrism in the History of International Law', in B. Fassbender and A. Peters (eds), *The Oxford Handbook of the History of International Law* (Oxford University Press 2012), pp. 1034–1057.

19   M. Koskenniemi, 'The Politics of International Law' [1990], *European Journal of International Law*, 1(1), 4–32.

20   R. Falk, 'The New States and the International Legal Order' [1966], *Recueil de Cours*, 118(1), 34–43.

21   D. Desierto, 'Postcolonial International Law Discourses on Regional Developments in South and Southeast Asia' [2008], *International Journal of Legal Information*, 36(3), 387–431.

Burma and Ceylon have also contributed significantly to the development of international law.[22] These contributions are seen in areas such as the use of treaties, diplomatic protocol and maritime principles on the freedom of the seas.[23] In the sixteenth century, the ancient civilization in India had specifically developed legislation regulating the conduct of states. This legislation laid out regulations on wars, treaties, asylum and the treatment of foreign nationals, the acquisition of territory, and laws on navigation and trade.[24]

## A comparative overview of the evolution of maritime cabotage law and public international law from seventeenth to twenty-first century

The aim of this section is to assess the evolution of the law of maritime cabotage and international law from their formative stages to their present status. The idea is to establish the converging and diverging points as both areas of the law developed. It is generally accepted that maritime cabotage law and international law did not start out at the same time. However, it appears that trade between nations was the common premise in the development of both areas of law. The *ius gentium* – often referred to as the first international law, was promulgated in 212 AD and was based on the commercial law in practice in the Mediterranean trade.[25] Regulations relating to the sea, and by extension maritime cabotage, was practised by some of the early trading nations. This contrasts with international law, which only really began to have a foothold among nations in the mid-nineteenth century.[26]

Although international law gradually gained global acceptance after the two world wars, maritime cabotage law has struggled to gain similar international acceptance. This is the case not only at international level, but perhaps surprisingly even at national level.[27] The difficulty with accepting maritime cabotage law at international level is attributed particularly to the lack of clarity on the agenda of an international maritime cabotage framework. On the other hand, the divisiveness at national level can be ascribed to the many national shipping interests craving the maritime cabotage law of their country to be drafted, with their interests as the overriding parameter. For instance, indigenous shipowners would advocate for a protectionist maritime cabotage policy so that they could operate without competition from foreign shipowners. The same is true for indigenous shipbuilders. However, indigenous shippers would seek a liberal maritime cabotage policy that allows foreign shipowners to engage in the cabotage trade of the

22 R. Anand, *Development of Modern International Law and India* (Nomos 2005).
23 M. Sornarajah, 'The Asian Perspective to International Law in the Age of Globalization' [2001], *Singapore Journal of International & Corporative Law*, 5(1), 284–313.
24 C. Alexandrowicz, *An Introduction to the History of the Law of Nations in the East Indies* (Clarendon Press 1967).
25 For a more generic read on the issues, see: A. Kaczorowska, *Public International Law* (3rd edn, Routledge Cavendish 2005), p. 2.
26 For an extensive read, see the Custom of the Phoenicians and the Rhodian Sea Law.
27 A detailed discussion of the different maritime cabotage legislation and policies of various sovereign maritime countries appears in later chapters.

country. This is because the cost of shipping cargo on an indigenous vessel is generally much higher than the cost of shipping similar cargo on a foreign vessel.[28]

There is evidence that documented legislation of maritime cabotage existed in England as far back as 1382.[29] In this book, however, a more recent starting point is picked to assess the development of both maritime cabotage law and international law. Therefore, the period between the seventeenth and twenty-first centuries has been selected for a comparative overview of both areas of law. An assessment of the formative period of both maritime cabotage law and international law will reveal the challenges that faced many countries at that time. The seventeenth century witnessed several events in both maritime and international law. The 1648 Peace of Westphalia, the 1651 Navigation Laws and the emergence of Hugo Grotius are highlights of how both areas of the law have evolved. Hugo Grotius is often referred to as the father of international law and his works on international law and freedom of the seas are much celebrated because of the important part they played in the evolution of both areas of the law. However, many scholars argue that Grotius's postulations on international law principles were not entirely groundbreaking even in that era. It is readily pointed out that his work and philosophy were heavily influenced by Alberico Gentili's 1598 *De Jure Belli*.[30] We will see in this section the intricate mechanism involved in transitioning from the legal mechanism of the Middle Ages to the present international legal framework under the 'Law of Nations'.[31]

The multilateral agreement system was a popular mechanism for building relationships among nations in the medieval period. This system is still very much in use today. However, one of the weaknesses of multilateral agreements under the medieval legal system was that parties to the agreement were likely to withdraw from any agreed commitments at the slightest provocation. The ease with which a state could withdraw from a commitment without repercussions fuelled the need for a binding international regulatory framework that compelled better compliance.[32]

---

28  For a general read, see: M. Brooks, 'Liberalization in Maritime Transport' [2009], International Transport Forum (Forum Paper 2). See also: J. Hodgson and M. Brooks, 'Towards a North American Cabotage Regime: A Canadian Perspective' [2007], *Canadian Journal of Transportation*, 1(1), 19–35.

29  5 Richard II. Stat. i, c. 3– the 1382 promulgation by King Richard II.

30  For a more specific read, see: J. Bentham, *Introduction to the Principles of Morals and Legislation* (London 1780). See also: G. Edmond, 'The Freedom of Histories: Reassessing Grotius on the Sea' [1995], *University of Wollongong Australia Law Text Culture*, 2(9), 179–217.

31  See: S. Neff, *War and the Law of Nations: A General History* (Cambridge University Press 2005).

32  See: L. Casey, and D. Rivkin, 'Making Law: The United Nations' Role in Formulating and Enforcing International Law', in B. Schaefer (ed.), *Conundrum: The Limits of the United Nations and the Search for Alternatives* (Rowman & Littlefield 2009), pp. 31–56.

Returning to the focus of this sub-chapter, the central theme in the development of international law in the seventeenth century was 'sovereignty'. At first, this was only common in Europe but it swiftly spread to other parts of the globe.[33] On the other hand, the central theme of maritime cabotage in the seventeenth century was the debate on the freedom of the seas. The question at the centre of this debate was whether the territorial seas should be free for use by all or whether in fact the sea could be subjected to nation ownership. In the eighteenth century, the central theme of international law was the speed with which the prioritization of national interests by sovereign nations accelerated. Furthermore, there were concerted efforts by Western powers to pursue peaceful relations by making better use of diplomacy and negotiations.[34] The law of maritime cabotage in the eighteenth century revolved around the debate surrounding the extent to which sovereign states could impose maritime cabotage jurisdiction over the territorial sea. A decrease in colonization by Western powers and the rise of nationalism and independent nations was the central theme of international law in the nineteenth century.[35] Sovereign states continued to pursue partnerships and build international relations to manage the risk of conflict.[36] Maritime cabotage law in the nineteenth century was characterised by the abolition of the British Navigation Act in 1849 and the protectionist cabotage law in 1854 respectively.[37] This was significant because Britain was one of the dominant powers at sea at the time. It is widely believed that Britain being an island nation brought an end to their protectionist maritime cabotage policy for fear that other nations of the world as they became stronger economically, could retaliate against Britain with similar protectionist policies.[38] The twentieth century witnessed changes in sovereign governance, technological advancement, and economic principles under international law. The central theme of that century was the unprecedented desire for peace and the determined effort of nations to avoid conflict where possible.[39]

---

33 Sovereignty is a concept said to have been first analysed systematically by Jean Bodin in his *Six Livres de la Republique* of 1576.

34 I. Kant, *Perpetual Peace: A Philosophical Sketch*. Translated by W. Hastie 1891 (Clark 1795).

35 For a broader take on the issues, see: G. Underhill, 'Global Governance and Political Economy: Public, Private and Political Authority in the Twenty-first Century', in J. Clarke and G. Edwards (eds), *Global Governance in the Twenty-first Century* (Palgrave Macmillan 2004), pp. 112–138.

36 H. Kissinger, 'The Congress of Vienna: A Reappraisal' (1956), *World Politics*, 8(2), 264–280.

37 House of Commons, 'Coasting Trade Bill' [1854], *Hansard*, 131, 462–466. 7 March.

38 For further reading, see: D. Coulter, 'Globalization of Maritime Commerce: The Rise of Hub Ports', in S. Tangredi (ed.), *Globalization and Maritime Power* (National Defence University 2009), pp. 133–142. In essence, the abolition of the protectionist maritime cabotage policy in Britain, signalled the beginning of other maritime nations enacting a maritime cabotage policy to suit their circumstances of the time.

39 For related views on the issues, see: R. Pastor, 'The Great Powers in an Age of Global Governance: Are They Still Great?', in J. Clarke and G. Edwards (eds), *Global Governance in the Twenty-first Century* (Palgrave Macmillan 2004), pp. 139–176.

On the other hand, maritime cabotage law in the twentieth century can be viewed in the context of the several attempts (albeit unsuccessful) to promote the much-needed international framework for maritime cabotage, often tied to a free trade agenda.[40] There have been unsuccessful attempts at the Uruguay Round, Doha Round and other high level WTO platforms to find common grounds among nations on an international harmonised maritime cabotage concept.[41] On that basis, there is room to argue that the inability to move forward with discussions on an international harmonised concept of maritime cabotage at both the Uruguay and Doha rounds should be viewed as missed opportunities. Furthermore, it is regrettable that progressive discussions on international harmonization of maritime cabotage services continues to be avoided or accorded little attention at relevant international forums.[42] The absence of an international regulatory framework means that individual nations retain the right to dictate which maritime cabotage approach policy to pursue. In the case of some developing countries, their maritime sectors are generally regarded by their governments as attractive investment opportunities for domestic and foreign investors.[43] As a result, these countries are likely to consider a protectionist maritime cabotage policy that reserves all maritime activities between two points on their maritime border to their national instrumentalities of commerce. This is despite the general acknowledgement that protectionist policies of this sort hamper the efficiency of maritime transport systems. Furthermore, such policies safeguard inefficient indigenous maritime cabotage service providers, thus increasing the cost of freight and consumer goods and services.[44] The twenty-first century has witnessed significant changes in how the role of international law is perceived in both developing countries and the industrialised nations whose influence is instrumental to the proper functioning of international law.[45] The consequence is that regionalization has become a more acceptable concept and there is more confidence among independent nations to synergise with each other. However, it is important that international law continues to function in a way that ensures that the sovereignty

40  A. Freudmann, 'WTO Urged to Avoid Cabotage Controversy' [1999], *Journal of Commerce*, 9 February.
41  P. Bossche, *The Law and Policy of the World Trade Organization: Text, Cases and Materials* (2nd edn, Cambridge University Press 2008).
42  See: A. Freudmann, 'WTO Urged to Avoid Cabotage Controversy' [1999], *Journal of Commerce*, 9 February. The director of shipping policy and external relations for the Chamber of Shipping (Mark Brownrigg) warned that the World Trade Organization's Millennium Round should not take on issues of domestic maritime cabotage even if it was desirable to do so, since maritime cabotage had no chance of universal acceptance. He argued that including maritime cabotage in the debate could scuttle chances for a broader agreement to limit protectionism.
43  A similar argument is presented in J. Drexhage and D. Murphy, *Sustainable Development: From Brundtland to Rio 2012* (IISD 2010).
44  See the 2007 ITC report on the 'Economic Effect of Significant U.S. Import Restraints'.
45  For a broader read on the issues, see: A. Harmes, *The Return of the State: Protestors, Power-Brokers and the New Global Compromise* (Douglas & McIntyre 2004).

of independent nations remains protected.[46] In contrast, maritime cabotage law in the twenty-first century has fallen firmly under the regulatory discretion of national governments. This is despite the fact that maritime cabotage law is recognized under both international law and transnational commercial treaties.[47] Furthermore, the contextual understanding of the law of maritime cabotage is no longer limited to trade and navigation. It now encompasses areas that hitherto fell under the company, immigration and labour legislations of sovereign nations. The maritime cabotage policies in many countries remain a political tool and, as such, tend to gravitate to protectionist maritime cabotage policies. That said, the law of maritime cabotage has also been gradually moving to align with the principles of cooperative international law. Hence, many countries have found a way to engage in each other's coastal waters through bilateral and multilateral understandings. Therefore, the idea of easing restrictions in the maritime cabotage sector in many nations does not sound as objectionable now as it once did in previous centuries.[48] For instance, the European Commission is open to the idea of allowing international maritime transport suppliers to move or reposition their equipment (i.e. empty containers) on their vessels between ports in a member state, provided that no revenue is involved.[49] However, allowing international players to engage in the maritime cabotage of a nation, even when no revenue is involved, would still present immediate and deep challenges. For instance, the European Community's proposal would still:

a   deny the home nation the opportunity to employ indigenous personnel;
b   hamper indigenous shipowners from providing such services for reward of freight and other revenues;
c   undermine the government of the home nation from generating revenue from those services;
d   provoke maritime and national security concerns.

Be that as it may, the proposal by the European Commission has been met by stiff opposition from EU shipowners. This demonstrates that any proposal that

---

46  For a general read on the issues, see: C. Staker, 'Jurisdiction. The Individual and the International Legal System', in M. Evans (ed.), *International Law* (4th edn, Oxford University Press 2014), pp. 309–335. There are many challenges facing International law in the twenty-first century and beyond, particularly in areas such as human rights, environment, domestic wars and foreign intervention, technological advancement and exploration of outer space and the sea bed. However, for the purpose of this book, maintaining the sovereign rights of nations is the key challenge.
47  See: L. Oppenheim, 'The Meaning of Coasting: Trade in Commercial Treaties' [1908], *Law Quarterly Review*, 24(3), 328–334.
48  For a broader read, see: G. Mailer, 'Europe, the American Crisis, and Scottish Evangelism: The Primacy of Foreign Policy in the Kirk?', in W. Mulligan and B. Simms (eds), *The Primacy of Foreign Policy in British History, 1660–2000: How Strategic Concerns Shaped Modern Britain* (Palgrave Macmillan 2010), pp. 119–136.
49  World Trade Organization, 'Communication from the European Communities and its Member States' [2005], TN/S/O/EEC/Rev.1. 05–2792. Council for Trade in Services Special Session. 29 June 2005.

fails to substantially accommodate the interests of domestic operators is likely to be challenged. It is suggested that more countries will embrace the concept of a regional maritime cabotage policy before the end of the twenty-first century. This idea is now being considered with less resistance than in the last quarter of the twentieth century. For instance, the EU maritime cabotage law allows member states to engage in maritime cabotage within the European Union.[50] The African Union has drafted a maritime transport charter that would open the regional maritime cabotage trade and services.[51] The idea of a regional maritime cabotage policy has also been considered in Asia, South America, North America and the Pacific regions.[52] However, the challenge with regional policies is the possibility of internal implosion. This is because the more advanced nations in the region may skew the scope and objective of the policy to their advantage and against that of the developing nations.[53]

On the other hand, many maritime nations in the twenty-first century have opted to compromise by accepting the idea of an international relay scheme. Hence, foreign vessels can engage in a nation's maritime cabotage trade if they are either arriving in the country on an international leg of the voyage or departing the country on an international voyage.[54] However, this scheme focuses on only one problem (i.e. the high freight cost) out of the many that surround the concept of a protectionist maritime cabotage policy.

Following the comparative overview of five decades of the development of both international and maritime cabotage law, what is clear is that both areas of law share some important central themes. These include sovereignty, development, national security and international services. Although the law of maritime cabotage and international law have developed under different frameworks, they have often converged to regulate national and international activities.[55] For instance, the International Law of the Sea is one of several international legislations whose provisions legislate for both international law and maritime cabotage law frameworks. International law and maritime cabotage law are particularly interrelated when they deal with sovereignty and the territorial sea. The Law of the Sea is prima facie rooted in public maritime law principles, even though it falls under the framework of international law. Nevertheless, it should be noted that maritime cabotage falls within the sovereign authority of a nation and at present there is no provision to divest such nation of its sovereign rights under international law.

50 See the provisions of Council Regulation (EEC) No. 3577/92.
51 See: Section 11 of the 1994 African Maritime Transport Charter. See also: Section 15 of the 2010 African Maritime Transport Charter – when it comes into force and replaces the 1994 charter.
52 See: ASEAN, MECOSUR, NAFTA and PACER maritime frameworks.
53 L. Weiss, 'Global Governance, National Strategies: How Industrialized States Make Room to Move Under the WTO' [2005], *Review of International Political Economy*, 12(5), 723–749.
54 See the cabotage policies of New Zealand and the Philippines.
55 See the provisions of the United Nations Law of the Sea 1982, which legislate for both public international law and maritime cabotage law.

## The legal habitat of maritime cabotage law and public international law

This section is focused on the sources of public international law and maritime cabotage law. Bearing in mind the different nature of both areas of law, identifying the sources from which these laws come into existence has an immediate bearing on the issues of who has authority to make the law, what is the scope of the law, and who is the law made to govern. The answers to these questions are not always as clear cut as might be expected. This is primarily because of the role of the sovereign state and the peculiarities of each state. However, to learn the sources of both areas of law, we must first understand the processes through which rules of maritime cabotage law and international law come into existence. Let us consider first the legal habitat of international law. We have already defined international law as the law governing the conduct between or among the nations of the world. This suggests that, at least in theory, every nation would provide some form of consent to abide with the provisions of the law. Furthermore, the threshold of obligations and liabilities should be the same for all the member nations of the world.

According to Article 38(1) of the Statute of the International Court of Justice, the sources of international law are:

a    International treaties or conventions (whether general or particular) which establish rules expressly recognized by the contesting states.
b    International custom, as evidence of a general practice accepted as law.
c    The general principles of law recognized by civilized nations.
d    Judicial decisions and the teachings of the most highly qualified publicists of the various nations, as subsidiary means for the determination of rules of law. However, this is subject to the provisions of Article 59. We note here that the provisions of Article 59 releases the ICJ from being bound by precedence. This means that the decision of the court applies only between the parties in a particular case and has no binding force on future cases.
e    In addition to the above, by Article 38(2), the power of the court to decide a case *ex aequo et bono* (i.e. according to what is equitable and good), if the parties agree thereto is a source of international law.

Before international law becomes enforceable it must go through the processes of signature, ratification, and entry into force. This means that the proposed text of a treaty cannot become law until such a time agreed, after it has acquired the stipulated number of ratifications by member states who are signatories to the convention. This is generally followed by the various member states incorporating the international law into their national legislative framework by an act of parliament or similar mechanism. For instance, the Carriage of Goods by Sea Act 1971 is a United Kingdom act of parliament that incorporates into English law the Hague-Visby Rules of

1968.[56] Finally, the United Nations serves as the central repository for all sources of international law.[57]

In contrast, the legal habitat of maritime cabotage law is not uniformly codified and there is no central repository. Rather, the sources of maritime cabotage law can be found in the various national legislations spanning across several sectors, in regional legislative frameworks and treaties, and in international conventions. It is this lack of harmonization or uniformity that is in large part responsible for the uncertain and complex nature of maritime cabotage law. For instance, in the national domain, a country may choose to exercise its right to adopt a protectionist, liberal or flexible maritime cabotage approach. For example, where a protectionist maritime cabotage approach is adopted, the objective is to reserve all maritime activities – at least in the territorial waters – to the national instrumentalities of commerce. This means that within the national domain, the legal habitat of maritime cabotage law may exist in at least two legislative instruments. There may be a single national maritime cabotage legislative framework. Alternatively, the maritime cabotage law provisions may be found in legislation regulating various sectors of a country. Where the latter is the case, the maritime cabotage law of a sovereign state may be found in acts of parliament, customs law, national constitutions, immigration acts, shipping laws and company law. Hence, a provision stipulating that ship crew be indigenous may conceivably be found in the labour or immigration laws of the state rather than part of a maritime cabotage legal framework.

Maritime cabotage within the regional domain is more harmonized and this minimizes the degree of complexity associated with the concept of maritime cabotage. In this context, the regional member states agree to sacrifice some of their sovereignty for the benefit of the communal interest. The norm is that the member states agree to a reciprocal removal of the barriers to free engagement in maritime activities in their territorial waters. As a result, there is only one set of legislative framework governing all the member states.[58]

Maritime cabotage is less conspicuous at international level. What is interesting about this is that the primary objective of a maritime cabotage regime is to keep international players such as foreign shipowners and others from engaging in the domestic maritime sector. What is not helpful is that over the years there has been no clarity regarding what the agenda of an international maritime cabotage framework might be. To this point, the provisions giving cover to the right of

---

56 The International Convention for the Unification of Certain Rules of Law Relating to Bills of Lading (1924)/First Protocol (1968)/Second Protocol (1979). The Hague–Visby Rules are a set of international rules for the international carriage of goods by sea that were drafted originally as the Hague Rules in Brussels in 1924. The Hague Rules are still enforceable in many countries that are yet to ratify the amended version of 1968.

57 See the third objective in the preamble of the Charter of the United Nations signed on 26 June 1945 in San Francisco, after the United Nations Conference on International Organization, and came into force on 24 October 1945.

58 See Council Regulation (EEC) No. 3577/92, which regulates maritime cabotage in the European Union and came into force in 1993.

sovereign states to implement a maritime cabotage regime in UNCLOS 1982 appear not to be sufficient.[59] Similarly, the decision of the Permanent Court of Arbitration in *The Republic of the Philippines v. The People's Republic of China*[60] should be welcome news for an international maritime cabotage agenda. However, it is not yet clear how much impact that decision will have given that both parties have since acted in a way that suggests a lack of willingness to comply with the ruling of the court. It appears we should look to the international legal framework of UNCLOS 1982 and the ruling of the Permanent Court of Arbitration as the legal habitat of international maritime cabotage, regardless of how unobtrusive maritime cabotage law at the international domain may seem.

## The intersection of internationality and national maritime frontiers

The relationship between international law and the domestic laws governing sovereign states is based on conformity. By that we mean that the domestic law should conform with rather than contradict the provisions of international law. Indeed, this could be reduced to understanding the mechanism by which international law is applied within domestic law. Moreover, it is important to remember the provisions of Article 27 of the Vienna Convention on the Law of Treaties, which state categorically that a state may not invoke the provisions of her domestic laws as a justification for failing to abide by her international law obligations. This is of course subject to the provisions of Article 46 of the same convention.[61] The provisions of Article 27 should not be used as a basis to suggest that the rule of international law must always prevail over domestic law rules. This is particularly evident where there is no consent to the rules of the international law by the state.[62]

We have so far discussed the concept of maritime cabotage from the perspective of sea boundaries. The discussion has mainly focused on the right of a sovereign state to decide whether to allow foreign entities to engage in maritime activities within the state's domestic waters. However, there is another perspective to this argument, which is: at what point does the nationalist agenda intersect with the international character of the maritime sector and what is the impact of such intersection. To a large extent this was central to the debate on closed versus open seas between two prominent jurists. In his 1609 treatise *mare liberum* (freedom of the seas), Hugo Grotius postulated that the sea is common to all and hence no nation should be entitled to claim

---

59 Article 2 of the United Nations Convention on the Law of the Sea 1982.
60 [2016] PCA Case No. 2013–19.
61 Article 46 stipulates that a state may not invoke the fact that its consent to be bound by a treaty has been expressed in violation of a provision of its internal law regarding competence to conclude treaties as invalidating its consent. The Vienna Convention was concluded on 23 May 1969 but its rulings did not come into force until 27 January 1980.
62 See the ruling of the Permanent Court of International Justice in *German Interests in Polish Upper Silesia (Germany v. Poland)* on 25 May 1926. (1926) PCIJ Series A no. 7.

proprietary rights over it.[63] However, John Selden advocated an alternative argument in his 1635 work on the *mare clausum* (closed sea). Selden argued that there was no reason why the sea could not be subjected to the kind of national possession similar to that enjoyed by landed proprietors.[64]

Bearing in mind these different views, there are two angles for looking at the intersection of internationality and national maritime frontiers. The first is where the mercantile realities in both the national and international domains fail to align. The other is where it has become imperative to recalibrate the national legislative framework to correspond with regional or international legislation such that, at a minimum, the two paradigms can operate in parallel.

Let us assess the first angle, where the mercantile realities do not align. Where a protectionist maritime cabotage regime restricts foreign vessels to their first port of call in the country, the objective is usually to give the indigenous shipowners the opportunity to either facilitate the onward transport of the cargo to its final destination or to get the cargo to a port where it will be placed on a foreign carrier. However, because indigenous shipowners typically lack the economies of scale available to international shipowners, there is usually a significant increase in the cost of domestic freighting of the cargo to its destination. The additional cost of freight is typically borne by the indigenous shippers in the imports and exports trade. An example of this is when the Malaysian government replaced a protectionist maritime cabotage policy with a flexible one in 2009 to assuage complaints about the high cost of transhipment made by indigenous shippers and consumers in the eastern part of Malaysia.[65] Prior to that change in policy, the protectionist maritime cabotage law did not allow foreign ships to call directly at ports in the eastern states of Malaysia. Hence, cargo destined for those states would usually be transhipped to domestic vessels at Port Klang in the west for onward carriage to its destination. Similarly, the lack of domestic capacity combined with huge dependence on foreign technical expertise led the Indonesian government to exempt the domestic oil and gas sector from their protectionist maritime cabotage Law 17 of 2008. The rationale behind this decision was that to act otherwise would have caused serious disruptions to an important sector of the Indonesian economy.[66]

Therefore, the domestic economy bears the brunt of the consequences when the mercantile realities of a nationalist agenda fail to align with the international

63  H. Grotius, 'Mare Liberum: The Freedom of the Seas or The Right Which Belongs to The Dutch To Take Part in the East Indian Trade', translated by R. Magoffin, in J. Scott (ed.), *Classics of International Law* (Oxford University Press 1916).

64  T. Fulton, *The Sovereignty of the Sea: An Historical Account of the Claims to England to the Dominion of the British Seas, And of the Evolution of the Territorial Waters: With Special Reference to the Right of Fishing And The Naval Salute* (William Blackwood 1911).

65  See the official letter exempting foreign vessels from the provisions of subsection 65 KA(1) of the Merchant Shipping Ordinance 1952, dated 1 June 2009. This directive came into force 3 June 2009. Note that under section 65KA of the Domestic Shipping Licence Board of Malaysia, non-Malaysian vessels are prohibited from engaging in domestic shipping.

66  See Indonesian Government Regulation 22/2011.

character of the maritime sector. This flies in the face of the argument that the rationale for a choice of a maritime cabotage approach is to facilitate national economic development.

Next, we consider the second angle, where there is need to recalibrate the national legislative frameworks. This usually occurs when the maritime cabotage law of a sovereign state conflicts with specific provisions of a regional or international legislative framework. When this happens, the expectation is that the national cabotage law will be amended to satisfy the provisions of the regional or international law. A good example of this is the application of the maritime cabotage legislative framework of the European Union, which became law in 1993. The EU Regulation is designed to allow Community shipowners the freedom to provide maritime transport services between member states in the European Union. This is subject to the proviso that they have satisfied the requirements and are eligible to carry out similar services in their home state. Prior to Council Regulation 3577/92 coming into force, member states in the European Union implemented different approaches to maritime cabotage. Some states (Greece, France, Spain, and Italy) had traditionally implemented a protectionist maritime cabotage regime, and thus there was need to amend their legislation to comply with the new European Union regulation. However, other states (United Kingdom Netherlands and Norway) had traditionally adopted a liberal or an open coast policy and did not need to make any changes to their legislation.[67] The same can be said about the proposed regional maritime cabotage framework of the African Union. The proposed legal framework advocates for a European Union-type liberal maritime cabotage approach within the African Union. Should this proposal become law, it will conflict with the protectionist maritime cabotage legislation of sovereign states within the African Union such as Nigeria. Thus, Nigeria would need to recalibrate her national maritime cabotage legislative framework so that it complies with the regional framework.

## The role of globalization in the development of maritime cabotage law

We have already discussed how the original concept of maritime cabotage was confined to navigating the seas along the coast of a sovereign state. We have also indicated that the original concept has since expanded in scope. A principal reason for this expansion is globalization. In basic terms, globalization may be defined as the desire to promote an integrated global economy facilitated by free trade, free movement of capital and maximizing the use of cheap labour. The result of this is a rapid increase in knowledge transfer, resource distribution and cross-boundary transportation of goods and services among the nations of the world. Furthermore, the advancement in technology has provided a platform for a near seamless transition of these resources.

67 See appendix 1 of Council Regulation (EEC) No. 3577/92 for EU member states' adaptation of their national laws to comply with EU maritime cabotage law.

This section is not concerned with a generic discussion on globalization – rather, it focuses specifically on how globalization has contributed to shaping the policy and legal framework of maritime cabotage within the national and regional domains. One way in which globalization has impacted national and regional maritime cabotage policies is the process of turning raw materials into a finished product. For instance, rather than processing raw materials at source into finished goods, economies of scale offer an opportunity to transport larger quantities of the raw materials for processing in locations nearer to the product markets. This is exemplified in the oil trade, where crude oil is refined into finished products far away from the exploration centre. The need to sustain global demand for finished products demands the exploration of very remote areas for the raw materials. Exploring these remote areas requires human labour and domestic transportation. Hence, whereas in the past a nation would generally have tolerated the exploration and transportation of its raw materials by foreign entities, this is no longer the case. Globalization has alerted all and enlightened national and regional governments to the benefit of reserving such domestic opportunities to indigenous people and national instrumentalities of commerce. Therefore, it is no surprise that the provisions of most national maritime cabotage frameworks stipulate that no merchandise shall be transported by water either directly or via a foreign port except in vessels owned and crewed by her citizens, built in the country and registered under the laws of the host cabotage country. These restrictions are not limited to the carriage of goods and persons or the provision of maritime services within domestic waters but also apply to exploration of natural resources and setting up principal places of business.[68]

Thus, globalization has shaped maritime cabotage law frameworks in such a way that the legislation of maritime cabotage laws by national and regional governments is now seen through the lens of protecting the domestic maritime sector from foreign competition. This is achieved by restricting foreign entities from accessing cargo and may be combined with offering incentives such as tax exemptions to indigenous maritime operators.

68 For a general read, see: S. Kumar and J. Hoffmann, 'Globalization: The Maritime Nexus', in C. Grammenos (ed.), *Handbook of Maritime Economics and Business* (Informa 2002), pp. 35–62.

# 3 The theory of developmental sovereignty

One of the issues that plague the concept of maritime cabotage is that one is never sure what rationale is used to justify the adoption of a specific maritime cabotage policy. Nevertheless, the general approach is that sovereign states base their choice of maritime cabotage policy on the need to promote national economic development. If this argument is to be considered, one is perfectly entitled to argue that the measure of economic development ought to be assessed with the aim of verifying whether the choice of maritime cabotage policy has indeed on balance contributed to the desired development. If one accepts this invitation, then, the theory of developmental sovereignty provides an appropriate mechanism for measuring economic development vis-à-vis the choice of maritime cabotage approach. In doing so, it must take into consideration the processes through which rules of maritime cabotage law come into existence. The importance of this theory goes further because it provides a pathway to a common understanding of the different approaches of maritime cabotage law. This is because it is not about making law based on reciprocity, reprisal or external pressure from other states – rather, it is about the practical impact that this law has on the state. One may ask: is this not the case with all law making? The short answer is no. This is because with the law of maritime cabotage, where the rationale of economic development on which the law is premised upon either does not exist or cannot be sustained, there is no purpose or agenda that that law serves. When this occurs, the state would be effectively contributing to self-destructing her economic progress by inventing a legal instrument that hinders economic development.

However, before we proceed further, we must understand the main purport of the theory of developmental sovereignty. This is useful because it provides the basis for the exploration of the maritime cabotage approach of various sovereign states in later chapters. The theory of developmental sovereignty states that

> The authority bestowed on a sovereign state under international law to enact legislation that regulates the performance of maritime activities between any two points of its littoral territory should be governed by the impact that such laws have on the economic development of the country.[1]

1 This is an original theory developed by the author.

This theory is a new conceptualization in legal theory and explains the shifting dynamics of the premise of modern maritime cabotage law. It is a new introduction to jurisprudence and forms the basis for understanding what is at the centre of the rationale for the choice of a maritime cabotage law policy. We have noted that the traditional premise of sovereignty that was long used to justify a maritime cabotage approach is now being challenged by the broader ideology of development. The theory of developmental sovereignty brings to the fore the important questions of what the common understanding of the law of maritime cabotage should be and what is its basis. It is suggested that this new theory reins in many of the inconsistencies surrounding the concept and application of the law of maritime cabotage. We will demonstrate this by applying the theory of developmental sovereignty to the different maritime cabotage approaches adopted in various sovereign states of the world.

One of the important elements of the theory of developmental sovereignty is the fact that it embodies the concept of 'sustainable development'. Thus, it asks the important questions whether the choice of maritime cabotage approach adopted by the sovereign state does indeed produce the desired tangible economic development, and secondly whether the approach and whatever economic development is achieved is sustainable. Generally, the ideas behind sustainable development imply the design of a strategy to support and maintain any development to be achieved.[2] Hence, in developing a maritime cabotage policy where the state's self-interest and self-identification are crucial in the shaping of policy at national, regional, or international levels, the theory of developmental sovereignty argues that a more realistic and pragmatic approach is essential. Moreover, what is of interest to us here is not why a law with such wide-ranging effect should exist or why the authority to implement such law should rest with a sovereign state. Rather, this section is interested in understanding whether there is indeed a correlation between the legislation and a positive economic impact as promised. It is of course always important to understand the historical, political and economic context surrounding the development of a specific maritime cabotage policy or approach by a sovereign state. As we shall see in later chapters, the process through which the maritime cabotage policy of a state is developed can be deeply political, thus overshadowing the technical and legal principles that should otherwise guide the policy reasoning.

Therefore, if the economic development of the sovereign state is the overriding objective for adopting a maritime cabotage policy, the state must demonstrate that the fundamentals exist for the law to achieve its desired objective. The fundamentals we are concerned here with are domestic capacity in the forms of; infrastructures, institutions, competent human resources, and the ability to develop technical and technological knowledge. A good example is section 3 of the Nigerian Maritime Cabotage Act of 2003, which stipulates that a vessel other than

---

2 See the 1987 'Report of the World Commission on Environment and Development: Our Common Future'. Transmitted to the General Assembly as an annex to document A/42/427 (The Brundtland Report).

a vessel wholly owned and crewed by Nigerian citizens, built in Nigeria and registered under the laws of Nigeria shall not engage in maritime activities within her domestic waters. The temptation here is to rush into assuming that this protectionist approach must be a good strategic agenda for the country. However, the deficiency of this legal provision becomes apparent when we step back to assess how much of this provision can be accomplished. Indeed, the Nigerian shipbuilding industry is yet to attain a level where it can build seagoing vessels on a commercial scale. Therefore, in the case of Nigeria, the maritime cabotage framework lacks pragmatism because it is not capable of delivering the promised economic impact. The theory of developmental sovereignty encourages the sovereign state to find a balance between how much development can be attained based on the country's domestic capacity and what areas would require dependence on external sources to progress and sustain the desired economic development. This has been proved to work successfully in Indonesia, where the domestic oil and gas sector was exempted, albeit temporarily, from the rather protectionist maritime cabotage policy.[3]

## The national framework of development

Many sovereign states are endowed with some form of resource whether natural or manmade with which they attempt to develop their national economy around. The manner in which this is approached will have a significant bearing on what economic development is achieved and how long it will take to achieve it. In many cases, there will need to have short, medium, and long-term plans on how to move the national economy forward. This will of course depend on the initial state of the economy at the time that the development framework is designed. Hence, it is expected that the national development framework of a developing economy would be different from that of an industrialized nation. In the former, the immediate objective of the framework would be to trigger growth while in the latter, the focus would be on sustaining the economic development and exploring new opportunities. Moreover, any such national framework of development will need to consider whether to pursue a protectionist, liberal or flexible policy in furtherance of its objectives.

In this section we will limit our focus to the national development framework within a maritime cabotage context. The idea behind a national framework of development is to articulate a country's vision, strategy and action plan for creating and sustaining economic development. At the heart of this there must be a well-defined government structure that enhances a system for capacity building, knowledge transfer, integrated planning and a mechanism for implementing the economic development policies. From a maritime cabotage law perspective, the idea is to contribute to the development of a strong and competitive economy by facilitating the growth of the domestic shipbuilding industry, promoting indigenous ship ownership, enhancing a competitive national ship register and employing

3 See: Government Regulation No. 22/2011 of the Republic of Indonesia.

domestic seafarers. Indeed, the United States has demonstrated through the protectionist Jones Act that it intends to continue to follow this national framework of development model. Over the years, this has been achieved by employing the full capacity of its political, social and economic systems to canvass support for the sustenance of the Jones Act.

However, we should note that there is not a one-size-fits-all formula for economic development. This is evident where different countries apply the same maritime cabotage approach but get very different results. In other words, a national framework that serves as a catalyst for the economic development in one country may be a growth barrier in another country. This explains why the Marshal Plan,[4] which was effective in redeveloping the economies of Western European countries after World War II, would fail as an economic development mechanism in Africa. If anything, that framework would be a burden and would thwart the progress that African countries have made towards economic growth and development. This is because the institutions and market access required for such a plan to be effective are fragile in most African countries.

Therefore, where a sovereign state has designated its maritime cabotage policy as a catalyst for economic development, it is suggested that its development framework should reflect a pragmatic approach. For example, there is no wisdom in legislating that vessels employed in the domestic waters must be built domestically if the country has no capacity to build such vessels or if there would be a cost saving by building the vessels in another country. Similarly, a cabotage regime that stipulates that vessels must employ only indigenous seamen would be anti-development if the country does not have sufficient competent indigenous seafarers. Furthermore, any such national framework of development should have a strategic plan towards long-term sustenance of the economic development achieved and a well-articulated contingency plan. Hence, as the United Kingdom prepares to withdraw her membership of the European Union, the British government will need a robust strategic plan to prepare for the effect that EU Regulation 3577/92 that regulates EU maritime cabotage law will have on her as a non-member state. The rancour of the divorce between the United Kingdom and the European Union has heightened following the declaration by the British government that she will formally leave the 1964 London Fisheries Convention in 2019. This means the UK will regain full control of her waters up to 12 nautical miles from her coast, thus prohibiting free access for other EU states. However, withdrawing from the Convention means UK vessels will also lose the right to fish in the 12 nautical miles territorial waters of other EU countries.[5]

---

4 The European Recovery Program (The Marshall Plan – named after the then US secretary of state, George Marshall) was a 1948 United States initiative to give more than $13 billion dollars in economic assistance to help with the rebuilding process of Western European countries after World War II.

5 It is noted that the London Fisheries Convention of 1964 is separate from the European Union Common Fisheries Policy that gives member states access between 12 and 200 nautical miles from the coast and is part of the Brexit negotiations.

Therefore, the national framework of development of any country should encapsulate a comprehensive strategy towards economic development. Furthermore, it should focus on the best approach of facilitating sustainable economic development using the resources at its disposal.

## Applying the theory of developmental sovereignty to the three approaches of maritime cabotage law

We stated earlier that the three main forms of a sovereign state's maritime cabotage policy are the protectionist, liberal and flexible approaches. In this section we will deal with how the theory of developmental sovereignty applies to these three approaches. We recall that one of the essential elements of this theory is that it reduces the many uncertainties surrounding the concept of maritime cabotage by asking which of these approaches best fits the dynamics of the cabotage state.

A classic protectionist maritime cabotage approach stipulates that vessels employed in the domestic waters of a country should be owned and crewed by citizens of the host country and that those vessels are built and registered in the host country. Nigeria and the United States of America are among the countries that have adopted this strict approach, although in the former case there is little alignment between the legal text and reality. Where this strict approach is adopted, the application of the theory of developmental sovereignty would require the following:

a   The country should have a strong and vibrant domestic shipbuilding industry with a clear comparative advantage over other shipbuilding nations.
b   There are indigenous persons or corporations with the capacity to own vessels.
c   The national ship register can provide appropriate and desirable advantages to indigenous shipowners.
d   There is a certified and accredited programme for the competency training of seagoing personnel.

A protectionist maritime cabotage policy will be an appropriate approach to promoting economic development if the above requirements are satisfied. Thus, it is not clear how the national economic development of a country may be triggered and sustained through a protectionist maritime cabotage policy in the absence of the above requirements. Indigenous shipowners in the United States engaged in the coastwise trades have no choice but to build and repair their vessels in the domestic shipyards at significant cost compared to building similar vessels in Asia. In Nigeria, the requirement that vessels must be built in domestic shipyards is not even pragmatic because the Nigerian domestic shipbuilding industry does not yet have the capacity to build vessels on a commercial scale. Therefore, the theory of developmental sovereignty suggests that it would be beneficial to the economic development of these two countries if the requirement that ships employed in domestic waters must be built in domestic shipyards is reconsidered.

The next step is to apply the theory of developmental sovereignty to the liberal maritime cabotage approach. Generally, this approach makes provision for foreign entities to carry out maritime activities in the coastal waters of a sovereign state. However, this does not necessarily mean that there are no restrictions at all. Thus, a liberal maritime cabotage policy will push for indigeneity to be preferred where possible in lieu of a comprehensive ban on foreign entities engaging in the coastal waters of the sovereign state. South Africa and New Zealand are two countries that adopt a very liberal maritime cabotage approach. The United Kingdom currently follows a liberal maritime cabotage policy, but it appears that one of the effects of Brexit is that it will revert to its nineteenth-century protectionist policies when it withdraws from the European Union. The EU maritime cabotage framework is often referred to as the model of a liberal maritime cabotage approach. However, we should quickly add that the benefits of the liberal maritime cabotage approach adopted in the EU only extends to member states. Thus, third party countries cannot expect to benefit from the EU maritime cabotage framework.

The principal shortcoming of a liberal maritime cabotage approach is the unintended consequence of impeding the growth and development of domestic enterprise. Thus, where a liberal maritime cabotage approach is adopted, applying the theory of developmental sovereignty would require the following:

a   The policy and legal framework should find a balance between supporting domestic enterprise and encouraging foreign entities to operate in the domestic maritime sector.
b   The policy framework should encourage competition while deterring unfair competition against domestic enterprise.
c   There should be a system to monitor that the liberal maritime cabotage approach continues to promote economic development in the interest of the state.

The successful implementation of a liberal maritime cabotage approach has some bearing on how much foreign involvement in the domestic maritime sector can contribute towards the economic development of the state. Therefore, the theory of developmental sovereignty assesses whether the access granted to foreign entities in the domestic maritime sector is effective in contributing towards the economic development of the state or whether it impedes the development of domestic capacity and enterprise.

Finally, let us consider how the theory of developmental sovereignty applies to the flexible maritime cabotage approach. The important point about this approach is that it is designed to alternate between the protectionist and liberal maritime cabotage approaches. This alternation may be periodic and often depends on the state of the economy of the sovereign state. The main advantage of the flexible maritime cabotage approach is that it offers the sovereign state the opportunity to adjust the policy to suit their present circumstances. However, the problem with this approach is the uncertainty for both the domestic and foreign entities. Although the liberal approach may favour foreign entities, these are only likely to pursue short-term investments because they know the policy could change. Similarly, the protectionist approach may not offer sufficient security to indigenous entities to encourage them to pursue long-term investments. Malaysia and India are two countries that have adopted the flexible maritime cabotage approach.

We have considered how the theory of developmental sovereignty applies to the protectionist and liberal maritime cabotage approaches. Furthermore, we note that the distinct feature of the flexible cabotage approach is the option to alternate. Thus, the result of applying the theory of developmental sovereignty to the flexible approach will depend on whether it has alternated to its protectionist or liberal form. Hence, the requirements as identified above regarding the protectionist and liberal policies will have to be satisfied.

## The role of national and regional governments

The role of the national and regional governments in deciding what maritime cabotage approach to adopt cannot be overstated. Indeed, the decision to adopt a particular maritime approach rests ultimately with the government of the sovereign state. However, the extent to which governments can detect the pace of economic development is not always clear. Hence, it could be argued that much of that decision-making process is based on the interaction between the polity and the economy. However, because the government is deemed to be the agent of the polity, it can leverage its influence over both the public and private sectors to drive the economic development of the state. The theory of developmental sovereignty captures this perfectly when it stipulates that the authority of government to enact laws should be controlled by a corresponding positive impact on the economic development of the state. This leads to a different but related question: would economic development fair better under a specific system of government regardless of the shifting dynamics of the society? To answer this would obviously require an understanding of the driving forces behind the quest for economic development. Perhaps the better approach is to consider the role that government plays in achieving a sustainable economic development programme based on the maritime cabotage policy adopted. It is an embedded responsibility of government to pursue economic development. But more importantly, it is the methodology employed that has a real bearing on how much success is achieved regarding promoting economic development. The result is very much dependent on the efficient execution of well-defined government strategy. It is important to note that because the circumstances of all states are likely to vary, the maritime cabotage policy adopted and the methodology applied must focus on dealing with the specific set of circumstances of the state in question.

Therefore, the role of government at national and regional level in triggering a sustainable economic programme based on the chosen maritime cabotage policy may be outlined as follows:

a   Enact appropriate maritime cabotage legislation and policies based on the theory of developmental sovereignty.
b   Develop appropriate legal and social framework to guide government policies.

c   Establish a robust monitoring and review mechanism to aid regular assessment of the impact of government policy on the economy.
d   Create an enabling environment to allow economic development to thrive.

In summary, to promote sustainable economic development based on the chosen maritime cabotage approach, a government should adopt a pragmatic and flexible agenda in the pursuit of realistic economic development objectives. Furthermore, it must leverage its capacity and authority to make appropriate changes to policies where they become a hindrance to economic development.

# 4 Theories of development and maritime cabotage

The term development lends itself to ambiguity and is understood differently depending on the perspective from which it is assessed. Therefore, it is important to establish the context in which we will be dealing with the subject matter. From a development economic perspective, the term 'development' generally refers to the extent to which economic growth in one sector produces a positive impact on other sectors of the economy while minimizing the cost of growth.[1] Therefore, the focus here is not on the frequently interchangeable term 'economic growth', which generally means an increase in size of output in a sector. In chapter 3, the concept of development was presented as the utilization of national maritime resources to improve the economy of the state. In this chapter we will be assessing some of the relevant development theories and how they fit in with the choice of maritime cabotage policy in different sovereign states. The idea is to extrapolate an understanding that is synonymous with the various approaches of maritime cabotage law from the various discourses on development. Furthermore, the theories of development that are relevant to the concept of maritime cabotage will be investigated and posited against the concept of 'developmental sovereignty'.

The term 'development' as used in this chapter is only concerned with the extent to which a maritime cabotage policy contributes to the economic development of a country. It is used here purely in its 'economic' context and only as it relates to national employment, revenue generation and building domestic maritime expertise.[2] Economic development is hereby defined as the growth witnessed in the domestic economy due to adopting a maritime cabotage approach.[3] In this context, the chosen maritime cabotage approach must be the primary stimulant of development opportunities in other sectors of the economy. These opportunities must encourage capacity building by utilizing the available capital, infrastructural and human resources.[4]

---

1 For a broader read, see: D. Goulet, *The Cruel Choice: A New Concept on the Theory of Development* (Atheneum 1971).
2 G. Rees and C. Smith, *Economic Development* (2nd edn, Macmillan Press 1998).
3 For a broader read, see: D. Weil, *Economic Growth* (3rd edn, Prentice Hall 2013).
4 For a general read, see: M. Ross, 'The Political Economy of the Resource Curse' [1999] *World Politics*, 51(2), 297–322.

However, there is the constant postulation that 'development' as defined above can only occur through the adoption of a liberal policy.[5] This argument suggests that there is no role for either government intervention, as dealt with in chapter 3, or protectionist policies to contribute to development. This assertion continues to be made even though, first, it flies in the face of the successes recorded in many East Asian countries. The Soviet Union recorded one of the fastest economic advancements in a relatively short period of time after World War 1 by applying a rigidly regulated government policy. Second, it is often conveniently forgotten how the developed nations of the world have not always adopted liberal and free trade policies as they developed. Indeed, their industrial sectors were developed on the back of protectionist trade tariffs and policies.[6] Nonetheless, the positive impact of government intervention through political and social controls in Asian economies such as Taiwan, South Korea, Hong Kong and Singapore is widely acknowledged.[7]

However, critics backed by international agencies such as the International Monetary Fund and the World Bank tend to attribute the successes recorded in these Asian economies to the adoption of open and free market policies.[8] These institutions claim that liberal policies facilitate export-oriented strategies and ensure there is little or no government intervention unless such intervention aids the establishment of a viable business environment.[9] Accordingly, there is a concerted effort to pursue a full frontal approach to imposing free market policies on the maritime sectors of developing countries.[10] The pursuit of these free market policies often occurs without consideration of the structural framework and resource mechanism needed to support such liberal maritime cabotage policies. This is important when we consider that one of the factors that contributed to the economic successes recorded in the Pacific Asian countries was the transfer of manufacturing processes from industrialized nations like Japan to developing nations with lower labour costs in the region.

The Asian countries referred to above benefited from a combination of factors. On the one hand, Singapore and Hong Kong had autonomous status as city-

5  M. Hendrickson, 'Trade Liberalisation, Trade Performance and Competitiveness in the Caribbean', in N. Duncan et al. (eds), *Caribbean Development Report* [2007], 1(1), 222–254,
6  See: A. Thirlwall, *Economics of Development* (9th edn, Palgrave Macmillan 2011).
7  S. Knowles and A. Garces-Ozanne, 'Government Intervention and Economic Performance in East Asia' [2003], *Economic Development and Cultural Change*, 51(2), 451–477.
8  S. Knowles and A. Garces, 'Measuring Government Intervention and Estimating its Effect on Output: With Reference to the High Performing Asian Economies', in H. W. Singer, N. Hatti and R. Tandon (eds), *Newly Industrializing Countries after the Asian Crisis*, vol. 4 (B. R. Publishing 2006), pp. 1723–1750.
9  M. Aoki et al., 'Beyond The East Asian Miracle: Introducing the Market Enhancing View: The Role of Government in East Asian Economic Development' [1997], *Comparative Institutional Analysis*, 1(1), 1–37.
10 For a broader read, see the 1983 and 1991 World Development Report by the World Bank.

states. This was in addition to them having the distinct advantage of serving as major commercial hubs for trading and transhipment.[11] On the other hand, Taiwan and South Korea had acquired the knowledge for significant industrial growth and developing infrastructure during the time they were colonized by Japan. Furthermore, they were recipients of huge amounts of aid and technical assistance from the United States during the Cold War.[12]

The overwhelming evidence of the development successes recorded in these Asian economies because of undisguised government intervention contrasts with the incorrect assertions by the international agencies on the actual catalyst of those economic successes. .[13] The criticisms levelled against the World Bank and its collaborators have led them to acknowledge the role played by the governments of the various nations.[14] However, these international agencies have applied a positive spin by describing the government intervention witnessed in these Asian countries as a market-friendly strategy. In doing so, they have attempted to incorporate what is otherwise an anti-free market policy into their preferred liberal policy framework agenda.[15] The international agencies have argued that even when protectionist policies in the form of government intervention work, they serve only to increase output levels rather than increasing productivity. They contend that such an increase in output is not sustainable.[16] To support their claim, they point to the collapse of the Soviet Union and the Pacific Asian crises of 1997/8.[17] However, we must remember that the liberal ideology promoted by these international agencies was ineffective in the first phase of the 1977–1978 International Monetary Fund (IMF) Rescue Package.[18]

The People's Republic of China and four other Asian countries tagged the 'Asian Transitional Economies' introduced market-oriented and outward-looking economic reform programmes in 1979 that contributed to accelerated GDP

11 D. Coulter, 'Globalization of Maritime Commerce: The Rise of Hub Ports', in S. Tangredi (ed.), *Globalization and Maritime Power* (National Defence University 2009), pp. 133–142.

12 C. Dixon, 'The Pacific Asian Challenge to Neoliberalism', in D. Simon and A. Narman (eds), *Development as Theory and Practice* (Prentice Hall 1999), pp. 205–229.

13 P. Warr, 'Poverty Reduction and Sectoral Growth in South-East Asia', in K. Sharma (ed.), *Trade Policy, Growth and Poverty in Asian Developing Countries* (Routledge 2003), pp. 172–186.

14 B. Granville and S. Mallick, 'Integrating Poverty Reduction in IMF-World Bank Models', in A. Paloni and M. Zanardi (eds), *The IMF, World Bank and Policy Reform* (Routledge 2006), pp. 183–200.

15 The World Bank, *The East Asian Miracle: Economic Growth and Public Policy* (Oxford University Press 1993).

16 K. Sharma and G. Herath, 'Trade Orientation, Growth and Poverty: What have We Learned From the Asia Experience', in K. Sharma (ed.), *Trade Policy, Growth and Poverty in Asian Developing Countries* (Routledge 2003), pp. 237–241.

17 S. Chirathivat, *Ten Years after the Asian Crisis: Toward Economic Sustainability in Southeast Asia* (Cambodia Foundation for Cooperation and Peace 2007).

18 N. Karunaratne, 'The Asian Miracle and Crisis: Rival Theories, The IMF Bailout and Policy Lessons' [1999], *Intereconomics*, January/February, 19–26.

growth rates.[19] However, despite the success of the reform policy, there has been little desire to dispense with the government intervention policies that served the West so well.[20] In China and the other Asian transitional economies it is expected that government will play an intervening or interfering role in the national economy and its market.[21]

It is acknowledged that trade liberalization as advocated for by the international agencies boosted confidence in foreign investment and provided access to international finance. It also expedited the export of capital from some of these Asian countries.[22] However, it can also be contested that such liberal policies exposed the vulnerability of these Asian countries to events (both regionally and internationally) that were beyond the scope of their national comprehension.[23] For instance, a major contributing factor to the 1997/8 Pacific Asian crises was the promotion and tacit imposition of open market policies. These liberal policies exposed those Asian economies to financial and related instabilities beyond their capacity.[24]

There is an irony here that is worth noting. The international agencies and industrialized nations are jointly and severally prepared to substitute the role of an interventionist government with market-oriented policies in developing nations.[25] In addition, they are ready to impose punitive sanctions on developing nations for rejecting these liberal policies.[26] In contrast, the economic crisis of 2008–2015 had an incisive negative impact on the economies of many advanced nations.[27] This is the clearest evidence yet that advanced nations are quick to resort to government intervention to stabilize their economies rather than wait for market forces to regularize matters.[28]

19 The other four countries were Vietnam, Laos, Cambodia and Myanmar (formerly known as Burma).
20 G. Crawford, 'The World Bank and Good Governance: Rethinking the State or Consolidating Neo-liberalism?', in A. Paloni and M. Zanardi (eds), *The IMF, World Bank and Policy Reform* (Routledge 2006), pp. 109–135.
21 J. Oi, 'The Role of the Local State in China's Transitional Economy' [1995], *China Quarterly*, 144(Special Issue: China's Transitional Economy), 1132–1149.
22 M. Shafaeddin, 'Trade Liberalization and Economic Reform in Developing Countries: Structural Change or De-industrialization?', in A. Paloni and M. Zanardi (eds), *The IMF, World Bank and Policy Reform* (Routledge 2006), pp. 155–182.
23 D. Harvey, *The New Imperialism* (Oxford University Press 2005).
24 P. Krugman, 'The Myth of Asia's Miracle' [1994], *Foreign Affairs*, 73(1), 62–78.
25 D. Rodrik, 'King Kong Meets Godzilla: The World Bank and the East Asian Miracle', in A. Fishlow et al. (eds), *Miracle or Design? Lessons from the East Asian Experience* (Overseas Development Council 1994), pp. 13–38.
26 B. Granville and S. Mallick, 'Integrating Poverty Reduction in IMF-World Bank Models', in A. Paloni and M. Zanardi (eds), *The IMF, World Bank and Policy Reform* (Routledge 2006), pp. 183–200.
27 D. Luttrell, T. Atkinson, and H. Rosenblum, 'Assessing the Costs and Consequences of the 2007–09 Financial Crisis and Its Aftermath' [2013], *Economic Letter*, 8(7), 1–4.
28 M. Ncube, *The Impact of Quantitative Easing in the US, Japan, the UK and Europe* (African Development Bank 2014).

During the 2008–2015 economic crises, there was a wave of government intervention in European countries and the United States. These governments engaged in a sustained period of quantitative easing to keep their respective economies afloat. Furthermore, they were proactive in intervening to prevent some key sectors of their economies from collapsing. Some sectors that benefited from government intervention in the United States and Europe include the automobile sector (Ford), real estate sector (Freddie Mac and Fannie Mae), companies (American International Group), institutions (Wall Street), and banks (Lloyd's Banking Group and Royal Bank of Scotland).[29] In Europe, it went further, with several European countries (Spain, Greece and Ireland) being bailed out by the governing council of the European Union.[30] Coincidentally and perhaps conveniently, the only punitive measures against some of these countries was lowering their credit rating.[31] Hence, there have been no retributive or devastating punitive measures imposed by international agencies such as the International Monetary Fund (IMF).[32]

This contrasts with what was witnessed during the 1997/8 Pacific Asian crises, when several of the countries were forced to sell their national assets and devalue their currencies.[33] Following the East Asian crisis, the Group of 7 (G7) proposed an enhanced International Monetary Fund (IMF) lending facility.[34] This would pre-emptively provide funds to pre-approved countries that were committed to adopting IMF-approved policies. The new IMF proposal was aimed at averting similar crises in the future. However, it was a revised strategy aimed at imposing the same kind of intrusive economic restructuring as it did in the aftermath of the 1997/8 East Asian

29  For an e.g. of the role of government intervention; Leyman Brothers was the fourth largest investment bank in the United States of America before the 2008 financial crisis. Following the crisis and with delay in government intervention, the bank went bankrupt. For a more detailed discourse on the impact of the financial crisis, see: P. Dicken, *Global Shift: Mapping the Changing Contours of the World Economy* (6th edn, SAGE Publications 2011).

30  Several years after the recession, Greece is still sinking under the weight of the crises and still receiving vast amount of money in sustained bailouts from the European Union.

31  S. Flanders, 'Moody's Cuts Italy, Spain and Portugal's Credit Ratings', *BBC News* (14 February 2014).

32  For a general read on the punitive measures that can be extended to developing economies, see: A. Young, 'Lessons from the East Asian NICs: A Contrarian View' [1994], *European Economic Review*, 38(3–4), 964–973.

33  T. Ito, 'Growth Crisis and the Future of Economic Recovery in East Asia', in J. Stiglitz and S. Yusuf (eds), *Rethinking the East Asian Miracle* (Oxford University Press 2001), pp. 55–94.

34  The Group of 7 (G7) (formerly the G6 before Canada joined in 1976 and now the G8 since Russia joined in 1998) is made up of the finance ministers and central bank governors of the top seven industrialized economies. They are: Canada, France, Germany, Italy, Japan, the United Kingdom and the United States of America. The officials of G7 meet periodically to discuss international economic and monetary issues. The European Union is also represented within the G7. The G7 constitutes more than half the global GDP.

crises.[35] The proposal would have hampered the recovery process rather than stimulate the desired growth in these struggling economies. First, none of the Asian countries involved in the East Asian crisis would have been eligible to benefit from this lending facility. Second, the method of disbursing the funds in phases would have caused uncertainty as to the availability of the funds. This was proved when Brazil took a loan under a similar plan in 1998. Brazil was forced to devalue its currency a few months later after failing to meet a variety of stringent fiscal conditions.[36]

The industrialized nations have continued to advocate for more liberalization and less protectionism. This can be attributed to the supposedly net benefits of comparative advantage derived from the connection between free trade and development.[37] However, advocating for more trade liberalization can be dangerous while there remains a gargantuan gap in development between industrialized and developing nations. The existence of this economic gap in development means there is now a real possibility that protectionist regionalized trading blocs will emerge.[38]

History and research has shown industrialization to be the catalyst of development. At the same time, it is a major contributor to the existing gap between industrialized and developing nations. It is not logical and lacks economic grounding to demand that every country industrializes to the level of becoming export-manufacturing countries. However, one way of narrowing the gap would be for governments of developing nations to consider a strategic development of the sectors of their economies that will give them a comparative advantage.[39] The capital market has gone global and it is now relatively easier to transfer technical knowledge. As a result, the pace of development today is bound to be quicker than that experienced by the industrialized countries. This is because of the speed with which capital and knowledge transfer can be processed with the aid of modern technology. In what appears to be a new trend, the economic growth of a sovereign state – which has been the usual measure of development – is being replaced gradually by a new measure of regional economic strength. In addition, international agencies and

35  M. Sarel, 'Growth in East Asia: What We Can and What We Cannot Infer' [1997], *Economic Issues*, 1(1), 1–22.

36  M. Goldstein, 'Debt Sustainability, Brazil, and the IMF' [2003], Institute Of International Economics, WP 03–1.

37  J. Powell, 'Protectionist Paradise?', in E. Hudgins (ed.), *Freedom to Trade: Refuting the New Protectionism* (Cato Institute 1997), pp. 57–68.

38  This has been evidenced by the European Union and North American Free Trade Area (NAFTA) trading blocs which, while liberalization is the binding principle among Member States, these blocs are protectionist towards non–member states. To some extent this has been replicated in the Pacific Asian Region with a significant percentage of trade taking place within that region – see: Association of Southeast Asian Nations (ASEAN) and Asia Pacific Economic Corporation (APEC).

39  For a related read, see: R. Wade, *Governing the Market: Economic Theory and the Role of Government in East Asian Industrialization* (Princeton University Press 1990).

market forces have become new agents of development and has deposed the government of a sovereign state from that role.[40]

However, we are yet to witness any tried and tested framework for development that will seamlessly accommodate the peculiarities of every nation or regional bloc. Hence, it is suggested that the better approach is for every country to make a critical assessment of their maritime capacity. Furthermore, a country should adopt a maritime cabotage approach that is sustainable and flexible enough to tolerate market forces and economic reality within the national, regional and international domains.[41]

## The linear stages of development theory

The linear stages of development are best illustrated by Rostow's 'stages of growth'.[42] The theory stipulates that the development of a country should naturally pass through different stages of economic growth.[43] In applying the principle of the linear stages of development, it is suggested that the maritime cabotage framework of a country should be designed to promote its gradual development. To successfully proceed from one stage of development to another, the basic conditions for development should be fulfilled by ensuring that the right mixture of investments and foreign aid are secured.[44] We will apply Rostow's model to the law of maritime cabotage and its impact on the economic development of a country. The model divides the stages of development into five levels, as discussed below.

The first level is *traditional society*. This is the base level where there is no strategic allocation of resources and there is very limited technical expertise or capital to develop the maritime sector.[45] The next level is *preconditions for take-off*. At this level, the gradual increase in technical expertise and use of technology within the maritime sector begins to stimulate economic development. This leads to an increase in maritime trade and the maritime sector starts to become attractive to investors.[46] The third level is *take-off*. This is the level where the manufacturing

40  J. Pieterse, *Development Theory* (2nd edn, SAGE Publications 2010).
41  For a general read, see: R. Lucas, 'On the Mechanics of Economic Development' [1988], *Journal of Monetary Economics*, 22(1), 3–42.
42  W. Rostow, *The Stages of Economic Growth: A Non-Communist Manifesto* (3rd edn, Cambridge University Press 1990).
43  S. Charusheela, *Structuralism and Individualism in Economic Analysis: The 'Contractionary Devaluation Debate' in Development Economics* (Routledge 2013).
44  S. Urata, 'Emergence of an FDI Trade Nexus and Economic Growth in East Asia', in J. Stiglitz and S. Yusuf (eds), *Rethinking the East Asian Miracle* (Oxford University Press 2001), pp. 409–460.
45  For a general read on the broader issue, see: Y. Itagaki, 'Criticism of Rostow's Stage Approach: The Concepts of Stage, System and Type' [2007], *Developing Economies*, 1 (1), 1–17.
46  For a broader read, see: B. Hoselitz, 'Economic Policy and Economic Development', in H. Aitken (ed.), *The State and Economic Growth* (Social Science Research Council 1959), pp. 325–352.

industries both within and outside the maritime sector grow rapidly. The growth in the manufacturing sector leads to an increase in investment, government revenue and employment in the maritime sector.[47] The idea that the higher the foreign investment received, the more accelerated the pace of growth, is adequately illustrated by the Harrod–Domar growth model.[48] The fourth level is *drive to maturity*. At this level, the development in the maritime sector is self-sustaining because appropriate maritime cabotage policy has been adopted. In addition, other sectors of the economy begin to feel the positive impact, which contributes to the overall development of the country.[49] Maritime countries in this category can export their technical expertise in maritime services and maritime technology. The fifth level is *high mass consumption*. At this level, the maritime sector becomes a major driving force of the economy and national development.[50] The continuous development in the maritime sector raises purchasing power, thereby triggering an increase in the demand for maritime services.[51]

Applying Rostow's growth model to the law of maritime cabotage has exposed some weaknesses in the linear stages of development theory. First, this theory assumes that all developing maritime nations possess the same natural and man-made characteristics. Hence, none of the levels can be skipped in the pursuit of economic development.[52] Second, the theory fails to stipulate the minimum and maximum period allocated to each development stage. Moreover, the theory does not specify the consequences for not achieving the desired level of economic development within the stipulated time.[53] Third, the assumption that all developing maritime nations will have the required capability to attract similar levels of foreign investment is not strictly true.[54] Furthermore, other than the maritime

---

47 For a comparative read on the issues, see: J. Parr, 'On the Regional Dimensions of Rostow's Theory of Growth' [2001], *Review of Urban & Regional Development Studies*, 13(1), 2–19.

48 This model is based on the linear stages theory and is often used by international agencies when dealing with policy issues in developing countries.

49 W. Rostow, 'The Take-off to self-Sustained Growth' [1956], *Economic Journal*, 66 (1), 25–48.

50 See for instance how the Republic of Singapore has developed into a modern city-state through the provision of maritime services that have contributed to the sustainable development of Singapore.

51 See for instance: R. Hung, and R. Li, 'Rostow's Stages of Growth Model, "Urban Bias" and Sustainable Development in India' [2013], *Journal of Contemporary Issues in Business Research*, 2(5), 170–188.

52 For a related read, see: G. Nagle, *Development and Underdevelopment* (Thomas Nelson 1998).

53 See: M. Baden hop, 'Economic Growth and Structure by Simon Kuznets' [1966], *Journal of Farm Economics*, 48(1), 148–150.

54 For instance, Taiwan and South Korea were better positioned than some of the other countries in the region to survive the East Asian crisis of 1997/8. This was because Taiwan and South Korea had acquired significant industrial development and infrastructure from being colonized by Japan. They were also recipients of huge amounts of aid and technical assistance from the United States of America during the Cold War.

cabotage policy adopted in a country, there are important determining factors in how the stages theory of development will work in each maritime country. These include: the peculiarities of the maritime nation, regional developments and external events occurring at the international level that are beyond the control of national governments.[55] The last point forms the cornerstone of the next development theory to be examined. This theory argues that developing maritime nations are not immune to events in the international system.

## The structural change development theory

The structural change theory is focused on understanding how developing economies move from the traditional subsistence economy to an industrially diverse manufacturing and service economy.[56] The two primary models of development that best represent the structural change development theory are: the Lewis model and the Chenery model. In this section, we will try to apply the principles of these models to the maritime cabotage concept.

### *The Lewis model*

The Lewis model, developed by William Arthur Lewis in 1954, dominated development theory between the 1960s and 1970s. The model focused on the importance of countries transforming their economic resources and structures from the low productivity of labour areas such as subsistence farming to the high productivity of labour areas associated with industrialization. The Lewis model is also known as the 'two sector model' or 'surplus labour model'. The model is a basic representation of the historical experience of economic growth in the West. It argues that the developing economies consist of two sectors, namely the traditional subsistence sector with surplus labour and a highly productive industrialized sector.[57] The model emphasizes the mechanism by which surplus labour in the subsistence sector is transferred to the industrialized sector.[58]

Generally, the subsistence sector is synonymous with underemployment, which leads to low marginal productivity of labour.[59] Hence, the transfer of labour out of the subsistence sector does not affect productivity in the economy. On the other hand, the transfer of labour from the subsistence sector to the industrial (e.g. maritime) sector increases labour supply and facilitates the

---

55 For instance, the Marshall Plan (European Recovery Program) was effective because the donor (USA) had a vested interest in the recovery of Europe after the devastation of the Second World War.

56 H. Chenery, *Structural Change and Development Policy* (Johns Hopkins University Press 1979).

57 M. Todaro and S. Smith, *Economic Development* (12th edn, Pearson Education 2015).

58 W. Lewis, 'Economic Development with Unlimited Supplies of Labour' [1954], *The Manchester School*, 22(2), 139–191.

59 For a general read, see: R. Nurkse, *Problems of Capital Formation in Underdeveloped Countries* (Oxford University Press 1953).

industrialization of the economy. This is achieved through investments and capital accumulation, which leads to sustainable economic development.[60] However, there is a third sector as espoused by the Fisher-Clark model. This model focuses on the importance of a service sector as the index of development. The maritime services sector has indeed become an important indicator of economic development. In 2013, the maritime services sector in the United Kingdom contributed a total of £22.2 billion in GDP. The sector supported 489,400 jobs and generated £6.5 billion in tax to the Exchequer.[61] The Fisher-Clark model suggests that as the economy develops, the service sector will become more attractive to labour. Allen Fisher argued in 1935 that progress in economic development would establish a service sector that would be a tertiary sector distinct from the subsistence and industrial sectors. This concept was further developed in 1940 by Colin Clark to create the Fisher-Clark model. This model shares some similarities with the linear stage and the structural change theories of development because it argues that progress in capitalist economies is dependent on structural change.[62]

The Lewis model has some weaknesses and some of its theoretical assumptions have been criticized as invalid. The major assumptions of this model are reflective of the historical economic development of the West after World War II. These assumptions therefore do not capture the institutional and economic realities of most contemporary developing countries.[63] The debatable assumptions of this model are that:

a   The faster the rate of capital accumulation, the higher the rate of development in the industrial sector. This is debatable because the model assumes without any valid evidence, that there will be no capital flight and that all capital profits will be reinvested in the industrialization programme.

b   There are always full-employment opportunities in the industrialized sector but surplus labour in the subsistence sector. This is not valid in developing economies.

c   There is a competitive industrial sector labour market that guarantees constant wages, with the capacity to exhaust the supply of surplus labour from the subsistence sector. This is not valid because in developing economies, fluctuations in wages depend on a variety of factors. These include unemployment in the industrial sector and marginal productivity in the subsistence sector.

d   Diminishing returns in the industrial sector will force a return to reliance on labour from the subsistence sector. This is debatable because the industrial

60  J. Fei and G. Ranis, *Development of the Labor Surplus Economy: Theory and Policy* (Irwin 1964).
61  Oxford Economics, *The Economic Impact of the UK Maritime Services Sector* (Maritime UK 2015).
62  See: M. Todaro and S. Smith, *Economic Development* (12th edn, Pearson Education 2015).
63  S. Robinson et al., *Industrialization and Growth: A Comparative Study* (Oxford University Press 1986).

sector is likely to industrialize further and to depend less on labour from the subsistence sector.[64]

## The Chenery model

The Chenery model, often referred to as the 'patterns of development' empirical analysis, was developed by Hollis Chenery and his colleagues around 1975. There is some similarity between the Chenery and Lewis models. Chenery examined patterns of development for several developing countries after World War II and identified that the primary feature in the development process was transitioning from agricultural to industrial production.

The Chenery model focuses on the institutional, economic and industrial structures of a developing nation. Specifically, it focuses on the order in which these structures are gradually reformed so that the subsistence sector is replaced by the industrial sector as the primary catalyst of national economic development.[65] If this model is used as the basis for the chosen maritime cabotage regime of a state, then there must be a robust process of converting the resources from the subsistence sector to drive industrialization and economic development.[66]

The Chenery model suggests that investments and savings (private or government) are important conditions for development, as emphasised by the linear stages theory. However, it argues that these conditions are not in themselves sufficient.[67] This is because of the impact that domestic resource capacity and international factors can have on the economic development of the maritime sector. This includes, by extension, the economy of a developing nation. It is thus arguable that Chenery's model recognizes that the rate at which the maritime sector of a country develops does not depend only on the choice of maritime cabotage approach. In a developing economy, such development may be impeded or facilitated by international structures of which developing nations are without any choice an integrated part.[68] The criticisms associated with the Chenery model are identified below:

64 For a detailed discussion on the issues, see: P. Bauer and B. Yamey, *The Economic of Under Developed Countries* (Cambridge University Press 1957); M. Todaro and S. Smith, *Economic Development* (12th edn, Pearson Education 2015); P. Leeson, 'The Lewis Model and Development Theory' [1979], *The Manchester School*, 47(3), 196–210; W. Elkan, *An Introduction to Development Economics* (Penguin Books 1978).

65 For a broader read, see: M. Todaro and S. Smith, *Economic Development* (12th edn, Pearson Education 2015).

66 For a comparative analysis of this argument, see: D. Schilirò, 'Structural Change and Models of Structural Analysis: Theories, Principles and Methods' [2012], Munich Personal RePEc Archive, MPRA Paper No. 41817, 1–24,

67 M. Syrquin and H. Chenery, 'Patterns of Development, 1950–70' (Oxford University Press 1975).

68 R. Slow, 'A Contribution to the Theory of Economic Growth' [1956], *Quarterly Journal Of Economics*, 1(70), 65–94.

a   The model fails to critically analyze the set of circumstances in which one developing nation finds favour with the international system over another developing nation.

b   The model fails to examine the impact on the international system when there is a transition from a developing to an industrialized economy.[69] Perhaps this explains why developing (maritime) nations struggle to attract international assistance with finance, technology and international trade.

It is suggested that these failures are a combination of the poor internal policy choices of many developing countries and the unhelpful external influences from industrialized nations. It is the influence wielded by industrialized nations that happen to orchestrate events within the international system that is central to the next development theory.

## The international dependence revolution theory of development

The international dependence revolution theory of development has been the subject of much commentary from theorists who reject globalization because they view it as a modified form of colonization.[70] These theorists point to the influence that the industrialized nations have on international institutions with respect designing the international governing framework as the basis of their argument. The suggestion is that developing nations have little choice but to develop at a pace dictated by the industrialized nations.[71] The two models that best represent the 'dependence theory' are examined below. They will bring to the fore the pertinent political, policy, and economic issues that influence the development of the maritime sector of a country.[72]

### The neo-colonial dependence model

The neo-colonial dependence model posits that an international system that encourages unequally advantageous relationships between industrialized and developing maritime nations is unfair.[73] Proponents of this model contend that this unbalanced co-existence is central to the slow developmental pace experienced

69  S. Robinson et al., *Industrialization and Growth: A Comparative Study* (Oxford University Press 1986).

70  See: M. Weisbrot, 'Globalism on the Ropes', in R. Broad (ed.), *Global Backlash: Citizen Initiatives for a Just World Economy* (Rowman & Littlefield 2002), pp. 38–41. Also see: J. Gray and F. Dawn, *The Delusions of Global Capitalism* (New Press 2000).

71  For a broader read, see: G. Burtless et al., 'Globaphobia: Confronting Fears about Open Trade', in R. Broad (ed.), *Global Backlash: Citizen Initiatives for a Just World Economy* (Rowman & Littlefield 2002), pp. 23–25

72  For a deeper insight into how the global economy is developed through national sectoral growth, see: S. Anderson et al., *Field Guide to the Global Economy* (New Press 2000).

73  M. Todaro and S. Smith, *Economic development* (12th edn, Pearson Education 2015).

by developing nations.[74] The choice of an appropriate maritime cabotage policy in a developing country is often influenced by industrialized nations with vested interests.[75] Hence, under this model, the maritime sectors of developing economies are conditioned by the requirements of the industrialized nations.[76] Therefore, developing maritime nations are dependent on the power centres of the world, which decide whether they can industrialize their maritime sectors and at what pace.[77]

The neo-colonial dependence model can be said to be one of the vestiges of colonization. It allows industrialized nations to systematically ensure that they remain in control of the international economic, social and financial mechanisms. This enables them to continue to dictate the pace of economic development in their former colonies.[78] For example, industrialized nations have long understood that the country which sells its manufactured products has an advantage over another that exports only raw materials.[79] The country that exports manufactured products is generally more advanced in development terms than one that produces only raw materials. This is because manufactured products have a far more extensive market.[80] Moreover, finished goods are consumed at a higher rate, while raw materials are only used by manufacturers.[81] One cannot but ponder whether the very premise of the 'theory of comparative advantage' was to ensure that there will always be a gap between developing (maritime) countries and industrialized (maritime) nations. By specializing in the areas where they had a comparative advantage, developing nations continue to specialize in the production of raw materials and cheap labour (the subsistence sector). On the other hand, the industrialized nations are focused on specializing in research, development of new technologies and production of finished products (the industrial sector). Thus, the Philippines is the largest supplier of seafarers under cheap labour, while Europe continues to specialize in building sophisticated vessels. If there is an obvious

74 See: D. Isham, 'The Neo-Colonial Dependence Model and the Diverging Economic Paths of Chile and Argentina' [2012], *Indian Journal of Economics & Business*, 11(2), 303–321.

75 See for instance how China and India have been pressured by Europe and the United States to liberalize their maritime cabotage services, while the United States can keep its protectionist maritime cabotage law.

76 For a good example, see: R. Pepa, 'How U.S. Neocolonial Development Failed the Philippines', *News Junkie Post* (Philippines, 7 November 2013).

77 The power centres of the world are made up of industrialized nations in collaboration with international institutions, such as the World Bank, World Trade Organization and International Monetary Fund.

78 For a general read, see: V. Ferraro, 'Dependency Theory: An Introduction' in G. Secondi (ed.), *The Development Economics Reader* (Routledge 2008), pp. 58–64.

79 R. Lawrence and D. Weinstein, 'Trade and Growth Import Led or Export Led? Evidence from Japan and Korea', in J. Stiglitz and S. Yusuf (eds), *Rethinking the East Asian Miracle* (Oxford University Press 2001), pp. 379–408.

80 M. Syrquin, 'Patterns of Structural Change', in H. Chenery and T. Srinivasan (eds), *Handbook of Development Economics* (vol. 1, Elsevier 1989), pp. 205–273.

81 F. List, *The National System of Political Economy*, translated by G. Matile; including notes by H. Richelot and S. Colwell (1856 edn, J. B. Lippincott 1841).

question it is why developing nations cannot extricate themselves from the clut-ches of the international institutions. The obvious answer is that developing nations have involuntarily become dependent on industrialized nations. This is because the international system often leaves them with little or no choice.[82] The set of circumstances that lead to developing nations continuing to struggle while industrialized nations get more affluent is captured by the concept of dualism.[83]

## The false-paradigm model

This model of international dependency theory focuses on the tacit approach employed by the international system to ensure that developing economies remain dependent on them.[84] There are two methods where the false-paradigm model is applied. The first method involves the process in which industrialized nations intentionally adopt exploitative policies against developing nations. Furthermore, the method allows the industrialized nations to inadvertently overlook systematic problems that hinder growth in developing countries.[85] Hence, the industrialized nations subtly impose sophisticated development policies designed for indus-trialized (maritime) nations on developing (maritime) nations.[86]

However, these sophisticated policies invariably fail because of the fragile insti-tutional and social structures in many developing nations. This is because these Westernized policies are often proposed to developing maritime nations on the basis that the same policies were essential in the development of the industrialized nations.[87] This is demonstrated when international organizations encourage developing maritime countries to adopt liberal maritime cabotage policies regard-less of whether they possess the capacity to make such policies work. Furthermore, there is often little thought given to whether the available structures and resources in the country would benefit more from a different maritime cabotage approach.[88]

82 For a deeper insight on the issues, see: J. Stiglitz, 'From Miracle to Crisis to Recovery: Lessons from Four Decades of East Asian Experience', in J. Stiglitz and S. Yusuf (eds), *Rethinking the East Asian Miracle* (Oxford University Press 2001), pp. 509–526.
83 For a deeper discourse on the concept of dualism and the dualistic-development thesis, see: H. Singer, 'Dualism Revisited: A New Approach to the Problems of Dual Socie-ties in Developing Countries' [1970], *Journal of Development Studies*, 7(1), 60–61. Singer discusses dualism as a concept that illustrates the existence and persistence of increasing divergences between rich and poor nations and rich and poor peoples on various levels.
84 For a broader read, see: M. Todaro and S. Smith, *Economic Development* (12th edn, Pearson Education 2015).
85 R. Matison, 'Economic Growths False Paradigm', *The Market Oracle* (27 January 2014).
86 The World Bank, *The East Asian Miracle: Economic Growth and Public Policy, Sum-mary* (Oxford University Press 1993).
87 K. Jong-Il and L. Lau, 'The Sources of Economic Growth of the East Asian Newly Industrialized Countries' [1994], *Journal of the Japanese and International Economies*, 8(1), 235–271.
88 For a more detailed examination of this issue, see for a comparative analysis, the Structural Adjustment Programmes (SAP) economic policies designed for developing

For instance, the African Union was warned at the World Economic Forum in Davos in 2013 against establishing a protectionist regional maritime cabotage regime.[89] This warning was issued even though the European Union has implemented a similar protectionist maritime cabotage policy since 1993.[90]

The second method of the false-paradigm model is what may be referred to as 'indirect human capital flight'. In this case, individuals with high (maritime) technical expertise do not permanently migrate from developing to industrialized nations as suggested by the 'brain drain theory'.[91] Rather, people from the developing countries are trained in industrialized countries. They are then persuaded to embrace foreign (maritime) policies and economic concepts. Following the completion of their training, these individuals return to their respective developing countries to occupy positions in government or the private sector.[92] The result is that these foreign-trained experts often implement unsuitable policies that thwart rather than promote the economic development of their countries,[93] thus ensuring that developing nations continue to depend on industrialized nations.

International dependence theory suggests that developing countries should investigate the maritime policies originally designed for use in industrialized countries before they adopt them.[94] This theory is persuasive, if not compelling, in demonstrating the influence of industrialized nations on the maritime sectors in developing nations. Nonetheless, there are weaknesses within international dependence theory.

First, this theory attempts to put all the blame squarely at the feet of the industrialized nations. It is difficult to justify this position because under-development in many developing countries is amplified by the domestic government bureaucratic structures. It is suggested that these anti-development structures are established to serve a few indigenous elites.[95] Second, this theory suggests that developing nations should adopt a national policy of economic

countries in Africa, Asia and South America by the World Bank and the International Monetary Fund (IMF). The SAP policies demanded that developing countries adopt liberal policies in exchange for conditional loans.

89 G. Marle, 'Africa Presses for Cabotage Laws Despite Davos Warning', *The Loadstar* (London, 2 June 2013).

90 See: EEC Regulation 3577/92.

91 M. Cervantes and D. Guellec, 'The Brain Drain: Old Myths, New Realities' [2002], *OECD Observer*, No. 230, January, p. 4.

92 S. Morano-Foadi, 'Citizen Migration within the European Research Area: The Italian Example', in A. Arranz et al. (eds), *New Europe, New World? The European Union, Europe, and the Challenges of the 21st Century* (Peter Lang 2010), pp. 91–110.

93 This largely explains why in most developing countries there is little or no development of their maritime sectors even though the persons in charge and in the relevant government organizations have mainly been trained and educated in industrialized nations.

94 For a related argument, read: K. Jomo, 'Rethinking the Role of Government Policy in Southeast Asia', in J. Stiglitz and S. Yusuf (eds), *Rethinking the East Asian Miracle* (Oxford University Press 2001), pp. 461–508.

95 L. Pasinetti, *Structural Change and Economic Growth: A Theoretical Essay on the Dynamics of the Wealth of Nations* (Cambridge University Press 1983).

independence. This is unrealistic for many developing nations because they lack the capacity to implement and sustain such policies. Although these policies work effectively in controlling the economy of industrialized nations, they are often unsuitable for developing economies. For instance, China and India have tried the autarkic approach but failed to achieve the desired economic development. Since the 1990s, India, which traditionally operates a protectionist maritime cabotage policy, has consistently kept open the option of applying a liberal maritime cabotage policy when required. Indeed, India has exercised that option several times since then. On the other hand, China has begun to liberalize many of its maritime services sector, although a protective maritime cabotage regime remains its conventional approach.

## The neoclassical counterrevolution theory of development

This theory of development rejects the arguments put forward by international dependence revolution theory.[96] The counterrevolution theory of development argues that the slow pace of growth in developing nations is the consequence of an overdose of government intervention. It claims that these unnecessary interventions often result in policies that are poorly resourced and implemented wrongly.[97] Hence, minimizing the heavy-handed and excessive involvement of government in the economy of developing nations is central to this theory. The counterrevolution theorists submit that economic development can only be expected when the following conditions are satisfied:

a   Free trade and export expansion are promoted.
b   There is an inviting and friendly environment for foreign investors.
c   Government interference in the economy is eliminated or limited to acts of necessity.
d   Competitive free markets are encouraged to flourish.[98]

The counterrevolution theorists support their claim by making a comparison between the sluggish economies of Africa and Latin America with the vibrant economies of the Asian Tigers (South Korea, Taiwan, Singapore and Hong Kong).[99] The former are characterized by interventionist governments, whereas the latter have embraced free market policies. However, it should be noted that

96  The international dependence revolution theory puts the blame for the under-developed status of developing nations on the coercive tactics employed by industrialized nations and international institutions.
97  For a general read, see: M. Todaro and S. Smith, *Economic Development* (12th edn, Pearson Education 2015).
98  The larger point on these issues are made in: E. Nafziger, *Economic Development* (5th edn, Cambridge University Press 2012).
99  For a counter argument and more detailed discourse, see: J. Williamson, 'The Progress of Policy Reform in Latin America' [1990] *Policy Analyses in International Economics*, 28(J1), 1–83.

the basis for the economic development success recorded in these Asian countries do not really fit typical 'free market' ideology.[100] The counterrevolution theory of development has been replicated and applied under different guises such as the 'Washington Consensus'.[101] This framework stipulate policies that allow markets to function without trade barriers and subsidies from interventionist governments.[102]

International institutions like the World Bank encouraged developing (maritime) nations to implement the counterrevolution theory of development.[103] However, this theory failed to stimulate economic growth in developing countries.[104] The failure could be attributed to the refusal to acknowledge that the economic structural systems alone were not robust enough to overcome the deficiencies in developing economies.[105] The counterrevolution theory of development offers three approaches for its implementation, as will be outlined in the subsequent subchapters.

### The free market approach

The free market approach trusts in the efficiency of the market and the effectiveness of competition where the economy is devoid of government intervention.[106] Furthermore, this approach assumes that there is easy access to technology and information. Hence, the product and factor markets can correctly reflect the availability and value of products or resources.[107] Therefore, any

100 See the Asian Miracle Report.
101 This is the set of ten policies for crisis-stricken developing countries designed by the United States government and the international financial institutions based in Washington. These policies are believed to be necessary elements of first-stage policy reform that all countries should adopt to increase economic growth. At its heart is an emphasis on the importance of macroeconomic stability and integration into a globalized economy. These ideas proved very controversial within and outside of the Bretton Woods institutions. However, they were implemented through conditionality under International Monetary Fund (IMF) and World Bank guidance but are now being replaced by a post-Washington consensus.
102 G. Skinner, 'The Neoclassical Counterrevolution and Developing Economies: A Case Study of Political and Economic Changes in the Philippines' [2007], *Social Sciences Journal*, 7(1) Article 12, 51–58.
103 S. Yusuf, 'The East Asian Miracle at the Millennium', in J. Stiglitz and S. Yusuf (eds), *Rethinking the East Asian Miracle* (Oxford University Press 2001), pp. 1–54.
104 K. Hoff and J. Stiglitz, 'Modern Economic Theory and Development', in G. Meier and J. Stiglitz (eds), *Frontiers of Development Economics: The Future in Perspective* (World Bank and Oxford University Press 2000), pp. 389–485.
105 I. Adelman, 'Fallacies in Development Theory and Their Implications for Policy' [1999], Working Paper No. 887, University of California.
106 J. Toye, *Dilemmas of Development: Reflections on the Counter-Revolution in Development Theory and Policy* (Blackwell 1987).
107 For a broad read, see: A. Portes, 'Neoliberalism and the Sociology of Development: Emerging Trends and Unanticipated Facts' [1997], *Population and Development Review*, 23(2), 229–259.

intervention by a government or its agents is distortive and negates economic development.[108]

The weakness with this approach is the assumption that in the absence of government intervention, the 'free market' approach is immune to failure in a developing economy where many factors are not under the control of government.[109] Furthermore, it seems at the very least highly speculative to suggest that markets in developing economies are efficient and that any imperfections that may exist (in their maritime sectors) are irrelevant or caused by government intervention.[110] Moreover, the ease of access to information and technology in developing economies as purported by this approach is debatable and even unrealistic.[111]

If we apply this approach under the law of maritime cabotage of a country, the argument would appear to be that the product market (shipbuilding, construction of terminals and storage facilities) would indicate when there is need for new investment. Thus, the labour market (naval architects, seamen, project managers and maritime lawyers) would react accordingly by creating employment opportunities.[112]

### *The public choice approach*

The public choice approach contends that an economy devoid of government intervention has a good chance of experiencing progressive economic development. The theory argues that governments are an encompassment of special interest groups that are mainly interested in securing their welfare at the expense of the wider society.[113] The theory therefore suggests that a national government is likely to be reckless with the allocation of resources because it is not answerable to a superior authority in the society.[114] Nonetheless, regardless of its appeal to argue that the economy can function efficiently without government, it is not practical. The world financial and economic crisis, which started in 2008 and lasted for more than half a decade, is evidence of the desirability and importance of

108 For further reading, see: M. Todaro and S. Smith, *Economic Development* (12th edn, Pearson Education 2015).
109 See: B. Granville and S. Mallick, 'Integrating Poverty Reduction in IMF-World Bank Models', in A. Paloni and M. Zanardi (eds), *The IMF, World Bank and Policy Reform* (Routledge 2006), pp.183–200.
110 R. Wade, *Governing the Market: Economic Theory and the Role of Government in East Asian Industrialization* (Princeton University Press 1990).
111 For a related argument, see: OECD, *Foreign Direct Investment for Development: Maximizing Benefits, Minimizing Costs* (OECD Publication 2002).
112 See: F. Smith, 'Sustainable Development: A Free Market Perspective' [1994], *Boston College Environmental Affairs Law Review*, 28(2), 297–308.
113 U. Medury, 'Effective Governance: The New Public Management Perspective', in P. Sahni and U. Medury (eds), *Governance for Development: Issues and Strategies* (Prentice-Hall 2003), pp. 20–32.
114 For a slightly different perspective to the argument see: W. Rasmussen et al., 'Evaluation of State Economic Development Incentives from a Firm's Perspective' [1982], *Business Economics*, 17(3), 23–29.

government intervention in the sustainable economic development of any country. Furthermore, it is arguable whether such an approach is even desirable as an economic development option for both developing and industrialized nations.[115] For instance, the maritime sector of developing nations would struggle without government intervention to support infant industries. Moreover, local investors rely on government incentives to develop to a level where they can attract foreign investors. For instance, capacity building and economic development would benefit from the construction of capital-intensive maritime infrastructures such as seaports, terminals and storage facilities. However, applying the public choice approach to maritime cabotage, it is not clear how much development can be achieved in developing countries without government intervention.[116] Hence, while an overbearing government intervention in the domestic economy is not desirable, a 'zero government intervention' practice could be disastrous for the economy of a country.[117]

### The market-friendly approach

The market-friendly approach differs from the two counterrevolution theory of development approaches discussed above. This is because, unlike the free market approach, it acknowledges the shortcomings that exist in the economic structures of developing nations.[118] The propensity for poor information, lack of technology, and inferior technical expertise are prevalent in developing nations. The presence of these deficiencies means that without government intervention, the market will be prone to failure.[119] The market-friendly approach recognizes that government has a role to play in stimulating the economic development (in the maritime sector) of a developing nation. However, this approach emphasizes that any such government intervention must be unbiased and market friendly. This entails proactive investment in infrastructures and creating an environment for private enterprise to thrive in.[120]

The neoclassical counterrevolution theory of development argues that the best method of provoking economic development is based on the government allowing the market to operate freely. A market-friendly intervention should therefore only be considered if and when there is a real need.[121] However, the drawback is that this argument does not hold true for both industrialized and developing

---

115 E. Butler, 'Public Choice: A Primer' (Institute of Economic Affairs, 2012).
116 For a contemporary analysis, see: A. Samuelson, *Foundations of Economic Analysis* (Harvard University Press 1947).
117 In support of this argument (albeit from a different perspective) see: R. Wade, *Governing the Market: Economic Theory and the Role of Government in East Asian Industrialization* (Princeton University Press 1990).
118 M. Cypher, *The Process of Economic Development* (Routledge 2014).
119 A. Singh, 'The Market-Friendly Approach to Development" vs. an "Industrialised Policy": A Critique of the World Development Report 1991 and an Alternative Policy Perspective' [1993], INEF Report Heft 4/1993, 2–42.
120 T. Bartik, 'The Market Failure Approach to Regional Economic Development Policy' [1990], *Economic Development Quarterly*, 40(4), 361–370.
121 R. Wade, *Governing the Market: Economic Theory and the Role of Government in East Asian Industrialization* (Princeton University Press 1990)

nations.[122] This is because many developing (maritime) nations lack the standards of organization and the structures available in industrialized nations.[123] Hence, a liberal maritime cabotage policy that has been designed for an industrial nation may fail to produce the same positive effect in a developing nation because of institutional, political, behavioural and technological differences.[124]

We have assessed the four theories of economic development and observed the various dynamics of economic development in both industrialized and developing nations. The theorists we have considered suggest that different permutations are required to arrive at the best framework that will guarantee economic development in different countries.[125] With so many uncertainties as to which approach a developing (maritime) nation should adopt among development economists, it is imperative that no economic development policy should be taken at face value.[126] Rather, developing (maritime) nations should opt for a case-by-case analysis of their maritime capacity. This will enable them to choose a maritime cabotage policy with the necessary modification that best complements the structural reality of the country in question.[127]

The notion that economic development is driven solely by either the market or the government, and that the two are incompatible, is theoretical hypothesis.[128] Every economy will have areas in which the market is efficient and areas that are dependent on government efficiency.[129] However, there will be other areas in which neither the market nor the government can claim efficiency. Hence, the market and the government need to work together to promote economic development.[130] The international community has gradually begun to accept the

122 B. Balassa, *The Newly Industrializing Countries in the World Economy* (Pergamon 1981).
123 B. Gurtner, 'The Financial and Economic Crisis and Developing Countries' [2010], *International Development Policy*, 1(1), 189–213.
124 N. Adler, E. Yazhemsky and R. Tarverdyan, 'A Framework to Measure the Relative Socio-Economic Performance of Developing Countries' [2010], *Socio-Economic Planning Sciences*, 44(3), 73–88.
125 See the economic development theories as expounded by theorists such as: Leibenstein, Streeten, Lewis, Rosenstein-Rodan, Bhagwati, Rostow, Hirshman, Krueger, Chenery, Nurkse, Myrdal and Scitovsky.
126 For a wider read, see: A. Fforde, *Understanding Development Economics: Its Challenge to Development Studies* (Routledge 2013).
127 R. Lucas, 'On the Mechanics of Economic Development' [1988], *Journal of Monetary Economics*, 22(1), 3–42.
128 R. Auty, 'Aid and Rent-driven Growth: Mauritania, Kenya, and Mozambique Compared', in G. Mavrotas (ed.), *Foreign Aid for Development Issues, Challenges, and the New Agenda* (Oxford University Press 2010).
129 For a comparative analysis, see: W. Bonefeld, 'Freedom and the Strong State: On German Ordoliberalism' [2012], *New Political Economy*, 17(5), 633–656.
130 New development theories such as the new growth theory, the big push and the o-ring theory of development have emerged in recent times and attempt to redress the deficiencies of the classic theories of development. The new theories are unanimous in their recognition that, for sustainable development to occur, all actors (government, institutions, public and private sectors, both domestic and international) must be incentivized to work productively and collectively, directly

important role that the government plays in the economic development process. This is because it is evident that the 'market' cannot operate in a vacuum. Rather, it needs the government to provide legal and regulatory frameworks to facilitate capacity building and economic development.[131]

Finally, the review of relevant economic development theories illustrates that no one theory can be said to be comprehensive. Rather, international economic development benefits from a circuitous route that harmonizes various theories. Each theory of development may emphasize a paradigm, but they also complement each other such that a comprehensive and sustainable economic development agenda can be fostered.[132]

and indirectly, to identify suitable theories and models for sustainable development. However, as these theories are relatively new, it might yet take some time to evaluate how well it fits into the systems and structures of developing (maritime) nations.

131 World Bank, *World Development Report 1991: The Challenge of Development* (Oxford University Press 1991).

132 World Bank, 'New Directions in Development Thinking', in G. Secondi (ed.), *The Development Economics Reader* (Routledge 2008), pp. 9–27.

# 5 The concepts of economic development and competition law

At the centre of the concepts of economic development and competition law lies the pursuit of facilitating capacity building and fostering the economic empowerment of a geographical entity using domestic and external resources. One may view economic development as the measure of the final product, and competition law as the methodology for achieving that product. There is a noticeable increase in the number of countries embracing competition law as the pathway to economic development. The rationale behind this approach is that liberal and free market policies provide for the unrestrained interaction of competitive forces that will yield the best allocation of economic resources, best market prices and high quality of goods and services within a conducive business and market environment.[1] However, this should not be taken to mean that competition law is necessarily the basis for triggering economic development. Moreover, while competition law may have been useful in sustaining the economic growth in industrialized countries, there is no evidence that it has been the main catalyst of economic development in a developing economy.

We have identified in previous chapters that the three approaches which sovereign states adopt in maritime cabotage law are: protectionist, liberal and flexible. It is the liberal maritime cabotage approach that most lends itself to the idea of competition law. From a maritime cabotage perspective, a liberal approach aims to achieve the highest quality of services at the best prices by inviting all interested players to compete on equal terms. However, the domestic players often lack the resources to compete at the same level as the foreign players. Hence, they are likely to view this open invitation as a threat to their survival. Therefore, the idea of promoting economic development very much hinges on appropriate government regulation, influence and intervention, as we shall see later in this chapter.

An effective system designed to accommodate the concept of economic development and competition law requires a comprehensive assessment of the available resources in the country and the country's capacity to implement an economic development-driven competition legal framework. Such assessment will lead to an understanding of the present state of the national economy with regard to its strengths, weaknesses, opportunities and threats. This will avoid the introduction

---

1 Northern Pacific Railway Co. v. United States, 356 U.S. 1 (1958).

of complicated competition law policies in developing countries that lack the capacity to implement or benefit from a sophisticated competition law system. Indeed, the disparity between the system of competition law and the capacity of the sovereign state to implement such policy successfully forms part of the wider challenge that developing countries face in achieving economic development based on the traditional international competition law system. Hence, there is no guarantee that a liberal maritime cabotage approach that works in one country will have the same effect in another country. Therefore, different countries will apply different maritime cabotage approaches according to their circumstances, even if that means it is something other than a liberal approach. There is simply no formula for harmonizing the different unique circumstances in various countries to facilitate a strict enforcement of a model system of promoting economic development based on an exclusive competition law system.

## A review of the interface between the concepts of economic development and competition law within the context of maritime cabotage law

At first, it might appear unimportant to examine the interplay between competition law and development economics. This perception arises because both disciplines evolved in relative ignorance of each other and therefore for a long time addressed different questions.[2] The disciplines were traditionally isolated from each other because the mutual benefits they offer received little attention. However, the expansion of competition law in developing countries has helped change that view. There is now a new direction that encourages contemporary research to explore how economic development in developing countries might be enhanced through competition law.[3] Further exploratory research has also been pursued to ascertain an appropriate competition legislative framework for a developing economy.[4] Hence, there is now a gradual recognition of the connection between these two disciplines. However, if we are to understand the nature of this connection, we must first understand why these two disciplines started out on diverging paths.[5] Further, it would be useful to grasp the traditional conceptions that they represent in different intellectual ideologies.[6]

2 See: L. Ioannis, A. Mateus and A. Raslan, 'Is There Tension Between Development Economics and Competition?', in D. Sokol, T. Cheng and L. Ioannis (eds), *Competition Law and Development* (Stanford University Press 2013), pp. 35–51.
3 A. Bhattacharjea, 'Who Needs Antitrust? Or, Is Developing-Country Antitrust Different? A Historical Comparative Analysis', in D. Sokol, T. Cheng and L. Ioannis (eds), *Competition Law and Development* (Stanford University Press 2013), pp. 52–65.
4 M. Furse, *Competition Law of the EC and UK* (6th edn, Oxford University Press 2008).
5 For a broad read on this, see; D. Gerber, 'Economic Development and Global Competition Law Convergence', in D. Sokol, T. Cheng and L. Ioannis (eds), *Competition Law and Development* (Stanford University Press 2013), pp. 13–34.
6 See: V. Dhall, 'Competition Law and Consumer Protection: Insights into Their Interrelationship', in H. Qaqaya and G. Lipimile (eds), *The Effects of Anti-Competitive*

Following the assessment of the different theories of economic development in chapter 4, it is tempting to accept unchallenged that an important paradigm of economic development is an economy that encourages competition to thrive. However, one can argue that while competition law plays an important role in facilitating economic development, there are severe limitations to what it can contribute to economic development based on the unique circumstances in different sovereign states. Therefore, it is useful to understand the context in which competition law is applied in this section. In effect, this section is not concerned with the historical development of competition law. It merely queries how the international framework of competition law interfaces with economic development from a maritime cabotage law perspective.

Modern competition law points to the *Sherman Antitrust Act* of 1890 in the United States as its origin. It was passed to prohibit certain business activities deemed to be anti-competitive.[7] In *Spectrum Sports Inc. v. McQuillan*, [8] the United States Supreme Court ruled that the Sherman Act was designed to protect not organizations from the mechanisms of the market but rather the public against market failure. Thus, the act was passed with the aim of protecting competition rather than, as widely believed, competitors. In contrast, competition law in the European Union tends to protect competitors over marketplace competition. Articles 101 to 109 of the Treaty on the Functioning of the European Union reminds us of its regulatory control over cartels, market dominance, mergers and state aid.[9] European Union competition law as it applies to maritime transport services is regulated by Regulation 1/2003 and, where relevant, Regulation 1419/2006. The latter regulation repealed Regulation 4056/86 in 2008 because it appeared to undermine the Commission's policy on fair competition.[10] We should emphasize that the idea of competition law was not a phenomenon brought about by the Sherman Act. Indeed, competition law is said to have been borrowed from the Constitution of Zeno and was practised in an organized

*Business Practices on Developing Countries and Their Development Prospects* (UNCTAD, 2008), pp. 3–42.

7  15 U.S.C. §§ 1–7 and amended by the Clayton Act in 1914 (15 U.S.C. § 12–27). The Sherman Act was passed in 1890. The act is not directed against conduct that is competitive (however severe such competitive conduct is), but is concerned with unfair conduct that tends to destroy competition.

8  [1993] 506 U.S. 447.

9  See: Articles 101 to 109 of the Treaty on the Functioning of the European Union. There are four main areas of competitive practices which these sections of the treaty focus on: (a) Cartels, or control of collusion and other anti-competitive practices, under article 101 of the Treaty on the Functioning of the European Union (TFEU); (b) Market Dominance, or preventing the abuse of firms' dominant market positions under article 102 TFEU; (c) Mergers, control of proposed mergers, acquisitions and joint ventures involving companies that have a certain, defined amount of turnover in the EU, according to the Merger Regulation; (d) State aid, control of direct and indirect aid given by Member States of the European Union to companies under TFEU Article 107.

10 For a comprehensive read on the wider issues surrounding this subject matter, see: V. Power, *EU Shipping Law* (3rd edn, Informa 2015).

manner long before the act.[11] The objective and methodology of competition law may vary according to jurisdiction. This means that it is not always possible to give a standard definition of competition law or describe with certainty the scope of its application in various jurisdictions. For instance, competition law is better known as 'antitrust' law in the United States and 'anti-monopoly' law in jurisdictions such as Russia and China, which suggests that their objective and regulatory scopes are different. Therefore, competition law is one of those phenomena best defined by understanding their purpose. The primary purpose of competition law is to prevent or remedy circumstances where the free market system has failed.[12] Thus, fair competition in the market economy is an important objective of competition law. However, whether such fair competition leads directly to economic development is the question that needs to be answered. This is a characteristic shared with the law of maritime cabotage because the same question is central to whether a liberal or protectionist maritime cabotage approach is the best catalyst for economic development.[13]

In the countries where a liberal maritime cabotage policy is adopted, the relationship between the law of maritime cabotage and competition law is obvious. This is because both areas of the law share the same goals of deregulating market access, avoiding government subsidies and privatising national assets.[14] This assumes that fair and effective competition provides business enterprises with the platform to strive for efficiency in the cost of production and provision of (maritime) services.[15] Thus, the three important elements that should be satisfied by competition law can be stated as follows. First, there should be prohibition of agreements or practices that restrict or repress free trading and competition between (maritime) businesses in a country. Second, there must be prevention of intimidating or abusive behaviour resulting from one company dominating a

11 K. Cseres, 'Competition Law and Consumer Protection' (Kluwer Law International, 2005). It has been suggested that the Sherman Act was derived from the Constitution of Zeno, which was promulgated in 483 AD. Zeno was emperor of the Eastern Roman Empire from 474 to 491 AD. There seems to be tacit acknowledgement of an earlier competition law by Senator Sherman himself when he informed the Senate that his bill did 'not announce a new principle of law but applied old and well-recognized principles of the common law to the complicated jurisdiction of our State and Federal Government'.

12 J. Crotty, 'The Neoliberal Paradox: The Impact of Destructive Product Market Competition and Modern Financial Markets on Non-Financial Corporation Performance in the Neoliberal Era', in G. Epstein (ed.), *Financialization and the World Economy* (Edward Elgar 2005), 77–110.

13 An in-depth analysis of the different approaches to the law of maritime cabotage as adopted by different maritime countries around the world is scheduled for later chapters.

14 For a related read, see: A. Pera, 'Deregulation and Privatisation in an Economy-wide Context' [1989], *OECD Economic Studies*, 12(2), 159–204.

15 P. Mehta et al., 'Competition Policy and Consumer Policy: Complementarities and Conflicts in the Promotion of Consumer Welfare', in H. Qaqaya and G. Lipimile (eds), *The Effects of Anti-Competitive Business Practices on Developing Countries and Their Development Prospects* (UNCTAD 2008), pp. 43–71.

market, or of anti-competitive practices that tend to lead to such a dominant position. Third, there must be supervision of the mergers and acquisitions of large corporations. This includes some joint ventures that can threaten the competitive process in a country.[16]

We have indicated above that the applicable system of competition law varies according to jurisdiction. Nonetheless, the anti-trust laws in the United States and European Union competition law tend to dominate both academic and industry debates. The competition laws in both jurisdictions are designed with the same objective in mind, albeit that they employ different methodologies.[17] On the one hand, the antitrust law in the United States focuses on the activities of the dominant organizations. It aims to ascertain whether their conduct, such as joint venture or merger, will create inefficiency in the market by raising price and lowering output.[18] On the other hand, the European Union competition law focuses on monitoring the major players to ascertain whether they contemplate mergers or joint ventures to prevent other players from accessing the market.[19]

The need for an international competition policy framework has not always been met with widespread enthusiasm or a common resolve. The United States and the European Union start from different positions on this question. Europe has generally indicated a strong desire for regulating competition policy at the international level. However, this idea has provoked considerable opposition in the United States, although there appears to be a softening of that stance.[20] An example of this new position is the report produced by the International Competition Policy Advisory Committee (ICPAC), which acknowledged an increasing trend of US antitrust cases with an international dimension.[21] Thus, the prospect of the United States' gravitating towards the EU's position suggests a need to establish a basic competition regulatory framework at the international level. However, this development should not ignore the fact that the United States antitrust law and the EU competition law evoke some very pertinent points for

16  For a broad take on the issues, see: M. Taylor, *International Competition Law: A New Dimension for the WTO?* (2nd edn, Cambridge University Press 2006).

17  M. Stucke, 'Is competition always good?' [2013], *Journal of Antitrust Enforcement*, 1(1), 162–197.

18  R. Cass, 'Competition in Antitrust Regulation: Law beyond Limits' [2009], *Journal of Competition Law & Economics*, 6(1), 119–152.

19  E. Fox, 'Competition, Development and Regional Integration: In Search of a Competition Law Fit for Developing Countries' [2012], New York University Law and Economics Research Paper No. 11-04. However, see the GATS Telecommunications Agreement and Annex, which serves as the rare exception.

20  For a read on the broader issues, see: M. Stucke, 'Is Competition Always Good?' [2013], *Journal of Antitrust Enforcement*, 1(1), 162–197; J. Jackson, 'Sovereignty – Modern: A New Approach to an Outdated Concept' [2003], *American Journal of International Law*, 97(1), 782–802.

21  See the final report of the International Competition Policy Advisory Committee to the Attorney General and Assistant Attorney General for Antitrust. Dated 28 February 2000.

consideration, particularly from a developing nation's perspective. The first point is that it appears that developing (maritime) nations have little choice other than to adopt either the antitrust laws of the United States or the competition law of the European Union.[22] The challenge with this is that these developing nations often lack the capacity to implement successfully either of these sophisticated competition law systems. The second point is the debate as to whether developing (maritime) nations should choose a pathway that follows a different direction to the one charted by industrialized (maritime) nations.[23] This is because of the common issues that characterize developing (maritime) nations such as scarce expertise, sluggish markets, scarce financial capital and tight access to markets.[24] It is suggested that these common issues justify the design of a 'bespoke' competition law framework that addresses the peculiar deficiencies in these developing nations.[25] This is not to suggest that the pursuit of such a bespoke approach should undermine the interaction between developing and industrialized nations under bilateral or multilateral agreements frameworks.[26] The agenda must be to develop a competition law system that facilitates national economic development based on competition economics.[27]

We have discussed at length the relationship between competition law and economic development such that we might be in danger of forgetting that the ideologies behind the concepts are different. The focus of competition law is the market. It assumes that there will always be a market economy where competition is at play.[28] On the other hand, economic development is concerned with macroeconomics. This involves managing the performance and structure of the national, regional and global economy.[29]

However, there is a critical point that warrants serious consideration when examining the interface between competition law and economic development. If we accept that different countries are at different stages of economic development, then we should query the extent to which a variation in the design framework of

22 S. Phang, 'Competition Law and the International Transport Sectors' [2009], *Competition Law Review*, 5(2), 193–213.
23 For a general read, see: E. Elhauge and D. Geradin, *Global Antitrust Law and Economics* (2nd edn, Thomson Reuters 2011).
24 For a wider read and support argument, see: B. Paasman, 'Multilateral Rules on Competition Policy: An Overview of the Debate' [1999], *ECLAC – SERIE Comercio Internacional*, 2(4), 1–55.
25 For an expansion of this argument, see: T. Howell et al., 'China's New Anti-Monopoly Law: A Perspective from the United States' [2009], *Pacific Rim Law & Policy Journal*, 18(1), 53–95.
26 Department for International Development, 'Competition Policy, Law and Developing Countries', Trade Matters Series (September 2001).
27 A. Rodríguez, 'The Role of Merger Policy in Recently Liberalized Economies' (Monterey Institute of Advanced Technological Studies, 1996).
28 J. Podolny, 'A Status-based Model of Market Competition' [1993], *American Journal of Sociology*, 98(4), 829–872.
29 See: I. Lianos, A. Mateus and A. Raslan, 'Development Economics and Competition: A Parallel Intellectual History' [2012], Centre for Law, Economics and Society (CLES) Working Paper Series, 1/2012.

competition law is necessary or even desirable.[30] The choices for competition provision and enforcement design are dictated by a spectrum of factors, including the social, economic and political environment. Therefore, countries should tailor their domestic competition law framework and the institutions that enforce the laws to suit their national structures.[31] The alternative, which is to design a 'one size fits all' framework of competition law for industrialized and developing economies, is likely to create more problems than proffer solutions.[32] One may suggest that competition law plays a major role in the national or regional framework of maritime cabotage law. This is because regardless of the choice of maritime cabotage law approach, a country will invariably be choosing to either encourage or impede the competition process within its economy.[33] Therefore, to function as an efficient facilitator of the development process, competition law should be complemented by compatible policies that support economic development.[34] Hence, the influence of competition law on the economic development of a (maritime) nation depends on the extent to which such an interface stimulates the desired economic development in the economy.[35]

The distinctive features of competition law and development economics have been examined above. Competition law deals with markets and the competition that supposedly occurs in the market economy. Meanwhile, development economics deals with the management of the macro-economy of the sovereign nation. This explains why the two fields of study traditionally set out on divergent paths. However, we have noted that contemporary studies have since sought a convergence of the fields. This allows us to explore how the interface between competition law and economic development aligns with the choice of a maritime cabotage approach.

The gap between competition law and development economics is continually narrowing as different schools of thought strive to find the convergent point between these two phenomena.[36] This is significant because industrial

---

30  For more on this, see: V. Ghosal, 'Resource Constraints and Competition Law Enforcement: Theoretical Considerations and Observations from Selected Cross-country Data', in D. Sokol, T. Cheng and L. Ioannis (eds), *Competition Law and Development* (Stanford University Press 2013), pp. 90–114.

31  R. Lucas, 'On the Mechanics of Economic Development' [1988], *Journal of Monetary Economics*, 22(1), 3–42.

32  For a similar argument, see: P. Mehta et al., 'Competition Policy and Consumer Policy: Complementarities and Conflicts in the Promotion of Consumer Welfare', in H. Qaqaya and G. Lipimile (eds), *The Effects of Anti-Competitive Business Practices on Developing Countries and Their Development Prospects* (UNCTAD 2008), pp. 43–71.

33  See a similar argument from a different perspective in: F. Marcos, 'Do Developing Countries Need Competition Law and Policy?' (Instituto de Empresa Business School, 2006).

34  M. Solow, 'A Contribution to the Theory of Economic Growth' [1956], *Quarterly Journal of Economics*, 1(70), 65–94.

35  UNCTAD, 'The Role of Competition Policy in Promoting Economic Development: The Appropriate Design and Effectiveness of Competition Law and Policy', TD/RBP/CONF.7/3, (UNCTAD Secretariat, 2010).

36  D. Gerber, 'Economic Development and Global Competition Law Convergence', in D. Sokol, T. Cheng and L. Ioannis (eds), *Competition Law and Development* (Stanford University Press 2013), pp. 13–34.

organization economists depict that the interaction between innovation and the economy is illustrative of the importance of competition in productivity growth.[37] Furthermore, empirical research has demonstrated the importance of competition. It is suggested that efficiency is achieved where there is (perfect) competition between businesses that contribute to economic development within the national, regional or international framework.[38] However, there is a counter-argument that suggests that mismanaged competition could be destructive, particularly where competitive opportunities in the market are limited. The other situation is where some players in the market have become so powerful that they threaten the competitive process. Both situations may negate the economic development unless steps are taken to regulate the conduct of such players.[39] Thus, development economists have argued that managing the macro-economics of a nation requires enforcing a suitable competition law. It is suggested that those who advocate for a liberal maritime cabotage approach would argue that this is vital to facilitating the interaction between competition law, growth and economic development within the maritime cabotage law context.[40]

We have identified that a fundamental principle of competition law is the balancing of economic efficiency and development. This suggests that promoting economic efficiency is an explicit objective of competition policy in many jurisdictions.[41] Hence, the interface between competition law and economic development is concerned with two questions. The first question relates to the manner in which the effective implementation of competition law contributes positively to economic development. The second question is concerned with the probable negative consequences that could arise from implementing a flawed competition law framework.[42] As such, the interface between competition and development can only truly be comprehended when economic development is viewed from a 'dynamic

---

37  For a detailed discussion and analysis on this subject, see: E. Brouwer et al., 'Market Structure, Innovation and Productivity: A Marriage with Chemistry', in G. Gelauff et al. (eds), *Fostering Productivity: Patterns, Determinants and Policy Implications* (Elsevier 2004), pp. 199–212.

38  M. Gal, 'The Ecology of Antitrust: Preconditions for Competition Law Enforcement in Developing Countries', in P. Brunsick et al. (eds), *Competition, Competitiveness and Development: Lessons From Developing Countries* (UNCTAD 2004), pp. 20–38.

39  See: D. Sokol and A. Stephan, 'Prioritizing Cartel Enforcement in Developing World Competition Agencies', in D. Sokol, T. Cheng and L. Ioannis (eds), *Competition Law and Development* (Stanford University Press 2013), pp. 137–154.

40  See similar argument in: I. Lianos, A. Mateus and A. Raslan, 'Development Economics and Competition: A Parallel Intellectual History' [2012], Centre for Law, Economics and Society (CLES) Working Paper Series, 1/2012.

41  A. Fels and W. Ng, 'Rethinking Competition Advocacy in Developing Countries', in D. Sokol, T. Cheng and L. Ioannis (eds), *Competition Law and Development* (Stanford University Press 2013), pp. 182–198.

42  For an in-depth analysis on these issues, see: M. Gal, 'The Ecology of Antitrust: Preconditions for Competition Law Enforcement in Developing Countries', in P. Brunsick et al. (eds), *Competition, Competitiveness and Development: Lessons From Developing Countries* (UNCTAD 2004), pp. 20–38.

efficiency' perspective.[43] This allows concentrated focus on sustainable balancing of the short- and long-term economic objectives of a country.[44]

Nevertheless, it is symbolic that there is no international framework for both the law of maritime cabotage and competition law even though the issues in these areas of the law have a global impact.[45] The International Competition Network (ICN),[46] which addresses global competition issues and promotes open and competitive markets for businesses and consumers, is an informal organization whose declarations are not legally binding.[47] The absence of an international framework on competition law is significant if we are to accept that fair competition results in the provision of goods and services at competitive prices, promotes efficient productivity, and stimulates sustainable economic development. Perhaps a useful example of the role of competition in a maritime cabotage law context was when consumers in Sabah and Sarawak States paid higher prices for goods and sea transport services under a protectionist maritime cabotage regime in Malaysia. This lends support to the proposition that vigorous competition often compels businesses to improve their efficiency. This is because the competition for resources within the economy engineers the movement of resources from the weak uncompetitive sectors towards the more competitive sectors.[48] This encourages domestic capacity building and promotes sustainable economic development in the country. Furthermore, the factor markets and institutions that control market operations are vital in enhancing the effects of competition law on the optimal economic development of a country.[49] Also, competition in product markets

43 R. Gilbert and S. Steven, 'Incorporating Dynamic Efficiency Concerns in Merger Analysis: The Use of Innovation Markets' [1995], *Antitrust Law Journal*, 63(2), 569–602.

44 World Trade Organization, 'The Fundamental Principles of Competition Policy' (WT/WGTCP/W/127, 7 June 1999).

45 E. Fox, 'Competition, Development and Regional Integration: In Search of a Competition Law Fit for Developing Countries' [2012], Law and Economics Research Paper Series, Working Paper 11/04. However, see the GATS Telecommunications Agreement and Annex, which serves as the rare exception.

46 The International Competition Network (ICN) was established from the recommendations of the International Competition Policy Advisory Committee (ICPAC). The ICPAC was formed in 1997 to address global competition problems within the context of economic globalization. It focused on issues such as multi-jurisdictional merger review, the interface between trade and competition, and the future direction for cooperation between competition agencies. Hence, ICN was launched on 25 October 2001 by top antitrust officials from 14 jurisdictions: Australia, Canada, European Union, France, Germany, Israel, Italy, Japan, Korea, Mexico, South Africa, United Kingdom, United States and Zambia.

47 International Competition Network, 'ICN Factsheet and Key Messages' (ICN 2009).

48 This is the exact argument postulated by the Rostow's model of growth, which has been treated in sufficient detail in chapter 4. For a wider read, see: C. Teo, 'Competition Policy and Economic Growth' [2003], paper for the ASEAN Conference on Fair Competition Law and Policy in the ASEAN Free Trade Area in Bali, 4–8 March 2003. Singapore: Ministry of Trade and Industry, Singapore Government.

49 R. Gilbert, 'Competition and Innovation' [2006], *Journal of Industrial Organization Education*, 1(1), 8, 1–30.

stimulates both product and process innovations that contribute to national economic development.[50]

This is because competition encourages industries to boost productivity by focusing on innovative development strategies for the national economy.[51] However, there is a generally accepted exception to the proposition that competition is the key to economic development. Protecting the infant industry appears to be the only argument where (foreign) competition is generally deemed to be undesirable and protectionism may be excused.[52] This tacit acceptance of protectionism is tied to the objective of encouraging economic development. This is achieved by enabling the domestic industry to grow to a level where it can entertain competition without being unduly disadvantaged.[53] However, it is also true that sheltering domestic firms from competition for longer than necessary can be harmful to the economic development of the country.[54]

When liberal policies such as trade deregulation and privatization are adopted as the path to economic development, the anticipated benefits of such liberalization may be lost without an effective competition law.[55] Thus, competition is encouraged in countries where liberal maritime cabotage policies are adopted. Liberal policy advocates argue that adequate implementation of competition law in a country increases investor confidence and attracts foreign investment.[56] A country whose economy and markets are reinforced by competition policy is likely to benefit from such foreign investment. This is because foreign investors are encouraged to support capacity building by investing in capital and human resources, with the overall aim of contributing to the economic development of the country.[57] Furthermore, the interface between competition law and economic development is evident in areas of infrastructural development and technological advancement.[58] Many maritime nations seek to develop their maritime sectors. However, to achieve the desired

50 G. Bonanno and B. Haworth, 'Intensity of Competition and the Choice between Product and Process Innovation' [1998], *International Journal of Industrial Organization*, 16(4), 495–510.

51 B. Rodger and A. MacCulloch, *Competition Law and Policy in the EC and UK* (4th edn, Routledge-Cavendish 2009).

52 J. Delacroix and J. Bornon, 'Can Protectionism Ever Be Respectable: A Skeptic's Case for the Cultural Exception, with Special Reference to French Movies' [2005], *Independent Review*, 9(3), 353–374.

53 M. Melitz, 'When and How Should Infant Industries be Protected?' [2005], *Journal of International Economics*, 66, 177–196.

54 See: S. Evenett, *What is the Relationship between Competition Law and Policy and Economic Development?* (University of Oxford 2005).

55 J. Stiglitz, 'Trade and the Developing World: A New Agenda' [1999], *Current History Magazine*, 98 (631), pp. 387–393.

56 M. Porter, *The Competitive Advantage of Nations* (Free Press 1990).

57 World Trade Organization, 'Synthesis Paper on the Relationship of Trade and Competition Policy to Development and Economic Growth', WT/WGTCP/W/80 (WTO, 18 September 1998).

58 K. Schmidt, Managerial Incentives and Product Market Competition [1997], *Review of Economic Studies*, 64(2), 191–213.

development, they must first choose whether to pursue a liberal or protectionist (maritime cabotage) policy.[59] It is argued that with a liberal maritime cabotage regime, there is a fusion of ideology between 'economic development' and 'competition'. This is because both legal concepts (law of maritime cabotage and competition law) aim for an improved economy by facilitating growth in various sectors.[60] Therefore, there is a theoretical argument that implementing a liberal (maritime cabotage) policy without a robust competition law may encourage a different kind of problem such as cartelization, which impedes economic development.[61] Hence, effective enforcement of competition policy requires a high degree of accountability and monitoring. This in turn relies heavily on good governance, which is an important principle of sustainable development law.[62] Also, the implementation of competition rules can provide incentives for industries to improve efficiency by avoiding wasteful practices.[63] This is because competition law improves economic regulation and supports economic development by encouraging innovation, industrialization and human resource development.[64]

Competition law and policy affects economic development in two ways. On the one hand, government might intervene to control competition where a specific sector of an economy is protected to encourage its development.[65] This is the 'infant industry' argument, which encourages staving off competition to give a domestic infant industry the chance to grow. This is often accompanied by government support in the form of subsidies, loans and grants. On the other hand, where there is a monopolistic economic system, encouraging free markets and fair competition would neutralise this monopoly.[66]

59 See later chapters where the choice of maritime cabotage approach adopted by different countries has been given sufficient treatment.
60 For a critical examination of this issue from a slightly different perspective, see: H. Pack, 'Technological Change and Growth in East Asia Macro versus Micro Perspectives', in J. Stiglitz and S. Yusuf (eds), *Rethinking the East Asian Miracle* (Oxford University Press 2001), pp. 95–142.
61 For a broader take on the issues, see: D. Sokol, and A. Stephan, 'Prioritizing Cartel Enforcement in Developing World Competition Agencies', in D. Sokol, T. Cheng and L. Ioannis (eds), *Competition Law and Development* (Stanford University Press 2013), pp. 137–154.
62 D. Schneiderman, 'Globalisation, Governance, and Investment Rules', in J. Clarke and G. Edwards (eds), *Global Governance in the Twenty-first Century* (Palgrave Macmillan 2004), pp. 67–94.
63 P. Van Cayseele, 'Market Structure and Innovation: A Survey of the Last Twenty Years' [1998], *De Economist*, 146(3), 391–417.
64 T. Arthur, 'Competition Law and Development: Lessons from the U.S. Experience', in D. Sokol, T. Cheng and L. Ioannis (eds), *Competition Law and Development* (Stanford University Press 2013), pp. 66–78.
65 See: Z. Onis, 'The Limits of Neoliberalism: Toward A Reformulation of Development Theory' [1995], *Journal of Economic Issues*, 29(1), 97–119.
66 M. Gehring, 'Sustainable Competition Law: for the 2003 Fifth Session of the Ministerial Conference of the World Trade Organization', WTO (Cancun, 10–14 September 2003).

## State aid in a maritime cabotage law context

State aid may be defined as the process whereby national or regional governments interrupt market forces by providing some form of relief, usually to indigenous businesses. It usually takes the form of a financial grant, exception or relaxation of the rules, or a reduction in the normal financial obligations of the state aid recipient. Just as competition, as discussed in the previous section, lends itself to a liberal maritime cabotage approach, state aid is very much an element of a protectionist maritime cabotage approach. It generally distorts competition and attempts to put the beneficiary businesses at an advantage over their competitors. Hence, state aid is deemed a protectionist policy mechanism because it threatens to introduce unfair competition into the market.

In the European Union, the Treaty for the Functioning of the European Union's (TFEU) competition rules declares the provision of state aid by member states to be incompatible with the internal market.[67] This general principle as contained in Article 107(1) of the TFEU is however derogated by the provisions of Article 107(2) and 107(3). The distinction between the provisions of the two articles is that while at least one of the aims of giving state aid must be satisfied under Article 107(2), such compulsoriness is not required under Article 107(3). Hence, the aims under that article may only be considered but need not be satisfied. In general, Article 107(2) permits state aid, provided that such aid has one of the three specified aims that is compatible with the internal market. For state aid to be compatible with the internal market, it must satisfy one of the following aims:

a   Aid should have a social character and be granted to individual consumers, provided that it is granted without discrimination related to the origin of the products concerned
b   Aid to make good the damage caused by natural disasters or exceptional occurrences.
c   Aid granted to the economy of certain areas of the Federal Republic of Germany affected by the division of Germany, provided such aid is required to compensate for the economic disadvantages caused by that division.[68]

Furthermore, Article 107(3) permits other objectives that may be considered compatible with the internal market. These objectives are outlined below:

---

67  See: Article 107(1) of the Treaty for the Functioning of the European Union: 'Save as otherwise provided in the Treaties, any aid granted by a member state or through state resources in any form whatsoever which distorts or threatens to distort competition by favouring certain undertakings or the production of certain goods shall, in so far as it affects trade between Member States, be incompatible with the internal market'.
68  This point comes with a proviso that five years after the entry into force of the Treaty of Lisbon, the Council, acting on a proposal from the Commission, may adopt a decision repealing it.

a   Aid to promote the economic development of areas where the standard of living is abnormally low or where there is serious underemployment, and of the regions referred to in Article 349, in view of their structural, economic and social situation.

b   Aid to promote the execution of an important project of common European interest or to remedy a serious disturbance in the economy of a member state.

c   Aid to facilitate the development of certain economic activities or of certain economic areas, where such aid does not adversely affect trading conditions to an extent contrary to the common interest.

d   Aid to promote culture and heritage conservation where such aid does not affect trading conditions and competition in the Union to an extent that is contrary to the common interest.

e   Such other categories of aid as may be specified by decision of the Council on a proposal from the Commission.

In addition to the above points, the Commission is empowered to control, monitor and review the administering of state aid to ensure that it remains compatible with the internal market, bearing in mind the relevant economic, political and social considerations.[69] Under EU law, it is important that for aid to be considered under the above regulations, such aid must be given by a member state. Where such aid is given by a non-member state, the appropriate regime for consideration is under the EU dumping law.[70]

Outside the European Union, state aid would normally take the form of government subsidy to indigenous ship owners to build ships in domestic shipyards, train and employ indigenous seafarers, and document their vessels with the domestic ship registers. It may also include mandatorily requiring certain seagoing positions such as master, chief officer and chief engineer to be reserved to indigenous seafarers only. Furthermore, cargo and passenger quota may be reserved exclusively to domestic carriers providing cabotage services. For instance, the Chinese government has been known to give financial subsidy to encourage the sustenance of state-owned vessels built in Chinese shipyards.

## Government regulation, influence and intervention

In this section, we will be looking at how government intervenes to regulate or influence the provision of maritime cabotage services within the domestic waters of the state. Liberal commentators are usually quick to assert that any such government intervention is counter-productive to the objectives of fair competition. By this they mean that government intervention is prone to thwarting economic development. However, we saw in chapter 4 that this proposition is not only incorrect but disingenuous: available evidence paints a rather different picture from that indicated by many liberal commentators. Many Asian countries during

69 See: Article 108 of the Treaty of the Functioning of the European Union.
70 See: Council Regulation No. 1225/2009.

the 1997/8 Pacific-Asian crisis recorded remarkable feat of economic development primarily on the back of government regulation, influence and intervention.[71] Moreover, one can argue that the idea of government intervention has always been construed narrowly. The general belief is that when government intervenes, it usually does so on the back of a protectionist policy aimed at giving domestic players an unfair advantage. However, it appears that there is no reason why government cannot intervene to promote liberal policies and encourage fair competition. Indeed, this is already demonstrated in the European Union. We would recall that the Commission under Article 108 of the Treaty of the Functioning of the European Union is empowered to monitor and intervene where the provision of state aid by a member state becomes incompatible with the internal market. If we accept that government intervention can be ambiguous, we have the basis for focusing our attention on the 'why' and 'how' government intervention impacts economic development within a maritime cabotage law context.

Government influence and intervention take different forms and can be applied at different stages of the economic development plan. However, the principal means by which governments can influence the pace and rate of economic development through maritime cabotage is by applying its legislative- and policy-making mechanism. This includes enacting statutory laws, enforcing judicial decisions and developing new government policies. This allows the government to influence fiscal and monetary policies, state aid and related subsidies and the business environment. The last item is particularly significant because the business environment affords government the opportunity to control business activities. This can take the form of legislation, cargo reservation or fiscal intervention.

Where regional governance is concerned, the control enjoyed by sovereign states is subject to the higher authority of the regional government. This has been demonstrated by the relationship between the governing Council of the European Union and governments of the member states. This means that sovereign states cannot influence or intervene through any mechanism if to do so would be incompatible with the objectives of the regional government. When a group of sovereign states agree to commit themselves to the laws of a supranational government, they do so with the knowledge and expectation that the supranational laws will interfere and often supersede the national laws of the state. Thus, in the context of maritime cabotage law, the regional maritime cabotage policy or legal framework will apply to all member states of the supranational body. This means that individuals or businesses which by their physical presence within the territorial waters or land of the cabotage state or by the nature of their business should be regulated under the laws of the cabotage state would now submit to the laws of the supranational government.

---

71 S. Knowles and A. Garces-Ozanne, 'Government Intervention and Economic Performance in East Asia' [2003], *Economic Development and Cultural Change*, 51(2), 451–477.

# 6   The variants of maritime cabotage

We have discussed in some detail that the three forms in which maritime cabotage law is applied in different sovereign states are; protectionist, liberal and flexible approaches. Thus, we have looked at the law of maritime cabotage as the process of government choosing one of the three approaches and applying it in one geographical entity known as the sovereign state. In simple terms, we have viewed maritime cabotage law as a one approach-one country arrangement. Although this is the norm and in most countries, there are exceptions. The geographical characteristics of some countries means that it is not always possible or desirable for the government to adopt one maritime cabotage approach for the country. Hence, a liberal maritime cabotage approach may be applied in some parts of the country while a protectionist cabotage regime is implemented in other parts of the same country. Perhaps we should note that the financial and resource cost of implementing a variant of maritime cabotage law in some sectors of the economy may exceed by far the overall possible economic returns in that country. For instance, a report from the Federal Reserve Bank of New York in 2012 revealed the impact of the Jones Act on island and inland waterways. The report concluded that it costs an estimated $3,063 to ship a 20-foot container from the east coast of the United States to the island of Puerto Rico. The same shipment costs $1,504 to nearby Santo Domingo (Dominican Republic) and $1,687 to Kingston (Jamaica). Similarly, it cost $8,700 to ship a 40-foot container from Los Angeles to Honolulu, while the same shipment from Los Angeles to Shanghai costs only $790.[1]

The law of maritime cabotage has three principal variants, namely island cabotage, mainland cabotage and general cabotage. Any one of these or a combination of all three may be implemented in a country depending on the maritime and geographical characteristics of the country. For instance, the objective of liberalizing maritime cabotage in the European Union required member states to ensure that their national legislation complied with Council Regulation (EEC) No.

---

1 See the *Report on the Competitiveness of Puerto Rico's Economy* by the Federal Reserve Bank of New York, dated 29 July 2012. For a broader take on these issues, see: B. Slattery, B. Riley and N. Loris, 'Sink the Jones Act: Restoring America's Competitive Advantage in Maritime-Related Industries' [2014], *Backgrounder*, No. 2886, 1–9.

3577/92. However, Greece expressed concern that some of her islands are sufficiently close to Turkey to pose serious threats to Greece's national security. Therefore, Greece argued unsuccessfully to be allowed to continue to implement its protectionist maritime cabotage policy in these island regions even though other parts of its territorial waters were liberalized.[2] Other southern member states had similar concerns about their island regions. Some countries may opt to implement an approach of maritime cabotage law in their niche maritime sector without imposing a sweeping national maritime cabotage policy across all of its territorial waters. Generally, where this is the case, such measures are often necessitated by an obligation not to distort the provision of essential services. This is evident in island regions, where it is crucial to avoid disrupting what is often the only means of transport for goods and passengers between islands and between islands and the mainland territory. The provision of these essential services is usually maintained using public service bligations (PSOs), public service contacts (PSCs) and public service compensations (PSCs). A comprehensive discussion of these public service provisions is outside the scope of this section. Nevertheless, it is useful to provide a basic outline of these public service schemes that are applied specifically to ease the challenges that arise with island cabotage.

First, public service obligation refers to the requirement defined or determined by a competent authority to ensure public transport services in the general interest of the public. This obligation must be such that if an operator were considering its own commercial interests, that operator would not assume such responsibility or would not assume it to the same extent or under the same conditions without reward.[3] Second, public service contract refers to one or more legally binding acts confirming the agreement between a competent authority and a public service operator. This agreement entrusts the management and operation of public transport services to that public service operator subject to the responsibilities under public service obligations. The competent authority may choose to provide the services or entrust the provision of such services to an internal operator. Alternatively, it may opt to regulate such agreement through an individual legislative or regulatory act.[4] Third, public service compensation refers to any benefit granted directly or indirectly to the public service operator by a competent authority from public funds during the period of implementation of a public service obligation or relating to that period.[5] This benefit is usually financial in the form of state aid.

2  See the Commission's letter of formal notice to Greece dated 3 February 2004. IP/04/159.
3  Article 2(e) of Regulation (EC) No 1370/2007 of the European Parliament and of the Council of 23 October 2007 on Public Passenger Transport Services by Rail and by Road and Repealing Council Regulations (EEC) Nos 1191/69 and 1107/70.
4  Article 2(i) of Regulation (EC) No 1370/2007 of the European Parliament and of the Council of 23 October 2007 on Public Passenger Transport Services by Rail and by Road and Repealing Council Regulations (EEC) Nos 1191/69 and 1107/70.
5  Article 2(g) of Regulation (EC) No 1370/2007 of the European Parliament and of the Council of 23 October 2007 on Public Passenger Transport Services by Rail and by Road and Repealing Council Regulations (EEC) Nos 1191/69 and 1107/70.

The general technique used in applying public service agreements in countries is to impose a sweeping protectionist law that is often tempered with brief exemptions to some services and sectors. Indonesia reverted to implementing a protectionist maritime cabotage law in 2008 but granted exemption to the oil and gas sector. Similarly, India and Malaysia have in the past granted periodic exemptions from their traditional protectionist maritime cabotage law.

We will see in later chapters that the assessment of different national legislation on maritime cabotage reveals the dilemma that many countries must deal with. In adopting a maritime cabotage regime, the government may need to decide whether to exempt, even periodically, some sectors or maritime services from the general application of the national maritime cabotage law. Such exemptions or waivers usually elicit strong opinions from many of the different stakeholders. One can argue that in this dilemma lies the fundamental question of what the driving factors behind the choice of maritime cabotage approach might be. Indeed, the answer depends on how the government understands and views the objectives of its maritime cabotage laws. On the one hand the government may be focused on facilitating an effective maritime cabotage regime that contributes to its economic development. On the other hand, the government may adopt a popular but ineffective maritime cabotage approach, thereby consigning the development of its maritime sector to a slow but inevitable demise. A good example is the maritime cabotage law in Nigeria. Although it was popular when it first became law, it is so ineffective that it is now sabotaging the once desired economic development of the Nigerian maritime sector. The situation, although not as bad, is not very different in Australia, where successive governments tend to favour a different kind of maritime cabotage law approach. For those operating maritime services in Australia's coastal waters, this means that it is difficult to know what kind of law will apply to them in the short, medium or long term. It is not difficult to understand how this kind of uncertainty hampers economic development.

The three variants of maritime cabotage are examined below. However, we should first look at some of their distinct characteristics. For instance, island cabotage is the most problematic variant of maritime cabotage because the government is faced with sensitive issues relating to public service. However, mainland cabotage is the variant that generates most debate on whether a liberal or protectionist approach is best for a country. The third variant, general cabotage, is the one that is most subjected to competition and complaints from other modes of domestic transport network such as road and rail. The European Union maritime cabotage framework is a useful example of a regime that accommodates the different variants of maritime cabotage. However, we should note that the general cabotage variant is excluded from the scope of Council Regulation 3577/92. The services that would normally fall within the scope of the general cabotage variant are covered under the different Council Regulation (EEC) No. 3921/91. This regulation governs the transport of goods or passengers on the inland waterways within a member state by non-resident carriers.[6]

6 See the provisions of Council Regulation (EEC) No. 3921/91.

With each variant of maritime cabotage, the cabotage host state is tasked with considering different conditions of access to nationals and non-nationals depending on the nature of the maritime activity being pursued. Perhaps this explains why a country may apply both the protectionist and liberal maritime cabotage approaches concurrently. This would take the form of applying a liberal maritime cabotage approach in the mainland region while adopting a more protectionist approach in the island region of the same country. This is evident in the European Union, where maritime cabotage rules in the island regions are more protectionist than what applies in the mainland territories. For instance, protectionist crewing requirements and fiscal policies such as state aid are permitted in the island regions of member states of the European Union, even though a liberal maritime cabotage framework is the operative regime in the European Union bloc itself. Therefore, the application of maritime cabotage law in any country may depend very much on the applicable variants of maritime cabotage.

Therefore, this section does not set out to propose that applying a liberal or protectionist policy to any of the maritime cabotage variants is the correct approach. Nevertheless, it does accept that the role of the regulator is bound to be different at each end of the protectionist–liberal continuum. Thus, what is predictable is that some policies may fit better with a government-controlled approach, whereas other policies may be better suited to market-driven choices.

## Island cabotage

Island cabotage is the most complicated of the three variants of maritime cabotage because of its often isolated and detached location. Littoral countries are challenged with providing sustainable maritime services in its island regions without compromising on the development and sovereignty issues that are fundamental to maritime cabotage. According to its most basic definition, island cabotage is the sea carriage of cargo between ports situated on the mainland and on one or more of the islands, or between ports situated on the islands of the same country.[7] It is arguable that islands almost assume the status of a quasi-state; they often require special legislations and policies that are different from the applicable regulations in the mainland territories of the country. The physical nature of islands means that the regulation of cabotage in these regions bears distinct characteristics from other variants of maritime cabotage. The regulation is therefore more complex from both policy formulation and implementation points of view. Generally, islands are challenged with access problems that affect the quality and volume of the transport services provided in the region because of their fragmented nature.[8]

One of the consequences of poor accessibility due to an overburdened transport network is the high price of consumer goods paid by the islanders and industries

---

7  See: Article 2(1)(c) of Council Regulation 3577/92.
8  For a broad read on the issues, see: M. Lekakou and T. Vitsounis, 'Market Concentration in Coastal Shipping and Limitations to Island's Accessibility' [2011], *Research in Transportation Business & Management*, 2(1), 74–82.

operating on islands. This is in part due to the imbalance in the traffic flow of more imports compared to very little export. The peculiar nature of islands demands that any legal or policy framework must be both pragmatic and flexible to cater successfully for the diverse characteristics of island regions. This may explain why maritime services in island regions within the European Union are still monopolized within a protectionist framework despite the EU liberal regional maritime cabotage policy. In comparison, the island cabotage regulations in the Economic and Social Commission for Asia and the Pacific (ESCAP) region is not as developed as that of the European Union. For instance, the maritime cabotage policy in the ESCAP region focuses on a narrow range of maritime services compared to what is obtainable in the European Union maritime cabotage framework.[9] The challenges faced in these islands include remoteness from the major global markets, low trade volumes, imbalance in economic activities among islands, lack of stable and efficient transport services covering the long distance between ports, and the expensive shipping costs to the islands.

A regional maritime cabotage policy framework has been proposed for the ESCAP region to mitigate against some of the challenges facing island cabotage. This would facilitate the provision of maritime services on a larger economy of scale.[10] This would create a better platform to tackle effectively, the worrisome issues identified above. The proposed regional maritime cabotage framework has not been implemented because of concerns that it would result in a monumental disruption to maritime transport activities in the region. Nonetheless, it is suggested that any such envisaged disruption could be minimized by experimenting with a sub-regional maritime cabotage framework before implementing the full regional maritime cabotage policy in the Pacific Island region.[11] The strategic option to experiment with a smaller group of countries may be particularly useful. This is because countries that by their nature are made up of islands and are separated by the sea but remain under one sovereignty are typically plagued by the lack of access and exit to road and rail transport network. Moreover, the option of air transport is marginal due to expense, frequency and availability. Therefore, islanders are left with little choice but to rely on internal waterways as a primary mode of transport for goods and passengers to sustain their economies.[12]

Discussions on the best policy framework for regulating island cabotage have generated strong debates at both national and supranational level due to its diverse and even more complicated nature. Greece, Italy, Portugal and Spain were very reluctant to accept the idea of liberalizing maritime cabotage services in their

---

9   The point is elaborated further in: R. Petrova, 'Cabotage and the European Community Common Maritime Policy: Moving towards Free provision of Services in Maritime Transport' [1997], *Fordham International Law Journal*, 21(3), 1–76.

10   For a broader read, see: R. Greaves, *EC Transport Law* (Pearson Education 2010).

11   For a more general read, see: G. Lee, 'Inter-Island Shipping Development in the ASEAN and the Pacific Region', in Korean Maritime Institute (ed.), *Seminar on the Development of an Integrated Transport and Logistics system in ASEAN countries and Pacific sub region* (KMI 2012).

12   See the provisions of Article 3(4) and Article 4 of Council Regulation 3577/92.

islands as required under the European Union maritime cabotage framework. It took pressure from both the European Commission and the judicial decisions of the Court of Justice of the European Union to make these countries liberalize maritime cabotage in their island regions. The distinct characteristics of islands is further demonstration that several delicate issues must be considered when formulating a national maritime cabotage policy framework. Therefore, attempting to develop a singular national maritime cabotage approach that also caters for all the characteristics of island cabotage is likely to be futile. This is because any framework must be sufficiently and effectively pragmatic and flexible to tackle the difficulties of maritime cabotage in these fragmented regions. For instance, any legislative framework designed to regulate maritime cabotage in islands must make provision for several complexities. These complexities include: large islands near major international shipping routes (Reunion Island close to the Indian Ocean), the presence of archipelagos (the Comoros), mountainous islands with multiple harbours (Honshu Island in Japan), and small inshore islands (The Carracks and Little Carracks Islands in England).[13]

Such legislative framework must first find a way to dovetail with the distinctive characteristics of insular maritime cabotage. In doing so, it must give due regard to the considerable seasonal variation in demand for transport and maritime services. Second, sovereign nations with more than one island evince the significance of coastal transport in catering for the needs and ensuring the continued socioeconomic integration of these island territories.[14] Therefore, the major concern with island territories seems to be that allowing foreign competition may endanger the provision of regular coastal services to islands. Therefore the failure by market forces to service island routes adequately would force government intervention to correct the irregularity. The risk with providing island transport services relate on the one hand to the uncertainty of long-term commitments by foreign operators and on the other hand to the volatility of pricing for services provided by foreign operators. Thus, finding an appropriate solution to the maritime cabotage problems in island regions have compelled many national governments that have sovereignty over their insular regions to resort to public service agreements.

Therefore, a major consideration for the littoral nations in regulating maritime cabotage in their islands is whether they can maintain maritime transport services through public service obligations (PSO) or public service contracts (PSC).[15] Where such public service agreement measures are applicable, it imposes an obligation on service providers to ensure that the standards of continuity, regularity, capacity and pricing are sustained. However, it also raises an entirely different but pertinent question: should insular maritime cabotage fall entirely within the ambit of public service? There is no short or easy answer to this question as it requires a

13  For more on this, see: CPMR Islands Commission, 'Consultation on the 5th Maritime Cabotage Report' (CPMR, 2009), p. 1.
14  For more on this, see: R. Greaves, *EC Transport Law* (Pearson Education 2010).
15  For the definition of Public Service Obligation and Public Service Contract, see; Article 2(e) and 2(i) respectively of Regulation (EC) No. 1370/2007 of the European Parliament and of the Council, 23 October 2007.

cross-examination of both the financial criteria and all the material facts. More-over, it appears that in attempting to answer this question, one should appreciate the advantages and understand the shortcomings of the free market within the context of island cabotage.[16] Hence, many governments have opted to regulate island cabotage by imposing either public service obligations or engaging in public service contracts. This is done to ensure continuous, unimpeded and sufficient transport and maritime services within the framework of maritime cabotage.[17] Indeed, this is buttressed by Article 4 of Council Regulation 3577/92, which allows member states of the European Union to conclude these kinds of contracts from, to and between domestic islands. This is only subject to the proviso that these contracts shall be non-discriminatory to all EU operators.

On the issue of non-discrimination, a pertinent question arises when a member state puts out a tender for a public service contract. It should be considered whether a successful bidder could demand to take over vessels and crews from the previous operator, without contravening the non-discriminatory principle of Council Regulation 3577/92. The Commission's position is that such a request would likely derogate from the non-discriminatory principle of Council Regulation (EEC) No. 3577/92.[18] This is because such a request would give unfair advantage to the incumbent operator if the successful bidder shares a stake with the previous operator. Furthermore, such a request would prevent EU shipowners from bidding with their own vessels. Nevertheless, the Commission argues that the taking over of vessels in such circumstances should not be forbidden altogether. This is particularly important in those circumstances where the provision of island services could be prejudiced in the absence of a viable alternative.[19] For example, Spain stipulated a prior administrative authorization scheme. Although the European Court of Justice (ECJ) decided in the Analir case[20] that prior administrative authorization schemes are compatible with the European Union maritime cabotage regulation, such scheme is subject to the proviso that:

a   The member state provides evidence that there is a real need for state inter-vention arising from the inadequacy of the regular transport services under conditions of free competition.

16  For more on this, see: A. Mikroulea, 'Competition and Public Service in Greek Cabotage', in A. Antapassis, L. Athanassiou and E. Rosaeg (eds), *Competition and Regulation in Shipping and Shipping Related Industries* (Martinus Nijhoff 2009), pp. 185–206
17  For a reference of where PSO and PSC are applied within the EU, see the island cabotage transport services in Italy, Greece and the United Kingdom.
18  See Article 4 of Council Regulation (EEC) No. 3577/92.
19  For a broader analysis on the issue, see: European Commission, 'Communication from the Commission: On the interpretation of Council Regulation (EEC) No. 3577/92 applying the principle of freedom to provide services to maritime transport within Member States (maritime cabotage)' (EC 2014) COM(2014) 232 final.
20  *Asociación Profesional de Empresas Navieras de Líneas Regulares (Analir) and others v Administración General del Estado* case [2001] C-205/99.

b    The member state must demonstrate that the prior administrative authorization is necessary and proportionate to the aim pursued.

c    The member state should show that the devised scheme is based on objective and non-discriminatory criteria that are transparent to the undertakings concerned.

It should be noted that the freedom to provide maritime services within the European Union constitutes the rule, whereas the imposition of a public service regime may be considered as the exception. Therefore, island transport services and related maritime services do not automatically constitute public interest service within the European Union.[21] One may suggest that it should be considered whether a country should implement protectionist maritime cabotage policies under the guise of public service agreements, regardless of whether that country can sustain this mechanism. Alternatively, there is a strong economic argument for liberalizing insular maritime cabotage services rather than expending huge resources on public service agreement schemes.

## Mainland cabotage

Mainland cabotage is the best-known variant of cabotage and dominates most debates on the concept of cabotage. In basic terms, it may be defined as the carriage of passengers or goods by sea between ports situated on the mainland or the main territory of the same sovereign nation without calling at ports on the islands.[22] The scope of mainland cabotage generally covers the maritime activities between seaports including carriage of goods and passengers between ports, transhipments, ship agencies, seismic activities and upstream activities. In the European Union, offshore services appear to be classed as a distinct variant of maritime cabotage. However, in many countries, the oil and gas sector is a major part of mainland cabotage. This explains why the maritime cabotage policy framework is often designed with mainland cabotage as its primary focus. From a policy implementation perspective, the legislation for mainland cabotage is easily distinguished from island cabotage that requires policy adjustments to accommodate their special characteristics.[23] In the European Union, providers of mainland cabotage services are somewhat liberated from the protectionist strictures, such as crewing requirements, that exist within EU island cabotage.[24] Generally, the situation in many countries is that the scope of activities falling under mainland cabotage is the widest of the three variants of maritime cabotage.[25]

---

21  This is the result of the European single market framework and Council Regulation (EEC) No. 3577/92.

22  Article 2(1)(a) of Council Regulation 3577/92.

23  See discussion on the broader issues in: A. Sefara, 'Achieving Access to the Maritime Transport Services Market in the European Union: A Critical Discussion of Cabotage Services' [2014], *Australian Journal of Maritime & Ocean Affairs*, 6(2), 106–110.

24  See: Articles 3(2) and 3(3) of EU Regulation 3577/92.

25  For a related discussion on the issues, see: M. Rowbotham, *Introduction to Marine Cargo Management* (2nd edn, Routledge 2014).

The United Nations Conference on Trade and Development (UNCTAD) may have unwittingly contributed to developing the principles that have sustained mainland cabotage by adopting the 1974 UNCTAD Code of Conduct for Liner Conferences.[26] The UNCTAD Code established the 40:40:20 multilateral agreement formula that allocates the percentage of cargo for carriage to the various parties. Under this arrangement, 40 per cent of cargo is each allocated to the national flag vessels of the importing and exporting countries respectively. The remaining 20 per cent of cargo is open to competition from vessels of other national flags.[27] The provisions of the UNCTAD Code have several loopholes and are not robust enough. They require an elaborate and complex regulatory mechanism to function effectively. The UNCTAD Code is often applied simultaneously with incompatible national legislations, thereby rendering it ineffective. For instance, the Philippines adopted the UNCTAD 40:40:20 cargo formula in 1982. However, there was no repeal of an earlier government decree that reserved all government cargoes to the Philippine national flag carriers. In Venezuela, 50 per cent of all cargo is reserved to its national flag vessels even though it is a signatory to the UNCTAD code. And the Republic of Korea reserves 100 per cent of all liner cargoes for Korean flag vessels while still a signatory to the code.

Around the time that the UNCTAD Code was introduced, the developing nations had become dissatisfied with and frustrated by their continued exclusion from the closed European and Japanese conferences. Hence, they welcomed the introduction of the Code. The closed conferences dominated by Europe and Japan were used to influence and control their trades with developing countries. The closed conference system increased protectionist measures against developing countries and impeded their efforts to develop their national merchant fleets to carry a significant share of their own cargo.[28] It is important to remember that the size of the national merchant fleet of a country was at the time seen as an important symbol of national sovereignty and power. The concerns expressed by developing nations were just. However, it appears their agitation was more a common response to the growing political chaos in international shipping in the 1970s than a desire to integrate national developmental policies.[29] For instance, the two successive oil crises in the mid-1970s caused the stagnation of seaborne trade that subsequently worsened the surplus of world shipping tonnage.[30] This forced

---

26 The UNCTAD Code was adopted in Geneva in April 1974 and was ratified in April 1983 with the signatory of 58 countries representing over 25% of the world's liner tonnage (in 1974) and it came into force in October 1983.

27 See: UNCTAD, 'Guidelines towards the Application of the Convention on a Code of Conduct for Liner Conferences' (UNCTAD Secretariat, 1986).

28 For more on this, see: L. Kanuk, 'UNCTAD Code of Conduct for Liner Conferences: Trade Milestone or Millstone – Time Will Soon Tell, The Perspectives' [1984], *Northwestern Journal of International Law & Business*, 6(2), 357–372.

29 For more, see: D. McNally, 'Turbulence in the World Economy' [1999], *Monthly Review*, 51(2), 38–52.

30 J. Tapia Granados, 'From the Oil Crisis to the Great Recession: Five Crisis of the World Economy' (University of Michigan, 2013).

major changes in maritime transport, particularly in Europe but also in other parts of the world involved in the import–export chain of petroleum products.[31]

Consequently, mainland cabotage became an attractive option as many developing nations employed flag-discriminatory and other protectionist practices. This allowed them to control trade and other maritime activities in their mainland territories, through their national instrumentalities of commerce.[32] Mainland cabotage policies, particularly in developing nations, are sustained through second national ship registers that often doubles as open registries.[33] The increasing influence of the open registries intensively challenged the dominance of traditional maritime nations who hitherto had dominated mainland cabotage in the territorial waters of developing nations.[34] The biggest category of activities for mainland cabotage is in the oil and gas and container trades. In many maritime cabotage countries, indigenous shipowners demand a protectionist mainland maritime cabotage law that allows them to carry out maritime activities in their territorial waters without foreign competition. The carriage of containerized goods and, in some cases, empty containers are the principal maritime activities in the mainland cabotage trades of Malaysia, India, China and the USA. However, it is the transportation of petroleum products that is central to the mainland cabotage trades in Indonesia, the USA and Nigeria.

## General maritime cabotage

General maritime cabotage is the reservation of maritime activities in the coastal and inland waterways of a country to the national maritime instrumentalities of commerce of the host country. This variant of maritime cabotage is the most exposed to competition from both foreign shipping interests and the domestic national land transport modes of road and rail. On the one hand, foreign ship operators always seek to control the shipment of cargo from end to end where possible. On the other hand, most of the cargo that is carried through the inland waterways can also be carried through other modes of transport. Hence, the road and rail transport network offers a viable alternative to shipment through the inland waterways. On this specific point, however, it appears that shipment through the inland waterways retains one advantage over the other modes of domestic transport. For instance, maritime cabotage in inland waterways in the

---

31  For a detailed read, see: L. Butcher, 'Shipping: EU Policy' [2010], House of Commons Library Report (SN/BT/55).

32  See: R. Petrova, 'Cabotage and the European Community Common Maritime Policy: Moving towards Free provision of Services in Maritime Transport' [1997], *Fordham International Law Journal*, 21(3), 1–76.

33  For a broad discussion on flag registry, see: R. Carlisle, *Sovereignty for Sale: The Origins and Evolution of the Panamanian and Liberian Flags of Convenience* (MD Naval Institute Press 1981).

34  A. Cafruny, 'Flags of Convenience', in R. Jones (ed.), *Routledge Encyclopaedia of International Political Economy* (Routledge 2002).

Netherlands receives huge support for reducing greenhouse gases by minimizing surface transportation of goods by road and rail.[35]

Another challenge with the general maritime cabotage variant is the duplicity and conflict between regulatory powers at the national and state levels of government in many countries. A good example of this multi-regulatory conflict can be seen in Nigeria, where the establishment of the Lagos State Waterways Authority (LASWA) by the Lagos state government in 2008 conflicts to an extent with the regulatory mechanism of the general maritime cabotage framework in the country.[36] LASWA is empowered to regulate any maritime activity and the operation of any type of vessel within the waterways, rivers, creeks, lakes, tidelands and lagoons within the boundaries of Lagos State.[37] However, these powers are a duplication of the existing provisions of the National Inland Waterways Authority (NIWA), which also regulates maritime activities in the federal inland waterways below the low water baseline.[38] These agencies challenge or duplicate the functions of the Nigerian Maritime Administration and Safety Agency (NIMASA), which is the principal regulatory agency for maritime cabotage in Nigeria as legislated in the 2003 Cabotage Act.[39]

Hence, the triplication of regulatory powers by the different agencies is confusing as it may not always be clear to an operator when it is under the state or federal cabotage regulatory regime when carrying out general maritime cabotage in inland waterways. This is particularly relevant to those operators involved in the transportation of oil and gas cargo through state inland waterways. Further confusion arises where shipping operators in Nigeria are required to comply with state and federal regimes when, for instance, the performance of their contractual duty of carriage of goods or passengers means they must deal with both mainland and general maritime cabotage. These confusions are further complicated by the fact that the power to legislate on shipping and navigation in the inland waterways of Nigeria rests with the National Assembly, not the State House of Assembly.[40] This

---

35 For more on this, see: B. Parameswaran, *The Liberalization of Maritime Transport Services* (Springer 2004).

36 The Lagos State Waterways Authority (LASWA) was established by the Lagos State Waterways Authority Act 2008 (Law No. 13 of 22/7/08). This was formed following the repeal of several sections of the National Inland Waterways Authority Act 1997 as it relates to Lagos State. LASWA is responsible for regulating, developing and managing all aspects of the waterways of Lagos State. This includes the granting of ferry licenses, dredging and concessions for the operation of terminals to the private sector. Furthermore, they are tasked with creating an enabling long-term regulatory environment that would attract significant private sector involvement in the provision of water transport services.

37 Sections 4 and 5 of Lagos State Waterways Authority Act 2008 (Law No. 13 of 22/7/08).

38 See sections 8, 9, 23 and the Second Schedule of the 1997 NIWA Act.

39 See: the Nigerian Maritime Administration and Safety Agency (NIMASA) Act, 2007. See also: The Coastal and Inland Shipping (Cabotage) Act No. 5 of 2003 of the Laws of the Federation of Nigeria.

40 See: item 36 of the Exclusive Legislative List in the 1999 Constitution. Furthermore, see: section 4 of the Constitution the National Assembly.

overlap of functions and uncertainty over the appropriate maritime cabotage regulator also exists in the United States, where maritime operators must comply with both state and federal legislations. In the European Union, not all inland waterway transport services in a member state are of a maritime nature and thus classified as maritime cabotage services under Regulation 3577/92. Hence, those transport services fall within the ambit of Council Regulation 3921/91, which regulates the transport of goods and passengers by inland waterway within a member state by non-resident carriers.[41]

The confusion and uncertainties that operators of general maritime cabotage face means that feeder service operators that dominate this variant of maritime cabotage are significantly at risk of violating the state or federal laws unless the rules governing feeder services of international cargo are relaxed. This will involve granting foreign suppliers of maritime transport services, under general cabotage rules, the freedom to move or reposition their equipment such as empty containers using their own vessels in the inland waterways. Moreover, any such relaxation of the rules must be subject to the proviso that no revenue is generated from the provision of such services.[42]

41 See the decision in: Case C 17/13 [2014] *Alpina River Cruises GmbH and Nicko Tours GmbH v Ministero delle infrastrutture e dei trasporti – Capitaneria di Porto di Chioggia*. Judgment of the court (Third Chamber) 27 March 2014.
42 For those interested in a more comprehensive read on the specific issues, see: B. Parameswaran, *The Liberalization of Maritime Transport Services* (Springer 2004).

# 7 The theoretical framework of maritime cabotage law

The objective of this chapter is to assess the ideology behind the concept of maritime cabotage. The assessment of any ideology is difficult because there is often no custom matrix for claiming a monopoly on understanding the underlying theories upon which different ideologies are based. Therefore, to understand the ideology behind the concept of maritime cabotage, we must first consider the theoretical framework of this area of law. This requires a two-step process. First, we will need to assess the maritime cabotage legislations of selected sovereign maritime countries. Second, we will identify and set a theme for querying the rationales behind the different approaches of maritime cabotage adopted in these sovereign states. We have established that the general premise for enacting maritime cabotage law in many countries is strongly connected to sovereignty and economic development rationales. These two rationales represent the strongest pillars of the theoretical framework of the maritime cabotage concept.

The choice of a maritime cabotage approach in a country depends very much on the theoretical framework guiding government decisions on specific issues. Therefore, the overall maritime capacity of the country influences how these theoretical frameworks fit with the maritime cabotage agenda of the country. In that respect, many countries see adopting a maritime cabotage approach as essential because it reaffirms their sovereign authority, promotes economic development, shores up national security and stimulates their domestic maritime sector. However, we have stated previously that the concept of maritime cabotage is experiencing a gradual shift from a territorial sovereignty ideology towards one that employs the national instrumentalities of commerce to facilitate economic development.[1]

The first challenge is that the theoretical framework must accommodate the various interests that the choice of maritime cabotage approach impinges on. Those interests include: indigenous shipowners, foreign ship-owning companies, shipbuilding companies, indigenous seamen, domestic shippers and other ancillary

---

1 The drive for the national development ideology is perhaps tempered within the European Union maritime cabotage framework because the regulation governing maritime cabotage within the European Union, i.e. Council Regulation (EEC) No. 3577/92, emphasizes a regional or supranational development ideology.

maritime service providers. Therefore, one may argue that the theoretical framework of maritime cabotage law is shaped according to the influence of one or more of these interests. For instance, the framework of maritime cabotage in the United States is influenced by the need to protect indigenous shipowners and domestic seamen. However, the maritime cabotage framework in Malaysia is influenced by domestic shippers.

The difficulty with understanding the theoretical framework of a maritime cabotage concept is underlined by the fact that sovereign states are at liberty to dictate how wide and stringent their maritime cabotage laws should be. This is demonstrated in many countries where the enforcement of maritime cabotage laws has an extended force in other areas such as company laws, immigration laws and labour laws. Hence, the degree to which the maritime cabotage concept impinges on the economic development agenda of the country is determined by the theoretical framework that it adopts.[2] This economic development-based agenda of maritime cabotage and the methodology of achieving this objective is what the theory of developmental sovereignty espouses. The theory argues that the inconsistencies that complicate and impede the common understanding of a maritime cabotage concept can be challenged by adopting a practical theoretical framework which promotes economic development.

As the concept of maritime cabotage now covers a wider range of commercial maritime activities, the theoretical and legislative frameworks of maritime cabotage law in many countries have become more focused on promoting the national economic development agenda. It is suggested that when the earliest known documented law of maritime cabotage was enacted under Richard II of England in 1382, it was not envisaged that it would become this complex phenomenon.[3] The common debate on national maritime cabotage policy is that indigenous maritime operators argue that the domestic waters of the country should be subjected to the same protection from foreign competition accorded other domestic modes of transport such as road, rail and air. The problem with this view is that it overlooks the very distinctive element of internationality that is associated with sea transport and services. Nevertheless, even in countries with strong protectionist maritime cabotage laws, the general perception is that such laws overwhelmingly serve the interest of indigenous shipowners.[4] Accordingly, the domestic shippers are generally left with the burden of higher freight prices. In Sabah and Sarawak states of Malaysia, the higher consumer prices on goods caused by the additional cost of transhipment between the international and domestic vessels forced the Malaysian government to switch to a more liberal maritime cabotage policy. However, advocates of a protectionist maritime cabotage regime argue that a

2  For a related argument, see: L. Taylor, 'The Revival of the Liberal creed: The IMF and the World Bank in a Globalized Economy' [1997], *World Development*, 25(2), 145–152.
3  See: 5 Richard II. Stat. i, c. 3.
4  See a related discussion in: World Economic Forum, *Enabling Trade: Valuing Growth Opportunities* (Bain & Company and the World Bank 2013). See also: Transportation Institute, *Jones Act/Domestic Shipping* (Transportation Institute 2009).

liberal regime poses a threat to national security and impedes national economic development. Thus, implementing anything less than a strict protectionist maritime cabotage law would be an infringement of sovereign rights. This view is common in the strict maritime cabotage regimes of the United States and Japan.

It should be noted that there is no evidence to support the widely held view that countries with deregulated maritime cabotage policies are in any danger of losing their sovereignty or that their national security is at risk. As we will see in later chapters South Africa and New Zealand provide sufficient evidence that a liberalized maritime cabotage policy is neither a barrier to national economic development nor a national security loophole. Similarly, the European Union implements a substantially liberalized maritime cabotage regime among its member states without any noticeable adverse effects.[5] The theoretical maritime cabotage framework employed in the European Union allows member states to cede some of their sovereignty in return for an inclusive economic development, based on a larger economy of scale.[6] The advantages of such a harmonized maritime cabotage concept has removed some complexities surrounding the concept of maritime cabotage law. Furthermore, the harmonized framework allows the policy to be monitored for inconsistencies and to record the progress made on economic development.

## The international law theory on maritime cabotage law

International law is the set of rules that governs relationships between nations. However, several events in the international domain perhaps allow one to question the effectiveness of this set of rules in regulating multi-national relationships.[7] For instance, Russia's annexation of Crimea, the Iraq invasion by the United States coalition forces, the rise of global terrorism and the increasing threats of piracy exposes the limited authority of international law. Nevertheless, the area of international law that this chapter is focused on is 'The Law of the Sea'. It covers issues relating to sovereignty, sovereign rights, and jurisdiction over a nation's territorial waters. The principal legal instrument for this area of international law is the United Nations Convention on the Law of the Sea.[8] This legal framework defines the responsibilities and determines the limits of the maritime zones that a sovereign nation is entitled to.[9] The 'law of the sea' has been instrumental in the resolution of many international law disputes bordering on maritime cabotage, even

---

5 See: Council Regulation (EEC) No. 3577/92 of 7 December 1992; applying the Principle of Freedom to Provide Services to Maritime Transport Within Member States (Maritime Cabotage); O.J. L 364.
6 European Commission, 'Europe 2020: A Strategy for Smart, Sustainable and Inclusive Growth' (European Commission, 2010).
7 See: L. Oppenheim, 'The Subjects of the Law of Nations', in R. Roxburgh (ed.), *International Law: A Treatise* (vol. 1, 3rd edn, Lawbook Exchange 2005), pp. 125–300.
8 The 1982 Convention, which largely replaced four 1958 Geneva treaties (on: The Territorial Sea and Contiguous Zone; The Continental Shelf; The High Seas; The Fishing and Conservation of Living Resources of the High Seas), came into force in 1994.
9 See: *El Salvador v. Honduras*. ICJ Rep. 1990.

before coming into force. Some of these disputes include landmark cases like *Denmark v Norway*,[10] *Eritrea v Yemen*,[11] and *The Qatar v Bahrain*.[12] The *Eritrea v. Yemen* arbitration is one of the most significant international dispute resolutions of the end of the twentieth century. It resolved the ownership issues of the southern islands of the Red Sea, which had lingered on since the end of World War I.[13] Other notable cases are *Libya v Malta*[14] and *Tunisia v Libya*,[15] both of which were concerned with the delimitation of the continental shelf between both nations. In *Canada v France*[16] and *Cameroon v Nigeria*,[17] the court of arbitration's decisions on ownership and maritime delimitation issues were heavily guided by the United Nations Convention on the Law of the Sea 1982 (UNCLOS).

The territorial sea is inherent in statehood and is automatically assigned to the coastal nation.[18] We should note that under international law, countries can only claim sovereignty over a 12-mile stretch of the sea, which constitute the territorial sea measured from the coastline.[19] Traditionally, the territorial sea is that part of coastal waters where states have absolute sovereignty to apply their maritime cabotage law. Therefore, coastal states may only possess sovereign *rights* in the rest of the maritime zones. The distinction between having sovereignty and claiming sovereign rights is that in the former, the country has full legislative jurisdiction, while in the latter it has exclusive access but not total control. It is also important to remember that the part of the sea known as the high seas is free for all under international law and is exempt from the authority of the coastal state.[20] Many maritime nations exercise their maritime cabotage authority within their 12 nautical miles of territorial waters as recommended under international law. However, some countries extend these maritime cabotage rights up to 200 miles from the baseline of their territorial waters.[21]

10 1993 ICJ Rep 38 [Judgement 14 June 1993]. This dealt with the maritime delimitation dispute between Greenland and Jan Mayen.
11 (1998) XXII RIAA 211, (1999) 119 ILR 1, (2001) 40 ILM 900, ICGJ 379 (PCA 1998). For details of the judgement on both the first and second stage awards, see court documents from The Hague dated 9 October 1998 and 17 December 1999 respectively.
12 1995 ICJ Rep on Jurisdiction and Admissibility [Judgement 15 February 1995].
13 See: The 2005 decision of the Permanent Court of Arbitration on the Eritrea-Yemen Arbitration Awards 1998 and 1999.
14 1985 ICJ Rep 13 [Judgement 3 June 1985].
15 1982 ICJ Rep 18 [Judgement 24 February 1982].
16 31 ILM 1145 (1992) [Judgement 10 June 1992].
17 ICJ Reports of Judgements, Advisory Opinions and Orders 1998 [Judgement 11 June 1998].
18 *UK v. Norway* (The Anglo- Norwegian Fisheries Case) [1951] ICJ Rep 116: as per Judge McNair.
19 Article 2 of the United Nations Convention on the Law of the Sea 1982.
20 For more on this, see: M. Dixon, *International Law* (5th edn, Oxford University Press 2005).
21 Article 56 of the United Nations Convention on the Law of the Sea 1982.

In the past, the debate over maritime sovereignty often arose because of wars and conflicts among maritime nations that threatened national security. However, the issues of sovereignty in coastal waters now arise primarily because maritime nations hope to accrue economic benefits either by exercising sovereignty or by claiming sovereign rights. Early doctrinal debates on maritime cabotage, dating back to the fifteenth and sixteenth centuries, were concerned with whether a nation possessed the right to appropriate any part of the sea to its exclusive sovereignty.[22] It is granted that these debates occurred at a time when some maritime activities such as hydrographic survey and offshore exploration were either non-existent or uncommon. Therefore, the debates centred on two fundamental issues. The first issue was national security –i.e. protecting the maritime entity from external threats. The second issue was trade – i.e. control of navigation, access to markets, custom and tax regimes.[23] In the end a balance was attained that would accommodate both sides of the argument. Thus, maritime nations had sovereignty over the territorial seas extending 12 nautical miles from the nation's baseline. In part this was an attempt to cater for the national security concerns.[24] However, in the waters regarded as the high seas, national security concerns were superseded by commercial interests and hence the seas were free from any nation's jurisdiction or sovereignty.[25]

## Revisiting the doctrines of *mare liberum, mare clausum* and *de dominio maris*

The concepts of *mare liberum* (free open seas to all nations), *mare clausum* (closed seas under the sovereign right of a nation) and *de dominio maris* (on the dominion of the seas) were embodied by the Roman legal philosophy.[26] The arguments raised by these three ideological concepts were:

a   whether the seas should be free from all control;
b   whether a sovereign nation should be allowed to exercise control over its seas;
c   how far out from the baseline of the coastal state such control should be permitted.

22  These debates were indigenously termed 'The Battle of the Books' and were notably championed by Hugo Grotius and John Selden. See: S. Chester, 'Grotius, Selden and 400 Years of Controversy', *Slaw Legal Magazine* (Toronto, 1 November 2009).
23  See: E. Gold, *Maritime Transport: The Evolution of International Marine Policy and Shipping Law* (D. C. Heath & Co. 1981).
24  M. Evans, 'The Law of the Sea' in: M. Evans (ed.), *International Law* (2nd edn, Oxford University Press 2006), pp. 623–655.
25  H. Grotius, 'The Freedom of the Seas [1608]', translated by R. Magoffin, in J. Scott (ed.), (Oxford University Press 1916).
26  For more on this, see: A. Dewar, 'The Freedom of the Seas' [1930], *Journal of the Royal Institute of International Affairs*, 9(1), 63–67.

These divergent views by three distinguished scholars demonstrate the difficulty in striking a satisfactory balance between the three concepts.[27] The current regulatory approaches of maritime cabotage law (protectionist, liberal and flexible) mirror to a large extent the conceptual arguments put forward by Grotius, Selden and Van Bynkershoek on the status of the territorial seas.

The Dutch jurist Hugo Grotius published the *mare liberum* (freedom of the seas) in 1609, asserting that the seas were incapable of being dominated. He argued that the sea should be available to be used freely by all invested maritime interests.[28] Grotius further argued that it was irresponsible for a maritime nation to claim sovereignty over a large part of the sea that it was incapable of policing.[29] Therefore, if a nation is incapable of claiming possession of the sea, it means that the sea could not be subject to the sovereignty of that nation.[30] In essence, the *mare liberum* doctrine postulated that the sea is common to all and no nation ought to have proprietary rights over it.[31] As the doctrine of *mare liberum* gathered support, resentment grew among scholars who held a different view to Grotius' postulation.

In response to Grotius position, the book *Mare Clausum* (closed sea) was published in 1635 by the English jurist John Selden.[32] Selden's work opposed the principles of *mare liberum* and instead advanced the legal principle that certain bodies of water could be claimed under the exclusive jurisdiction of a nation. Selden's *mare clausum* principle argued that in accordance with natural law and the law of nations the sea was virtually as capable of being appropriated as the land.[33] Furthermore, Selden reasoned that the opportunity for foreign vessels to engage in the territorial waters of another nation should be viewed as a privilege similar to those enjoyed by landed proprietors.[34]

However, the current concept of the territorial sea may be attributed to Pontanus, a Dutch jurist who abandoned the distinction between sovereignty and

27  See: E. Papastavridis, *The Interception of Vessels on the High Seas: Contemporary Challenges to the Legal Order of the Oceans* (Hart Publishing 2013).
28  H. Grotius, 'Mare Liberum: The Freedom of the Seas or The Right Which Belongs To The Dutch To Take Part in the East Indian Trade', translated by R. Magoffin, in J. Scott (ed.), *Classics of International Law* (Oxford University Press 1916).
29  H. Grotius, 'Mare Liberum: The Freedom of the Seas or The Right Which Belongs To The Dutch To Take Part in the East Indian Trade', translated by R. Magoffin, in J. Scott (ed.), *Classics of International Law* (Oxford University Press 1916).
30  For a broader read, see: J. O'Brien, *International Law* (Cavendish Publishing 2001).
31  L. Oppenheim, *International Law: A Treatise* (vol. 1, Longmans, Green & Co 1905).
32  See: H. Thornton, 'John Selden's Response to Hugo Grotius: The Argument for Closed Seas' [2006], *International Journal of Maritime History*, 18(2), 105–128. A good discussion on the broader issues can also be seen in: R. Rayfuse, *Non-Flag State Enforcement in High Seas Fisheries* (Martinus Nijhoff 2004).
33  For a broader discussion, see: D. Armitage, *The Ideological Origins of the British Empire* (Cambridge University Press 2000).
34  See: T. Fulton, *The Sovereignty of the Sea: An Historical Account of the Claims to England to the Dominion of the British Seas, And of the Evolution of the Territorial Waters: With Special Reference to the Right of Fishing and The Naval Salute* (William Blackwood 1911).

ownership of the high sea as put forward by Grotius.[35] Pontanus in his 1637
*dominium maris adjacentes* argued that sovereignty accorded a nation the power
of excluding external entities from its sovereign activities. He took a more practical
approach and sought to distinguish between the high seas and the territorial seas.
He argued that while the high sea should be free for all, the territorial sea could be
subjected to state ownership and exclusive jurisdiction.[36] Thus, Pontanus' theory
of *dominium maris adjacentes (1637)* was a compromise of the theories of *mare
liberum* and *mare clausum*.

Another Dutch jurist, Cornelius Bynkershoek, suggested a compromise
between the disparate views of the other jurists in his 1702 essay 'De Dominio
Maris'. Bynkershoek argued that a coastal nation should be entitled to claim
dominion over as much of the sea as it could effectively control and protect.[37]
Bynkershoek set out the doctrine of the freedom of the high seas and sovereignty
over territorial waters to coastal nations. On the one hand he opposed Selden's
*mare clausum* doctrine by suggesting that sovereignty must be extended outward
from the coastline up to the limit of the power of arms (*terrae potestas finitur ubi
finitur armorum vis*). This established the famous cannon-shot rule.[38] On the
other hand he disagreed with Grotius's doctrine of *mare liberum* by suggesting
that some parts of the sea should be subjected to sovereign control. We should
remember that the territorial sea as conceived in this period was not an ideal
compromise. However, it did meet the various political, commercial and strategic
needs at a time when national and commercial policies of most nations shared
similar objectives. This was in addition to playing a key role in the politics of the
free or closed territorial seas.[39] Bynkershoek's views contributed to the cannon-
shot or three-mile rule, which prevailed in the main until the 1982 United
Nations Convention on the Law of the Sea. The UNCLOS Convention expanded
the principle of dominion of the territorial sea to 12 nautical miles.[40] Furthermore,
UNCLOS 1982 provides that a coastal state is eligible to claim a territorial sea of
12 nautical miles, a contiguous zone of 24 nm, an Exclusive Economic Zone
(EEZ), and a continental shelf zone of 200 nm.[41] In some cases a further continental shelf zone could be claimed if the natural prolongation of that shelf
extends further.[42] Thus, the sovereignty of coastal states over their maritime zones
is limited to the territorial sea. They have sovereign rights to enjoy and explore the

35 R. Churchill and A. Lowe, *The Law of the Sea* (2nd edn, Manchester University Press
   1988).
36 J. Pontanus, *Discussiones Historicae de Mari Libero: Adversus Johannem Seldenum.*
   (Harderwyck 1637).
37 P. Potter, *The Freedom of the Seas in History, Law and Politics* (Longmans 1924).
38 J. Reddie, *Researches, Historical and Critical, IN Maritime International Law*
   (Thomas Clark 1844).
39 E. Gold, *Maritime Transport: The Evolution of International Marine Policy and Shipping Law* (D. C. Heath & Co. 1981).
40 Article 2 of the United Nations Convention on the Law of the Sea 1982.
41 See respectively, Articles 3, 33, 57 of The United Nations Convention on the Law of
   the Sea 1982.
42 See; Part VI of The United Nations Convention on the Law of the Sea 1982.

resources of the other maritime zones. However, these rights are not exclusive because other neighbouring coastal states have the same rights to these zones.[43]

The arguments surrounding the different maritime cabotage approaches are at present not very different from the arguments that surrounded the free or closed seas in the sixteenth century. If anything, it is even more rooted in the national, commercial and political benefits that the sovereign nation could claim.[44] It is suggested that the respective arguments over the freedom of the seas were not because any of the parties were prioritizing the interests of the international community.[45] Rather, these arguments were born out of a biased desire to develop and protect the source of wealth of the respective countries.[46] For instance, the closed sea policy was beneficial for England because she had a head start in colonizing many countries.[47] Hence, England embraced a territorial sovereignty ideology. It proceeded to restrict trade in and from those colonized nations to itself or to other countries that England gave permission.[48] On the other hand, an open coast policy was more appealing to the Dutch and so they took a pragmatic approach and pursued a commercial philosophy of maritime trade to promote and sustain their economic development.[49] England had championed a closed sea policy for more than three centuries up until 1854, when it abolished its protectionist policies and became a principal proponent of an open sea policy.[50] One may argue that the United Kingdom did not adopt a liberal policy out of conviction that it was the better economic choice. Rather, the repeal of the protectionist maritime cabotage policy was a calculated attempt to protect the national interest of the United Kingdom. The driving force behind this repeal was fear of retaliatory practices by other sovereign nations emboldened to embrace protectionist maritime cabotage policies.[51] It was vehemently argued that any form of retaliatory practice by other sovereign nations would be detrimental to England and its

43  For more on this, see: D. Rothwell and T. Stephens, *The International Law of the Sea* (Hart Publishing 2010).

44  For a supportive discussion on the issue although from a slightly different perspective, see: J. Moore, 'UNCLOS Key to Increasing Navigational Freedom' [2008], *Texas Review of Law & Politics*, 12(2), 459–467.

45  See: H. Hannum, *Autonomy, Sovereignty and Self-determination: The Accommodation of Conflicting Rights* (2nd edn, Pennsylvania University Press 1996).

46  For a general discussion on the issue, see: J. Kraska, 'Grasping the Influence Of Law On Sea Power' [2009], *Naval War College Review*, 62(3), 113–135.

47  D. Armitage, *The Ideological Origins of the British Empire* (Cambridge University Press 2000).

48  H. Thornton, 'John Selden's Response to Hugo Grotius: The Argument for Closed Seas' [2006], *International Journal of Maritime History*, 18(2), 105–128.

49  H. Grotius, 'Mare Liberum: The Freedom of the Seas or The Right Which Belongs To The Dutch To Take Part in the East Indian Trade', translated by R. Magoffin, in J. Scott (ed.), *Classics of International Law* (Oxford University Press 1916).

50  (5 Richard II. Stat. i, c. 3). The protectionist maritime cabotage policy of the United Kingdom can be traced as far back as 1382 under the reign of Richard II. This protectionist policy was finally abolished in 1854.

51  J. Lalor, *Coasting Trade: Cyclopaedia of Political Science, Political Economy, and of the Political History of the United States* (Maynard, Merrill, & Co 1881).

trade.[52] Ironically, by repealing the protectionist maritime cabotage laws, the interests of the United Kingdom were served better by Grotius' *mare liberum*, which they had hitherto condemned, than by Selden's *mare clausum*, which they originally sponsored.[53]

The *mare liberum* and *mare clausum* arguments may have been historically centred on sovereignty and sea trade supremacy.[54] However, the current debates surrounding the choice of maritime cabotage approach are centred more on economic development and sovereignty rationales.[55] Nevertheless, what has not changed much is the degree to which political consideration drives the debate on the choice of national and regional maritime cabotage approaches.[56]

## The international institutions perspective

In chapter 4 we assessed the theories of development and the different impacts they have when applied to industrialized and developing nations. What was clear from that assessment is that developing maritime nations are likely to adopt a maritime cabotage policy that aligns with the agenda of the international institutions or their agents.[57] At first, these Westernised policies appear enticing and harmless. They promise to conserve domestic savings while helping developing economies to industrialize.[58] However, it often emerges that acceptance of these policies is fraught with serious challenges.[59] For example, the international institutions often seek to be involved in dictating the domestic economic agenda of the recipient developing nation.[60] Indeed, this is the basis for the argument put forward by dependency theorists.[61] The combined effect of

52  See: House of Commons, 'Coasting Trade Bill', *Hansard*, 131, 462–466 (London, 7 March 1854).

53  For a highly intellectual analysis on this intricate subject matter, see; B. Hayton, *The South China Sea: The Struggle for Power in Asia* (Yale University Press 2014).

54  V. Grey, 'Freedom of the Seas' [1930], *Foreign Affairs*, 8(3), 325–335.

55  See: M. Igbokwe, 'Advocacy Paper for the Promulgation of a Nigerian Maritime Cabotage Law: Draft Modalities for Implementation of Coastal and Inland Shipping (Cabotage) Act' (NMA, 2001).

56  For an in-depth examination on the issue, see: B. Slattery, B. Riley, and N. Loris, 'Sink the Jones Act: Restoring America's Competitive Advantage in Maritime-Related Industries' [2014], The Heritage Foundation, No. 2886; D. Johnston, *The International Law of Fisheries: A Framework for Policy-Oriented Inquiries* (New Haven Press 1987); M. Brooks, 'Liberalisation in Maritime Transport' [2009], OECD/ITF; D. Hackston, G. English, R. Taylor and J. MacDonald 'Research Study on the Coasting Trade Act' [2005], Research and Traffic Group.

57  For a general discussion on the issue, see: D. Rodrik, *The Developing Countries' Hazardous Obsession with Global Integration* (Harvard University Press 2001).

58  L. Taylor, 'The Revival of the Liberal creed: The IMF and the World Bank in a Globalized Economy' [1997], *World Development*, 25(2), 145–152.

59  A. Young, 'Lessons From the East Asian NICs: A Contrarian View' [1994], *European Economic Review*, 38(3–4), 964–973.

60  For a broader discussion, see: J. Cypher and J. Dietz, *The Process of Economic Development* (3rd edn, Routledge 2009).

61  See the section in chapter 4, where the International Dependence Revolution Theory of Development has been given sufficient attention.

adopting inappropriate policies and the international institutions getting involved in the affairs of the developing countries often has a negative impact. Furthermore, the negative impact that is experienced by these countries is often under-acknowledged. This is because the governments of these developing nations, fearing criticism for their failed adoption of these policies, continue to exaggerate the benefits of these Westernised policies. In addition, these international institutions have since become experts at disguising their modus operandi such that they can pretend to offer policies that appear different but will eventually have the same negative impact.[62] It is suggested that it not coincidence that the Organization of Economic Cooperation Development (OECD), World Bank, International Monetary Fund (IMF), World Trade Organization (WTO) and European Commission often work together to promote global liberalization in trade and services.[63] They are usually supported by powerful business lobbying groups representing the logistics and supply chain interests of the global corporations.[64] However, for the purpose of this sub-chapter, we will focus on the WTO and the OECD. Both organizations aim to facilitate world trade free of protectionism. The activities of some of these international institutions impact the maritime cabotage policies and regulations of developing countries directly or indirectly. For example, the International Transport Workers' Federation (ITF) has continually advocated the vital importance of maritime cabotage in the development of a maritime country. The organization has historically supported this principle as one way of securing the long-term sustainable and fair distribution of employment for indigenous seafarers.[65] The International Monetary Fund (IMF) and World Bank continue to facilitate the replacing of trade barriers with liberal policies. This remains the case even when such liberal policies do not suit some countries.[66]

### World Trade Organization (WTO) dimension

The World Trade Organisation (WTO) commenced operations in 1995 as a successor to the General Agreement on Tariffs and Trade (GATT). The organization was formed in 1948 to drive forward the concept of international liberalization in trades and services.[67] This objective is captured clearly under the 'national treatment' principle that is contained in all four major WTO agreements. They include: Article 3 of General Agreement on Tariffs and Trade 1947 and 1994 (GATT),

62  P. Krugman, 'The Myth of Asia's Miracle' [1994], *Foreign Affairs*, 73(1), 62–78.
63  R. Kanbur, 'Economic Policy, Distribution and Poverty: The Nature of Disagreements' [2001], *World Development*, 29(6), 1083–1094.
64  W. Knight, *A Changing United Nations: Multilateral Evolution and the Quest for Global Governance* (Macmillan 2000).
65  ITF, 'Transport: The WTO's Problem Industry', *Transport International Magazine* (London, 11 April 2003).
66  For a more specific understanding of these issues, see: N. Karunaratne, 'The Asian Miracle and Crisis: Rival Theories, The IMF Bailout and Policy Lessons' [1999], *Intereconomics*, January/February, 19–26.
67  GATT, 'The Marrakech Agreement: Agreement Establishing the World Trade Organization' [1994], United Nations. Signed 15 April 1994. GATT was established in 1947 and is the predecessor to the WTO, which was created in 1995.

Article 17 of General Agreement on Trade in Services 1995 (GATS), Article 3 of the Agreement on Trade Related Aspects of Intellectual Property Rights 1995 (TRIPS), and Article 2 of the Agreement on Trade Related Investment Measures 1995 (TRIMs). The national treatment principle prohibits any WTO member country from discriminating between foreign imported goods/services and domestically produced goods/services using internal taxation or regulatory measures. The idea is to avoid giving a competitive advantage to goods and services produced within the domestic economy, thereby disadvantaging imported goods and services.[68]

As the only global organization dealing with trade between nations, one of the objectives of WTO is to facilitate a seamless global transport system. However, while there has been progress on the liberalization of some transport sectors, the WTO has made no progress in tackling the multifaceted and controversial concept of maritime cabotage. There has been no significant desire to bring maritime cabotage under the umbrella of its GATS framework.[69] This raises serious questions because at its basic, the concept of maritime cabotage aligns with a protectionist agenda that contradicts the liberalization policies and principles of the WTO. Hence, while the deadlock in discussions on maritime cabotage lingers on, maritime nations continue to be at liberty to legislate for more complex and protectionist maritime cabotage policies. One may argue that this challenge the liberalization campaign of the World Trade Organization.[70] Furthermore, the missed opportunities at the Uruguay and Doha Rounds demonstrate the challenges faced by the WTO in pursuing the international harmonization of a maritime cabotage concept. The members of WTO agreed at the Uruguay round to finalize discussions on the harmonization of maritime cabotage at the Doha round.[71] However, while other areas of maritime transport services have been considered and negotiated, maritime cabotage was not even an agenda item at the Doha round.[72]

In the meantime, the United States, whose maritime cabotage law is unparalleled in its stringency, has refused to participate in the maritime cabotage discussions.[73] Its reluctance to liberalise its regulations has led to other countries like Canada, Japan and China refusing to renegotiate the protectionist policies of their maritime cabotage regime.[74] It is noted that a provision in the GATT

---

68 For a full text of the provisions of Article 3 of GATT, see the General Agreement on Trade and Tariffs 1994.
69 See: A. Freudmann, 'WTO Urged to Avoid Cabotage Controversy' [1999], *Journal of Commerce*, 9 February.
70 For a more general discussion, see: C. Liu, *Maritime Transport Services in the Law of the Sea and the World Trade Organization* (Peter Lang 2009).
71 K. Kennedy, 'GATT 1994', in P. Macrory, A. Appleton and M. Plummer (eds), *The World Trade Organization: Legal, Economic and Political Analysis* (vol. 1, Springer 2007), pp. 91–182.
72 C. VanGrasstek, *The History and Future of the World Trade Organization* (WTO 2013).
73 B. Gootiiz and A. Mattoo, 'Services in Doha: What's on the Table?' [2009] Policy Research Working Paper 4903.
74 See: M. Brooks, 'Liberalization in Maritime Transport. International Transport Forum' [2009], OECD/ITF Forum Paper 2009-2.

exempts statutes in force before its establishment in 1947. Consequently, protectionist maritime cabotage policies such as the United States Jones Act enjoy an exemption even though they are generally acknowledged to contravene the WTO rules.[75]

### Organization of Economic Cooperation Development (OECD) dimension

The Organization for Economic Cooperation and Development (OECD) sought to promote harmonized shipping policies and free competition in 1987 through the 'Common Principles of Shipping Policy for Member Countries' initiative.[76] Although a non-binding policy, OECD member countries agreed not to introduce any new measures under this framework that would restrict competitive access.[77] The objective was to promote open shipping policies that encourage trade and investment among member countries of the OECD.[78] According to an OECD report on common principles of shipping policy, the organization acknowledged that maritime cabotage is widely practised by both OECD and non-OECD members. However, the report claimed that there is no concrete evidence to support some of the commonly held beliefs surrounding the concept of maritime cabotage. This includes its purported importance in maintaining domestic transport capability and its significance as an inhibitor of foreign influence in domestic transport services.[79]

Many maritime nations, whether they are members or non-members of the OECD, recognize the importance of a maritime cabotage policy in facilitating the growth and economic development of their maritime sector. On one hand, the United States argues that the Jones Act is as much an issue of sovereignty as it is a shipping issue. Therefore, there is the need to sustain an indigenous merchant fleet manned by its nationals for trade and defence purposes. Similarly, the case for implementing a maritime cabotage law in Nigeria is based on the economic development agenda.[80] On the other hand there continues to be a major debate about the overall effectiveness of a protectionist maritime cabotage policy. This is partly because the liberal maritime cabotage laws applied in some Western economies have not produced serious adverse outcomes. This would suggest that there may be no basis for scepticism in relation to liberalizing national and regional

75 See: Paragraph 3a of the General Agreement on Tariffs and Trade 1994.
76 OECD, 'Recommendation of the Council Concerning Common Principles of Shipping Policy for Member Countries' (C (2000) 124/FINAL, OECD 2001).
77 OECD, 'Understanding on Common Shipping Principles' (Paris, 9 June 1993).
78 For a general discussion on the issue, see: L. Blanco, *Shipping Conferences under EC Antitrust Law: Criticism of a Legal Paradox* (Hart Publishing 2007).
79 W. Hubner, 'Regulatory Issues in International Maritime Transport' (OECD, 2001).
80 See the comments of Michael McKay, National President of American Maritime Officers to European Union Dredging Agency (EUDA) in 2002. See also: M. Igbokwe, 'Advocacy Paper for the Promulgation of a Nigerian Maritime Cabotage Law: Present and potential problems of cabotage and recommended solutions' presented on the Public Hearing of the Nigerian cabotage Bill, at the House Committee on Transport, National Assembly complex, Abuja in April 2001.

maritime cabotage policies. Moreover, liberal policies when applied to other sectors of an economy have tended to encourage investment, growth and economic development.[81] However, for the many reasons we have identified, these theories on liberalization have not proven effective in poor developing economies. Therefore, one may suggest that the national regulatory authorities should test their chosen maritime cabotage approach against the realities of the market rather than speculating on theoretical consequences.[82] For the free and non-discriminatory treatment within the OECD Common Principles of Shipping policy framework to be effective, the different strengths and weaknesses of the various member countries must be considered within the framework. The liberalization of maritime cabotage law can be facilitated by identifying the least complex areas. This will allow for the most conflicting areas of the policy to be tackled in the long term.[83]

We have stated that maritime cabotage trade and services have been liberalized within the European Union for member states. However, the liberalization of maritime cabotage in other OECD member countries has not progressed at the same pace as liberalization in other maritime services. While some deregulation has occurred in other maritime transport sectors, there are still significant maritime cabotage restrictions in the domestic maritime trades and services of major OECD nations.[84] Strict protectionist maritime cabotage laws are still heavily maintained in the United States, Japan, China, Nigeria, Indonesia and Canada. The preservation of the national fleet is a common reason for adopting a protectionist maritime cabotage approach. However, Panama and Liberia, with their almost non-existent maritime cabotage laws, boast of more vessels flying their respective flags than the stringently protectionist United States. Furthermore, the establishment of second registers allow shipowners to retain the national flag while enjoying the benefits of open registers.[85]

The European Union is associated with implementing a liberal maritime cabotage regime. We should note that the EU liberal maritime cabotage policy is reserved for its member states and does not extend to non-European Union countries. Thus, like many other OECD industrialized countries, the European Union implements a protectionist maritime cabotage policy for the world at large.[86] The drawback of the European Union maritime cabotage regulation is that it extends a protectionist maritime cabotage policy over the wide geographical area of the European Union. Nevertheless, the EU's liberal maritime cabotage

---

81  See: J. Lalor, 'Coasting Trade' [1881] *Cyclopaedia of Political Science, Political Economy, and of the Political History of the United States*, 1(1).
82  B. Parameswaran, *The Liberalization of Maritime Transport Services* (Springer 2004).
83  See: J. Frittelli, 'Federal Freight Policy: An Overview' *Congressional Research Service Report for Congress* (Washington, 2 October 2012).
84  For a related argument, see: BXA, 'U.S. Shipbuilding and Repair: National Security Assessment of the U.S. Shipbuilding and Repair Industry' (BXA, 2001).
85  OECD, 'Ownership and Control of Ships' (OECD, 2003).
86  See: Council Regulation (EEC) No. 3577/92. In this book, the EU is seen as implementing a liberal maritime cabotage regime under its supranational framework for member states.

regime provides credible evidence to counter the weak argument that a liberal maritime cabotage policy poses threats to national sovereignty and hampers economic development.[87] This is particularly evident where the volume of cargo available at the level of domestic shipping trade is so small such that a liberal maritime cabotage policy would have no significant impact on vessel demand.[88] A good, albeit not recent, example that illustrates the point perfectly is the statistics obtained on Chilean maritime cabotage in 2001. The Chilean maritime cabotage trade accounted for 25 per cent of its port traffic. However, the maritime cabotage trade's share in sea-borne commerce registered by shipping companies was 14.5 per cent, which was less than its share in port traffic.[89]

Many OECD member countries with a protectionist maritime cabotage approach would be inclined to consider a relaxation of their protectionist measures.[90] This would require the major OECD countries, like China, Canada, Japan and the United States, to offer reasonable concessions in their overly protectionist maritime cabotage trade and services policies.[91] However, such reform would likely be opposed by advocates of a protectionist regime, even though evidence suggests that protectionist policies do more to increase domestic freight than protect a country's shipping capability.[92] This strongly held view further complicates the already vexed concept of maritime cabotage.[93]

87  See: R. Petrova, 'Cabotage and the European Community Common Maritime Policy: Moving towards Free provision of Services in Maritime Transport' [1997], *Fordham International Law Journal*, 21(3), 1–76.

88  W. Hubner, 'Regulatory Issues in International Maritime Transport' (OECD, 2001).

89  J. Hoffmann, 'Maritime Cabotage Services: Prospects and Challenges' [2001], *Bulletin on Trade Facilitation and Transport in Latin America and the Caribbean*, 183 (11), 1–7. It should perhaps be added that each vessel engaged in carrying cargo within the Chilean maritime cabotage trade goes through two ports but is only counted once as sea traffic.

90  Commission of the European Communities, 'Towards a Future Maritime Policy for the Union: A European Vision for the Oceans and Seas' [2006], Green Paper, Volume II – Annex, Com(2006) 275 final, {SEC (2006) 689}.

91  See: J. Hodgson and M. Brooks, 'Canada's Maritime Cabotage Policy: A Report for Transport Canada' (Dalhousie University, 2004).

92  W. Hubner, 'Regulatory Issues in International Maritime Transport' (OECD, 2001). See also: American Maritime Partnership, 'Why We Need the Jones Act' (AMP, 2011). Moreover, one of the key points for those advocating for the abolition of the Jones Act in the United States is that the cost of labour in America is too expensive. Hence it is not attractive to employ American crew or build ships in America.

93  For a general discussion on the issue, see: D. Hackston, G. English, R. Taylor and J. MacDonald, 'Research Study on the Coasting Trade Act' (Research and Traffic Group, 2005).

# 8 The regulatory approaches of maritime cabotage law

This chapter is the precursor to chapters 9, 10 and 11. It introduces the different approaches of maritime cabotage law that we have identified in previous chapters. Those approaches will receive comprehensive consideration in the chapters that follow. Hence, this chapter will provide an understanding of the driving forces behind the appeal of each of these approaches.

Maritime nations with significant coastline recognize the importance of a robust domestic maritime sector and the need to regulate access to their coastal waters. This has led to countries adopting some form of maritime cabotage regime to ensure the continued viability of its coastal trade.[1] We have identified the three regulatory regimes of maritime cabotage law as protectionist, liberal and flexible. It is important to note that there is no such thing as best maritime cabotage approach. However, a case could be made for why one approach might be the best fit for a country. This depends on the characteristics and capacity of the host cabotage country as espoused by the 'theory of developmental sovereignty' in chapter 3.

The maritime cabotage policy in many countries is shaped by the desire to balance the competing interests of the foreign and domestic players in a country's maritime sector. This means that some countries will seek to procure maritime services at the best market rate, while others act under the guise of a sovereign entity to supply maritime services at over the global market rate.[2] This is illustrated in the liberal-protectionist maritime cabotage law spectrum. For instance, a liberal maritime cabotage approach is said to be vital for free-market competition because it eliminates distortions that prevent free interplay of market forces.[3] However, many countries place coastal trade and services in the same context as their domestic transport system. For this group of countries, it is vital that coastal trade

---

1 See: S. Galbraith, 'Thinking Outside the Box on Coastal shipping and Cabotage', *Maritime Trade Intelligence* (Victoria, 1 December 2014).
2 See: J. Mattos and M. Acosta, 'Maritime Transport Liberalization and the Challenges to Further its Implementation in Chile' [2003] CEPAL – SERIE Comercio internacional, 43.
3 For a comparative analysis on the specific issue, see: F. Bliss, 'Rethinking Restrictions on Cabotage: Moving to Free Trade in Passenger Aviation' [1994], *Suffolk Transnational Law Review*, 17(2), 382–407.

and services are reserved to national vessels and indigenous crews or to the maritime operators of other countries whose activities they can regulate. If this remains the case, these countries will consistently regard the prospect of opening their maritime cabotage trade to foreign competition as non-negotiable. This is because maritime cabotage is seen as concerning domestic trade in which foreign flags cannot engage as a right but to which they may be admitted as an act of grace.[4] This is perhaps too rigid a view given the expanding range of maritime activities that may now fall within the ambit of modern maritime cabotage law. The international nature of shipping and market forces driving competition for comparative or absolute advantages means that beyond foreign vessels in domestic waters, other factors that influence modern maritime cabotage law should be considered.[5] Whether a maritime cabotage policy addresses issues of the national shipping industry or those of foreign shipping, there will invariably be domestic and international consequences. Hence, it is suggested that maritime cabotage policies ought to be a matter beyond domestic national concerns.[6] The expanding scope of maritime cabotage law means that different states are likely to approach their maritime cabotage policy differently based on their domestic needs. The category assigned to the shipbuilding industry of a country offers useful insight into the rationale behind its maritime cabotage policy. The shipbuilding industry may be considered part of the shipping sector dealing with maritime transport or part of the manufacturing sector promoting industrialization, or the shipbuilding industry may form part of the national defence capability ensuring national security.[7] For example, the United States considers shipbuilding as part of her shipping sector and national defence capabilities. However, Canada views shipbuilding as part of their manufacturing industry.

Furthermore, the maritime cabotage law of some countries expands beyond the basic reservation of coastal trade to their domestic registered vessels.[8] The law in these countries require that vessels used to perform maritime cabotage services should be built in the host country.[9] Moreover, the law in these countries also demand that all or a significant majority of the crew employed on these vessels should be nationals of the cabotage country.[10] Furthermore, services such as

---

4 See: Indian Mercantile Marine Committee, 'Indian Mercantile Marine Committee 1923–24: Report' (Delhi, 1924), p. 24.

5 See: David Ricardo's 1817 theory on comparative advantage. See also: Adam Smith's theory on absolute advantage in his 1776 publication, *An Inquiry in to the Nature and Causes of the Wealth of Nations.*

6 For a broader read on the issue, see: M. Brooks, 'The Jones Act Under NAFTA and Its Effects on the Canadian Shipbuilding Industry (Research Paper)', *Atlantic Institute for Market Studies (AIMS)*, (September 2006).

7 J. Darling, *Report of Inquiry on the Coasting Trade of Canada and Related Marine Activity* (Canadian Transport Commission 1970).

8 For a supplementary discourse on the issue, see: Independent Consumer & Competition Commission, 'Final Report: Review of the PNG Coastal Shipping Industry' (16 February 2007).

9 See: 46 U.S.C. App. § 833, 46 U.S.C. 50101 and 46 U.S.C. 55102.

10 See Section 3 of *The Coastal and Inland Shipping (Cabotage) Act*, No. 5 of 2003 of the Laws of the Federation of Nigeria.

exploration, hydrographic survey and other seismic activities are now frequently covered under the maritime cabotage regulations of countries.[11] This illustrates further how the scope of activities has expanded within the area of maritime cabotage law.[12] The problem with this is that the requirements of building vessels domestically and employing indigenous seafarers as identified align better with regulatory policies on manufacturing, labour and immigration law.

The widening scope of maritime cabotage takes it outside the context in which it is currently understood under international law.[13] Therefore, one may argue that there is a good case for establishing an international maritime cabotage law framework that takes into account the concepts of sovereignty, commerce, and economic development.[14]

We have stated that the maritime cabotage approach adopted in a country is based broadly on sovereignty and economic development rationales. Each maritime cabotage approach has requirements that may include: shipbuilding, ship ownership, ship registration and crewing.[15] In this book we have categorized a country's maritime cabotage approach according to how protectionist, liberal or flexible the maritime cabotage policy of that country is. The more onerous the requirements of a country's maritime cabotage law, the more protectionist a regime we have considered the country to have, and vice versa. However, some countries periodically alternate between a protectionist and a liberal approach. In this book we refer to those countries as adopting a flexible maritime cabotage approach.[16] This is illustrated in Table 8.1.

## The protectionist, liberal and flexible maritime cabotage law approaches

The law of maritime cabotage is used as an important legal instrument in a range of policy settings that are required to secure a strong and sustainable indigenous maritime sector in a country.[17] In some maritime jurisdictions, the choice of

11 For instance, see: Section 2(1) of *Canadian Coastal Trading Act 1992* for the meaning and scope of coasting trade in Canada.

12 League of Nations, *Article 5 of the Statue on the Regime of Navigable Waterways of International Concern* (LON 1921). See also: E. De Vattel, *The Law of Nations* (Book 1, Article 288, T. & J. Y. Johnson 1758).

13 For a broader discussion on the issue, see: B. Marten, *Port State Jurisdiction and the Regulation of International Merchant Shipping* (Springer 2014).

14 See: J. Jackson, 'Sovereignty - Modern: A New Approach to an Outdated Concept' [2003], *American Journal of International Law*, 97(1), 782–802. See also: V. Wee, 'China Cabotage Rules Benefit Hong Kong: HIT', *Seatrade Global* (Beijing, 10 October 2013).

15 See: C. Liu, *Maritime Transport Services in the Law of the Sea and the World Trade Organization* (Peter Lang 2009).

16 The categorization of countries with respect to the maritime cabotage approach they adopt as used in this book is designed by the author. The author accepts that other countries and scholars may have a different categorization.

17 See: W. Oyedemi, 'Cabotage Regulations and the Challenges of Outer Continental Shelf Development in the United States' [2012], *Houston Journal of International Law*, 34(3), 607–651.

maritime cabotage approach is influenced by the need to ensure reliability in the provision of maritime services. This was evident in chapter 6 when we considered island cabotage. This is in addition to protecting the country's capacity to maintain price stability in its domestic maritime markets.[18]

However, based on the theory of developmental sovereignty, this book presents a new and different argument, which is that an appropriate maritime cabotage regime should provide the country with the benefits that flow from a diverse maritime economic cluster. This ensures a continuous availability of the expertise needed to stimulate the country's economic development agenda.[19] There is evidence that an appropriate maritime cabotage approach contributes to the development of the domestic freight services market.[20] However, because of the degree of control a country has over its territorial waters, it must bear the burden of ensuring that its maritime cabotage policy is regulated in a way that bolsters the economic development of the country.[21] This can only be achieved by adopting an appropriate maritime cabotage law approach that results in a robust domestic maritime sector.[22]

We must now turn to the important question of why maritime activities in the coastal waters of a country are regulated differently from other domestic modes of transportation. From a practical perspective there are many ways of answering this question. However, the problem with following a practical approach is the challenge of dealing with the many different variables that exist in each maritime cabotage country. Therefore, we will adopt the theoretical, albeit conservative, approach to the question. The short answer to the question involves going back to the 'battle of the books', which debated the concepts of open and closed seas. The argument for open seas was championed by Grotius, but Selden put forward a compelling counter-argument for why the seas should not be open to all.[23] Nevertheless, the objective answer to the question lies with the flag state and the international nature of shipping.[24] First, sea transport has traditionally been regarded as an international venture that requires minimal disruptive regulation. A simple example of this is the lack of maritime equivalents to the provisions for

18 A good discussion on this can be seen in: A. Mikroulea, 'Competition and Public Service in Greek Cabotage', in A. Antapassis, L. Athanassiou and E. Rosaeg (eds), *Competition and Regulation in Shipping and Shipping Related Industries* (Martinus Nijhoff 2009), pp. 185–206.

19 See: J. Zheng, Q. Meng, and Z. Sun, 'Impact Analysis of Maritime Cabotage Legislations on Liner Hub-and-Spoke Shipping Network Design' [2014] *European Journal of Operational Research*, 234(3), 874–884

20 For more on this, see: R. Greaves, *EC Transport Law* (Pearson Education 2010).

21 See: C. Whitehurst, *American Domestic Shipping in Domestic Ships* (AEI Press 1985).

22 For a similar discussion, see: Australian Shipowners Association, 'Options Paper: Approaches to Regulating Coastal Shipping in Australia' (ASS, 2014).

23 For a more expansive discourse on the subject matter, see: E. Gold, *Maritime Transport: The Evolution of International Marine Policy and Shipping Law* (D. C. Heath & Co. 1981).

24 For a broader discussion, see: A. Cafruny, 'Flags of Convenience', in R. Jones (ed.), *Routledge Encyclopaedia of International Political Economy* (Routledge 2002).

'innocent passage' in road and rail transport. Second, whereas all domestic road and rail transport service providers are subjected to the same cost structures in their country of operation, shipowners base their operating cost on many other external factors including the requirements of their flag states. For example, international shipping companies can make use of economies of scale to offer cheaper maritime services compared to their domestic rivals.[25] One may suggest that the strategic benefits of a viable national maritime sector dictate that maritime transport should be regulated differently to other transport modes. The exception being the aviation sector, which also has a cabotage concept.[26]

We have indicated that the categorization of the different maritime cabotage approaches as used in this book is purely the opinion of the author. In some countries, the maritime cabotage approaches discussed here may very well operate under different terms. Furthermore, we should note that however sensible it may seem, it is inaccurate to assume that countries adopting the same maritime cabotage approach do so for the same underlying reasons. The fact is that different countries may very well adopt the same maritime cabotage policy but with different motivations and rationales. A useful example, as we shall see in the chapters that follow, is that the protectionist maritime cabotage law in the United States is premised on national security and maritime labour. However, the protectionist maritime cabotage regime in Brazil is borne out of the need for national economic development and capacity building.

## Outline of the maritime cabotage regimes of various countries

We have established that there is neither a right nor a wrong nor a one-size-fits-all maritime cabotage approach. This does not mean that a country may not adopt an inappropriate maritime cabotage approach that fails to deliver the desired objectives. At this point it is useful to explain the criteria employed in the selection of maritime countries whose maritime cabotage legislations have been selected for investigation in this book. In selecting the countries with a maritime cabotage regime, consideration has been given to:

25  For a similar argument but based on a broad regional perspective, see: J. Hoffmann, 'Maritime Cabotage Services: Prospects and Challenges' [2001], *Bulletin on Trade Facilitation and Transport in Latin America and the Caribbean* (FAL Bulletin), 183 (11), 1–7.
26  For in-depth discussions on maritime cabotage, see the following: N. Hesse, 'International Air Law: Some Questions on Aviation Cabotage' [1953], *McGill Law Journal*, 1(1), 129–140; P. Mendes, *Cabotage in Air Transport Regulation* (Martinus Nijhoff 1992); The 1919 Paris Convention (formally, the Convention Relating to the Regulation of Aerial Navigation) signed in Paris, on 13 October 1919; and J. Cooper, 'Aviation Cabotage and Territory' [1952], *US and Canadian Aviation Reports*, 1(1) 256–272.

*Table 8.1* The different maritime cabotage approaches

| Maritime cabotage requirements | Maritime cabotage activities | Countries with a protectionist approach | Countries with a liberal approach | Countries with a flexible approach |
|---|---|---|---|---|
| Built and re-built requirements | Carriage of goods and passengers | United States of America | European Union | Russia |
| Manning | Towage | Canada | South Africa | India |
| Vessel flag/registration | Salvage | Nigeria | New Zealand | Malaysia |
| Vessel ownership | Oil drilling | Indonesia | | Australia |
| Principal place of business | Seismic activities: e.g. excavation of mineral resources | Japan | | Chile |
| | | China | | |
| | | Brazil | | |
| | | Philippines | | |

a  Countries and regions with a prominent maritime cabotage regime.
b  Geographically, every continent is represented by at least two nations.
c  Countries that constitute industrial, economic, strategic, and political power brokers, e.g. BRICS and ASEAN nations.

There are several countries – for example, South Korea, known for its ship-building prowess, and countries in the Central American region – that have not been specifically selected for analysis. Nevertheless, the maritime cabotage regimes in these countries have been referred to where necessary to emphasize important elements of maritime cabotage law.

# 9 The protectionist maritime cabotage approach

A protectionist maritime cabotage approach often departs radically from the basic principles of reserving coastal trade for indigenous registered vessels. It covers a wide scope of maritime activities and imposes onerous requirements on maritime operators looking to engage in maritime cabotage trade and services. In some jurisdictions, the protectionist maritime cabotage approach requires that:

a   the vessel should be documented, registered and fly the flag of the host nation. In addition, the principal place of business should be in the host nation.
b   the vessel should be owned by people that satisfy the nationality and indigenous person's requirements test of the host country.
c   the vessel should be crewed by persons that satisfy the nationality and indigenous person's requirements test of that host nation.
d   the vessel should be built, re-built and repaired in the host cabotage nation.

In some countries, the protectionist maritime cabotage approach extends to maritime activities up to 200 miles from the coast, which includes the Exclusive Economic Zone (EEZ) and the Continental Shelf. An example of this is the maritime cabotage policy in Canada. Such a protectionist approach covers not only maritime transport within the reserved sea area but also maritime services such as seismic activities, towage, hydrographic surveys, oil spills and sometimes salvage services.[1] We will now consider some of the protectionist maritime cabotage law regimes.

## United States of America: Section 27 of the Merchant Marine Act of 1920 (the Jones Act)

The protectionist maritime cabotage law in the United States is one of the relics of British colonisation. It is an inheritance from when the United States was a British

---

1 See: W. Oyedemi, 'Cabotage Regulations and the Challenges of Outer Continental Shelf Development in the United States' [2012], *Houston Journal of International Law*, 34(3), 607–651.

colony.[2] From then onwards, the United States has maintained what is probably the most stringent form of maritime cabotage law in the world. The Merchant Marine Act of 1920 (the Jones Act) is the applicable law regulating maritime cabotage in the United States.[3] The Jones Act stipulates strict adherence to ship construction, flag state, crewing and ownership requirements.[4] The Act has occasionally been relaxed during emergencies and natural disasters, as was the case during hurricane Katrina in 2005 and hurricane Sandy in 2012. In the aftermath of hurricane Sandy, foreign bulk carriers carrying fuel could enter more than one port to help facilitate supply of gas in the New York area.

Maritime cabotage in the United States can be traced back to the Tariff Act of 1789, when the first Congress imposed a higher tariff on merchandise transported on foreign vessels.[5] However, the Tariff Act only encouraged preference to be given to vessels built in a domestic shipyard, registered in the United States, owned by indigenous shipowner and employing indigenous crew, rather than compulsorily reserving coastwise trade services to vessels that satisfied these requirements. Another act passed later that year defined a United States vessel as one built in the United States, registered in the United States and flying the American flag, and owned wholly by American citizens.[6] Section 4 of the Navigation Act of 1817 then raised the regulatory bar by prohibiting foreign vessels from partaking in the United States coastal trade.[7] The Navigation Act of 1817 was strengthened further by the United States Congress by enacting the Prevention of Smuggling Act of 1886.[8] Hence, under the more stringent act, goods transported on a foreign vessel between ports in the United States' northern frontiers via a foreign port by transhipment were subject to forfeiture. In the same year, the protectionist policy in the coastal waters of the United States was extended beyond merchandise on ships to include passengers by enactment of the

2   W. Marvin, *The American Merchant Marine: Its History and Romance from 1620 to 1902* (Charles Scribner 1902).
3   The Merchant Marine Act of 1920 is popularly called the Jones Act – so named after Senator Wesley Jones who sponsored the bill.
4   46 U.S.C. 81, 121 and 551.
5   1 Stat. 24: An Act for laying a Duty on Goods, Wares and Merchandises Imported into the United States [4 July 1789]. This was the 11th act enacted by this Congress.
6   Section 1 of an Act for Registering and Clearing Vessels, Regulating the Coasting Trade, and for Other Purposes, 1789. Dated 1 September 1789, passed into law 29 September 1789. Repealed 31 December 1792.
7   Section 4 of an Act Concerning the Navigation of the United States. Approved 1 March 1817.
8   Section 20 of an Act Further to Prevent Smuggling and for Other Purposes. 18 July 1866. 14 Stat. 178. The scope of the act covered: Merchandise at any port in the United States on the northern, north-eastern or north-western frontiers thereof, laden upon any vessel belonging wholly or in part to a subject or subjects of a foreign country or countries, and taken thence to a foreign port or place to be re-laden and reshipped to any other port in the United States on said frontiers, either by the same or any other vessel, foreign or American, with the intent to evade the provisions relating to the transportation of merchandise from one port of the United States to another port of the United States.

Passenger Vessel Services Act 1886. This act applied the same United States build, crew, ownership and flag requirements for cargo vessels to passenger vessels.[9] However, the Prevention of Smuggling Act of 1886 and the Navigation Act of 1817 were both circumvented in 1892 in *United States v. 250 Kegs of Nails*.[10] In this case, the court held that the transportation of cargo between ports in the United States via a foreign port that involved transhipment was outside the scope of the maritime cabotage laws of the United States, regardless of the intentions of the cargo owners. Following the decision in this case, the United States Congress moved swiftly and in 1893 it amended the 1817 Navigation Act. The amendment prohibited shipment between two ports in the United States on a foreign vessel via a foreign port.[11] This was further amended in 1898 to cover 'any part of such a voyage'.[12]

The Merchant Marine Act 1920 was conceived originally to sustain the merchant marine fleet after World War I. The act is now the law regulating coastwise trade in the United States and is tagged 'super cabotage' and 'the mother of all cabotage laws' by critics. Section 27 of the Merchant Marine Act 1920 states:

> No merchandise shall be transported by water, or by land and water, on penalty of forfeiture of the merchandise between points in the United States either directly or via a foreign port, or for any part of the transportation, in any other vessel than a vessel built in and documented under the laws of the United States, crewed by American citizens and owned by persons who are citizens of the United States.[13]

These requirements apply to all maritime activities between ports in the United States mainland and the non-contiguous states of Alaska, Hawaii, Puerto Rico and Guam. However, the outlying territory of Guam is exempt from complying with the compulsory United States 'built requirement' of the Merchant Marine Act under the 'Guam Exemption'.[14] Nonetheless, this exemption is of little benefit as the natural westbound trade lane from the United States west coast passes through Honolulu (Hawaii). This effectively ties Guam to the United States ship build requirement for its interstate trade. All four non-contiguous states have long sought for an exemption from the requirements of the Merchant Marine Act of 1920.

---

9  Section 8 of the Passenger Vessel Services Act of 19 June 1886. 24 Stat. 81. 46 U.S. C. 55103.
10  52 F. 231 (S.D. Cal. 1892), 61 F. 410 (9th Cir. 1894).
11  Act of 15 February 1893. 27 Stat. 455.
12  Act of 17 February 1898. 30 Stat. 248.
13  46 U.S.C. App. § 833, 46 U.S.C. 50101 and 46 U.S.C. 55102.
14  See: Petition and Memorials (POM) – 545: A Resolution Adopted by the Legislature of Guam; to the Committee of Commerce, Science and Transportation. Resolution No. 303. Congressional Record – Senate, V.144, Pt. 15, 22 September 1998.

The stringent protectionist maritime cabotage regulation in the United States also covers maritime activities like; coastwise transport of passengers,[15] salvage,[16] oil spill,[17] towing[18] and dredging.[19] Furthermore, Section 446 of the Tariff Act of 1930 imposes a 50 per cent ad valorem duty on the cost of repairs performed on United States-flagged ships in a foreign country.[20] In addition, Section 2 of the 1916 Shipping Act stipulates that only the citizens of the United States can be owners of a coastwise trade vessel.[21]

In essence, the Merchant Marine Act of 1920 is just a more stringent version of the 1789 and 1898 acts. There has been pressure to repeal or reform the Merchant Marine Act of 1920 because of the high cost of building ships in the United States and the cost of transporting goods and passengers within the United States on coastwise eligible vessels. . The report of a study conducted by the United States International Trade Commission (ITC) in 1991 suggested that the Jones Act was responsible for the high cost of domestic shipping.[22] The Commission submitted that the cost of transporting cabotage cargo in a coastwise vessel is far higher than the worldwide ocean transportation rates.[23] The period from 1995 to 1999 witnessed the first legislative struggle to repeal the Merchant Marine Act of 1920. Like the 'battle of the books' between Grotius and Selden in the seventeenth century, two groups emerged arguing from opposite sides of the maritime cabotage policy in the United States. On one hand, the Jones Act Reform Coalition (JARC) formed by domestic shippers, sought to repeal or substantially reform the Jones Act.[24] On the other hand, the American Maritime Partnership (AMP), formed by a coalition of maritime operators, defended the protectionist regime of the Merchant Marine Act of 1920 against any such reforms.[25]

In 1996, the JARC's efforts led to legislation in the United States Congress known as the Shipping Competition Act.[26] This bill sought among other things to

15  46 U.S.C. 55103.
16  46 U.S.C. 80104.
17  46 U.S.C. 55113.
18  Act of 11 June 1940. 46 U.S.C. 55111.
19  46 U.S.C. 55109.
20  19 U.S.C. 1466 – also known as the Smoot Hawley Tariff.
21  Ch. 451, H.R. 15455, Public No. 260. Shipping Act 1916. Dated 7 September 1916.
22  ITC Report No. 2422: The Economic Effects of Significant U.S. Import Restraints – Phase III (Services with a Computable General Equilibrium Analysis of Significant U. S. Import Restraints), Inv. 332–262. September 1991.
23  The ITC acknowledged in a 12 June congressional testimony that the study may have erred in calculating cost.
24  J. Lewis, 'Veiled Waters: Examining the Jones Act's Consumer Welfare Effect' [2013], *Issues in Political Economy*, 22(1), 77–107. The Jones Act Reform Coalition (JARC) was formed by Rob Quartel in 1995.
25  See: American Maritime Partnership, 'Why We Need the Jones Act' (AMP, 2011). The American Maritime Partnership (AMP) was formerly known as the Maritime Cabotage Task Force (MCTF).
26  A Bill to Reform the Coastwise, Inter-coastal, and non-contiguous Trade Shipping laws, and for other Purposes. 104th Congress, 2D Session, H.R. 4006. Dated 2 August 1996.

permit the use of foreign-built and foreign-flagged vessels. However, such vessels still had to be owned, operated or chartered by defined United States citizens to be considered eligible to engage in the coastal trade of the United States. This effort was unsuccessful as JARC failed to obtain enough support for the bill to be considered by Congress.[27] Another bill titled 'Open America's Waters Act', which claimed that the Jones Act hinders free trade and favours labour union over consumers, was also unsuccessful in repealing the Jones Act in 2010.[28] Finally, suggestions that the Merchant Marine Act could be relaxed under the Transatlantic Trade and Investment Partnership (TTIP) has since fallen through because the United States insisted that the Act was non-negotiable. The TTIP aims to remove twenty-first-century trade barriers and to promote regulatory coherence through various degrees of transatlantic convergence.[29] On the other hand, attempts to make the Merchant Marine Act even more stringent have also failed. For instance, in the mid-seventies, the United States Congress considered but decided against legislations that would have required a certain percentage of goods destined for the United States to be carried on vessels that were registered in the United States and flying the flag of the United States of America.[30] Furthermore, there were two failed proposals in 1974 and 1977 respectively for the Energy Transportation Security acts.[31] These acts stipulated that about 30 per cent of all petroleum products imported into the United States should be transported on United States registered and flagged vessels. Thus, the Merchant Marine Act of 1920 has remained largely unchanged since coming into force.

Nevertheless, there have been some modifications to the 1920 Merchant Marine Act over the years. Some of the modifications made the laws more stringent, while others relaxed it by introducing some exemptions. For example, the first proviso to the Merchant Marine Act of 1920 was introduced by a 1935 act and stipulated that:

27 K. Magee, 'U.S. Cabotage Laws: Protective or Damaging? A Strategy to Improve Cruise Vessel Competitiveness and Traffic to U.S. Ports' (Monterey Institute of International Studies, 2002).
28 A Bill to Repeal the Jones Act Restrictions on Coastwise Trade and for Other Purposes. 111th Congress, 2D Session. S. 3525. Dated 25 June 2010.
29 See: D. Hamilton and P. Schwartz, *A Transatlantic Free Trade Area: A Boost to Economic Growth?* (New Direction – The Foundation for European Reform 2012).
30 For a detailed read, see: J. Kilgour, The Energy Transportation Security Act of 1974 [1976], *J. Mar. L. & Com.*, 7(4).
31 See: H.R. 8193 (The Cargo Preference Bill); The Energy Transportation Security Act of 1974. United States House Committee on Merchant Marine and Fisheries. Congress of the United States. 1974. Hearing on: Energy Transportation Security Act of 1974. Ninety-third Congress, first and second sessions, on H.R.8183: Subcommittee on Merchant Marine. 9 October 1973. Serial No. 93–26. Washington: U.S. Govt. Printing Office. This bill actually passed Congress but was vetoed by President Gerald Ford. See also: S. 61 – The Energy Transportation Security Act of 1977. 10 January 1977. United States Senate Committee on Commerce, Science, and Transportation. 1977. Hearing on: Energy Transportation Security Act of 1977. Ninety-fifth Congress, first session, on S.61: July 28, October 5 and 7, 1977. Serial No. 95–43. Washington: U.S. Govt. Printing Office.

Any vessel above 200 gross tons, which acquired the legal right to engage in coastwise trade because it was built in or documented by the laws of the United States but later sold foreign in whole or in part or placed in foreign registry, loses that right to engage in coastwise trade.[32]

A second proviso added by a 1956 act stated that 'vessels rebuilt outside the United States will also forfeit any previously acquired legal right to engage in the coastwise trade by virtue of having been built in or documented under the laws of the United States'.[33]

Initially, the provision only applied to vessels over 500 tons, but this was revised in 1988 and it now applies to all vessels engaged in coastwise trade regardless of tonnage. Shipowners sought to circumvent the second proviso by building large parts of the ship overseas and bringing them to shipyards in the United States to be installed into a Jones Act-eligible vessel. However, the amendment of the second proviso in 1960 blocked this loophole. The new provision stated that the foreign construction of any major component of a vessel's hull or superstructure would render that vessel ineligible for coastwise trading.[34]

Other modifications have provided some exemptions to the Merchant Marine Act of 1920. For instance, the Bowaters Amendment was enacted in 1958 by creating a new section 27A of the Merchant Marine Act 1920. The new section exempts foreign companies based in the United States that own vessels for the carriage of their own merchandise for their own account from the Jones Act citizenship requirements.[35] Furthermore, section 1113(d) of the 1996 Coast Guard Authorization Act creates an exception to the Jones Act requirements that vessels employed in the coastwise trade must be built in the United States and owned by her citizens. Under the Coast Guard Authorization Act, a vessel built in the United States but owned by a non-American citizen could be endorsed for coastwise trade. However, this is subject to the proviso that the vessel must be on demise charter to a coastwise-eligible citizen of the United States for at least three years.[36]

The Merchant Marine Act of 1920 receives huge support from the United States government. Thus, every loophole exploited by shippers and shipowners is meticulously closed with legislative enactments by the United States Congress. One of the most contentious aspects of the Jones Act is the build/re-build requirement. There are several issues that the 'second proviso' raises and which

32  Ch. 355, 49 Stat. 442: An Act to Amend Section 27 of the Merchant Marine Act 1920. 2 July 1935. H.R. 115, Public No. 191. See also: 46 U.S.C. App. § 833.
33  Ch. 600, 70 Stat. 544: An Act to amend the Shipping Laws, to prohibit the Operation in the Coastwise Trade of vessels Rebuilt Outside the United States, and for other purposes. 14 July 1956. H.R. 6025, Public Law 714. See also: 46 U.S.C. App. § 833.
34  Act of July 5, 1960, Pub. L. No. 86–583, § 1, 74 Stat. 321, 321.
35  Public Law 85–902, 72 Stat. 1736: An Act to Amend Section 27 of the Merchant Marine Act 1920 (Bowaters Amendment). H.R. 9833, 2 September 1958.
36  Public Law 104–324, 110 Stat. 3971: An Act to Authorise Appropriations for the United States Coast Guard and for other Purposes. S.1004. Dated 19 October 1996.

has led to several litigations.[37] The primary issue is that in attempting to save costs on shipbuilding, shipowners opt to construct large parts of the ship's structures in foreign shipyards before transporting them to the United States to be installed on their vessels.[38] This is a less expensive way for shipowners to rebuild their vessel while ensuring that they remain eligible for coastwise trade. The Jones Act plays an important role in providing employment of labour and generating internal revenue. Nevertheless, it is responsible for the high cost of domestic freight. Critics have argued that it is significantly more expensive to build/re-build ships in the United States than to do the same in Asia.[39] The direct consequence of the price differential is that shipowners engaged in the coastwise trade are forced to operate with vessels that are significantly older than the international average.[40] In turn, these vessels have become too expensive to operate and are a pollution threat to the marine environment.[41]

### *Judicial decisions arising from the Merchant Marine Act of 1920 (Jones Act)*

#### *United States v. 250 Kegs of Nails* [42]

This was the first case that put the maritime cabotage laws of the United States to test. The facts of this case are that merchandise was carried on a foreign vessel (Belgian flagged) from New York to California. The vessel sailed via a foreign port (Antwerp port, Belgium), where the cargo was transhipped onto a British-flagged vessel for onward shipment to the United States. Upon arrival of the cargo in California, the 'collector of customs' brought a forfeiture action against the cargo owner for contravening the maritime cabotage laws of the United States. The United States government initiated legal action against the foreign shipowners and the cargo owners. The court decided against the government that there was no breach of either the 1817 Navigation Act[43] or the 1866 Anti-smuggling Act.[44] The court's decision was based largely on the fact that both acts only covered domestic shipping between ports in the United States.

---

37  See the issues raised in: *Shipbuilders Council of America, Inc. v. United States Coast Guard.* 4th Cir. 08-21-2009, Duncan, Circuit Judge, Nos 08–1546 and 08–1702. This is one of the leading cases that highlights the complexities of the issues in this area.

38  W. Gray, 'Performance of Major US Shipyards in 20th/21st Century' [2008], *Journal of Ship Production*, 24(4), 202–213.

39  Drewry Maritime Research, 'US Cabotage Protection Gets More Expensive', *Container Insight Weekly* (London, 17 November 2013).

40  C. Grabow, 'U.S. Maritime Sector Among the Jones Act's Biggest victims', CATO Institute (Washington, 28 June 2018).

41  See: R. Pouch, 'The U.S. Merchant Marine and Maritime Industry in Review' [1999], *Proceedings Magazine*, 125(5), 1, 155.

42  52 F. 231 (S.D. Cal. 1892), 61 F. 410 (9th Cir. 1894).

43  An Act Concerning the Navigation of the United States. Approved 1 March 1817.

44  An Act Further to Prevent Smuggling and for Other Purposes. 18th July 1866. 14 Stat. 178.

Hence, even though the intent of the cargo owners was to transport cargo between two ports in the United States, the stop over and transhipment in a foreign port (Antwerp) had disrupted the continuity of the voyage. Consequently, the activity was outside the scope of both acts. The court argued that upon proper interpretation, the plain and ordinary meaning of the words 'to transport goods from one domestic port to another' could only be to carry goods in one continuous voyage. The court further reasoned that the wording of the relevant provision could not reasonably mean to carry cargo in two distinct and separate voyages, or in two different vessels.[45] Following this decision, the United States Congress moved swiftly to amend the 1817 Navigation Act in 1893. The amendment prohibited shipment on a foreign vessel between two ports in the United States via a foreign port.[46] In 1898, the amendment was extended to include 'any part of such a voyage'.[47]

### Marine Carrier Corp. v. Fowler[48]

This case involved a vessel (*The Observer*) that was built by joining several parts of other vessels (jumboize). The Observer sought to engage in coastwise trade pursuant to the provisions of the Jones Act. *The Observer's* origin began with the tanker *Wapello*, constructed in 1953 in an American shipyard for Panamanian owners and registry. The *Wapello* was later taken apart in a Japanese shipyard, and its fore body was joined to the stern of an American-built tanker, *Esso Chittagong* which was sold and registered foreign. The result of this coupling was the Liberian-registered vessel, *Santa Helena*. The *Santa Helena* was also later dismantled and her fore body previously that of the *Wapello* was attached to the stern of the 1943 American-built, owned and coastwise enrolled vessel, the *Trustco*, in a United States shipyard. The result of this attachment was the vessel in question, the *Observer*. As a result of the build and ownership requirements of the Jones Act, the question before the court was whether the *Observer* was eligible to engage in coastwise trade. This question arose because of a dispute on whether the *Santa Helena*, one of the predecessors of the *Observer*, had the right to engage in coastwise trade. Due to the provisos added to the Merchant Marine Act of 1920, the eligibility of the *Wapello,* and consequently that of the *Observer* to coastwise trade rights was also disputed . The first proviso states:

> No vessel having at any time acquired the lawful right to engage in the coastwise trade, either by virtue of having been built in, or documented under the laws of the United States, and later sold foreign in whole, or in part, or

---

45 For a broader discourse, see: R. McGeorge, 'United States Coastwise Trading Restrictions: A Comparison of Recent Customs Service Rulings with the Legislative Purpose of the Jones Act and the Demands of a Global Economy' [1990], *Northwestern Journal of International Law & Business*, 11(1), 62–86.
46 Act of 15 February 1893. 27 Stat. 455.
47 Act of 17 February 1898. 30 Stat. 248.
48 429 F.2d 702 (1970).

placed under foreign registry, shall hereafter acquire the right to engage in the coastwise trade.[49]

The second proviso that was added to make the Merchant Marine Act more stringent states:

> Provided further, that no vessel of more than five hundred gross tons which has acquired the lawful right to engage in the coastwise trade, either by virtue of having been built in or documented under the laws of the United States, and which has later been rebuilt outside the United States, its Territories (not including trust territories), or its possessions shall have the right thereafter to engage in the coastwise trade.[50]

It is important to bear the following in mind. The *Observer's* fore body, previously the fore body of the *Wapello*, constitutes 75 per cent of its total length. However, the *Observer's* stern, erstwhile the stern of the *Trustco*, is more important than the forepart. This is because the *Trustco* was constructed in the United States and owned by Americans since construction. Employing a vessel in the United States coastwise trade is premised on two conditions that such vessels must be built in the United States and owned by American citizens.[51] This statutory requirement contributes to the inconsistency and difficulty in interpreting the language of the first proviso. On one hand, the proviso can be interpreted as suggesting that it only applies to vessels sold foreign after acquiring the lawful right to the coastwise trade. On the other hand, the proviso seems to apply to all vessels sold foreign after being built in the United States. Therefore, it was important determine first, the *Wapello's* eligibility to partake in coastwise trade.

The appellee, Marine Carriers, argued that the first interpretation of the proviso applied to the *Wapello*. They argued that since she was never owned by an American citizen before being sold and registered foreign, the *Wapello* did not at any time acquire the lawful right to engage in coastwise trade. Hence, she could not lose rights that were never acquired in the first place. They argued further that, on coming under American ownership for the first time, she should be conferred with the lawful right to coastwise trade. However, the appellants contested that the second interpretation of the first proviso applied to the *Wapello* because, having been built in the United States before being sold foreign, she forever forfeited her lawful right to engage in the coastwise trade.

---

49 Ch. 355, 49 Stat. 442: An Act to Amend Section 27 of the Merchant Marine Act, 1920. H.R. 115. Public No. 191. Dated 2 July 1935. See also: 46 U.S.C. App. § 833.

50 Ch. 600, 70 Stat. 544: An Act to amend the Shipping Laws, to prohibit the Operation in the Coastwise Trade of vessels Rebuilt Outside the United States, and for other purposes. 14 July 1956. H.R. 6025, Public Law 714. See also: 46 U.S.C. §§ 12101, 12132. App. § 833. The provision only applied to vessels over 500 tons initially, but has since 1988 been revised to apply to all vessels engaged in coastwise trade regardless of tonnage. This was in addition to the prior amendment in 1960.

51 46 U.S.C. 12112.

The court reconciled the seeming contradiction in the language of the proviso by deciding that a vessel built in the United States acquired a conditional right to engage in the coastwise trade. However, that condition is subject to the vessel being owned by an American citizen. In reaching this decision, the court made an important assumption that the 'lawful right' as contained in the proviso referred to any lawful right, conditional or unconditional. Thus, viewing the proviso in its new but now more consistent language, the court accepted the appellant's interpretation and concluded that the *Wapello* had acquired the lawful right to engage in the coastwise trade because she was built in the United States. Hence, by being sold foreign, she had irrevocably forfeited that lawful right in pursuit of the provisions of the statutory instrument. The *Wapello* was therefore ineligible for coastwise trade. In reaching this decision, the court relied on the committee reports of both the United States Senate and House of Representatives. These reports expressly explained that the proviso's aim was to prevent the following two kinds of vessels from acquiring lawful rights to participate in coastwise trade:

a   Vessels built in or documented under the laws of the United States and later sold foreign.

b   Vessels built in the United States for foreign countries or foreign purchasers.[52]

The *Wapello* fell within the context of the second instance. Having ruled the *Wapello* ineligible, the court had to decide on the status of the *Observer*. Being a rebuilt ship in a United States shipyard, was the *Observer* a rebuilt *Santa Helena*, which contributed the *Wapello's* fore body to the *Observer*, or a rebuilt *Trustco*, which contributed her stern to the *Observer*? If the *Observer* was a rebuilt *Santa Helena*, then the *Observer* could not acquire the lawful right to engage in coastwise trade under the first proviso. This is because the *Santa Helena* would have irrevocably forfeited her lawful right to engage in coastwise trade because of her tarnished lineage with the *Wapello* and *Esso Chittagong*, both of which were sold foreign. Also, under the second proviso, vessels rebuilt outside the United States are excluded from engaging in coastwise trade.[53] The *Santa Helena* was rebuilt in Japan and would therefore be prohibited by the second proviso from acquiring lawful rights to engage in coastwise trade.

However, if the *Observer* was a rebuilt *Trustco*, the *Observer* would be eligible to engage in coastwise trade because the *Trustco* was built in the United States and owned by American citizens at all times. Moreover, the rebuilding process in which the *Trustco* contributed its stern to produce the *Observer*, also took place in the United States. Therefore, the *Trustco* complied with both the first and second provisos of Section 27 of the Merchant Marine Act of 1920. The challenge that

---

52  See: S. Rep. No. 870, 74th Congress, 1st Session (1935) and H.R. Rep. No. 118, 74th Congress, 1st Session (1935).

53  Ch. 600, 70 Stat. 544: An Act to amend the Shipping Laws, to prohibit the Operation in the Coastwise Trade of vessels Rebuilt Outside the United States, and for other purposes. 14 July 1956. H.R. 6025, Public Law 714.

was now before the court was to decide the coastwise trade status of the *Observer*, which was a vessel produced by the joining of an eligible coastwise trade vessel to an ineligible coastwise trade vessel. To make that decision, the court had to decide first whether the *Observer* was a rebuilt *Santa Helena* or a rebuilt *Trustco*. However, the court did not determine which body the Observer inherited and the case was referred for trial but was never retried. The *Observer* continued to trade internationally and was stranded in the Suez Canal during hostilities between Egypt and Israel in 1970. She was not returned to her owners until during the 1976 dredging of the canal. The appellants, Marine Carriers, were by this time reluctant to pursue the case because of the lapse in time and the vessel's damaged condition when she was returned. This case demonstrates some of the legal complexities of the United States Jones Act with both provisos of the Act still generating confusion on the eligibility of some rebuilt vessels to engage in coastwise trade under the maritime cabotage laws of the United States.[54]

## *Shipbuilders Council of America et al. v United States of America et al.*[55]

In this case, the draft of an oil rig was too deep for the rig to be repaired at a shipyard. As such, the rig was loaded onto a foreign submersible barge at a coastwise point. Thereafter, the barge was raised and towed with the rig on board to a shipyard at another coastwise point. The oil rig was repaired there while still stationed on the deck of the barge. After the repairs, the barge returned to the coastwise point where the rig was loaded. There, the barge was submerged and the rig was offloaded. This operation was sanctioned by Customs as complying with the relevant provisions of the Merchant Marine Act of 1920. Their understanding was that the loading and unloading of the cargo occurred at the same place. However, this was to be later challenged in court out of fear that a precedent may be set. In the lower court, it was held that the repair carried out on the oil rig was the purpose of the voyage. Hence, the shipyard was the true destination of the voyage and the rig was transported on a foreign vessel between two coastwise points in the United States, thereby contravening the provisions of 19 C.F.R. § 4.80b(a). This decision was reversed in the Court of Appeals on a technicality because the plaintiff's challenge to the ruling was out of time and should never have been heard in the lower court in the first place. Nevertheless, the upper court suggested that the oil rig could not be described as 'merchandise' pursuant to the provisions of 19 C.F.R. § 4.80b(a).[56] By that suggestion, the upper court provided some form of tacit judicial support to the original Customs Ruling .

54 See: *The Shipbuilders Council of America, Inc. and Pasha Hawaii Transport Lines LLC. v. U.S. Coast Guard and Matson Navigation Company, Inc* [2009]. Case No. 1:07cv1234. APA, 5 U.S.C. §§ 704.
55 868 F. 2d 452 (DC Cir. 1989). Decided March 3, 1989 in the United States Court of Appeals, District of Columbia Circuit. Nos 88–5095, 88–5119.
56 See: 19 Code of Federal regulation (C.F.R.) § 4.80b(a), which stipulates thus: *Effect of manufacturing or processing at intermediate port or place*: A coastwise transportation of merchandise takes place, within the meaning of the coastwise laws, when

This case raises an important question particularly under a protectionist maritime cabotage regime like that obtained in the United States. The question is can there be justification for applying maritime cabotage law to all maritime activities occurring in domestic waters or should the purpose of the maritime activity be a determinant It is not difficult to understand the decision of the lower court for the following reasons. First, the foreign barge sailed with its domestic cargo between two coastwise points of the coastal waters of the United States. Second, the time spent at the repair yard would take the operation beyond the ordinary definition of a 'stopping service'. Therefore, the repair shipyard had for all purposes become a destination point, distinct from the point of origin regardless of whether the rig was unloaded from the barge. Furthermore, pursuant to the provisions of the Merchant Marine Act of 1920, the use of a foreign rig incontrovertibly denied an eligible coastwise vessel the opportunity to perform that transport service in return for a remuneration. Moreover, it does not appear as though the stricken rig had posed enough real risk to the environment or safety of people to meet the emergency threshold that would trigger the waiver of the Merchant Marine Act of 1920.

The Custom ruling and the upper court appeared to place too much emphasis on the fact that the rig was not unloaded from the barge at the repair shipyard. However, they failed to consider whether unloading the rig would have made the the repair operation more challenging or prevented it altogether. If so, then the point about unloading the cargo is invalid. This case contrasts the decision in *Alpina and Nicko Tours v Chioggia Port Authority.* [57] Here, the Court of Justice of the European Union held that all maritime transport services provided for remuneration in coastal waters are covered under Regulation 3577/92, regardless of whether they start and end with the same cargo in the same port.[58] Importantly, the *Alpina* case re-emphasized the definition of a port as any infrastructure temporary or small scale that serves as a terminal for the loading and discharging of cargo for carriage by sea.[59]

merchandise laden at a point embraced within the coastwise laws ('coastwise point') is unladen at another coastwise point, regardless of the origin or ultimate destination of the merchandise. However, merchandise is not transported coastwise if at an intermediate port or place other than a coastwise point (that is at a foreign port or place, or at a port or place in a territory or possession of the United States not subject to the coastwise laws), it is manufactured or processed into a new and different product, and the new and different product thereafter is transported to a coastwise point.

57 Case C 17/13: Alpina River Cruises GmbH and Nicko Tours GmbH v Ministero delle infrastrutture e dei trasporti — Capitaneria di Porto di Chioggia. Judgment of the Court (Third Chamber), 27 March 2014.

58 For a different application of the law of maritime cabotage, see: Article 40 of the Navigation and Maritime Trade Law 'NMTL' of Mexico (Article 40 Ley de Navegación y Comercio Marítimos), which entered into force in 2006.

59 A port was defined as stated above in; Commission of the European Communities v Kingdom of Spain Case C-323/03 [2006] ECR I-2161; 9 March 2006.

*American Maritime Association v. Blumenthal*[60]

In the *Blumenthal* case, Hess Corporation used a foreign-flagged vessel to transport crude oil from Alaska to its refinery in the Virgin Islands. The refined products were then shipped back on a foreign vessel to the United States. The question before the court was whether such activity violated the provisions of the Merchant Marine Act of 1920. The district and circuit courts had ruled against the plaintiffs that the refining process produced eleven new products distinctly different from the crude oil that left Alaska. The court found such degree of change in the original product as conclusive evidence that the products from the refinery were new and distinct from the cargo of Alaskan crude oil. Moreover, as the two different cargoes were carried on two separate voyages, this could not be deemed as transhipment and hence there was no violation of the Merchant Marine Act. The plaintiffs appealed the decision to the Court of Appeal and argued that, irrespective of the changes undergone by the original crude oil product, the defendant's actions violated the 'continuity' requirement as construed within the meaning of the Merchant Marine Act of 1920. They contended that the defendant's utmost desire was to engage in coastwise trade between Alaska and other points in the United States using a foreign vessel. The appellant also argued that the original cargo did not change significantly to such a degree that it lost its identity and thus qualified as a different cargo.

The point on 'continuity' is important because in 1893, the United States Congress amended the Merchant Marine Act to prohibit the transhipment of goods following the decision in *United States v. 250 Kegs of Nails*.[61] On the question of 'intent', the court held that the 'intent' of a shipper to send goods to a final destination is immaterial. What is important is the degree of change to which the goods have undergone as a matter of fact in the course of business. On the question of the product alteration, the court held that the nature of the original cargo had changed sufficiently enough to render them new products without violating the provisions of the Jones Act.

The impact of this decision is that, under the maritime cabotage laws of the United States, it is essential that products are new and distinct from the original product. A mere change in the grade of a product is not sufficient.

*Recent rulings of United States Customs and Border Protection*

The legal position in *American Maritime Association v Blumenthal*[62] has now been bolstered by two rulings made by the United States Customs and Border Protection in 2014 and 2015 respectively. Pursuant to the provisions of 19 C.F.R. § 4.80b(a), a coastwise endorsement is not required if, at an intermediate port or

---

60 590 F. 2d 1156 (1978). District of Columbia Circuit. See also: the decision of the District Court; 458 F. Supp. 849 (1977)
61 52 F. 231 (S.D. Cal. 1892), 61 F. 410 (9th Cir. 1894).
62 590 F. 2d 1156 (1978). District of Columbia Circuit. See also: the decision of the District Court; 458 F. Supp. 849 (1977).

place other than a coastwise point, the merchandise is processed into a 'new and different product' and the new and different product thereafter is transported to a coastwise point.[63] The first ruling dealt with an inquiry about adding conventional regular gasoline blendstock (CBOB) and reformulated blendstock for oxygenate blending (RBOB) to undenatured ethanol, to produce a denatured ethanol fuel grade. The question was whether this would create a new and distinct product to satisfy the provisions of 19 C.F.R. § 4.80b(a). The Customs and Border Protection (CBP) responded by issuing Ruling H254877 in 2014 stating that undenatured ethyl alcohol and the fuel grade denatured ethyl alcohol were simply different grades of the same original product with no apparent chemical or structural difference. Therefore, transporting a different grade of the original product on a non-coastwise-qualified vessel would contravene the stipulations as laid out in 46 U.S.C § 55102. However, in response to a similar query, the CBP issued Ruling H259293 in 2015, stating that the blending of alkylate, reformate, light naphtha, heavy naphtha, raffinate, butane, catalytic cracked gasoline and heavy aromatics to produce CBOB, RBOB, 87-octane index conventional gasoline and 93-octane index conventional gasoline would result in a new and distinct product within the meaning of 19 C.F.R. § 4.80b(a) and thus would not violate 46 U.S.C § 55102. Thus, to satisfy the relevant provisions of the maritime cabotage laws of the United States, new and distinct products must result from whatever refining or reformulating process the original product has undergone.

The cases examined above illustrate the stringent nature of the 1920 Merchant Marine Act and in particular the 'built requirement' provisions that contravenes the World Trade Organisation rules. However, the Act enjoys an exemption from WTO rules because of a GATT provision that exempts statutes in force before its creation in 1947.[64] Nevertheless, the WTO is supposed to have periodic reviews to prevent the exempted law from being made more stringent.[65]

## Analyzing the 1920 Merchant Marine Act

The Merchant Marine Act of 1920 (Jones Act) is viewed in the United States as a vital legal instrument for maintaining a dependable marine fleet for emergency purposes and national security issues. The argument is that a reliable merchant marine fleet is required to facilitate logistical contingencies in the event of crises or threats. Therefore, the Jones Act is necessary to protect the interests of the United States and to sustain the industrial base for shipbuilding in the United States.[66] To

---

63 *United States v. 250 Kegs of Nails.* 52 F. 231 (S.D. Cal. 1892), 61 F. 410 (9th Cir. 1894).
64 A. Stoler, 'The Current State of the WTO'. Paper presented at Workshop on the EU, the US and the WTO, Institute for International Business, Economics and Law (California, 28 February–1 March 2003).
65 R. Joshi, 'WTO Review Fears Derail Proposed Jones Act Amendment', *Lloyd's List* (London, 28 October 2009).
66 See: I. Arnsdorf, 'U.S. Shipbuilding Is Highest in Almost 20 Years on Shale Energy', *Bloomberg Newletter* (New York, 18 September 2013).

this point, a new bill[67] from both Houses of Congress has provided the strongest congressional statement of support for the Jones Act since the 1936 Merchant Marine Act.[68] The 'emergency crisis and national security' justifications may have carried some validity in the past. However, this is no longer the case because neither of these arguments reflect the actual maritime cabotage practices in the United States. Hence, these justifications have no impact on United States national security or the revitalizing of her shipbuilding sector.[69] The steady decline in the number of commercial vessels built in the United States indicates clearly the disconnect between the theoretical justifications of the Jones Act and the reality of the maritime sector of the United States.[70] According to the United States Department of Transport, 1072 Jones Act-eligible commercial vessels were built in the United States in 1955. However, the number of domestic built coastwise vessels fell to 193 by the year 2000, and by 2014, only 90 commercial vessels were built in shipyards across the United States under the Jones Act programme.[71] Furthermore, the United States Department of Defence has admitted to frequently leasing foreign vessels to execute missions that required additional sealift capacity.[72] This is in addition to the Military Sealift Command (MSC) shipping more than one-fifth of its dry cargo on foreign-chartered vessels to deployed United States armed forces during the Persian Gulf conflict. Furthermore, the Maritime Administration's Ready Reserve Force (RRF) has 30 foreign-built vessels out of the 46 vessels in its fleet.[73] The RRF was established to support the rapid worldwide deployment of United States military forces and to respond to other emergencies as they affect the interests of

67  See the National Defense Authorization Act (H.R. 3979).
68  Sec. 101. 46 App. U.S.C. 1101 – Fostering Development and Maintenance of Merchant Marine: the 1936 Act was enacted to further the development and maintenance of an adequate and well-balanced American merchant marine; to promote the commerce of the United States; and to aid in the national defence. In addition to the establishment of the United States Maritime Commission, the Act also established federal subsidies for the construction and operation of merchant ships by citizens of the United States.
69  See: S. Galbraith, 'Thinking Outside the Box on Coastal Shipping and Cabotage', *Maritime Trade Intelligence* (Victoria, 1 December 2014).
70  See: B. Edmonson, 'Navy Official Calls for a Fleet of Dual-Use Marine Highway Ships' [2011], *Journal of Commerce*, 13 July.
71  Maritime Administration, 'United States Flag Privately Owned Merchant Fleet: 2000–2014' (U.S. Department of Transportation, 2014).
72  The Official Department of Defence Congressional Research Service Report states: '[MSC] charters ships (from the commercial market) to meet the requirements of DOD components and respond to changes in the operational environment. Unfortunately, very few commercial ships with high military utility have been constructed in U.S. shipyards in the past 20 years. Consequently, when MSC has a requirement to charter a vessel, nearly all of the offers are for foreign-built ships. In cases where the need is immediate or subject to change, due to the operational environment or other factors, a commercial charter is the only practical way to obtain the capability.'
73  Maritime Administration, 'The Maritime Administration's Ready Reserve Force' (U.S. Department of Transportation, 2014).

the United States.[74] This proves that the Merchant Marine Act of 1920 is not necessary for emergencies or dealing with national security issues. Rather, the stringent provisions of the Act may deprive the relevant agencies, the needed resources to perform their tasks efficiently. Therefore, one can argue that if foreign vessels have been employed in the United States military service in wartime, then the argument that employing foreign vessels for commercial use poses a security risk is not logical. Hence, the idea of subjecting the national economy to the inefficiencies of a protectionist Jones Act regime for the claimed security benefits is disingenuous.

It is suggested that factors such as disparities in corporate taxation, over-regulation of the industry, absence of robust competition and a lack of a coherent national maritime policy have all contributed to and explain better the decline of the United States merchant marine. The continued preservation of the Merchant Marine Act, which reserves maritime cabotage cargo to only American-flagged vessels, is becoming more disadvantageous to indigenous shippers and ship-owners.[75] For example, a 2,890 TEU vessel scheduled for delivery between 2003 and 2006 from a shipyard in the United States cost around $125 million. This was around four times higher than the market price in Asia at the time. The cost of building a 3,600 TEU vessel in a shipyard in the United States in 2013 was approximately $209 million. In contrast, a comparably sized vessel was built for less than a fifth of that price in Asia.[76] The prohibitive cost of constructing any kind of vessel in the United States underlines the negative impact of the stringent maritime cabotage laws being implemented in the United States.[77] The high price of protecting American domestic trade by insisting on United States-flagged ships suggests that there is need for reconsideration. This is particularly imperative at a time when protectionist China is moving towards introducing some liberal measures into its maritime cabotage sector.[78] One of the more recent case studies that illustrate the impact of the Merchant Marine Act of 1920 is the rock salt market. The United States is one of the largest producers of rock salt used to de-ice roads during snow and ice storms. However, it is cheaper for states like Maryland and Virginia to import the bulk of their rock salt from Chile rather than from the Port of South Louisiana.[79] This was highlighted in 2014 when the state of New Jersey was prevented from transporting rock salt on a foreign ship from Maine in response to an emergency disaster. The cargo was only 400 miles from New

---

74 See: R. O'Rourke, 'DOD Leases of Foreign-Built Ships: Background for Congress', Congressional Research Service Report for Congress, 7–5700 - RS22454 (Washington, 28 May 2010).
75 For more, see: J. Lewis, 'Veiled Waters: Examining the Jones Act's Consumer Welfare Effect' [2013], *Issues in Political Economy*, 22(1), 77–107.
76 Drewry Maritime Research, 'US Cabotage Protection Gets More Expensive', *Container Insight Weekly* (London, 17 November 2013).
77 See: W. Gray, 'Performance of Major US Shipyards in 20th/21st Century' [2008], *Journal of Ship Production*, 24(4), 202–213.
78 See: The Maritime Executive, 'Shanghai's New Cabotage Laws: A Disappointment', MarEX, 2013).
79 J. Rodrigue et al., *The Geography of Transport Systems* (3rd edn, Routledge 2013).

Jersey, and a foreign vessel would have required about two days to deliver the cargo. However, it took about a month to find an eligible Jones Act vessel to transport the cargo. If any impetus were required to reconsider reforming the strict Merchant Marine Act of 1920, then the liberal maritime cabotage legal framework of the European Union would readily provide such stimulus.

It was agreed during the negotiations that established the WTO that non-conforming measures that were grandfathered in the General Agreement on Tariffs and Trade (GATT) should be eliminated. These included pre-1947 measures that were incompatibility with GATT principles. However, the United States insisted that the Jones Act was sacrosanct and must be retained.[80] This special exemption is documented in paragraph 3 of GATT 1994.[81] The continued exemption of the protectionist Jones Act many years after the establishment of the WTO is a systemic concern.[82] The European Union and Japan opposed upholding the grandfathering of rights under the new institution. Ironically, that did not prevent them from seeking special dispensation of their own.[83]

This would not be the only time that the United States has declined to include the Merchant Marine Act in a trade agreement. It requested specifically for the Merchant Marine Act to be exempted from the NAFTA negotiations even though Canada and Mexico favoured a liberal maritime cabotage policy in all the NAFTA member countries.[84] Indeed, at the same time as NAFTA members were negotiating three-way liberal regional maritime cabotage policy, the Merchant Marine Act was made more protectionist by the 'Byrnes–Tollefson' Amendment.[85] This amendment precludes Canadian shipyards from providing repairs to United States military vessels.

There are legislative attempts to use the Providing for Our Workforce and Energy Resources (POWER) Act[86] to extend the ambit of the Jones Act to cover offshore renewable energy services. The POWER Act tightens a loophole in

---

80  C. VanGrasstek, 'The History and Future of the World Trade Organization' (World Trade Organization, 2013).

81  A. Stoler, 'The Current State of the WTO', paper presented at Workshop on the EU, the US and the WTO (Institute for International Business, Economics and Law, Stanford University, 28 February–1 March 2003).

82  WTO, 'How Can the WTO Help Harness Globalization?', World Trade Organization Forum (Geneva, 4–5 October 2007). As per speech by a member of the Hong Kong Delegation.

83  C. VanGrasstek, 'The History and Future of the World Trade Organization' (The World Trade Organization, 2013).

84  The position taken by the United States encouraged Mexico to preserve its domestic maritime cabotage environment under Annex I Schedule of Mexico. Therefore, marine cabotage, towing, stevedoring and all investments over 49% in port facilities are reserved for Mexican nationals. Canada followed in Mexico's footsteps and restricted Canada's coasting trade to Canadian-flagged and crewed vessels under Annex II-CIII and Annex II-C-XIII.

85  10 U.S.C. § 7309: US Code - Section 7309: Construction of vessels in foreign shipyards: prohibition. 107 Stat. 1710. 30 November 1993.

86  The United States House of Representatives passed the POWER Act (H.R. 2360) on 7 December 2011.

existing legislation that permits foreign vessels and workers to install and service offshore renewable energy resources. The Act stipulates that the building and servicing of renewable energy resources on the Outer Continental Shelf (OCS) should be exclusively performed by American maritime workers. The Outer Continental Shelf refers to all submerged lands lying three miles offshore seaward of state coastal waters. It also includes areas outside of the lands beneath navigable waters and in which the subsoil and seabed appertain to the United States and are subject to her jurisdiction.[87] This area is regulated by the Outer Continental Shelf Lands Act (OCSLA). The Act extends the scope of the United States federal law that applies up to 200 nautical miles from the territorial sea baseline to the subsoil and seabed of the outer continental shelf.[88] The OCSLA also covers all structures (excluding vessels) permanently or temporarily attached to the seabed for the purpose of developing, producing or exploring for oil. Therefore, the POWER Act would expand OCSLA, which governs offshore gas and oil production, to include all offshore energy activities.[89] Hence, renewable-energy workers would be brought under the Merchant Marine Act of 1920. Thus, all energy production from the Outer Continental Shelf waters off the coasts of the United States would need to be serviced and transported by the Jones Act fleet without foreign competition.

## Canada: Coasting Trade Act 1992, Canadian Shipping Act, Part X, 1936

The coasting trade law and policy in Canada can be traced to the 1763 Treaty of Paris.[90] At that time, Canada had just become a British colony and its maritime commerce was under British control. The Canadian Parliament first had powers to regulate shipping in Canadian waters in 1867 through the British North American Act. Even so, any law that was passed in Canada had to be consistent with the laws of the United Kingdom.[91] The enactment of the Canada Shipping Act in 1934 gave Canadian shipping laws total independence from British laws.[92]

87 The Outer Continental Shelf Lands Act (OCSLA): 43 U.S.C. § 1331 et seq., the Act of 7 August 1953, as amended through P.L. 106–580, Dec. 29, 2000.
88 C. Johnson, 'Advances in Marine Spatial Planning: Zoning Earth's Last Frontier' [2014], *Journal of Environmental Law and Litigation*, 29(1), 191–246.
89 See: S. Kalen, 'Cruise Control and Speed Bumps: Energy Policy and Limits for Outer Continental Shelf Leasing' [2013], *Environmental & Energy Law & Policy Journal*, 7 (2), 155–189.
90 The Treaty of Paris was signed 10 February 1763 in Paris by Britain, France and Spain. Portugal also agreed to the Treaty. This treaty gave Britain undisputed supremacy over maritime commerce.
91 J. Hodgson and M. Brooks, 'Towards a North American Cabotage Regime: A Canadian Perspective' [2007], *Canadian Journal of Transportation*, 1(1), 19–35.
92 The Canada Shipping Act of 1934 came into force in 1936. The Merchant Shipping Agreement of 1931 still allowed British vessels free access to the coasting trade while non-British ships were levied duty. This agreement became defunct in 1979 when all parties to the Agreement agreed to withdraw.

Canada has the longest coastline of any country in the world, with 202,080 kilometres. Thus, the government is under pressure by both protectionist and liberal campaigners to maximize the benefits of her long coastline. The protectionists argue that Canada should extend the scope of her maritime cabotage law to cover the outmost permissible limit and ensure that the national security interest of the country is secured.[93] This includes the renewing and maintaining of the national fleet to safeguard her domestic and international trade, which is vital to the sustenance of Canada's sovereignty and prosperity.[94] However, the liberalists argue that rather than more protectionism of the maritime cabotage trade and services, the solution lies in Canada opening up her coastal trade and services to foreign expertise to compensate for areas of domestic shortage.[95]

The coasting trade law and policy in Canada, as embodied in the Canadian Coasting Trade Act 1992, is the result of three commissions of inquiry. These are: the Spence Commission (1957), the Macpherson Commission (1959) and the Darling Commission (1970). The objective of these commissions was to determine the most appropriate maritime transport policy for Canada. Following the enactment of the Canada Shipping Act, the Spence Commission was set up in 1957. The Commission was tasked with evaluating the consequences of reserving Canada's coasting trade only to vessels registered with and flying the Canadian flag. Furthermore, the Commission was required to analyze the probable effect of lifting the restriction so that vessels of all flags (not limited to the Commonwealth) could access the coasting trade.[96] The Spence Commission submitted that a protectionist maritime cabotage regime was not in the economic interest of Canada. Moreover, Commonwealth (particularly British) vessels already provided sufficient competition to nullify the negative effect of a liberal coasting trade policy.[97] Two years after the findings of the Spence Commission, the MacPherson Royal Commission was set up in 1959. Although it was not focused specifically on maritime cabotage transport, it was the MacPherson Report that recommended free competition between the different transport modes in Canada.[98] Furthermore, it produced the 1967 National Transportation Act.[99] Nevertheless, the Darling Report

93 S. Chapelski, 'CETA: Opening up Canadian Waterways to Foreign Vessels' (Bull Housser, 2014).
94 National Shipbuilding and Procurement Strategy Secretariat, 'Results of the National Shipbuilding and Procurement Strategy' (Government of Canada, 19 October 2011).
95 See: M. Brooks, 'Maritime Cabotage: International Market Issues in the Liberalisation of Domestic Shipping', in A. Chircop et al. (eds), *The Regulation of International Shipping: International and Comparative Perspectives* (Martinus Nijhoff 2012), pp. 293–324.
96 See: J. Francois, H. Arce, K, Reinert and J. Flynn, 'Commercial Policy and the Domestic Carrying Trade' [1996], *Canadian Journal of Economics*, 29(1), 181–198.
97 See: Government of Canada, 'Report of the Royal Commission on Coasting Trade (The Spence Commission)', *Queen's Printer* (Ottawa, 9 December 1957).
98 Government of Canada, *Report on the Royal Commission on Transportation (The Macpherson Commission 1959)* (Queen's Printer 1961).
99 A New Transportation Act 1987 (identical to the 1967 Act) came to be as a result of the Freedom to Move Initiative.

of 1970 advocated for coasting trade in Canada to be reserved for Canadian vessels. The report recommended that the application of the protectionist policy should extend to the Canadian continental shelf. The policy would also cover activities such as dredging and salvage, including vessels such as seismographic vessels and supply and support ships. This report laid the foundation for the present coasting trade law and policy in Canada.[100]

Despite the recommendations of the Darling Report, the Coasting Trade Act was not enacted until 1992.[101] The Coasting Trade Act 1992 states that 'No foreign ship or non-duty paid ship shall, except under and in accordance with a licence, engage in the coasting trade'.[102] This Act replaced the Canada Shipping Act of 1936 as the governing regulation for the coasting trade of Canada. However, the 1936 Canada Shipping Act, which was itself amended and is now the Canada Shipping Act 2001, still regulates other areas of Canadian shipping apart from coasting trade.[103] Nevertheless, fishing vessels, research vessels and vessels responding to emergency marine pollution are exempted from the provision of Section 3(1) of the Act. Furthermore, the Act allows for temporary entry of foreign vessels, if there are no available or suitable Canadian registered duties paid or Canadian built vessels to perform the required tasks.[104] The Coasting Trade Act covers moveable drilling platforms, seismic vessels used in the exploration, exploitation, extraction and transportation of oil, gas and other mineral resources. The Act also applies to offshore waters of the continental shelf up to the 200-mile limit.[105] The Coasting Trade Act regulates Canada's maritime cabotage trades and services together with other legislative instruments such as the 2001 Canada Shipping Act, which defines a Canadian vessel,[106] and the 1986 Custom Act, which defines Canadian water.[107] Maritime cabotage in Canada is reserved to Canadian vessels built in Canada or duty-paid. However, foreign vessels may still engage in the Canadian coastal trade through the waiver and licence system. Since 2012, foreign seismic vessels have been exempted from the requirement to obtain coasting trade licenses when undertaking exploration for oil and gas resources on Canada's continental shelf. However, such vessels must still obtain the license for activities conducted in the territorial seas of Canada.[108] The Coasting Trade Act prioritizes participation in the Canadian

100 J. Darling, *Report of Inquiry on the Coasting Trade of Canada and Related Marine Activity* (Canadian Transport Commission 1970).
101 The Coasting Trade Act received assent on the 23 June 1992.
102 Section 3(1) of the Coasting Trade Act 1992.
103 The 2001 Canada Shipping Act replaced the older (1936) CSA on 1 July 2007.
104 For more on this, see: J. Hodgson and M. Brooks, 'Towards a North American Cabotage Regime: A Canadian Perspective' [2007], *Canadian Journal of Transportation*, 1(1), 19–35.
105 See Section 2(1) of Canadian Coastal Trading Act 1992 for the meaning and scope of coasting trade in Canada.
106 Section 2 of Canada Shipping Act 2001.
107 Section 2 of Canadian Custom Act 1986.
108 See: PF Collins, *Temporary Importation of Vessels into Canada's Coasting Trade: Information for Contractors and Vessel Operators* (PF Collins 2014).

coasting trade in the following order: (a) Canadian-flagged duty-paid or Canadian-built vessels, (b) Canadian-flagged non-duty paid vessels, and (c) foreign vessels.

One of the most contentious issues with the Canadian Coastal Trade Act was the 25 per cent duty that was levied on foreign-built vessels.[109] In a strict sense, this levy was not a shipping policy but a Canadian industry policy aimed at protecting the Canadian shipbuilding industry. The Canadian Shipowners Association criticized the levy as constituting an obstacle in replacing its ageing vessels, particularly specialised vessels that cannot be built in Canadian shipyards. It claimed that the tariff added more than $10 million to the purchase of a ship built overseas.[110] In 2010, the 25 per cent tariff was waived on imports of all general cargo vessels, tankers and ferries longer than 129 metres. The government claimed that waiving this tariff is expected to save shipowners $25 million per year over the next decade.[111] Another issue with the Canadian maritime cabotage policy is the Canadian Coast Guard's unique vessel regulatory regime that requires an operator to convert its vessel to meet specific Canadian coastal waters regulations.[112]

Negotiations were concluded on the Canada-European Union Comprehensive Economic and Trade Agreement (CETA) in 2014. This is designed to be a comprehensive trade agreement that encompasses all elements of modern trade.[113] According to the terms of the agreement, Canada aims to remove trade restrictions in exchange for preferential access into the European Union market that is Canada's second most important trade and investment partner, with more than 500 million consumers and a GDP of $18 trillion.[114] However, the proposed CETA agreement appear to be inconsistent with the provisions of the Coasting Trade Act of 1992 because it opens Canadian waterways to EU and other foreign vessels.[115] For instance, under the proposed CETA agreement:

a   European Union companies can use non-Canadian vessels to reposition their empty containers between ports in Canada, on a non-revenue basis.

109 J. Hodgson and M. Brooks, 'Towards a North American Cabotage Regime: A Canadian Perspective' [2007], *Canadian Journal of Transportation*, 1(1), 19–35.
110 MariNova Consulting Ltd, *Research and Traffic Group Gardner Pinfold CPCS* (Marine Transportation Study: Phase II Final Report 2009).
111 Government of Canada, *Government of Canada Announces New Tariff Measures for Ships for a More Competitive Canadian Economy* (Department of Finance Canada 2010).
112 M. Brooks, *NAFTA and Short Sea Shipping Corridors* (Australia Institute of Market Studies 2005).
113 S. Chapelski, 'CETA: Opening up Canadian Waterways to Foreign Vessels' (Bull Housser, 2014)
114 See: Environmental Hansard, 'MPs Resumed Discussion about the Government's Fisheries Investment Fund Commitment to Newfoundland and Labrador', House of Commons Debates, 41st Parliament, 2nd Session, No. 167 (London, 2 February 2015).
115 See: Consolidated Comprehensive Economic and Trade Agreement (CETA) text between CANADA and the European Union. Published 26 September 2014, pp. 278–282.

b   European Union registered vessels can be used to provide feeder services for cargo between Ports in Canada. In particular, for the provisions of feeder services between the ports of Halifax and Montreal, both bulk and containerized cargo for continuous service could be performed using vessels on EU first registries. For containerized cargo on a single voyage where it is part of an international leg, vessels on EU first or second registries will be eligible to perform the service.

c   European Union companies would be able to use vessels of any registry for commercial dredging services contracted by private entities.

d   For federally procured dredging contracts, European Union companies will be permitted to bid on contracts exceeding the procurement thresholds for construction services using EU registered, built or modified vessels. These procurement thresholds are the same as those currently found in the World Trade Organization's Agreement on Government Procurement and stands at C$7.8 million.

We shall now look at some of the judicial decisions that have shaped the maritime cabotage policy of Canada into one of the most protectionist in the world.[116]

### *Judicial decisions arising from Canadian cabotage law*

Judicial decisions from the Canadian courts on maritime cabotage disputes are not readily available. Nevertheless, the Canadian Transport Agency, which functions as a quasi-judicial tribunal and an economic regulator, has laid down some important decisions.

### *The RV Northern Access* [117]

The applicant, Logix Marine acting on behalf of TGS-NOPEC Geophysical Company ASA, applied for a temporary coasting trade license. They intended to use *RV Northern Access*, a Cyprus-registered seismic research vessel, to conduct multi-client 2-D seismic survey in Canadian waters from 30 June 2001 to 30 November 2001. The defendant, Geophysical Service Incorporated (GSI), countered the applicant's application by offering their Canadian-registered vessel, *GSI Admiral*, for the service.

The applicant outlined several reasons why *GSI Admiral* was neither suitable nor available to conduct the survey activity described. These included: the vessel's lack of experience in the type of activity proposed, its lack of up-to-date

---

116 For more on this see: M. Brooks, 'Maritime Cabotage: International Market Issues in the Liberalisation of Domestic Shipping', in A. Chircop et al. (eds), *The Regulation of International Shipping: International and Comparative Perspectives* (Martinus Nijhoff 2012), pp. 293–324.

117 Decision No. 447-W-2001. File No. W9125/L22/01–1. Decided 9 August 2001.

equipment and inferior technology on board the vessel. Also, they referenced the fact that the defendant's recent use of a foreign vessel to conduct another seismic survey was indicative of the unsuitability or unavailability of *GSI Admiral.*

The defendant (GSI) counter-argued that as a Canadian vessel, *GSI Admiral* was available and more than suitable to conduct the proposed survey activity. Therefore, the vessel had priority over any foreign vessel. Furthermore, they submitted that a Canadian-flagged vessel owned by a Canadian company, employing Canadian crew, would contribute more to the Canadian economy. In addition, GSI contended that the Coasting Trade Act does not require Canadian vessel owners to argue the fine points of a recording equipment and software on board a vessel as such argument was an attempt to detract attention from the suitability and availability of *GSI Admiral.* They claimed that any equipment identified by the applicant was already on board *GSI Admiral,* or could be easily installed.

Thus, the issue for determination before the Canadian Transport Agency was whether there was a suitable Canadian vessel available to provide the proposed seismic survey in accordance with the provisions of the Coasting Trade Act.[118] It was held by the Canadian Transport Agency that, pursuant to the provisions of the Coasting Trade Act, a Canadian or non-duty paid vessel offered to conduct an activity in Canadian waters need not be identical to the foreign vessel. Such a Canadian vessel need only be suitable to perform the activity described in the application, even if it would be required to acquire additional equipment where necessary. The Agency found that the equipment on *GSI Admiral,* although not identical to that of *RV Northern Access,* was suitable to perform the activity described in the coasting trade license application. On the issue of lack of experience, the Agency found that the absence of previous experience of a refitted vessel in a specified area of work cannot be interpreted as the unsuitability of the vessel for the work.

The applicant had also failed to adduce substantive evidence that the Canadian vessel would not be available on the required dates. The Canadian Transport Agency therefore determined that, pursuant to the provisions of the Coasting Trade Act, *GSI Admiral* was a suitable Canadian vessel available to perform the service described in the application.

### Concluding analysis of the Canadian maritime cabotage law and policy

Canada has maintained a stringent protectionist maritime cabotage law and policy dating back to before the confederation in 1867. The only time that Canada considered liberalizing their maritime cabotage law was during the Spence Commission and NAFTA (now USMCA Trade agreements) maritime cabotage negotiations. Canada was open to the idea of a North American Free Trade Agreement (NAFTA – now USMCA) cabotage policy similar to that adopted by the European Union. The then proposed NAFTA cabotage framework would have provided access to trade without restraint and freedom to provide maritime services in the North American region for vessels and nationals from

---

118 See sections 4(1a and 1b), 5(a and b) and 8(1) of the Coasting Trade Act 1992.

member countries in North America. However, the then NAFTA cabotage policy failed to materialize because the United States was opposed to the idea of opening their coastal trade to foreign nations regardless of their regional connections.[119] Hence, the difference between Canadian and United States maritime cabotage law is the domestic shipbuilding requirement. Whereas ships built in foreign countries are prohibited from engaging in the coastwise trade of the United States, such foreign-built vessels can participate in the Canadian coasting trade.

## Nigeria: Coastal and Inland Shipping (Cabotage) Act No. 5 of 2003

Nigeria had no operative maritime cabotage law prior to 2004. Hence, the territorial sea of Nigeria was open to all. All vessels were free to participate in Nigeria's maritime cabotage trade and services regardless of who owned them, where they were built or registered and the nationalities of her crew.[120] The closest that Nigeria came to restricting maritime trade to her national instrumentalities of commerce was when it adopted the 40:40:20 cargo-sharing formula of the UNCTAD Liner Code.[121]

The Nigerian maritime sector is dominated by foreign vessels with foreign crews, to the disadvantage of indigenous shipowners and seafarers. This is particularly evident in the oil and gas industry. Therefore, enacting the Nigerian maritime Cabotage Act was heralded as the catalyst that would give indigenous shipowners an advantage over foreign shipowners in the maritime trade and services that occur in Nigerian territorial waters. However, many years after the Act was passed into law, it has failed to deliver on its objectives. Hence, Nigerian shipowners and seafarers complaint of being marginalized in Nigeria's coastal trade and services has triggered efforts to reform the ineffective Act.[122]

Nigerian maritime cabotage law is governed by the Coastal and Inland Shipping (Cabotage) Act, No. 5 of 2003 of the Laws of the Federation of Nigeria.[123] Other legislations that complement the Nigerian Cabotage Act are: the Merchant Shipping Act 2007, Nigerian Maritime Administration and Safety Agency (NIMASA) Act 2007, and Nigerian Oil and Gas Industry Content Development (Local Content) Act 2010.[124] Section 3 of the 2003 Coastal and Inland Shipping (Cabotage) Act states:

119 For more on this, see: J. Hodgson and M. Brooks, 'Towards A North American Cabotage Regime: A Canadian Perspective' [2007], *Canadian Journal of Transportation*, 1(1), 19–35.
120 For more on this, see: M. Igbokwe, 'Advocacy Paper for the promulgation of a Nigerian Maritime Cabotage Law: Draft Modalities for Implementation of Coastal and Inland Shipping (Cabotage) Act' (Nigerian Maritime Authority, 2001).
121 See: section 9 of National Shipping Policy Act Cap. 279 of the Laws of the Federation of Nigeria 1990. This act was formerly promulgated as the National Shipping Policy Decree No. 10 of 1987.
122 See: HB. 12.03.256. A Bill for An Act to Amend The Coastal and Inland Shipping (Cabotage) Act, No. 5 of 2003 and for Related Matters.
123 Enacted into Law on 30 April 2003 but came into force 1 May 2004.
124 See the 2007 maritime Cabotage Guidelines on the Implementation of Coast and Inland Shipping (Cabotage) Act, issued by the Federal Ministry of Transportation.

A vessel other than a vessel wholly owned and manned by a Nigerian citizen, built and registered in Nigeria shall not engage in the domestic coastal carriage of cargo and passengers within the Coastal, Territorial, Inland Waters, Island or any point within the waters of the Exclusive Economic Zone of Nigeria.[125]

Furthermore, rebuilt vessels can engage in coastal trade only if the entire rebuilding takes place in Nigeria. This includes the construction of any major components of the hull or superstructure of the vessel.[126] The cabotage law also covers maritime services such as towage and salvage operations. However, the strict provision of section 3 of the Act is tempered in later sections through the provision of waivers to foreign vessels.[127] The waiver provisions are generally abused and hence foreign vessels continue to gain unrestricted access to perform cabotage services.[128] The arbitrary use of the waiver mechanism contradicts the idea that waivers should only be used in exceptional cases. In Nigeria, the waiver provision introduces bureaucratic barriers and gives the minister of transport an unwarranted degree of discretionary authority. Furthermore, the lack of a framework like that of the EU to monitor and report periodically on the impact of the Cabotage Act means there is no basis for evaluating the effectiveness of the Act. Moreover, the success of Nigerian maritime cabotage law is hindered by lack of national capacity, the complacency of the regulator and lax implementation of the Cabotage Act. With regards to vessel ownership, section 23 of the Cabotage Act stipulates that vessels seeking to engage in cabotage trade and services must do so under one of the following ownership structures:

a   The Nigerian Ownership structure: The vessel is wholly and beneficially owned by Nigerian citizens, or Nigerian company, and all the shares in the vessel must be held by Nigerian citizens free from any encumbrance to any foreigner.
b   Bareboat Charter Structure: The charterer must be a Nigerian or a wholly owned Nigerian company, who has full control and management of the vessel. Where the vessel is financed, the terms of the charter must be more than five years.
c   Joint Venture Ownership Structure: A minimum of 60per cent of the shares of the ship owning company must be held freely by Nigerian Citizens. It appears that this joint venture structure contradicts the 'wholly owned' stipulation in section 3 of the Cabotage Act.

---

125 See also: section 6 of the 2003 Cabotage Act.
126 See: sections 4(1), 5, 8(1a) and 7 respectively of the 2003 Cabotage Act. This is similar to the built requirement of the Jones Act.
127 See: sections 9–12 and 14 of the Nigerian Maritime Cabotage Act 2003 for waiver and licence provisions respectively.
128 See section 21 of the Act, which prohibits foreign vessels without licence from trading in Nigerian coastal waters.

However, the above ownership structures are subject to sections 9–12 of the Coastal and Inland Shipping (Cabotage) Act. In addition, vessels undertaking maritime cabotage activities must comply with the applicable provisions of the Merchant Shipping Act 2007, which deals with shipping, registration, licensing of ships and other related matters in Nigeria. The new maritime cabotage amendment Bill attempts to redress the contentious issue surrounding the definition of a ship in the Cabotage Act.[129] However, the Bill creates a new loophole that would allow ineligible maritime cabotage operators to circumvent the Cabotage Act by providing maritime services 'via a foreign port'. The Bill appears to exclude the clause in the cabotage Act which prohibits foreign vessels from engaging in maritime cabotage in Nigerian territorial waters via a foreign port.[130] The consequences of excluding this clause is covered above in *United States v 250 Kegs of Nails.*[131]

The federal government introduced a new guideline to offer indigenous shipping interests more protection from foreign domination and to correct some of the negative impact of the Cabotage Act, including the inconsiderate granting of waivers. The guideline requires any vessel requiring a waiver to submit an application 60 days before her arrival in Nigeria's territorial waters. Thereafter, the maritime cabotage regulatory agency (NIMASA) shall publish a notice of cabotage waiver application on its website within 48 hours of receiving the application. The 'Notice' will request notifications of objections to be made within seven days by indigenous shipowners with the capacity to perform the maritime cabotage activity in question. In addition, all maintenance and repair of the vessel throughout the duration of the waiver must take place in Nigeria. Also, the guideline proposes a compulsory 2 per cent surcharge on vessels engaged in Nigeria's maritime cabotage and emphasizes the mandatory employment, training and use of Nigerian seafarers. The 2 per cent surcharge contributes to the Cabotage Vessel Financing Fund (CVFF) aimed at promoting the indigenous capacity on ship acquisition. However, the Nigerian Shipowners Association (NISA) has rejected the guideline and has demanded instead that the waiver clause be expunged from the Cabotage Act.

One of the biggest issues facing Nigerian maritime cabotage law is that foreign shipowners seek to circumvent it by not restricting their maritime activities to Nigerian territorial waters. These foreign shipowners set up their operations in a triangular dimension to trade across West African waters. Hence, although the bulk of their activities occur within the Nigerian territorial waters, this strategy ensures that those activities are outside the ambit of the Nigerian cabotage law.[132]

---

129 See the decision in: *Noble Drilling v NIMASA and Minister of Transport* [2008]. FHC/L/CS/78/2008.
130 See: sections 2(a) to 2(c) of Nigerian Inland and Coastal Shipping (Cabotage) Act 2003.
131 52 F. 231 (S.D. Cal. 1892), 61 F. 410 (9th Cir. 1894).
132 See the decision of the Federal High Court of Nigeria in *ISAN and Pokat v. MBX*, where this strategy was employed to good effect.

There are several controversies surrounding the maritime Cabotage Act since it came into force in 2004. Many of these have ended up in court where the Cabotage Act has been tested and found to be lacking the necessary robustness to combat the challenges for which it was enacted. We shall now assess some of these judicial decisions.

## *Judicial decisions from Nigerian cabotage law*

### *ISAN and Pokat v. MBX[133]*

This was an early maritime cabotage case to reach the Nigerian courts. The indigenous shipowners, who hoped in vain to benefit from the Cabotage Act, had organized themselves as vigilantes. Their aim was to monitor the Nigerian coastal waters for foreign vessels that provide maritime transport services in Nigerian territorial waters. In this case, the plaintiffs – the Indigenous Shipowners Association of Nigeria (ISAN) and Pokat Nigeria Limited, an indigenous shipping company – had before a Nigerian Federal High Court accused a foreign shipping company, MBX Shipping Limited of St. Vincent and Grenades, of using its foreign vessel, *MT Markhambet*, to transport petroleum product between points in the Nigerian coastal waters. The plaintiffs alleged that the defendant's act contravened several provisions of the Nigerian Inland and Coastal Shipping (Cabotage) Act.[134] The vessel was alleged to have lifted 10,000 litres of petroleum products from a point within Nigerian coastal waters to Ibafon petroleum products jetty in Apapa, Lagos. Therefore, the plaintiffs requested the court to detain the vessel and put her in the custody of the Admiralty Marshal of the Federal High Court. This request was granted and an interim injunction was issued to restrain the defendants from obtaining the port clearance with which the ship could escape from Nigerian jurisdiction.[135]

Amongst several alleged breaches, the plaintiffs relied heavily on the breach of section 5 of the Cabotage Act. The section reserves carriage of petroleum products and the provision of ancillary services within Nigerian territorial waters to vessels whose beneficial ownership resides wholly in a Nigerian citizen.[136] The

---

133 Suit No. FHC/L/CS/703/2009.
134 Specifically, it was alleged that the defendant and her vessel contravened sections 2,3,5,9,11,12,15,22,23,29,33 of the Nigerian Inland and Coastal Shipping (Cabotage) Act 2003.
135 Section 33 of the Coastal and Inland Shipping (Cabotage) Act stipulates that: Notwithstanding the provisions of any other laws, no port clearance-shall be granted to a vessel engaged in domestic coastal shipping unless the owner, charterer, master or agent satisfies the proper customs or such other authority authorized to issue port clearance that the vessel is licensed to engage in domestic shipping or has the prescribed waiver.
136 Section 5 of the Coastal and Inland Shipping (Cabotage) Act, No. 5 of 2003 of the Laws of the Federation of Nigeria, states: 'A vessel, tug or barge of whatever type other than a vessel, tug and barge whose beneficial ownership resides wholly in a Nigeria citizen shall not engage in the carriage or materials or supply services to and

defendant, MBX Shipping Ltd, denied the accusation and claimed that its vessel loaded the said petroleum product in a foreign country (Cotonou – Republic of Benin) and not in Nigeria. Hence, the company and its vessel could not be said to have breached the Nigerian Cabotage Act.

The Court held that the defendant did not contravene the Cabotage Act because the overwhelming evidence on the bill of loading indicated that the vessel was loaded outside Nigerian waters in Cotonou (Benin Republic) and not within the territorial waters of Nigeria. The decision of the court undermined the fact that there was no refinery in Cotonou at that time to warrant the loading of petroleum product from that country. Hence, it was not possible for the vessel to load at the purported loading port. Furthermore, this decision greatly undermined the authority and impact of the Coastal and Inland Shipping (Cabotage) Act.

Since there is no known crude oil refinery in Cotonou, it would appear that a mother vessel loaded the petroleum cargo originally at a port in Nigeria and sailed outside of the Nigerian coastal boundary.[137] This mother vessel then anchored near Nigerian waters to transfer her cargo to the smaller vessel (*MT Markhambet*), which then carried the cargo of petroleum product from that boundary point back to Nigeria.[138] A combination of this strategy and the lack of evidence by the plaintiff gave the court no option than to arrive at the unpopular decision.

The court decided that the reach of the operative maritime cabotage law in Nigeria extends only as far as her territorial waters. By the court's reasoning, the effective point of loading was for all purposes outside the legal territory of the Nigerian waters regardless of the defendants' disingenuous overall intent.[139] However, it appears that in making this ruling, the court failed to take into consideration the express provisions of sections 2(a) to 2(c) of the Coastal and Inland Shipping (Cabotage) Act, which categorically prohibit the use of a foreign port to circumvent the Act. This case is a classic demonstration of how foreign shipowners set up their operations in a triangular dimension with the sole intention of circumventing the Coastal and Inland Shipping (Cabotage) Act.[140]

from oil rigs, platforms and installations or the carriage of petroleum products between oil rigs, platforms and installations whether offshore or onshore or within any ports or points in Nigerian waters'.

137 See: Commission of the European Communities v Kingdom of Spain Case C-323/03 [2006] ECR I-2161, 9 March 2006. In this case, a port has been defined as encompassing any infrastructure (be it temporary or small scale) that serves as a terminal for the loading and discharging of cargo for carriage by sea.

138 See: *United States v. 250 Kegs of Nails* [1892]. 52 F. 231 (S.D. Cal. 1892), 61 F. 410 (9th Cir. 1894). See also: *American Maritime Association v. Blumenthal* [1978] 590 F. 2d 1156 (1978). District of Columbia Circuit. See also: the decision of the District Court; 458 F. Supp. 849 (1977).

139 See: *United States v. 250 Kegs of Nails*. 52 F. 231 (S.D. Cal. 1892), 61 F. 410 (9th Cir. 1894).

140 There have since been suggestions that the lack of evidence which hampered the plaintiff's argument in Court was caused by the intentional lack of cooperation by the national maritime regulatory body NIMASA.

*Noble Drilling v. NIMASA and Minister of Transport*[141]

This case attempted to clarify sections 2, 5 and 22(5) of the Coastal and Inland Shipping (Cabotage) Act, No. 5 of 2003. The plaintiff, an offshore drilling contractor operating in Nigeria, disagreed with the given definition of a ship.[142] The plaintiff argued that offshore drilling did not constitute maritime cabotage activity, pursuant to the relevant provisions of the Coastal and Inland Shipping (Cabotage) Act. The defendant is the regulating authority on maritime cabotage in Nigeria, claimed that section 2 of the Cabotage Act applies effectively to all maritime-related commercial activities occurring on, in or under Nigerian waters. Therefore, the relevant questions for the court were:

a   Whether drilling operations fell within the definition of maritime cabotage under the Coastal and Inland Shipping (Cabotage) Act, No. 5 of 2003.
b   Whether, upon the proper interpretation of section 2 of the Coastal and Inland Shipping (Cabotage) Act, drilling rigs fell within the definition of a vessel as contained in the Act.

In its decision, the Court ruled that a drilling rig is not a vessel as contemplated by section 2 of the Coastal and Inland Shipping (Cabotage) Act. The ratio decidendi for this decision was that there was no specific or express mention of a drilling rig under section 22(5) of the Act for cabotage registration. The Court argued further that under section 2 of the Act, the process of navigation in which a vessel must be engaged was a horizontal movement. Hence, a drilling rig that operates in a vertical movement, bringing oil from the sub-sea to the surface of the sea, cannot be classified as a vessel for the purposes of the Nigerian cabotage law.[143]

The problem with the narrow interpretation of the Act preferred by the court is that it undermines the objective of setting up cabotage legislation in the first place. Perhaps, an awareness of the different approach adopted in other jurisdictions might have yielded a different result. For instance, in the Ley de Navegación y Comercio Marítimos 2006, which is the Mexican equivalent of the Nigerian Coastal and Inland Shipping (Cabotage) Act, a maritime object is defined broadly for the purpose of maritime cabotage. The Ley de Navegación defines a ship as including:

141  Suit No. FHC/L/CS/78/2008.
142  Section 2 of the Coastal and Inland Shipping (Cabotage) Act defines a vessel as including any description of vessel, ship, boat, hovercraft or craft, including air cushion vehicles and dynamically supported craft, designed, used or capable of being used solely or partly for marine navigation and used for the carriage on, through or under water of persons or property without regard to method or lack of propulsion.
143  However, section 444 of the Merchant Shipping Act 2007, section 26 of the Admiralty Jurisdiction Act 1991 and section 22(5m) of the Cabotage Act suggest that sections 2 and 22(5) of the Cabotage Act should be construed to include drilling rig in the Act's definition of 'vessels'. The defendants have since appealed the decision.

any construction designed to navigate over or under waterways or any other floating or fixed structure which, without having been designed and built to sail or navigate, is susceptible of being moved over water by its own means or by a vessel, or built on water, to fulfil its operational purposes.[144]

One disagrees with the court's ruling in this case because prima facie, section 22(5)(m) of the Act expressly provides that 'any other craft or vessel used for carriage on, through or underwater of persons, property or any substance whatsoever' should be subjected to the cabotage registration. Moreover, even without the express provisions of section 22(5)(m) of the Act, one can argue that section 22(5)(m) of the Act should be regarded as an indicative rather than an exhaustive list.[145]

## *Polmaz Limited v. Nigerian National Petroleum Corporation*[146]

In this case, the court considered the standing of an indigenous shipping company to seek the court's interpretation of relevant provisions of the Coastal and Inland Shipping (Cabotage) Act. The plaintiff, Polmaz Limited, brought an action in the Lagos Federal High Court against the Nigerian National Petroleum Corporation (NNPC) and eight other defendants. They were accused of engaging in business with foreign vessels within Nigerian coastal waters contrary to the provisions of the Coastal and Inland Shipping (Cabotage) Act. The plaintiff outlined the grounds for its grievance before the court as follows:

a  The provisions of the Cabotage Act and the Merchant Shipping Act preclude foreign vessels not registered in Nigeria from engaging in domestic coastal trade.
b  The plaintiff was a Nigerian company engaged in the shipping business in Nigeria, but has been deprived of business opportunities through the actions of the defendants.
c  The Cabotage Act was enacted to promote business opportunities for indigenous shipping companies, of which it qualified.
d  NIMASA, which has been vested with the power by the minister of transport to ensure compliance with the Cabotage Act, had failed to perform its statutory duty. Thus, jeopardizing the plaintiff's business interests.

Some of the defendants filed a preliminary objection to the plaintiff's application on the basis that the plaintiff lacked the standing to commence and maintain the action. They contended that the Coastal and Inland Shipping (Cabotage) Act and the Nigerian Maritime Administration and Safety Agency (NIMASA) Act vest the

---

144 Article 2(iv) and (v) of Ley de Navegación y Comercio Marítimos 2006.
145 See the decision in: *Commission v. Hellenic Republic*, Case C-251/04 [2007] ECR I–67 (Second Chamber).
146 FHC/L/CS/1270/13.

power to enforce infractions solely on the Minister of Transport through NIMASA. Therefore, the plaintiff lacked the *locus standi* to pursue this action.

The relevant sections of the legislations in this case are: section 30(1) of the Coastal and Inland Shipping (Cabotage) Act, No. 5 of 2003, and section 22(1)(L) of the NIMASA Act, both of which set out the relevant statutory enforcement provisions.[147]

Section 30(1) of the Coastal and Inland Shipping (Cabotage) Act, stipulates that: 'The Minister shall immediately after the commencement of this Act create an enforcement unit within the National Maritime Authority (now NIMASA) with appropriate operational guidelines and shall designate the officers in that unit as enforcement officers.'

Section 22(1)(L) of the NIMASA Act states similarly that 'the functions and duties of the Agency shall be to enforce and administer the provisions of the Nigerian Cabotage Act 2003'. These provisions seem to suggest that the power to enforce the Coastal and Inland Shipping (Cabotage) Act resides firstly with the minister of transport, who acts through NIMASA, and secondly with NIMASA as the national regulating agency.

In its ruling, the court held that a party has a right to approach the court for interpretation of a statute through an originating summons and to seek declaratory relief, irrespective of whether such relief would confer any benefit to that party.[148] Therefore, the courts would wilfully interpret the provisions of the Coastal and Inland Shipping (Cabotage) Act to confer *locus standi* on indigenous shipowners so that they have unhindered access to the courts. This would encourage them to register any infractions of the Nigerian Cabotage Act that impinge on the economic fortunes of Nigerians. Further to this, the court submitted that the statement in the Act's recital states that it is 'An Act to restrict the use of foreign vessels in domestic coastal trade, to promote the development of indigenous tonnage and establish a cabotage vessel financing fund and related matters.'

Therefore, it can be deduced that the Coastal and Inland Shipping (Cabotage) Act was not designed to sabotage indigenous vessel owners. Rather, it was promulgated to cure the mischief and correct the imbalance faced by indigenous shipowners in a similar position to the plaintiff.[149]

Thus, the court decided that the provision of an enforcement unit by a minister of transport would not prevent a litigant with valid grievance from approaching the court for interpretation of the law, regardless of whether it confers any benefit to him. This decision has clarified the right of a party to be heard in Nigeria, particularly with regards to the administration of the Coastal and Inland Shipping

---

147 The Nigerian Maritime Administration and Safety Agency Act 2007 was assented to on 25 May 2007.

148 The court reasoned that while the reliefs claimed were important in the determination of jurisdiction, it had to be careful in invoking standing with regard to an issue relating purely to an originating summons filed to construe a legal provision and followed up with declaratory relief.

149 See the Recital at the very beginning of the Coastal and Inland Shipping (Cabotage) Act, No. 5 of 2003 of the Laws of the Federation of Nigeria.

(Cabotage) Act. As a result, persons other than the minister of transport can approach the court where the minister fails to ensure compliance with the Cabotage Act.[150]

## Analysis of Nigerian maritime cabotage law

In theory, Nigeria has since 2004 adopted a protectionist maritime cabotage law and policy similar to that of the United States The objective of the Coastal and Inland Shipping (Cabotage) Act is to stimulate the development of indigenous capacity in the Nigerian maritime sector. This development ranges from vessel construction to maritime business entrepreneurship. However, Nigeria as a developing country lacks the capacity with regard to relevant infrastructures and expertise to apply such a protectionist approach. The economic development agenda of the kind envisaged in enacting the Coastal and Inland Shipping (Cabotage) Act illustrates the importance of the theory of developmental sovereignty.

Nigeria has around thirteen seaports and several commercial cities that rely on the inefficient transport network system to move cargo. The Lagos seaports are the busiest because the city is the commercial hub of Nigeria and the destination port of choice for most foreign vessels on international voyages. This situation should generate opportunities for domestic shipowners to transport containers and other cargo destined for other commercial cities in the country. However, this is not the case as containers destined for these other commercial cities are carried by land on trucks. The immediate problems with land transportation are that it is more expensive than sea transport, more time consuming and increases air and noise pollution.[151]

Furthermore, apart from the unavailability of domestic vessels that reach international standard, there is the issue of non-navigable seaways linking the other seaports in Nigeria. Both seaports and seaways need dredging to facilitate sea transport around the country, and to allow domestic vessels when they become available to serve the domestic maritime sector better.

One of the fallouts from Nigeria's maritime Coastal and Inland Shipping (Cabotage) Act appears to be that indigenous shipowners are only interested in the wet market, as demonstrated by all the case law considered above. Hence, the many opportunities available in other shipping markets are not explored. Finally, the Coastal and Inland Shipping (Cabotage) Act is fraught with several challenging issues. For instance, the Act requires that vessels seeking to engage in the

150 See: E. Akabogu, 'Nigeria: Aggrieved Ship Owners Can Bring Action to Enforce Cabotage Claims', Akabogu & Associates, 6 February 2015.
151 For a reflection on the View of the Nigerian Government on the state of her maritime sector and the impact of the Nigerian Maritime Cabotage Act, see: Ngozi Okonjo-Iweala's speech at the Presidential Retreat on 'Maritime Safety: Harnessing the Potential of Nigeria's Maritime Sector for Sustainable Economic Development'. Held 23 July 2012 in Abuja.

Nigerian coasting trade must be built in Nigeria. This is a requirement that cannot be satisfied currently due to lack of technical and infrastructural capacity.

## Indonesia: Maritime Law No.17 of 2008

Indonesia is the world's largest archipelago nation with 17,000 islands and a long maritime tradition going back to the fifth century 'tributary trade' .[152] Hence, it has experimented with deregulation and re-regulation of her maritime cabotage policies but it now operates a protectionist maritime cabotage approach that is regulated through a combination of a cabotage law and several government and ministerial decrees.

Indonesia enforced a protectionist maritime cabotage policy for the first time in the mid-1970s. This protectionist measure lasted until the 1985 government deregulation exercise.[153] At that time, the Indonesian maritime cabotage policy was more protectionist than those of many other maritime countries. This was because the scope of Indonesia's maritime cabotage law extended into inter-regional shipping, including Bangkok and parts of Cambodia.[154] It was the 1985 Presidential Instruction that opened up Indonesian ports to foreign ships by deregulating customs and relaxing trans-shipment controls.[155] This deregulation exercise caused the collapse of the protectionist trade agreement between the Indonesian National Shipowners Association and Singapore Shipowners Association (INSA–SSA Agreement).[156] Although Article 5 of government regulation PP17/1988 reserved coastal trades for Indonesian flag vessels, maritime cabotage was significantly weakened because foreign vessels could trade between Indonesian ports providing they appointed a local agent, which did not need to be an Indonesian company.[157] Also, regulation PP17/1988 made it easier to charter foreign vessels under a simplified licence system for coastal trades in the absence of

152 G. Tibbetts, 'Arab Navigation in the Archipelago', in T. Hellwig and E. Tagliacozzo (eds), *The Indonesia Reader: History, Culture, Politics* (Duke University Press 2009, pp. 48–53. 'Tributary trade' was the practice during the 5th and 6th centuries whereby foreign merchants from afar used Indonesia as their safe base before sailing on to China with the emperors' barbarian vassals. This was at a time when China was yet to undertake long voyages overseas, hence they had to rely on foreign shipping for their imports.

153 For more on this, see: D. Howard, 'The 2008 Shipping Law: Deregulation or Re-regulation?' [2008], *Bulletin of Indonesian Economic Studies*, 44(3), pp. 383–406.

154 For a related discussion, see: M. Brooks, *Fleet Development and the Control of Shipping in Southeast Asia* (Institute of Southeast Asian Studies 1985).

155 See: Inpres 4/1985 on 'Policy on the Flow of Goods to Support Economic Activities'. It must be noted that a Presidential Instruction does not carry the same weight as a legislative instrument.

156 See: PDP Australia Pty Ltd and Meyrick & Associates, 2005, 'Promoting Efficient and Competitive Intra – ASEAN Shipping Services – Indonesia Country Report' (Final Report). The trade agreement allowed Singapore and Indonesia to share trade between the two countries.

157 See: V. Bellamy, 'The Implementation of Cabotage Principle in Indonesia', *HG.Org Legal Resources* (Jakarta, 22 August 2010).

suitable Indonesian flagged vessels.[158] However, using chartered foreign vessels for cabotage services in Indonesia under regulation PP17/1988 was subject to the proviso that foreign vessels on long-term charters must ensure that the crew consists of at least 50 per cent Indonesian nationals after six months. Furthermore, Law 21/1992 on shipping was enacted and it brought along with it strong regulatory powers.[159] It appeared to support further protectionist maritime legislation in Indonesia and encouraged the application of maritime cabotage law, albeit with the option to opt out. It required the use of vessels flying the Indonesian flag for maritime trade and services in Indonesia's territorial waters. However, it offered that cabotage law could be suspended if Indonesian-flagged vessels were inadequate for its coastal trade.

Government Regulation 82/1999 introduced a more stringent version of a protectionist maritime cabotage law. Article 3 of Regulation 82/1999 stipulated that domestic cargo be carried in Indonesian-flagged vessels by Indonesian companies between Indonesian ports. Furthermore, Article 4 of PP 82/1999 instructed that foreign vessels could only be used for domestic coastal trading when Indonesian-flagged vessels were not available to perform the required service.[160] However, even the exceptional use of such foreign vessels under PP 82/1999 was subject to the following caveats:

a   The foreign vessel must be on a lease or charter by an Indonesian shipping company.
b   The foreign vessels had to be classed in a classification society recognised by the Indonesian government.[161]

The PP 82/1999 was boosted further by the Presidential Instruction of 2005 on the Development of the National Shipping Industry (Inpres 5/2005). Also, Article 3 of Ministerial Decree 71/2005 protects the maritime cabotage law principles enshrined in Inpres 5/2005. Ministerial Decree 71/2005 stipulated that a stringent new law should be implemented ahead of schedule in the event that there was an adequate supply of Indonesian vessels.[162] Therefore, the Presidential Instruction of 2005 formed the basis for enacting Law 17 of 2008 on shipping, which presently

---

158 Government Regulation (PP) 17/1988. Maintenance and Operation of Sea Transport. This replaced the PP2/1969.
159 Enacted in 1992 and repealing the colonial Shipping Law 1936.
160 See: N. Kurniasari, 'Connecting Indonesia's Maritime Cabotage and the 1982 United Nations Convention on the Law of the Sea' [2011], *Indonesian Journal of International Law*, 8(4), 716–734.
161 See articles 3 and 4 of Government Regulation 82/1999 on Sea Transport. This regulation repealed Government Regulation 17/1988.
162 The Indonesian government's philosophy to continue to develop their maritime sector through protectionist mechanisms to continue to promote and empower domestic indigenous interests was echoed more recently when the new Indonesian president, Joko Widodo, was sworn into office. See: V. Shekhar and J. Liow, *Indonesia as a Maritime Power: Jokowi's Vision, Strategies, and Obstacles Ahead* (Brookings Institution Press 2014).

regulates maritime cabotage in Indonesia.[163] Furthermore, Government Regulation 20/2010 was promulgated to implement Law 17/2008. The relevant provisions of Law 17 of 2008 are:

- Article 8(1), which states: 'All domestic activities of sea transportation must be carried by Indonesian shipping companies employing Indonesian flagged vessels and manned by Indonesian citizens.'
- Article 8(2) stipulates that: Foreign ships are prohibited from carrying passengers and/or goods between islands and between ports within Indonesian territorial waters.

Vessels that engage in the Indonesian coastal trade must be registered in Indonesia and must be owned by Indonesian citizens or business entities domiciled in Indonesia.[164] This is in addition to the requirement that, where the business is a joint venture, the foreign investment is limited to a maximum of 49 per cent ownership.[165] However, in what appears to be a contradiction, Article 6 of Indonesian Government Regulation No. 20 of 1994 permits up to 95 per cent of foreign investment in Indonesian companies. Also, the new legal instrument makes provisions for waivers and an annual licence system in the event that a suitably qualified Indonesian vessel is unavailable.[166]

Although Law 17 of 2008 came into force in 2011, the Indonesian oil and gas sector was exempted from the immediate application of the new protectionist maritime cabotage law. The was to avoid disrupting operations in a sector that is critical to the functioning of the Indonesian economy.[167] As the oil and gas offshore production sector depends on foreign technical expertise, the government set an oil production target in 2012 of one million barrels per day to assess its domestic capacity to take control of the oil and gas sector when the maritime cabotage law finally applies.[168] However, Government Regulation 22/2011 was promulgated to delay the implementation of Law 17 of 2008 with regard to some offshore oil and gas vessels. The vessels covered by the exemption are those in 'Category C' of the offshore sector pursuant to Law 17/ 2008.[169]

---

163 Law 17 of 2008 repealed Law 21/1992.
164 See Article 158 of Law 17 of 2008.
165 See Presidential Instruction 77/2007 and Presidential Instruction 117/2007 on Foreign Investment.
166 See Article 29 of Law 17 of 2008, which deals with vessels wholly owned or fully crewed by Indonesian citizens and vessels built in Indonesia.
167 See the broader discussion of the issue: V. Shekhar and J. Liow, *Indonesia as a Maritime Power: Jokowi's Vision, Strategies, and Obstacles Ahead* (Brookings Institution Press 2014).
168 See: International Energy Agency, 'Energy Supply Security: Emergency Response of Partner Countries 2014 – Indonesia' (OECD/IEA Publications, 2014), p. 8.
169 The vessels in category C include: jack-up rig, semi-submersible rig, drilling vessels, pipe/cable laying vessels and 3-D seismic vessels.

Due to this exemption, Government Regulation 22/2011 was issued to amend Government Regulation 20/2010.[170]

Thus, Article 206(a) of Government Regulation 22/2011 stipulates that a foreign vessel can conduct activities exclusive of passenger and/or goods transportation in Indonesian waters if there are insufficient or unavailable Indonesian-flag vessels to provide the required service.[171] However, such foreign vessels are obligated to obtain a permit or licence before commencing operations in Indonesian coastal waters.[172] In addition, Ministerial Regulation 48 of 2011 was issued to implement further the principles of the Indonesian maritime cabotage law as stipulated in Government Regulation No. 22 of 2011. Article 2(1) of Ministerial Regulation 48/2011 states:

> Foreign ships can perform other activities that do not include passenger transport activities and/or goods in the domestic sea freight activities in Indonesian waters as long as the Indonesian flagged vessels are not yet available or not sufficiently available.

Ministerial Regulation 48 strictly regulates the procedures and requirements for the use of foreign-flagged vessels in offshore oil and gas activities. This includes the duration of each operation, the permit procedures and what activities are covered by the permit. There is nonetheless an important caveat: the permit may only be granted in the event of non-availability or insufficient supply of Indonesian-flagged vessels.[173] Furthermore, Ministerial Regulation 48/2011 on maritime cabotage has been revised into Regulation 10/2014. This new regulation eliminates offshore support vessels (OSV) from the list of vessels that foreign companies were allowed to operate. In addition, foreign dredging ships with a capacity less than five thousand gross tonnage (GT) that were allowed previously to engage in Indonesia's coastal trade and services can no longer do so under the new Regulation No. 10/2014. Such foreign dredging ships must now be over five thousand gross tonnage before they are permitted to provide maritime cabotage services in Indonesia. Furthermore, the exemptions for oil and gas survey vessels, offshore constructions vessels, underwater works, dredging, and salvage vessels expired at the end of 2014. The exemptions for jack-up rigs, semi-submersibles,

---

170 GR 20/2010 was the implementing regulation for Law 17/2008, which was supposed to apply the cabotage principle to all ships engaged in all commercial maritime activities in Indonesia's territorial waters by 7 May 2011. As a result of the exemption of certain offshore oil and gas vessels, GR 22/2011 had to be issued to amend GR 20/2010 on the application dates of cabotage principles on these offshore oil and gas vessels.

171 The activities outside passenger and/goods contemplated by GR 22/2011 include: oil and gas survey, drilling, offshore construction, supports for offshore operation, dredging, salvage and underwater services.

172 See Article 29 of Law 17 of 2008 of the Republic of Indonesia.

173 For more on this, see: M. Cefali, *Oil and Gas Industry: An Exception in Newly Effective Indonesian Cabotage Regulation* (MA Law 2011).

deep-water drillships and tender-assist and swamp bridge rigs were expected to expire at the end of 2015.[174]

After experimenting with a liberal approach, Indonesia has returned to the protectionist approach of maritime cabotage with the exemption of the domestic oil and gas sector. The protectionist maritime cabotage approach has always been canvassed for by the INSA because it argues that a liberal maritime cabotage approach is a dangerous economic policy for Indonesia. INSA insists that lessons should be learnt from the collapse of the INSA-SSA Agreement, which was caused by the liberal Inpres 4/1985. The collapse of this private sector bilateral agreement led to a severe disruption of Indonesian market share and caused domestic ship operators to lose about US$11 billion of income to foreign carriers and operators.[175] Since the implementation of the maritime cabotage law of 2005, the number of Indonesian-flagged ships has doubled to over 12,000 ships. This is because the new maritime cabotage law has encouraged existing shipowners to expand and new players to enter the industry.[176] Statistics from INSA show that the number of Indonesian vessels rose from 6,041 in 2005 to 12,536 by the middle of 2013. The rising number of vessels has also increased capacity from 5.67 million gross tonnage (GT) in 2005 to 17.89 million GT in 2013.[177] Indigenous shipowners and operators are confident that such growth is sustainable over a long period.

The Indonesian maritime cabotage law has become an important driver in the development of its maritime sector. As a result, Indonesia is positioned to become the regional shipping and transhipment hub.[178] To consolidate their regional advantage, the Ministry of Energy and Mineral Resources introduced Regulation 15/2013 in 2013.[179] The new regulation codifies oil and gas local content guidelines and tightens local content requirements for upstream oil and gas procurement by increasing the minimum local content target.[180] The immediate and substantial change imposed by Regulation 15/2013 was increasing the minimum local content for companies offering shipping services for projects in the oil and gas sector. These companies are now required to source 75 per cent of their components locally, up from 35 per cent previously. Also, the local content

174 At the end of 2015, the exemptions under Regulation No 10/2014 were scheduled for review. This was to assess what vessels are still in need of permits. See tables 9.2 and 9.3 for the exemption deadlines as detailed by the Indonesian Ministry of Transport.
175 For more on this, see: PDP Australia Pty Ltd and Meyrick & Associates, 'Promoting Efficient and Competitive Intra-ASEAN Shipping Services: The Philippines Country Report', Final Report (March 2005).
176 See: V. Wee, 'INSA sees Local Owners Dominating Offshore by 2015', *Seatrade Global* (Jakarta, 14 April 2014).
177 Indonesian National Shipowners Association, 'The Development of Container Traffic Carried By Domestic Vessels' (INSA, 2013).
178 See: V. Shekhar and J. Liow, *Indonesia as a Maritime Power: Jokowi's Vision, Strategies, and Obstacles Ahead* (Brookings Institution Press 2014).
179 Ministry of Energy and Mineral Resources (MEMR) Regulation No. 15 of 2013.
180 See: Pedoman Tata Kerja (PTK 007) – For Regulatory Guideline.

*Table 9.1* Previous maritime cabotage exemption deadlines in Indonesia as per MOT Regulation 48/2011

| Vessel type | Deadline |
|---|---|
| **Oil & gas survey:** | |
| a) Seismic survey | December 2014 |
| b) Geographical survey | December 2014 |
| c) Geotechnical survey | December 2014 |
| **Drilling:** | |
| a) Jack-up rig | December 2015 |
| b) Semi-submersible rig | December 2015 |
| c) Deep water drillship | December 2015 |
| d) Tender-assist rig | December 2015 |
| e) Swamp-barge rig | December 2015 |
| **Offshore Construction:** | |
| a) Derrick/crane, pipe/cable/subsea umbilical riser flexible (SURF) laying barge/vessel | December 2013 |
| b) Driving support vessel | December 2013 |
| **Offshore Operation support:** | |
| a) AHTS >5000bhp with DP ($DP_2/DP_3$) | December 2012 |
| b) PSV | December 2012 |
| **Dredging:** | |
| a) Drag-head suction hopper dredger | December 2013 |
| b) Trailing suction hopper dredger | December 2013 |

*Table 9.2* Revised maritime cabotage exemption deadlines in Indonesia as per MOT Regulation 10/2014

| Vessel type | Deadline |
|---|---|
| **Oil & gas survey:** | |
| a) Seismic survey | December 2014 |
| b) Geographical survey | December 2014 |
| c) Geotechnical survey | December 2014 |
| **Drilling:** | |
| a) Jack-up rig | December 2015 |
| b) Semi-submersible rig | December 2015 |
| c) Deep water drillship | December 2015 |
| d) Tender-assist rig | December 2015 |
| e) Swamp-barge rig | December 2015 |

*(Continued)*

*Table 9.2  (Cont.)*

| Vessel type | Deadline |
| --- | --- |
| **Offshore Construction:** | |
| a) Derrick/crane, pipe/cable/subsea umbilical riser flexible (SURF) laying barge/vessel | December 2014 |
| **Dredging:** | |
| a) Drag-head suction hopper dredger of more than 5,000 m3 | December 2014 |
| b) Trailing suction hopper dredger of more than 5,000 m3 | December 2014 |
| **Salvaging and underwater works:** | |
| a) Heavy floating cranes heavier than 300 tonnes | December 2014 |
| b) Heavy crane barges heavier than 300 tonnes | December 2014 |

minimum for all offshore oil and gas 'Engineering Procurement Construction & Infrastructure' (EPCI) projects and offshore drilling activities have been increased from 35 per cent to 45 per cent. These amendments only come into effect after 2016 and so it is a little early to fully assess its impact.[181] The local content target for offshore seismic activities has remained, surprisingly, at the already high 35 per cent, despite concerns that there is an acute lack of local content capacity and expertise in that field.[182] Other stipulations imposed by the new regulation include a requirement for 'domestic company' and two-thirds board representation accompanied by voting and management rights attached to shares.

The new protectionist maritime cabotage law in Indonesia has stimulated the domestic shipbuilding industry, which now has the capacity to build 19 different types of offshore vessel. The adoption of a measured but robust strategy that permits some flexibility and has fixed exemption deadlines corresponding with when the domestic industry is expected to develop enough capacity to support the oil and gas sector appears to be successful.[183] Nevertheless, the continued success of this strategy depends on whether the domestic shipping industry will acquire the requisite technical expertise to build and maintain sophisticated offshore vessels within the exemption period.

181 See: the text of Ministry of Energy and Mineral Resources (MEMR) Regulation 15/ 2013.
182 See: Global Business Guide Indonesia, 'Going Local: Understanding Indonesia's Local Content RequirementJakarta, 2014).
183 See Table 9.3, which is the revised exemption timetable for the application of the new protectionist maritime cabotage law in Indonesia to the oil and gas sector. This revised timetable became necessary when it became obvious that the domestic maritime sector was not ready to sustain its oil and gas sector as per MOT Regulation 48/2011.

# Japan: Ship Law No. 46 of 1899

Japan is a country with many islands, and this highlights the importance of maritime transport services in Japan. As a shipbuilding nation, Japan has traditionally been protectionist. Its protectionist regulations extend beyond its maritime industry to other sectors of the Japanese economy such as mining and aeronautics. Furthermore, the Japanese maritime cabotage law prohibits financing of vessels with foreign capital.[184] Foreign vessels are prohibited from participating in maritime activities in Japanese waters except on rare occasions when exemptions are made based on reciprocity or national agreements.

In 1912, the issue of whether British vessels were allowed to compete with Japanese ships in the coasting trade of Japan was raised in the British House of Commons.[185] It was also enquired whether Japanese ships were subject to any restrictions in respect of the British-Indian coasting trade.[186] However, under Article 21 of the third Anglo-Japanese Treaty of Commerce and Navigation of 1911, the coasting trade of the two countries was exempt from the provisions of the Treaty and retained in the legislative instruments of the respective countries.[187] There are suggestions that it was only in 1910 that Japan adopted the maritime cabotage policy of excluding foreign vessels from her coasting trade.[188] However, there is documented evidence that indicates that a protectionist maritime cabotage approach may have been adopted long before then. In 1636, all Japanese seaports apart from the port of Nagasaki were closed to foreign vessels. This confined the bulk of Japanese shipping to coastal routes using small-sized traditional wooden vessels. Furthermore, this led to the emergence of the common carrier and the evolution of the liner services. However, in 1853, Japan was ordered by the United States to open her coastal trade to vessels of foreign nations. This ultimatum caused disagreement within the Japanese government. Opinions were divided on how the Japanese maritime sector would benefit from a liberal policy and the impact that a liberal policy would have on indigenous shipowners.[189]

In a letter to Mitsubishi employees in 1876, the president of Mitsubishi, Iwasaki Yataro advocated for reserving coastal trade to indigenous shipowners. Yataro

184 T. Kvinge and A. Odegard, 'Protectionism or Legitimate Protection? On Public Regulation of Pay and Working Conditions in Norwegian Maritime Cabotage' (FAFO Report, 2010).
185 House of Commons, 'Japanese Ships (Coasting Trade)', Hansard 39, 1838–1839. 20 June 1912.
186 The British government had huge influence on Indian coasting trade. See: Indian Coasting Trade Act No. 5 of 1850 (An Act for Freedom of the Coasting Trade of India) passed by the Governor-General of India in Council on 5 March 1850.
187 The first Anglo-Japanese Treaty was signed in London on 30 January 1902 by Lord Lansdowne (British foreign secretary) and Hayashi Tadasu (Japanese minister in London). The Treaty was renewed and expanded in scope twice, in 1905 and 1911, before its demise in 1921, and was officially terminated in 1923.
188 See: S. Haji, *Economics of Shipping: A Study in Applied Economics* (Tata 1924), p. 355.
189 T. Chida and P. Davies, *The Japanese Shipping and Shipbuilding Industries: A History of their Modern Growth* (2nd edn, Bloomsbury Publishing 2012).

claimed that coastal trade was too important an issue to be handed over to the control of foreigners.[190] He argued that allowing the right of coastal trade to fall into the hands of foreigners in peacetime would mean loss of business and employment for Japanese people. Furthermore, ceding the coastal right to foreigners in wartime meant yielding the vital right to gather information to foreigners. From his perspective, this was tantamount to abandoning the rights of Japan as an independent country.[191] It is suggested that Yataro's letter was instrumental in the Japanese parliament's 1891 declaration that 'Neither foreigners or foreign craft would be allowed to engage in coastal trade in Japanese waters'.[192]

The Japanese maritime cabotage law is enshrined in the Japanese Ship Law No. 46 of 1899. Article 3 of the 1899 Ship Law states:

> Foreign vessels cannot conduct coastal shipping of cargo or passengers between ports in Japan unless to avoid capture or marine accident, or there is a provision in law or otherwise provided by treaty, or they have obtained a permit from the Ministry of Land, Infrastructure, Transport and Tourism.

Further to this, Article 1 of the 1899 Ship law defines a Japanese ship as:

> one possessed by a State organ, by a Japanese national, by a company established under the Japanese law if all its representatives and more than two-thirds of its officers are Japanese nationals, or by a foreign company if all its representatives are Japanese nationals.

In addition, the revised Coastal Shipping Act of Japan changed the licensing system for maritime cabotage operators from the permit to the current registration system in Japan. Thus, licensed operators became registered operators. This led to the abolition of the business categories of coastal shipping transportation and coastal ship leasing in Japan.[193]

In response to the criticisms of its protectionist maritime cabotage policy, Japan argues that its policy is premised on the duty of care owed to foreign vessels and their crew within Japanese territorial waters because it would be reckless and negligent of Japan to permit foreign vessels to engage in Japanese maritime cabotage operations. By their argument, to do so would expose foreign vessels to

---

190 For a more in-depth analysis on the issue, see: T. Okazaki, 'The Government Firm Relationship in Post-war Japan: The Success and Failure of Bureau Pluralism', in J. Stiglitz and S. Yusuf (eds), *Rethinking the East Asian Miracle* (Oxford University Press 2001), pp. 323–342.

191 I. Yataro, 'Patriotic Duty and Business Success: Letter to Mitsubishi Employees' (Mitsubishi, 1876).

192 See: A. Fraser, R. Mason and P. Mitchell, *Japan's Early Parliaments, 1890–1905: Structures, Issues and Trends* (Routledge 1995).

193 The revised Coastal Shipping Act was enacted on 1 April 2005. In addition to the introduced registration system, the revised Act strengthens the organizational control within shipping operators in terms of obligations for safety control procedures.

the challenges of navigating Japan's congested and hazardous coastal sea lanes, renowned for their extremely dangerous, intense and unpredictable weather changes. Thus, from their perspective, foreign vessels in Japanese coastal waters undertake a risky 'adventure' that could prejudice the Japanese coastal trade in the event of an accident.[194] Japan can point to the recent spate of accidents involving mostly United States vessels in Japanese waters as evidence to support their argument. Accidents in 2017 included: the running aground of the guided-missile cruiser *USS Antietam* while trying to anchor in Tokyo Bay – the ship damaged its propellers and spilled some 1,100 gallons of hydraulic oil into the water off the coast of Japan, prompting environmental concerns; the collision of *USS Fitzgerald* with the container ship *MC Crystal* off the coast of Japan, which resulted in the deaths of seven US sailors; the collision of *USS Benfold* with a Japanese tugboat in a bay off central Japan, which caused damage to the guided-missile destroyer.

A liberal maritime cabotage approach conflicts with Japan's national interests in several areas, including national defence, public safety measures and shipbuilding industry policies. Hence, the Japan Federation of Coastal Shipping Association (JCSA) argues that the current protectionist maritime cabotage approach prevents the decline of national flag vessels in coastal trade. At present, Japan does not rely on foreign flag vessels for the domestic transport of her industrial equipment and daily domestic cargo.[195] The organization has consistently argued that a liberal maritime cabotage approach would threaten the very existence of Japanese coastal shipping, pointing to what has befallen Japanese ocean-going vessels. Japan has witnessed its national ocean-going fleet depleted to such an extent that it is no longer a force on the high seas.[196]

In 2011, the share of cabotage shipping in the total domestic transportation traffic volume in Japanese waters approached 32 per cent.[197] This is an indication of the importance of coastal shipping to the Japanese economy and the degree to which it is threatening to replace truck transportation as the preferred method for long-distance and mass transportation.[198] However, high labour costs in Japan mean that a Japanese vessel with Japanese crew under a strict protectionist cabotage regime increases operations cost.[199] The consequence is that the domestic freight rate is higher than the international freight rate. This forces many Japanese

194 Japan Federation of Coastal Shipping Associations, 'Adherence to the Cabotage System' (JFCSA Secretariat, 2011).

195 For more on this, see: M. Asrofi, 'Cabotage Full Implementation vs Cabotage Relaxation', *Frost & Sullivan Market Insight* (Tokyo, July 2011).

196 For a related discuss, see: M. Brooks, *NAFTA and Short Sea Shipping Corridors* (Australia Institute of Market Studies 2005).

197 M. Grosso et al., 'Services Trade Restrictiveness Index (STRI): Transport and Courier Services' [2014], OECD Trade Policy Papers, No. 176.

198 Japan Federation of Coastal Shipping Association, *Coastal Shipping Cargo Transportation* (JFCSA 2011).

199 H. Yoshizaki et al., 'Integration of International and Cabotage Container Shipping in Brazil', in J. Bookbinder (ed.), *Handbook of Global Logistics: Transportation in International Supply Chain* (Springer Science & Business Media 2013), pp. 117–138.

shippers to tranship their cargo in one of the South Korean seaports to take advantage of the lower international freight rates.[200]

Therefore, if Japan were to adopt a liberal maritime cabotage approach, it would open Japan's maritime cabotage market to both regional and international competitors. The fear is that these competitors would engage in Japan's maritime cabotage trade with substandard vessels and cheap maritime labour. On the one hand this would have the advantage of lowering both the domestic freight rate and the price of consumer goods. On the other hand it would threaten the commercial existence of both Japanese shipowners and the country's shipping industry.[201] Japan has always reserved its coasting trade and the maritime activities in its territorial waters to Japanese vessels. Hence, it appears that the protectionist maritime cabotage approach in Japan will be maintained for the foreseeable future.[202] However, Japan expressed a willingness to grant international maritime transport operators access to some of her service markets on reasonable and non-discriminatory terms at the Doha Round of the WTO. These would include: pilotage services, pushing and towing services, provisioning, fuelling and watering services, shore-based operational services essential to ship operations, emergency repair services, anchorage, berths and berthing services.

## The People's Republic of China: Maritime Code of the People's Republic of China 1992

The aftermath of the Opium War of 1840–1842 and the subsequent military and diplomatic setbacks at the hands of foreign powers forced China to open up its economy to foreign merchants.. Thus, under the treaties imposed upon China, foreign interests were permitted to carry out maritime activities in Chinese territorial waters without restriction. These treaties allowed foreign interests to control the vital sectors of the Chinese economy ranging from the maritime sector to other service sectors.[203] Furthermore, in addition to controlling important government department such as customs, foreign nationals were not subject to received Chinese jurisdiction under the treaties.[204] The consequence of these imposed treaties was that China was open to foreign exploitation, making the development of the domestic maritime sector extremely difficult. For almost a century, the Chinese economy deteriorated slowly

---

200 See: J. Paul, 'Easing the Law on Container Transhipments Will Reduce Freight Rates and Boost Shipping', *Economic Times* (London, 6 September 2012).
201 For a broader discussion albeit an emotive one, see: Japan Federation of Coastal Shipping Associations, 'Adherence to the Cabotage System' (JFCSA, 2011).
202 House of Commons, 'Japanese Ships (Coasting Trade)', *Hansard* 39, 1838–1839, 20 June 1912.
203 For more on this, see: A. Eckstein, *China's Economic Revolution* (Cambridge University Press 1977).
204 See: A. Hussain et al., 'Effective Demand, Enterprise Reforms and Public Finance in China' [1991], *Economic Policy*, 6(12), 141–186.

but steadily to the point of near collapse before the intervention by the Communist Party in 1949.[205]

It was against this background that the new foreign trade policy of the Communist Party was formulated. It is therefore unsurprising that the People's Republic of China should have adopted a protectionist maritime cabotage law and policy, an approach that points to a desire for domestic economic development through stringent control measures of import and export activities. It also explains why contemporary China is reluctant to embrace a liberal maritime cabotage approach agenda designed to allow foreign interests another opportunity to monopolize Chinese coastal waters.[206]

Following the establishment of the new China in 1949, the Chinese shipping industry was confronted with numerous challenges. First, there was the need to reconsider the highly centrally controlled economic administrative model borrowed from Eastern Europe. This meant that the Chinese state bore both profits and losses arising from the maritime industry.[207] Second, the new Chinese state had to find a solution to the trade embargo policy imposed by Western countries, which forced China to continue to operate its maritime industry through the state.[208] The two issues highlighted above meant that China was compelled to depend on external support to operate and maintain her maritime sector.[209] Hence, China set about introducing international bilateral agreements with some countries. The objective of these bilateral agreements was to outsource the right to operate Chinese vessels to these foreign partners.[210] Furthermore, the Chinese government strategically leased vessels from overseas to sustain her maritime trade and services. China encouraged her foreign-based shipowners to make their vessels available to the Chinese state in exchange for preferential terms of service contracts.[211] However, with the lifting of the trade embargo policy imposed on China by Western countries, the Chinese government concentrated on developing a

205 N. Bajpai and V. Shastri, 'Port Development in Tamil Nadu: Lessons from Chinese Provinces', Development Discussion Paper No. 731 (Massachusetts, November 1999).

206 For a broader discussion on the issue, see: K. Wang, 'Foreign Trade Policy and Apparatus of the People's Republic of China' [1973], *Law and Contemporary Problems*, 38(2), 182–200.

207 See: Y. Qian, 'Government Control in Corporate Governance as a Transitional Institution Lessons from China', in J. Stiglitz and S. Yusuf (eds), *Rethinking the East Asian Miracle* (Oxford University Press 2001), pp. 295–322.

208 See: J. Lin and Y. Yao, 'Chinese Rural Industrialization in the Context of the East Asian Miracle', in J. Stiglitz and S. Yusuf (eds), *Rethinking the East Asian Miracle* (Oxford University Press 2001), pp. 143–196.

209 A. Hussain et al., 'Effective Demand, Enterprise Reforms and Public Finance in China' [1991], *Economic Policy*, 6(12), 141–186

210 The governments of China and Poland set up a Chinese-Polish joint stock shipping company in June 1951 allowing Chinese vessels to be operated by Poland and to fly the Polish flag. In July of the same year, the Chinese government entered into a similar agreement, entrusting the operation of Chinese vessels to Czechoslovakia.

211 See: K. Wang, 'Foreign Trade Policy and Apparatus of the People's Republic of China' [1973], *Law and Contemporary Problems*, 38(2), 182–200.

strong and vibrant national Chinese maritime sector. This led to a rapid growth in the Chinese shipbuilding industry. Hence, China was able to wrestle back control both politically and economically from the foreign nations to which they had previously ceded their operational shipping control.[212] The protectionist maritime cabotage approach in Chinese legislation is thought to date back to the 1963 Temporary Customs Law.[213] However, it is the 1992 Maritime Code of the People's Republic of China that currently regulates maritime cabotage in China. Article 4 of the Maritime Code states:

> Maritime transport and towage services between the ports of the People's Republic of China shall be undertaken by ships flying the national flag of the People's Republic of China, except as otherwise provided for by laws or administrative rules and regulations.
>
>   No foreign ships may engage in the maritime transport or towage services between the ports of the People's Republic of China unless permitted by the competent authorities of transport and communications under the State Council.[214]

Moreover, Article 7 of the 1987 Regulation on Waterway Transport Administration of the People's Republic of China further stipulates that 'wholly foreign capital enterprises and Sino-foreign (equity or contractual) joint-ventures shall not engage in the operations and management of water transport in Chinese coastal waters without the permission of a competent authority'.[215] Furthermore, Article 28 of the 2002 Regulations of the People's Republic of China on International Ocean Shipping states:

> Foreign international shipping operators may not operate the shipping business between Chinese ports; neither may they operate the shipping business between Chinese ports in disguised forms such as using rented Chinese ships or shipping space, or exchanging the shipping space, etc.[216]

In the period between 1949 and the 1980s, China's maritime cabotage and her cargo reservation policy was designed to ensure that national cargoes were carried

---

212 For a related discussion on the issue, see: G. Sun, and S. Zhang, 'Chinese Shipping Policy and the Impact of its Development', in T. Lee et al. (eds), *Shipping in China* (Ashgate 2002), pp. 4–17.

213 See: Li Xingang, 'Policy and Administrative Implications of the China Maritime Code 1992' [1996], *Logistics and Transportation Review*, 32(3), 301–318.

214 Article 4 of the Maritime Code of the People's Republic of China 1992. This Maritime Code was drafted over a 40-year period but entered into force on 1 July 1993.

215 The 1987 Regulation on Waterway Transport Administration. As amended 3 December 1997. Entered into force 1 October 1987.

216 See Article 45 of the same regulation for the consequences of breach by foreign companies. The regulation came into force 1 January 2002 and simultaneously repealed the 1990 PRC provisions on the Administration of International Ocean Shipping of Containers, as amended in 1998.

only by Chinese national vessels.[217] However, China eased her maritime cabotage legislation in 2003 to allow foreign shipping lines to move their empty containers between seaports in China. This had previously been considered domestic transportation of cargo and therefore subject to Chinese cabotage law.[218]

There has been pressure from Europe and the United States for China to open up its coastal waters to allow foreign vessels to engage in its maritime cabotage services. It is ironic that the United States and the EU would expect China to allow foreign vessels to carry out services in its coastal waters. This is because the United States implements a particularly stringent protectionist maritime cabotage policy. Also, the EU implements a protectionist maritime cabotage law in relation to third-party countries as the regime is liberalized within the Union and benefits member states only. Nevertheless, the vigorous campaign by these countries compelled the Chinese Ministry of Transport to carry out research on open coast policy. The research concluded there was no benefit in opening up the Chinese maritime cabotage business to foreign vessels.[219] Therefore, partaking in Chinese cabotage services requires that the vessel must possess a licence duly issued under the regulations of the Water Transport Administration of the People's Republic of China.[220]

China has a large population and is one of the biggest manufacturing countries in the world. Therefore, the adoption of a protectionist maritime cabotage approach has been justified by the need to create domestic employment, raise revenue and protect its sovereignty. Furthermore, the government argues that a liberal cabotage approach will impact negatively on both the domestic shipping industry and the status of Hong Kong as an international shipping hub. Also, a liberal policy would hamper the economic development of small and medium-sized ports in China.[221]

Foreign vessels may operate between Chinese ports in exceptional circumstances under a permit system. However, there are difficulties with obtaining permits and licences. This is in addition to the fact that foreign vessels are subject to various taxes and surcharges, which hands the advantage to Chinese vessels and crew. A vessel is deemed eligible for Chinese registration if the principal place of business of the shipowner or company is in China. In addition, 50 per cent of the capital investment of the company must be held by a Chinese citizen.[222]

217 The Ministry of Communication of the People's Republic of China, *China Shipping Development Report 1999* (Renmin Jiaotong Press 2000).
218 See: G. Rudder, 'China Revamps Cabotage for Empties' [2003] *Journal of Commerce*, 7 July. However, this amendment only applies to the shipping lines of countries who have signed relevant bilateral agreement with China [USA – 1991, EU – 1992, S/ Korea – 1993 and 2005].
219 M. Chen, 'China Will Not Open Its Cabotage to Foreign Vessels', *China Shipping Gazette*, No. 844 (Shanghai, 7 May 2010). The Chinese Ministry of Transport conducted the research through scientific research institutes in 2009.
220 See articles 13 and 14 of the Regulation of the Water Transport Administration of the People's Republic of China 1987 (as amended).
221 See: M. Chen, 'China Will Not Open its Cabotage to Foreign Vessels', *China Shipping Gazette*, No. 844 (Shanghai, 7 May 2010).
222 Article 2 of the Ship Registration Ordinance of the People's Republic of China 1994.

China implements some liberal policies in maritime transport services in areas such as access to the market and port-related services. However, this liberal approach does not include the Chinese coastal trade.[223] This is because China argues that coastal trade plays an integral part in China's economic development. Hence, adopting a protectionist maritime cabotage approach to facilitate the development of their domestic maritime sector is hugely beneficial to China and contributes to the phenomenal growth of southern Chinese ports.[224]

Although the Chinese maritime cabotage law prohibits foreign-flagged vessels from moving cargoes between its mainland coastal ports, this does not apply to Hong Kong because it is considered a foreign port for maritime cabotage purposes. China's protectionist maritime cabotage law benefits Hong Kong as it ensures that its port remains a key player in the market.[225] This allows Hong Kong and other Guangdong ports to complement each other by serving as cargo consolidating centres.[226] Thus, the Hong Kong port is well positioned to handle international transhipment cargoes without hindering its own independent development. This is one of the unique advantages under the 'one country, two systems' principle adopted by China.[227] China's perseverance with its protectionist cabotage approach ensures that Hong Kong continues to benefit from handling both southern China import and export cargo and Asian transhipments.[228]

Generally, China has demonstrated a willingness to relax certain aspects of its strict cabotage regime if doing so will promote Chinese economic development. For instance, cabotage regulations for cargo moving to and from Shanghai have been formally liberalized because of the establishment of the new China (Shanghai) Pilot Free Trade Zone (SH PFTZ).[229] The new policy formally permits

---

223 For a related discussion, see: M. Brooks, 'The Jones Act Under NAFTA and Its Effects on the Canadian Shipbuilding Industry', research paper (Atlantic Institute for Market Studies, September 2006).

224 Even at a growth rate regarded as slow by industry experts, China's transport ministry announced that in the first six months of 2012 China's cabotage dry bulk fleet grew by 9.2% to a total of 1,586 vessels compared to 21.7% growth for the whole of 2011; the tanker fleet expanded 2.7% to 1,125 vessels – an increase of 564,000 dwt in the first six months compared to 778,000 dwt for the whole of 2011; chemical and gas tankers grew 8.4% and 2.6%, respectively, to total 916,000dwt (248 vessels) and 158,000 dwt (63 vessels) and the coastal fleet of container vessels above 700 TEU has grown to 129 vessels, with a combined capacity of 420,000 TEU. See: Fairplay 24, 'China's Domestic Fleet Grows Slower', 27 July 2012.

225 See: C. Jin, 'Maritime Policy in China After WTO: Legal and Economic Approach' (Hong Kong Polytechnic University, 2006)

226 O. Merk and J. Li, 'The Competitiveness of Global Port-Cities: The Case of Hong Kong – China' [2013], OECD Regional Development Working Papers, 2013/16.

227 For more discussion, see: X. Li et al., 'The Application of WTO Rules in China and the Implications for Foreign Direct Investment' [2003], *Journal of World Investment*, 4(2), 343–364.

228 See: V. Wee, 'China Cabotage Rules Benefit Hong Kong: HIT', *Seatrade Global (Asia, Port and Logistics)*, (Shanghai, 10 October 2013).

229 For more on this, see: K. Zhang et al., 'China (Shanghai) Pilot Free Trade Zone' (PwC Group, 2014).

foreign vessels to carry cargo between Shanghai and other Chinese ports. This is subject to the provisos that the cargo is transhipped in Shanghai from deep-sea traffic and the foreign vessel must be under Chinese ownership. Previously, the formal position was that the carriage of such cargo could only be carried out by Chinese-owned and Chinese-flagged vessels. This requirement prevented Chinese companies such as COSCO and CSCL from engaging in coastal transport services using their foreign-flagged vessels.[230] However, the changes to the regulation are likely to have minimal impact because the relaxation of the cabotage rules only formally regulates what was already occurring.[231] Moreover, the relaxation of the cabotage rules does not apply to Chinese domestic cargo moving between Shanghai and other Chinese ports, that has not been transhipped in Shanghai from deep-sea traffic. Therefore, it appears that all the arguments by foreign interests on the dangers of a protectionist cabotage policy on the Chinese port industry and its economy have failed to persuade China to substantially reform its protectionist maritime cabotage law.[232]

Furthermore, China's activities in the East and South China seas are forceful indication of how it intends to pursue its domestic maritime cabotage policies. China has been assertive in claiming a large portion of the South China Sea by relying on what it calls its 'nine-dash line'.[233] This line covers a region that accounts for the transportation of around 40 per cent of the world's trade and the bulk of China's imported oil cargo via the Strait of Malacca.[234] Public discussions suggest that the action of the Chinese government prima facie contravenes the provisions of international law on maritime zones under the UNCLOS 1982 Convention. However, China contends that she cannot be blamed for protecting China's maritime and national security interests as they are only reacting to the actions of neighbouring countries in the South China Sea. The countries involved in the dispute accuse each other of trying to extend the limit of its territorial waters so it can have sovereignty to apply their respective maritime cabotage laws

---

230  For a broader perspective, see the arguments made earlier on the impact of liberalizing some aspects of the Chinese maritime policy in: C. Kevin et al., 'Maritime Policy in China after WTO: Impacts and Implications for Foreign Investment' [2005], *Journal of Maritime Law & Commerce*, 36(1), 77–139.

231  See: Drewry Maritime Research, 'Shanghai's New Cabotage Laws a Disappointment', *Insight Wk. 47* (Shanghai, 17 November 2013).

232  For a more comprehensive discussion on the issue, see: M. Brooks, 'Maritime Cabotage: International Market Issues in the Liberalisation of Domestic Shipping', in A. Chircop et al. (eds), *The Regulation of International Shipping: International and Comparative Perspectives* (Martinus Nijhoff 2012), pp. 293–324.

233  The 'Nine-Dash Line' is a relic of China's early-20th-century nationalist era, when it was first sketched to indicate China's view of its traditional prerogatives. The line has no international standing or recognition in international law and had been largely insignificant until China recently revived it. It now figures in all Chinese maps. Since 2012 it has been embossed in new passports issued to Chinese citizens. The 'Nine-Dash Line' was declared invalid by the Permanent Court of Arbitration in its 2016 ruling in *Philippines v China*.

234  For a related discussion, see: H. French, 'China's Dangerous Game', *The Atlantic* (Shanghai, November 2014).

and policies.[235] The dispute in the South China Sea centres on claims over islands. To that effect, Article 121 of UNCLOS 1982 provides that an island is a 'naturally formed area of land surrounded by water which is above water at high tide'. Hence, islands can generate all the maritime zones of territorial sea (12nm), a contiguous zone (24nm), an Exclusive Economic Zone (EEZ), and continental shelf zone (200nm). However, this is subject to the exception that:

a    Features such as 'rocks' that are incapable of sustaining human habitation or economic life of their own can generate only a territorial sea and a contiguous zone.
b    Features, which are entirely submerged, are not capable of generating any zones under the 1982 UNCLOS.[236]

The dispute in the South China Sea has revived the debate on the law of maritime cabotage from both the regional and international perspective.[237] This is evident in the cardinal ruling of the Permanent Court of Arbitration in *The Republic of the Philippines v. The People's Republic of China.* [238] The countries involved in the dispute in the South China Sea have territorial and jurisdictional claims. These include rights to exploit the region's projected extensive reserves of oil and gas.[239] We should note that all the countries involved in the dispute in the South China Sea implement a protectionist maritime cabotage law.[240] Attempts to set up a regional maritime cabotage policy under the ASEAN framework have been unsuccessful. For a graphic idea of the nature of the dispute, see Figure 9.1.

235  Freedom of navigation in the region is also a contentious issue, especially between the United States and China over the right of United States military vessels to operate in China's 200 nm Exclusive Economic Zone (EEZ).
236  R. Beckman, 'International Law, UNCLOS and the South China Sea', in C. Schofield et al., (eds), *Beyond Territorial Disputes in the South China Sea: Legal Frameworks for the Joint Development of Hydrocarbon Resources* (Edward Elgar 2013), pp. 47–93.
237  From a regional perspective, the claimants in the South China Sea dispute are: China, Taiwan, Vietnam, Malaysia, Brunei, Indonesia and the Philippines. From an international perspective, the countries that have special interests in the region and are therefore keen to avert what some commentators describe as having all the ingredients to start WW III are: the United States of America, Japan, South Korea, India Russia, Australia, the European Union and ASEAN.
238  [2016] PCA Case No. 2013–19.
239  The disputes concern the Spratly and Paracel islands and the Scarborouch reef, as well as maritime boundaries in the Gulf of Tonkin. There is a further dispute in the waters near the Indonesian Natuna Islands. The interests of different nations include the strategic control of important shipping lanes.
240  For an incisive discourse on the challenges of the South China Sea and the nature of the dispute, read the exquisite account in: B. Hayton, *The South China Sea: The Struggle for Power in Asia* (Yale University Press 2014). See also: C. Antrim and G. Galdorisi, 'Creeping Jurisdiction Must Stop' [2011], *U.S. Naval Institute Proceedings*, 137(4), 66–71.

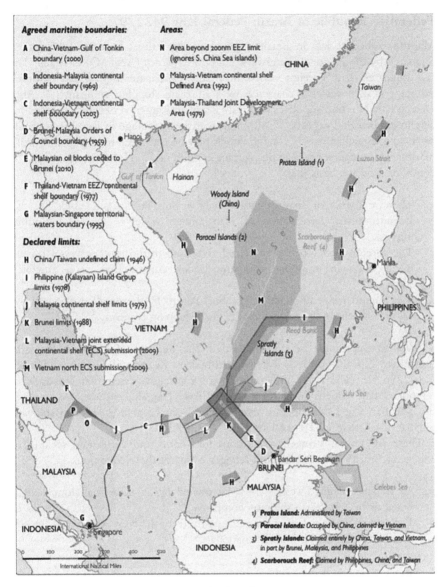

**Agreed maritime boundaries:**

A  China-Vietnam-Gulf of Tonkin boundary (2000)

B  Indonesia-Malaysia continental shelf boundary (1969)

C  Indonesia-Vietnam continental shelf boundary (2003)

D  Brunei-Malaysia Orders of Council boundary (1959)

E  Malaysian oil blocks ceded to Brunei (2010)

F  Thailand-Vietnam EEZ/continental shelf boundary (1977)

G  Malaysian-Singapore territorial waters boundary (1995)

**Declared limits:**

H  China/Taiwan undefined claim (1946)

I  Philippine (Kalayaan) Island Group limits (1978)

J  Malaysia continental shelf limits (1979)

K  Brunei limits (1988)

L  Malaysia-Vietnam joint extended continental shelf (ECS) submission (2009)

M  Vietnam north ECS submission (2009)

**Areas:**

N  Area beyond 200nm EEZ limit (ignores S. China Sea islands)

O  Malaysia-Vietnam continental shelf Defined Area (1992)

P  Malaysia-Thailand Joint Development Area (1979)

1) **Pratas Island:** Administered by Taiwan
2) **Paracel Islands:** Occupied by China, claimed by Vietnam
3) **Spratly Islands:** Claimed entirely by China, Taiwan, and Vietnam, in part by Brunei, Malaysia, and Philippines
4) **Scarborough Reef:** Claimed by Philippines, China, and Taiwan

*Figure 9.1* Sovereignty claims in the South China Sea
Source: The Library of the University of Texas.

## Federative Republic of Brazil: Federal Law 9432/97

Maritime cabotage law in Brazil is governed by Federal Law 9432/97 and is regulated by the National Waterways Transport Agency (ANTAQ) of Brazil. The law stipulates that 'Foreign vessels may only participate in Brazilian maritime cabotage if such vessel is chartered by a Brazilian shipping company'.[241] Also, Decree Law No. 666 stipulates that only Brazilian-flagged vessels may be used for certain imports and exports.[242] Although maritime cabotage in Brazil is generally reserved to Brazilian vessels, foreign vessels may be permitted to engage in Brazil's maritime cabotage services under certain conditions.[243] However, any waiver is conditional on the basis that:

a   There is absence or unavailability of suitable Brazilian flagged vessels.
b   Permitting the participation of such foreign vessel is justified by public interest.
c   The foreign vessel being chartered is to substitute another vessel owned by a Brazilian shipping company under construction at a Brazilian shipyard.[244]
d   The foreign vessel suspends her original flag to fly the Brazilian flag and the vessel is bareboat chartered by a Brazilian shipping company.[245]

Brazilian ships must be documented in the Registry of Maritime Property under Law No. 7652/88 or the Special Brazilian Registry (REB) under Decree No. 2256/97. The latter ship registry is for foreign vessels that are under a temporary flag suspension of their original flag. This allows these vessels to fly the Brazilian flag based on the vessel having been built in a Brazilian shipyard pursuant to Article 10(III) of Law No. 9432/97.

There are several stringent conditions for vessels and companies seeking to engage in Brazil's coastal trade and services. Some of these conditions are:

a   All Brazilian-flagged vessels must be owned by an individual domiciled in Brazil or by a Brazilian shipping company.[246]
b   The captain, the chief engineer and two-thirds of the crew of vessels flying the Brazilian flag must be Brazilian nationals.[247]

241 Chapter 5, Article 7 of Law No. 9432 of 1997.
242 Decree Law No. 666 of 2 July 1969: Establishing the Obligation to Transport with Brazilian Flag Vessels and Other Matters. Amended by Decree Law No. 687 of 17 July 1969.
243 See Article 178 of the Brazilian constitution 1988. As amended by the 7th Constitutional Amendment of 15 August 1995.
244 Chapter VI, Article 9 of Law No. 9432 of 1997. Assented 8 January 1997.
245 Chapter III, Article 3(II) of Law No. 9432 of 1997. See also; Chapter VI, Article 10 (III) of Law No. 9432/97.
246 Chapter III, Article 3(I) of Law No. 9432/97.
247 Chapter IV, Article 4 of Law No. 9432/97.

c For vessels registered in the Special Brazilian Registry (REB), the captain and the chief engineer must be Brazilian nationals.[248]

Article 2(2) of the Brazilian National Immigration Council Normative Resolution (NR) 72/06 stipulates that foreign crew members on ships engaged in Brazilian maritime cabotage are permitted to work for 30 days only. Hence, any foreign carrier employed on a continuous basis for longer than 90 days in Brazil's coastal waters must have a crew comprising one-fifth Brazilians on permanent employment.. Furthermore, with regard to foreign vessels operating for longer than 180 days, the workforce aboard must comprise one-third Brazilians working permanently.[249]

Brazilian maritime cabotage law is particularly stringent with regard to the requirements for providing services in its territorial waters. Even when circumstances permit foreign vessels to engage in coastal trade, such vessels must still satisfy technical, economic and financial, and tax and legal conditions.[250] Resolution No. 843-ANTAQ of 2007 provides that to operate as a Brazilian shipping company (EBN), an organization must be established and incorporated under Brazilian law and must meet:

a Technical requirements, which include owning at least one Brazilian-flagged vessel.
b Economic requirements, which includes a minimum capital stock or net assets of R$6,000,000.00 (six million reais) for maritime cabotage trade and services.
c Legal requirements, by showing documentation of its validity as a company registered and incorporated under Brazilian law as prescribed in Resolution No. 843/07.[251]

One of the objectives of the Brazilian maritime cabotage policy is to facilitate the development of capacity building in Brazilian ports. Therefore, special attention is given to cargo handling in port terminals.[252] The protectionist maritime cabotage regime thus does not extend to foreign companies that wish to invest in the Brazilian port sector. Law 12815/2013 continues in that tradition by encouraging foreign companies to invest in private port development in Brazil.

---

248 Chapter VII, Article 11(6) of Law No. 9432/97.
249 Article 3(3a and 3b) of the Brazilian National Immigration Council Normative Resolution (NR) 72 of 10 October 2006.
250 See: Chapter III, Article 3 of Resolution No. 843-ANTAQ of 2007. Assented 14 August 2007 and amended by Resolution No. 879-ANTAQ of 26 September 2007.
251 For the complete set of ANTAQ requirements and conditions, see: Section II, Article 5 (Technical); Section III, Article 6(b) (Economic); Section IV, Article 7 (Legal) of Resolution No. 843-ANTAQ of 2007.
252 See: Union of Brazilian Shipowners, 'The Brazilian Coastwise Traffic', *Syndarma* (Rio de Janeiro, 1 September 2010).

For instance, the container terminals at the Port of Suape and the Port of Itajai are controlled respectively by the ICTSI Group and the Maersk Group.

Brazil's maritime cabotage policy has contributed to its economic development and has encouraged shipowners to invest in the domestic maritime sector by purchasing Brazilian-built vessels.[253] Brazil is keen to develop her manufacturing sector and improve her expertise in the shipbuilding sector.[254] The national shipping industry is focused on the construction of both seagoing vessels and offshore units such as maritime support vessels, and floating production storage and offloading (FPSO) vessels for the oil sector.[255] Under the Fleet Modernization and Expansion Program (PROMEF), the Brazilian shipbuilding sector has taken just 13 years to attain the level of maturity that is comparable to the Chinese shipbuilding market.[256] The construction of all the ships in the PROMEF programme is expected to generate about 40,000 direct jobs, with more than 70,000 people targeted for training to operate in the revitalized shipbuilding industry.[257] Although the shipbuilding sector represents a great opportunity, this process has been slow and several domestic companies have experienced delays in the delivery of their new builds. These delays are attributed to the lack of expert capacity in the domestic shipyards to meet the high demand for new Brazilian builds.[258] This has prompted a debate on the necessity of adopting a maritime cabotage policy that reduces the tax burden thus making it easier to import vessels.[259] There is also debate on whether it might be more practical to apply more flexibility in the rules for chartering foreign vessels for use in coastal trade. As foreign crew are only permitted to take up employment within the coastal waters of Brazil for a limited period, the challenge is for qualified Brazilians to fill the skill gap within a reasonable time.[260]

The Brazilian cabotage law has recorded some important successes. In 2011, *Log-In Jacarandá*, the first container vessel built in Brazil this century, was commissioned into operation.[261] The launch of the vessel signalled the beginning of a new chapter in the Brazilian maritime sector in general, but in particular the resumption of shipbuilding in Brazil. The vessel was completed within the limits of

253 S. Adams, 'DNV GL to Class Two Pipe Laying Vessels at New Vard Promar Yard in Brazil', *DNV.GL* (Oslo, 6 November 2013).
254 See: H. Elstrodt et al., *Connecting Brazil to The World: A Part to Inclusive Growth* (McKinsey Global Institute 2014).
255 G. M. Vianna, 'Cabotage Industry Faces Major Challenges to Growth', Shipping & Transport – Brazil, *International Law Office* (22 August 2007).
256 The main players in the international shipbuilding industry, Japan, South Korea and China, have had 63, 53 and 23 years, respectively, to reach maturity in the sector.
257 For more on this, see: C. Campos, 'PROMEF: The Brazilian Shipbuilding Market is Booming', *Petrobas Magazine* (Rio de Janeiro, 11 February 2014).
258 See the discussion in: J. Leahy and S. Pearson, 'Rousseff's Dream of Brazilian Shipbuilding Titan in Deep Water', *Financial Times* (Rio de Janeiro, 25 January 2015).
259 See: J. Gabriel, 'Revitalisation of the Shipbuilding Industry' [2009], *Petrobas Magazine*, 58(1), 5–10
260 See: G. M. Vianna, 'Cabotage Industry Faces Major Challenges to Growth', Shipping & Transport – Brazil, *International Law Office* (Rio de Janeiro, 22 August 2007).
261 The gigantic Brazilian-built container vessel is capable of transporting 2,800 TEUs and is highly energy efficient; it also has outstanding operational stability.

its original budget and represents one of the biggest achievements of Brazilian maritime cabotage law.[262] The demand for domestic built-vessels in the Brazilian offshore oil and gas industry is fostered by Petrobras investing in the domestic building of a variety of vessels for the oil and gas sector. This includes a business plan to place orders of US$100 billion with Brazilian shipyards by 2020.[263] However, many of these Brazilian shipyards are struggling with financial or operational challenges. It is not clear whether these challenges are the inevitable part of the development process or evince the fundamental issues affecting the domestic shipbuilding sector in the long term.[264] Hence, although there is high demand for domestic shipbuilding, the domestic shipyards have struggled to accommodate capital and financial extensive projects. For instance, IESA Oleoe Gas secured a US$720 million contract with Petrobras to supply 24 gas compression modules for its FPSOs (Floating Production Storage and Offloading vessels).[265] Estaleiro Ilha S.A. (EISA) had 26 contracts estimated to be worth a total of US$1.6 billion.[266] Estaleiro Rio Grande (ERG) had an order book estimated to be worth US$6 billion including a US$ 3.5 billion contract with Petrobras to supply hulls for eight FPSOs by 2016.[267]

In the 1970s, backed by government support and incentives, Brazil had the world's fifth-largest merchant marine fleet and a shipbuilding industry with the world's second-largest order book. At the time, Brazil's shipbuilding sector employed over 40,000 workers directly. A further 100,000 people were indirectly employed.[268] However, in the face of little incentive and government

262 For more on this, see: V. Lopes, *Brazilian Cabotage Shipping Project* (Login 2011).
263 See: T. Rhodes and G. McDonald, 'Brazilian Shipyards: Industry in Crisis or Growing Pains?', *Lexology* (18 August 2014). Petrobas needs 70 new floating production platforms by 2030 to develop its huge pre-salt oil reserves. This is in addition to several drilling vessels, shuttle tankers, and installation vessels.
264 See: J. Leahy and S. Pearson, 'Rousseff's Dream of Brazilian Shipbuilding Titan in Deep Water', *Financial Times* (Rio de Janeiro, 25 January 2015).
265 The company was in a grave financial situation for some time, resulting in difficulties paying suppliers and staff, strikes and a failure to meet production schedules. It is reported that a solution has now been found, with Brazilian construction group Andrade Gutierrez agreeing to step in and take a stake in the shipyard.
266 The shipyard is reported to have suspended operations in 2014 amid serious liquidity problems resulting from poor administration, and is now seeking to secure urgent funding from foreign investors. These orders included a contract to supply five container ships, and two ore carriers to Log-In Logistica Intermodal, Brazil's largest cabotage company. For more information on these orders, see: T. Rhodes and G. McDonald, 'Brazilian Shipyards: Industry in Crisis or Growing Pains?', *Lexology* (18 August 2014).
267 This project, however, is experiencing delays and there was talk of Petrobras transferring part of this project away from Ecovix to speed things up. To improve performance and raise capital, Ecovix concluded a joint venture with Mitsubishi Heavy Industries in 2013, which allowed the Japanese company to acquire a 30% stake in the company.
268 The success of the sector, at that time, was due to a combination of domestic orders and government support through incentives given to encourage small shipyards to increase capacity.

support, the fortunes of the industry declined very quickly in the 1980s and by 2000 the Brazilian shipyards employed fewer than 1,000 people.[269] At present, Brazil's shipbuilding industry has rebounded through a combination of government support and developments in Brazil's offshore oil and gas industry. Government measures, such as better financing through an improved Merchant Marine Fund (Fundo da Marinha Mercante – FMM), and stringent maritime cabotage laws have stimulated growth in the domestic maritime and shipbuilding industry.[270]

Generally, it is accepted that domestic shipyards in Brazil are uncompetitive in comparison to its Asian competitors. This is due to a combination of factors such as high labour costs, shortage of skilled workers, lack of innovative technology, and management techniques. The consequence of these factors can be seen vividly in the frequent delays in the delivery dates of vessels, further compounded by several domestic shipyards undertaking large and technologically demanding projects against tight schedules.[271] The challenges faced by domestic shipyards have inevitably prompted speculation as to whether the investors in Brazil's domestic shipbuilding will continue to support the domestic shipyards.[272] Thus, it is necessary to ensure that an appropriate framework is put in place to promote the competitiveness and sustainability of domestic shipyards in the long term.[273] All indications suggest that these challenges are clearly surmountable, and domestic shipyards are now collaborating with foreign enterprises to improve their

269　See: T. Rhodes and G. McDonald, 'Brazilian Shipyards: Industry in Crisis or Growing Pains?', *Lexology* (18 August 2014).

270　The Brazilian Special Registry (REB) is a case in point. It was established to make Brazilian shipyards more competitive by reducing import and other taxes which would otherwise be payable on the importation of parts and components by national shipyards in the construction, maintenance and/or upgrade of a vessel. Vessels registered with the REB also have other benefits relating to financing, insurance and crewing. To register a vessel, the owner should be a Brazilian navigation company, authorized by the Brazilian Agency for Water Transport (ANTAQ), and the vessel generally has to be registered under the Brazilian flag.

271　In order to help address the high labour costs in the shipbuilding sector, the government has introduced measures to reduce the burden of social security payments. Thus, instead of being required to pay social security contributions (INSS) on employee salaries, it is now only payable at a discounted rate on invoices for the sale of a vessel, which helps with cash flow. Although this measure was only supposed to apply for 2014, the then Brazil president, Dilma Rousseff, announced that it will be made permanent.

272　The construction of the oil tanker, 'João Cândido' by the Atlantico Sul shipyard (EAS), illustrates the point on the impact of construction delays. This vessel was delivered 21 months late and incurred a 23% over the budget cost. In 2013, OSX Construção Naval entered into bankruptcy protection and had to suspend construction of its shipyard in Açu, Rio de Janeiro state. OSX's problems were linked to an over-reliance on contracts with sister oil company, OGX, which itself entered into bankruptcy protection following major production difficulties in its offshore fields. As such delays have become common over the past few years, some shipowners are taking a more active role in the supervision of projects, with critical parts, such as hull conversions, being done outside Brazil in some cases. This has raised concern among national shipyards that this might lead to the relaxation of the maritime cabotage law.

273　Petrobras has sought to allay such fears by denying that there is a threat to the sector's long-term future and confirming that it is in the company's interests to have a local and competitive industry close to its operations. However, the president of the state

all-round expertise. This is evidenced by improvements in projects undertaken by EAS since it entered into a joint venture with a Japanese consortium in 2013.[274] It is argued that a consolidated framework would encourage a stronger shipbuilding sector that is better positioned to compete internationally and improve the economics in Brazil's maritime sector.

## The Philippines: Tariff and Customs Code of the Philippines (RA 1937) and Domestic Shipping Development Act of 2004 (RA 9295)

The Philippines is an archipelago made up of over 7,100 islands. Therefore, the carriage services of goods and passengers between the islands are heavily reliant on maritime transport.[275] Furthermore, the Philippines is a significant player in the maritime labour market, with many Filipinos employed on domestic and international vessels. The protectionist maritime cabotage policy in the Philippines was adopted from the United States Merchant Marine Act during its colonial period. It is perhaps ironic that the Philippines pursue a protectionist maritime cabotage approach given the national policy to place Filipino seamen on foreign and domestic vessels around the world.[276] In its defence, the government of the Philippines claims that a protectionist maritime cabotage approach provides much-needed employment in the Philippines.[277]

There is no specific maritime cabotage law instrument in the Philippines. Instead, its maritime cabotage law can be found in several acts and the national Constitution.[278] The 1987 Constitution of the Republic of the Philippines stipulates a maximum of 40 per cent foreign equity in domestic shipping.[279] Generally, maritime cabotage in the Philippines is reserved only for national flag vessels by two laws. They are:

a   Republic Act (RA) 1937 or the Tariff and Customs Code of the Philippines
b   Republic Act (RA) 9295 or the Domestic Shipping Development Act of 2004.

company, Maria das Graças Foster, has stated that increasing production has higher priority than placing orders with national shipyards.

274 A number of shipyards are also investing heavily in productivity improvements. These businesses include EAS, ERG and Enseada Industria Naval in Bahia, which have invested a total of BRL 6.6 billion to create modern industrial parks.
275 According to the 2013 *Philippine Statistical Yearbook* published by the National Statistical Coordination Board (NSCB), 77.47 million metric tons of cargo and 49.5 million passengers were carried by sea in the coastal waters of the Philippines in 2012.
276 For more discussion on this issue, see: G. Llanto, E. Basilio, and L. Basilio, 'Competition Policy and Regulation in Ports and Shipping', Research Paper Series No. 2007–04, Philippine Institute for Development Studies, 2007.
277 See: M. Lorenzo, 'The Domestic Shipping Industry of the Philippines: A Situation Report', Maritime Industry Authority, 1997.
278 There are several bills in both houses of Congress that propose to repeal the protectionist maritime cabotage regime, but none have so far been enacted into law.
279 Article 12, section 11 of the 1987 Constitution of the Republic of the Philippines (see also sections 2 and 12 of the Constitution). See also: section 2 of the Domestic shipping Act 2004 – RA 9295.

Section 806 of Republic Act 1937 enacted in 1957 defines domestic ownership of a vessel as that which at least 75 per cent of the capital stock is vested in citizens of the Philippines.[280] Also, in the case of corporations engaged in maritime cabotage trade, the president or managing directors shall be citizens of the Philippines.[281] Further, Republic Act 9295 expressly stipulates that 'No franchise, certificate or any other form of authorization for the carriage of cargo or passenger, or both in the domestic trade, shall be granted except of domestic ship owners or operators'.[282]

Hence, foreign vessels are barred from transporting passengers or cargo between ports in the Philippine territorial waters. Nevertheless, foreign vessels may be granted special permit by the Maritime Industry Authority (MARINA) when no domestic vessel is available or suitable to provide the required service.[283] Further exemptions include honouring bilateral and international agreements like the port tariff policy issued by the government. This policy considers vessels trading in the Brunei-Indonesia-Malaysia-Philippines East Asian Growth Area (BIMP-EAGA) territory as domestic vessels.[284]

The nucleus of the Philippines maritime cabotage law is the Tariff and Customs Code (RA 1937). Under the Tariff and Customs Code Act, every non-transient vessel employed in the territorial waters of the Philippines must be registered in the Bureau of Customs within 15 days of the vessel becoming subject to such registration.[285] The right to engage in Philippine coastwise trade is limited to vessels carrying a certificate of Philippine registry and vessels duly licensed annually.[286] Although we have stated above that there is no specific maritime cabotage instrument in the Philippines, sections 905 and 1009 of the Tariff and Customs Code (RA 1937) of 1957 offer a good understanding of the country's maritime cabotage law. Section 905 of the Tariff and Customs Code stipulates as follows:

280 There appears to be contradiction between Article 12, section 11 of the Philippine Constitution, which demands 60 per cent indigenous shares to 40 per cent foreign shares, and section 806 of Republic Act 1937, which defines domestic ownership of vessels as 75 per cent of capital shares.
281 The requirement for qualification to be a Philippine-flagged vessel is particularly onerous, including: ownership, nationality qualifications, manning, residency prerequisites and immigration requirements.
282 See: section 5 (Authority to Operate) of the Domestic Shipping Act 2004 (RA 9295).
283 See: section 6 of the Domestic Shipping Act 2004 (RA 9295): 'Foreign Vessels Engaged in Trade and Commerce in the Philippines Territorial Waters.'
284 See Government Resolution No. 1470. See also: M. Lorenzo, 'The Domestic Shipping Industry of the Philippines: A Situation Report', Maritime Industry Authority, 1997.
285 See: section 802 of the Customs and Tariffs Republic Act (RA 1937) of 1957.
286 See: sections 902 (Vessels Eligible for Coastwise Trade) and 903 (Licence for Coastwise Trade), respectively, of the Customs and Tariffs Republic Act (RA 1937) of 1957.

Passengers shall not be received at one Philippine port for any other such port by a vessel not licensed for the coastwise trade, except upon special permission previously granted by the collector; and subject to the same qualification, articles embarked at a domestic port shall not be transported to any other port in the Philippines, either directly or by way of a foreign port, or for any part of the voyage, in any other vessel than one licensed for the coastwise trade.[287]

Section 1009 of the Tariff and Customs Code states:

Passengers or articles arriving from abroad upon a foreign vessel may be carried by the same vessel through any port of entry to the port of destination in the Philippines; and passengers departing from the Philippines or articles intended for export may be carried in a foreign vessel through a Philippine port.[288]

Section 1009 of the 1957 Tariff and Custom Code of the Philippines (TCCP) is often interpreted controversially as the liberal gateway to foreign ships engaging in the coastwise trade of the Philippines. The section permits foreign vessels to proceed beyond one domestic port to load cargo destined for a foreign port, or to discharge cargo from a foreign port.[289] This appears to contrast with the provisions of section 1001 of the same Act that restricts vessels engaged in foreign trade to the port of entry only.[290] This controversy led the Philippines Department of Justice to clarify that section 1009 of the Tariff and Custom Code cannot be construed as a legal platform and authority for permitting foreign vessels to engage in the coastwise trade of the Philippines. It emphasized that coastwise trade is a nationalized activity reserved for vessels that have satisfied the requirements of sections 902 and 903 of the Tariff and Custom Code.[291] The argument put forward by the Department of Justice with regard to section 1009 of the Tariff and Custom Code may be rejected. This is because a foreign vessel that loads and/or discharges cargo in more than one domestic port in a country is effectively engaging in that country's

287 Republic Act 1937 of 1957 – Transportation of Passengers and Goods between Philippine Ports.
288 Republic Act 1937 of 1957 – Clearance of Foreign Vessels to and From Coastwise Ports.
289 G. Llanto, and A. Navarro, 'Relaxing the Cabotage Restrictions in Maritime Transport', Senate Committee on Trade, Commerce and Entrepreneurship, 2014.
290 SEC. 1001: Ports Open to Vessels Engaged in Foreign Trade. - Duty of Vessel to Make Entry. - Vessels engaged in the foreign trade shall touch at ports of entry only, except as otherwise specially allowed; and every such vessel arriving within a customs collection district of the Philippines from a foreign port make entry at the port of entry for such district and shall be subject to the authority of the Collector of the while within his jurisdiction.
291 See Opinion No. 73, s. 1997 of the Philippines Department of Justice, dated 3 November 1997.

*Table 9.3* A snapshot of the legal provisions of Philippine maritime cabotage law

| Sections | Specific maritime cabotage provisions under the Tariff and Customs Code of the Philippines(RA 1937) |
|---|---|
| 801 | **Registration and Documentation of Vessels**<br>The Bureau of Customs is vested with exclusive authority over the registration and documentation of Philippine vessels. By it shall be kept and preserved the records of registration and of transfers and encumbrances of vessels; and by it shall be issued all certificates, licenses or other documents incident to registration and documentation, or otherwise requisite for Philippine vessels. |
| 810 | **Privileges Conferred by Certificate of Philippine Registry**<br>A certificate of Philippine registry confers upon the vessel the right to engage, consistently with law, in the Philippine coastwise trade and entitles it to the protection of the authorities and the flag of the Philippines in all ports and on the high seas, and at the same time secures to it the same privileges and subjects it to the same disabilities as, under the laws of the Philippines, pertain to foreign-built vessels transferred abroad to citizens of the Philippines. |
| 902 | **Vessels Eligible for Coastwise Trade**<br>The right to engage in the Philippine coastwise trade is limited to vessels carrying a certificate of Philippine registry. |
| 903 | **License for Coastwise Trade**<br>All vessels engaging in the coastwise trade must be duly licensed annually. |
| 905 | **Transportation of Passengers and Articles between Philippine Ports**<br>Passengers shall not be received at one Philippine port for any other such port by a vessel not licensed for the coastwise trade, except upon special permission previously granted by the collector; and subject to the same qualification, articles embarked at a domestic port shall not be transported to any other port in the Philippines, either directly or by way of a foreign port, or for any part of the voyage, in any other vessel than one licensed for the coastwise trade |
| 1009 | **Clearance of Foreign Vessels to and from Coastwise Ports**<br>Passengers or articles arriving from abroad upon a foreign vessel may be carried by the same vessel through any port of entry to the port of destination in the Philippines or articles intended for export may be carried in a foreign vessel through a Philippine port.<br>Upon such reasonable condition as he may impose, the Commissioner may clear foreign vessels for any port and authorize the conveyance therein of either articles or passengers brought from abroad upon such vessels; and he may likewise, upon such conditions as he may impose, allow a foreign vessel to take cargo and passengers at any port and convey the same, upon such vessel to a foreign port. |
| Sections | Specific Maritime Cabotage Provisions under the Domestic Shipping Development Act(RA 9295) |
| 5 | **Authority to Operate**<br>No franchise, certificate or any other form of authorization for the carriage of cargo or passenger, or both, in the domestic trade, shall be granted except to domestic shipowners or operators. |

*(Continued)*

Table 9.3 (Cont.)

| Sections | Specific Maritime Cabotage Provisions under the Domestic Shipping Development Act(RA 9295) |
|---|---|
| 6 | **Foreign Vessels Engaged in Trade and Commerce in Philippine Territorial Waters**<br>No foreign vessels shall be allowed to transport passengers or cargo between ports or places within the Philippine territorial waters, except upon the grant of Special Permit by the MARINA when no domestic vessel is available or suitable to provide the needed shipping service and public interest warrants the same. |

maritime cabotage services.[292] Regardless of the benefits of this provision, it is argued that section 1009 of the Tariff and Custom Code opens the door for competition with domestic shipowners and is contrary to what is generally accepted as a strict protectionist cabotage regime. The consequence of this loophole is that domestic shipowners are denied the opportunity to provide maritime services between two or more domestic maritime points in their country. Furthermore, the somewhat liberal loophole in section 1009 of the Tariff and Custom Code also appears to derogate from the specific provisions of RA 9295.[293] The different positions of these various legislative instruments are irreconcilable and therefore somewhat confusing with regard to the correct position of the law.[294]

There is always the possibility that a liberal approach would create competition with foreign companies dominating the cabotage trade and thus hindering development of domestic maritime capacity. Nevertheless, it is suggested that such a liberal approach would force a reduction in domestic freight rates, thereby lowering the prices of consumer goods. The Domestic Shipping Development Act (RA 9295) was viewed by many as a mechanism to deregulate further the domestic maritime sector in the country. However, while RA 9295 introduced a variety of reforms including liberalizing passenger rates, the Act reiterates and bolsters the protectionist maritime cabotage provisions as stipulated in RA 1937.[295] The port tariff policy, which categorizes vessels from BIMP-EAGA territory as domestic vessels for the purposes of maritime cabotage, has also attracted criticism from both sides of the debate.[296] Critics from both sides have latched on to

292 This of course excludes periods when foreign vessels are employed due to an emergency or disaster or when such foreign vessels are employed in a temporary capacity.
293 Section 1009 of the Tariff and Customs Code grants foreign vessels access to multiple ports. In contrast, other sections of RA 1937 and RA 9295 reserve maritime activities in the territorial waters of the Philippines to the domestic vessels and shipowners.
294 See Opinion No. 73, s. 1997 of the Philippines Department of Justice, dated 3 November 1997.
295 Other reforms introduced by RA9295 are: providing incentives to renew domestic fleet, toughening regulations on ship safety standards, identifying eligible ship classification societies, and stipulating for compulsory insurance coverage of passengers and cargoes.
296 In honour of international and bilateral agreements, the government of the Philippine issued the Port Tariff Policy, which exempts vessels trading in the Brunei-Indonesia-Malaysia-Philippines East Asian Growth Area (BIMP-EAGA) territory from the

this exemption to suggest that the maritime cabotage law is compromised. Protectionists suggest that the government has effectively opened up the coastwise trade to foreign competition at the expense of indigenous shippers and shipowners.[297] Liberalists argue that opening up the coastwise trade to selected countries only is counterproductive. They suggest that to take advantage of a larger economy of scale that would bring most benefit to the development of the Philippines economy, the better approach is to pursue an open coast policy for all countries.[298]

In what appears to be a change in policy, the government signed the Foreign Ships Co-Loading Act, which is a shift from the country's traditional maritime cabotage regime.[299] The amendments to the law are expected to lower shipping costs for export and import shipments as more foreign vessels can stop at multiple ports in the Philippines. Furthermore, the amended law will permit the carriage and co-loading of export cargos by foreign vessels within the coastal waters of the Philippines. This is in addition to allowing empty containers from overseas to be transhipped between two domestic ports. This amendment correlates with the Association of Southeast Asian Nations' idea of a unified common market. The objective of the common market is to reduce trade barriers and encourage free flow of goods, services, investment and skilled labour.[300] However, it is not immediately clear whether this amendment is a temporary measure or whether it repeals the other protectionist maritime cabotage laws in the Philippines. This is important because section 8 of the Foreign Ships Co-Loading Act still prohibits foreign vessels from the carriage of domestic cargo. Table 9.3 is a snapshot of relevant maritime cabotage legislation in the Philippines.

## *The Republic of the Philippines v. The People's Republic of China*[301]

The dispute between the Philippines and China in the South China Sea, which led to the cardinal ruling of the Permanent Court of Arbitration, has brought the debate on

protectionist coastwise trade restrictions imposed on foreigners. See also: Memorandum Order 237, which exempts passengers from the international ports of Mindanao from paying taxes.

297  For a comparative argument, see: D. Jati, 'Liberalised but Protected: Shipping Law Introduces New Cabotage Rules and Welcomes Private Sector Participation', Oxford Business Group, 2011.

298  See: G. Llanto and A. Navarro, 'The Impact of Trade Liberalization and Economic Integration on the Logistics Industry: Maritime Transport and Freight Forwarders', Discussion Paper Series No. 2012–19, Philippine Institute for Development Studies, 2012.

299  See: An Act Allowing Foreign Vessels to Transport and Co-Load Foreign Cargoes For Domestic Transhipment and For Other Purposes. Sixteenth Congress of the Republic of the Philippines. Second Regular Session. 15 June 2015.

300  See: G. Knowler, 'Philippine Ports Ready for Rising Volumes After Cabotage Law Change', *Journal of Commerce*, (New York, 12 August 2015).

301  [2016] PCA Case No. 2013–19.

maritime cabotage law to the fore from both regional and international perspectives.[302] The legal basis of this dispute in international law is the United Nations Convention on the Law of the Sea 1982 (UNCLOS 1982). The South China Sea lies to the south of China, to the west of the Philippines, to the east of Vietnam, and to the north of Malaysia, Brunei, Singapore and Indonesia. It is a crucial shipping lane, a rich fishing ground, home to a highly biodiverse coral reef ecosystem, and believed to hold substantial oil and gas resources. Generally, the dispute between the parties centres around the legal basis of maritime rights and entitlements in the South China Sea, the status of certain geographic features in the South China Sea, and the lawfulness of certain actions taken by China in the South China Sea. Specifically, the Philippines application to the court falls broadly into four areas, namely:

a   The Philippines asked the tribunal to rule on the source of the Parties' maritime rights, obligations, and entitlements in the South China Sea. Specifically, they asked the tribunal to determine that China's rights and entitlements in the disputed sea area are subject to the provisions of the Convention and not based on claims of historic rights. Therefore, the Philippines asked the tribunal to rule that China's claims to historic rights within its 'nine-dash line' marked on Chinese maps are without lawful effect to the extent that they exceed the entitlements that China would be allowed under the Convention.

b   The Philippines asked the tribunal to rule on the status of certain maritime features claimed by both China and the Philippines with respect to the entitlements to maritime zones that would be generated under the Convention by Scarborough Shoal and certain maritime features in the Spratly Islands. They asked the tribunal to declare whether these maritime features can properly be characterized as islands, rocks, low-tide elevations or submerged banks, which determines what maritime zones they can generate under the Convention.

c   The Philippines asked the tribunal to declare whether certain actions by China in the South China Sea with respect to fishing, oil exploration and navigation that has interfered with the Philippines' exercising her sovereign rights in jurisdictional waters under international law violates the provisions of the Convention. Furthermore, they sought a ruling on whether China's actions, which include large scale construction and fishing activities that have harmed the marine environment, breach international law.

d   The Philippines asked the tribunal to find that the large-scale land reclamation and construction of artificial islands in the Spratly Islands and other actions by China since the Philippines commenced arbitration proceedings have aggravated and extended the Parties' dispute unlawfully.

302 From a regional perspective, the claimants in the South China Sea dispute are: China, Taiwan, Vietnam, Malaysia, Brunei, Indonesia and the Philippines. From an international perspective, the countries who have special interests in the region and are therefore keen to avert what some commentators describe as having all the ingredients to start WW III are: The United States of America, Japan, South Korea, India Russia, Australia, the European Union, and ASEAN.

In response, China stated its position in several *note verbale* but declared that regardless of its statements, China had no intention of participating, accepting or recognizing the tribunal proceedings and its rulings on the matter.[303] China's position paper argued that the tribunal lacks jurisdiction because the issue at arbitration concerns the territorial sovereignty over the relevant maritime features in the South China Sea, which is beyond the scope of UNCLOS, therefore the Convention cannot apply. Moreover, China submitted that both parties have agreed to resolve their disputes through negotiations using bilateral instruments and the Declaration on the Conduct of Parties in the South China Sea. Therefore, the unilateral action by the Philippines to initiate arbitration on this matter was a breach of her obligations under international law. Lastly, China contested that the disputes submitted by the Philippines constitutes an integral part of maritime delimitation between the two countries and is covered in the Declaration filed by China in 2006 in accordance with Article 298 of the Convention. The 2006 Declaration of the People's Republic of China under Article 298 of the UNCLOS Convention states that China does not accept any of the procedures provided for in section 2 of Part XV of the Convention with respect to the categories of disputes referred to in paragraph 1 (a), (b) and (c) of Article 298 of the Convention. The Declaration on the Conduct of Parties in the South China Sea (DOC) confirms that sovereign states directly concerned undertake to resolve their territorial and jurisdictional disputes by peaceful means through friendly consultations and negotiations. It excludes inter alia; maritime delimitation disputes from compulsory arbitration and other compulsory dispute settlement procedures.

However, Articles 288 and 9 of Annex VII of UNCLOS 1982 state clearly that the objection to the tribunal's jurisdiction or the willful absence from the tribunal by one party to the proceedings cannot constitute a bar to the proceedings provided that prior to making its award, the arbitral tribunal has satisfied itself both that it has jurisdiction over the dispute and that the claim is well founded in fact and law.[304] Furthermore, pursuant to the provisions of Article 296(1) and Article 11 of Annex VII of UNCLOS, China remained a party to the arbitration and is bound by the award issued by the tribunal. To satisfy these requirements, the tribunal deemed China's informal communications as objection to jurisdiction and convened a separate hearing on its jurisdiction and admissibility as a preliminary question. Following the hearing, the tribunal issued the 'Award on Jurisdiction'

---

303 See: The 'Position Paper of the Government of the People's Republic of China on the Matter of Jurisdiction in the South China Sea Arbitration Initiated by the Republic of the Philippines', dated 7 December 2014 ('China's Position Paper'). See also: letters to members of the Tribunal from the Chinese Ambassador to the Kingdom of the Netherlands.

304 Article 288 of UNCLOS 1982 states: 'In the event of a dispute as to whether a court or tribunal has jurisdiction, the matter shall be settled by decision of that court or tribunal.' Also: Article 9 of Annex VII to UNCLOS 1982 states: If one of the parties to the dispute does not appear before the arbitral tribunal or fails to defend its case, the other party may request the tribunal to continue the proceedings and to make its award.

and Admissibility in 2015, which addressed the objections to jurisdiction set out in China's position paper and other questions on the scope of the tribunal's jurisdiction. Other issues were deferred for further consideration in conjunction with the merits of the Philippine claims.[305] A similar hearing was also held to determine the factual and legal basis for the claims. Therefore, the Permanent Court of Arbitration provided its award on the merits of the four main issues as outlined in the following:

### The 'nine-dash line' and China's claim to historic rights in the maritime areas of the South China Sea

The tribunal ruled that China's 'nine-dash line' has no legal basis and that China's claim to historic rights to resources was not compatible with the detailed allocation of rights and maritime zones under the Convention. It concluded that whatever historic rights to resources in the waters of the South China Sea that China may have had, such rights were effectively extinguished when the Convention came into force to the extent they were not compatible with the system of maritime zones in the Convention. The tribunal noted that the issue on pre-existing rights to resources is covered by the Convention. Generally, a country has no rights to petroleum or mineral resources and only limited rights to access fisheries in the EEZ where the coastal state cannot utilize their allowance. Furthermore, the tribunal acknowledged the existence of evidence that navigators and fishermen from China and other countries had historically engaged in activities in the islands in the South China Sea. However, the tribunal in re-emphasizing that the question of sovereignty was beyond its authority, stated that before the coming into force of the Convention, the waters of the South China Sea beyond the territorial waters were designated as part of the high seas. Therefore, it was open to all to fish and navigate freely. Furthermore, there was no evidence that, historically, China had exclusive control over the waters of the South China Sea such to allow her to prevent other countries from enjoying the resources in the area. Hence any activity performed by China in these waters represented her freedom like any other country in the high seas. Therefore, the tribunal concluded that China's claim to historic rights to resources in the maritime areas of the South China Sea beyond the rights provided for by the Convention in the sea areas falling within the 'nine-dash line' had no legal basis.

### The status of features in the South China Sea

The tribunal considered the status of features in the South China Sea and the entitlements to maritime areas under the Convention. This included evaluating whether certain coral reefs claimed by China are or are not above water at high tide. In making the award, the relevant provisions of the Convention are articles 13 and 121 of the Convention. Article 13 provides that maritime features above

---

305 For more on this, see the 'Award on Jurisdiction', dated 29 October 2015.

water at high tide can generate a 12-nautical mile territorial sea, whereas features that are submerged at high tide generate no entitlement to maritime zones. Article 121 provides that islands can generate 200 nm of EEZ and a continental shelf. However, rocks that cannot sustain human habitation or economic life of their own cannot give entitlement to an EEZ or continental shelf.

As many of the reefs in the South China Sea have undergone heavy artificial modification through land reclamation and construction, the tribunal adhered to the Convention principle of classifying maritime features based on their natural condition. Pursuant to Article 13 of the Convention and with the help of an independent expert hydrographer, the tribunal accepted the case as put forward by the Philippines that Scarborough Shoal, Johnson Reef, Cuarteron Reef and Fiery Cross Reef are high-tide features, and that Subi Reef, Hughes Reef, Mischief Reef and Second Thomas Shoal were submerged at high tide in their natural condition. However, it rejected the Philippines case on the status of Gaven Reef (North) and McKennan Reef, holding that both are high-tide features.

The tribunal then considered whether under Article 121 of the Convention, any of the maritime features claimed by China could generate 200 nm of EEZ and a continental shelf.[306] It determined that pursuant to Article 121 of the Convention, the entitlements a maritime feature can generate depends on the objective capacity of the feature in its natural condition to sustain either a stable community of people or economic activity that is neither dependent on outside resources nor purely extractive in nature. The tribunal observed that many features in the Spratly Islands are under the control of one or more of the littoral states and have been modified to enhance habitation on the features. It noted that such modified habitat does not prove the feature's capacity in its natural condition to sustain a stable human presence. The tribunal argued that historical evidence of habitation or economic life was necessary for the objective capacity of the features. As historical records showed that the Spratly Islands were used by personnel from several states, the tribunal determined that those economic activities were extractive in nature. Furthermore, the tribunal stated that temporary use of the features by fishing personnel was not inhabitation by a stable community. Therefore, the tribunal decided that all high-tide features in the Spratly are 'rocks' under Article 121 of the Convention and therefore cannot generate an exclusive economic zone or continental shelf.[307] Also, it was held that the Convention does not provide for a group of islands such as the Spratly Islands to generate maritime zones collectively as a unit.

306 The objective of Article 121 is to prevent less significant maritime features from generating large entitlements to maritime zones that would infringe on the entitlements of inhabited territory or on the high seas and the area of the seabed reserved for the common heritage of mankind.
307 The maritime features include: Itu Aba, Thitu, West York Island, Spratly Island, North-East Cay, South-West Cay.

## Chinese activities in the South China Sea

The tribunal considered the lawfulness of various actions by China in the South China Sea under the Convention. Following from the second issue above where the tribunal held that Mischief Reef, Second Thomas Shoal and Reed Bank are submerged at high tide, constitute part of the EEZ and continental shelf of the Philippines, and are not overlapped by any possible entitlement of China, it decided that under the Convention, the Philippines had sovereign rights to sea areas in its exclusive economic zone. Furthermore, the tribunal ruled that China had (a) interfered with Philippine petroleum exploration at Reed Bank, (b) attempted to prohibit fishing by Philippine vessels in the Philippines' EEZ, (c) protected Chinese fishermen and failed to prevent them from fishing within the Philippines' EEZ at Mischief Reef and Second Thomas Shoal, and (d) constructed installations and artificial islands at Mischief Reef without permission from the Philippines. Therefore, the tribunal ruled that China violated the Philippines' sovereign rights with respect to its EEZ and continental shelf.

The tribunal next examined traditional fishing at Scarborough Shoal and held that fishermen from the Philippines, China and other countries had traditional fishing rights in the area. As Scarborough Shoal generates an entitlement to a territorial sea, traditional fishing rights were not extinguished by the Convention because its surrounding waters are not part of the EEZ. Without authority or need to determine sovereignty over Scarborough Shoal, the tribunal held that China had breached her obligation to respect the traditional fishing rights of the Philippines by blocking its fishermen from accessing the Shoal after May 2012. Furthermore, the tribunal held that China had breached its obligations under the International Regulations for Preventing Collisions at Sea 1972 and Article 94 UNCLOS 1982 on maritime safety when Chinese law enforcement vessels physically obstructed the Philippine vessels from approaching or accessing the Shoal in 2012. The tribunal also found that China's large-scale land reclamation and construction of artificial islands at several features in the Spratly Islands endangered the coral reef and that China was in breach of its obligations under articles 192 and 194 of the Convention to preserve and protect the marine environment of fragile ecosystems and the habitat of threatened, or endangered species.

### Aggravation of the dispute between the parties

The tribunal considered whether China's activities such as the large-scale land reclamation and construction of artificial islands at several features in the Spratly Islands since the Philippines commenced arbitration proceedings aggravated the dispute between the parties. The tribunal noted that parties engaged in dispute settlement proceedings were obliged to refrain from aggravating the dispute during the settlement process. It was held that the below actions by China's constituted a breach of its obligations to do nothing that aggravates or extends the parties' disputes during the settlement process.

a    Building artificial island on Mischief Reef, a low-tide elevation in the Philippines EEZ
b    Taking actions that endangered the coral reef ecosystem
c    Engaging in activities that damaged evidence of the natural condition of the features

In conclusion, the argument as to whether, as claimed by China, this was a delimitation issue where the tribunal had no authority or an international law issue as claimed by the Philippines and accepted by the tribunal remains relevant to the positions taken by both parties irrespective of the tribunal's award. In turn, this has huge consequences on the binding effect of the award as anticipated under Article 11 of the Convention and the authority of the Permanent Court of Arbitration. China has declared an unwillingness to accept, respect or recognize the Award and the tribunal on this matter. However, in doing so, China has not set a new precedent but joins a small number of countries in undermining the authority of the International Court of Justice by rejecting and refusing to comply with its ruling without this having any consequences. In *Nicaragua v United States of America*,[308] the United States challenged the tribunal's jurisdiction, refused to participate in the award process, ultimately refused to comply with the resultant award, and blocked enforcement of the court judgement by the United Nations Security Council. Similarly, the Russian Federation refused to participate in arbitration proceedings or comply with the award in *The Arctic Sunrise Arbitration*.[309] The United Kingdom adopted a similar strategy in *Mauritius v. United Kingdom*.[310]

China's claim to ownership of large portions of the South China Sea based on historical rights is superficial at best. However, it may be suggested that a more significant point to ponder here is that other coastal states that have a stake and various claims in the South China Sea must take some responsibility for China's conduct. The fact that, for so long, China's claims and projections in the South China Sea area did not provoke questions by these states regarding its legitimacy appears to have given China the impetus to pursue its objectives without deferring to international law.

China stated in her position paper that both parties in the dispute have agreed through bilateral instruments and the Declaration on the Conduct of Parties in the South China Sea to settle their relevant disputes through negotiations. Although this argument had no influence on the tribunal's award, it now appears to be a significant point, judging from the reactions and actions of the Philippine government following the tribunal's award. However, the idea that the Philippine and

308 Military and Paramilitary Activities in and against Nicaragua (*Nicaragua v. United States of America*). Merits, Judgment. I.C.J. Reports 1986, p. 14.
309 *Kingdom of the Netherlands v. The Russian Federation*, PCA Case No. 2014–02, Award on the Merits (Perm. Ct. Arb. 2015).
310 Chagos Marine Protected Area Arbitration, *Mauritius v. United Kingdom*, Final Award, ICGJ 486 (PCA 2015), 18 March 2015, Permanent Court of Arbitration [PCA].

Chinese governments are now seeking amicable resolution of this dispute should be worrisome to all states. This is because if both countries were to proceed with that option, they would have succeeded in mutually agreeing to disregard both international law and the judgement of an international court. This would continue a strategy employed successfully by a small number of countries including the United States and the United Kingdom. The challenge here is that even if this amicable resolution between both parties were to succeed, it would probably be limited to tempering the feud between the Philippines and the Chinese. There is no evidence to indicate that all the other state parties involved in disputes in the South China Sea would also be satisfied.

# 10 The liberal maritime cabotage approach

A liberal maritime cabotage approach generally impose fewer requirements on operators conducting maritime cabotage activities in the coastal waters of a maritime nation. Normally, all vessels regardless of flag, ownership, place of build or nationality of crew can engage in the coastal trade and services of a liberal maritime cabotage nation. Generally, states adopt liberal maritime cabotage policies to promote economic development by encouraging competition.

In assessing the liberal maritime cabotage framework, we will not focus on countries without the necessary national instrumentalities of commerce to support a national maritime cabotage regime. This is because, in any case, there would be no maritime cabotage services in these countries without the foreign maritime presence. Rather, we will focus on countries with dedicated domestic maritime resources, functional institutional framework and reliable infrastructural facilities that can support domestic and international maritime activities. Contrary to the protectionist view, there is no evidence to suggest that countries with liberal maritime cabotage regime are threatened to any considerable degree by foreign vessels trading in their territorial waters. Rather, the presence of these foreign vessels contributes to the development of the domestic maritime sector. This is because allowing foreign vessels the privilege of engaging in coastal trade deprives indigenous shipowners of the opportunity to charge oppressive freight rates. Furthermore, the liberal system allows indigenous shipowners to be subject to the open competition essential to the proper development of their inventive energies.[1]

A liberal law is as advantageous in the maritime sector as it is in other sectors of the economy in countries with effective institutional and functional infrastructural facilities. We will now assess some countries that have adopted a liberal maritime cabotage approach.

---

1 For more on this, see: J. Lalor, 'Coasting Trade' [1881], *Cyclopedia of Political Science, Political Economy, and of the Political History of the United States*, vol. 1, *Abdication-Duty*. This very succinct commentary of John Joseph Lalor which though written in 1881, remains timelessly true even now beckons on all countries to be careful in their choice of maritime cabotage approach as illustrated in the theory of developmental sovereignty.

## The European Union: Council Regulation (EEC) No. 3577/92

The maritime cabotage policy in the European Union can be traced back to Council Regulation (EEC) No. 4055/86. This Regulation applied the principle of freedom to provide services to maritime transport between member states and between member states and third countries.[2] The desire to create a single European market (now the 'internal market') was the driving force that led to enacting this Regulation. Establishing the internal market formed the central theme in the Commission's 1985 white paper discussions.[3] Maritime cabotage was eventually liberalized in the European Union by Council Regulation 3577/92 and applies throughout the European Economic Area.[4]

The maritime cabotage framework in the European Union is described generally as the best illustration of an effective liberal maritime cabotage approach. Council Regulation 3577/92 came into force in 1993 and is designed to allow Community shipowners the freedom to provide maritime transport services between member states in the European Union. This is subject to the proviso that they have satisfied the requirements and are eligible to carry out similar services in their home state. In the strictest sense, the maritime cabotage framework in the EU is not liberal. This is because the liberal policy is limited to the European Union and does not extend to countries outside the European Union.[5] Furthermore, the Regulation does not necessarily include crew and fiscal requirements as some member states still set thresholds that must be met.[6] Moreover, the Regulation provides safeguard measures that permit member states to suspend the Regulation in the event of a serious disturbance in the internal transport market.[7]

The Regulation's objective of pursuing a liberal policy, as described in the third and fourth recitals in the preamble, is yet to be achieved in full. This is illustrated by the protectionist framework around island cabotage within the European Union. Article 3(2) of Council Regulation (EEC) No. 3577/92 effectively lays down an exception to the liberalization objective with respect to island cabotage. Article 3(2) provides that the law of the host state applies to all matters relating to

2  Council Regulation (EEC) 4055/86 of 22 December 1986, O.J. 1986 L 378/1 as amended by Regulation 3573/90.
3  European Commission, 'Completing the Internal Market: White Paper for the Commission to the European Council', European Commission, 1985.
4  Council Regulation (EEC) No. 3577/92 of 7 December 1992; Applying the Principle of Freedom to Provide Services to Maritime Transport within Member States (Maritime Cabotage); O.J. L 364. It should be noted that Non-EU member vessels can only engage in EU country cabotage based on a waiver or bilateral agreements, except in those EU countries (UK, Norway and Denmark) that traditionally have an open coast policy.
5  See: Article 1 of Council Regulation (EEC) No. 3577/92. See also: Article 3 of the same Regulation, which illustrates that the liberal policy does not extend to manning requirements.
6  See: Article 3 of Council Regulation (EEC) No. 3577/92 for Manning stipulations.
7  Article 5 of Council Regulation (EEC) No. 3577/92. Spain is the only member state to date to have used the safeguard measure in 1993 for two consecutive six-month periods.

crewing for vessels providing maritime transport services between islands. This is in addition to similar protectionist measures on fiscal and crewing requirements with regard to the freedom to provide maritime transport services within the European Union. Article 3(3) applies the law of the flag state to crew composition when island cabotage is preceded or followed by an international voyage carried out by a cargo vessel over 650 gt. This is bolstered by the express provisions of articles 1 and 3(1) of the Regulation that specify that the law of the flag state applies. Traditionally, the flag state is responsible for all issues relating to crewing, although the rules vary depending on the ship register. For instance, some member states in the EU impose strict nationality conditions that require all crew members to be EU nationals. Other member states are less strict and impose EU nationality requirements on the ship master, chief officer and chief engineer positions only. These different nationality requirements result in serious financial disparity between different registers.

In order to avoid distorting competition on the most sensitive routes, the Regulation stipulates that 'host' member states may impose their own crewing rules on ships carrying out island cabotage and ships smaller than 650 gt engaged in other kinds of maritime cabotage services.[8] However, to avoid negating the essence of Council Regulation 3577/92, flag state rules apply to cargo ships over 650 gt carrying out island cabotage where the voyage concerned follows or precedes a voyage to or from another state. This is referred to as consecutive cabotage.[9]

These provisions raise two issues that concern the extent of the host state's competence. The first issue relates to the leverage possessed by the host state in determining crewing requirements, where the law of the host state applies.[10] The second issue is concerned with the competent authority between the flag state and the host state with respect to consecutive cabotage. On the first issue where the applicable law is that of the host state, the Regulation does not specifically identify what responsibilities fall to the host state on matters relating to crewing. There are suggestions that the host state has unlimited competence. This is based on the express wordings of the Regulation, which refer to 'all matters relating to manning'. However, it is observed that the European Commission adopts a more conservative approach on the issue.

On the second issue, The Commission argues that the powers of the host state should be limited to protect the objective of Regulation 3577/92, which is the freedom to provide maritime transport services within the European Union. Therefore, the principle that allows host states to impose their crewing requirements on maritime cabotage services derogates from the liberal agenda of the Regulation.[11] The Commission suggests that the powers of the host state should

---

8  See: articles 3(1) and 3(2) of Council Regulation (EEC) No. 3577/92.
9  See: articles 3(1) of Council Regulation (EEC) No. 3577/92.
10 See: articles 3(1), 3(2), and 3(3) of Council Regulation (EEC) No. 3577/92.
11 See Article 9 of Council Regulation (EEC) No. 3577/92, which stipulates that any member state wishing to avail itself of the possibility to apply its own rules to matters relating to crewing should consult the Commission. Furthermore, Article 9 states that

be limited to the right to stipulate the required proportion of EU nationals on board ships carrying out island cabotage and on vessels smaller than 650gt. Therefore, a member state may:

a   Require the crews of such vessels to be composed entirely of EU nationals.
b   Require the seafarers on board to have social insurance cover in the EU.
c   With regards to working conditions, impose the minimum wage rules in force in the country.
d   With regard to the rules on safety and training (including the languages spoken on board), member states may do no more than require compliance with the EU or international rules in force (STCW and SOLAS Conventions), without disproportionately restricting the freedom to provide services.[12]

Furthermore, an ancillary issue for consideration is whether feeder services fall within the scope of Regulation 4055/86, which does not impose any flag requirement. Alternatively, whether such services are to be considered cabotage services under Regulation 3577/92 where there is a flag requirement.[13] Feeder services are generally considered as cabotage services in member states with the exception of France and Portugal, where maritime transport services are reserved for EU-flagged vessels. However, the freedom to provide feeder services is free for all in member states that implement an open coast policy.[14]

Although EU legislation on maritime cabotage was effective from 1993, some member states were granted flexibility to facilitate full compliance with the law.

the scope and content of envisaged measures will be subject to a case-by-case analysis in the light of the principles of necessity and proportionality.

12  See: European Commission, 'Communication from the Commission: on the interpretation of Council Regulation (EEC) No. 3577/92 applying the principle of freedom to provide services to maritime transport within Member States (maritime cabotage)', European Commission COM(2014) 232 final (Brussels, 22 April 2014).

13  Feeder services (also known as relay of international cargo services) are international services by which a carrier discharges cargo from a vessel that has sailed from a point of departure to transfer the same cargo on to another vessel which continues the journey to a port of destination. The service is normally carried out under a through bill of lading. For instance, where the feeder service consists of pre- or onward transportation of cargo between two ports of a member state X (a) with a destination in member state Y or a third country or (b) coming from member state Y or a third country, member state X could reserve such feeder services for EU-flagged vessels.

14  The Commission has acknowledged the substantial savings in the cost of transport and the contribution to better efficiency of services that can be achieved if companies can perform feeder services for the carriage of international cargo following or preceding an international voyage. These associated benefits mean that the provision of feeder services is increasingly the subject of negotiations in trade agreement discussions. The Commission believes there is scope to explore these benefits through better cooperation by member states. For more on the issue, see: European Commission, 'Communication from the Commission: On the interpretation of Council Regulation (EEC) No. 3577/92 applying the principle of freedom to provide services to maritime transport within Member States (maritime cabotage), COM(2014) 232 final (Brussels, 22 April 2014).

For instance, Greece was allowed an extended period until 2004 to comply with the new Regulation. However, by 2002 maritime cabotage in Greece was fully liberalized. Furthermore, by opening her maritime market in 2010 to cruise ships registered in a third country, Greece succeeded in liberalizing its maritime cabotage market beyond the scope required by the EU Regulation.[15] Nevertheless, it was not until 2011 that Greece aligned fully with the EU maritime cabotage regulation. The delay was because of a series of amendments introduced by Ministerial Decision 3323.1/02/08, presidential decrees 38/2011 and 44/2011, and Law 3922/2011.[16] In the case of other member states, island cabotage and mainland passenger operations were not liberalized until 1999.[17]

Prior to Council Regulation 3577/92 coming into force, member states in the European Union implemented different approaches to maritime cabotage. Greece, France, Spain, and Italy applied protectionist maritime cabotage regulations, and were required to amend their legislations to comply with the new European Union regulation. However, the United Kingdom, Netherlands, and Norway had traditionally operated an open coast policy and did not need to make any changes to their legislations.[18] The scope of the EU maritime cabotage law is captured in Article 1 of the EU Regulation 3577/92, which stipulates that:

> As from January 1, 1993, freedom to provide maritime transport services within a Member State (maritime cabotage) shall apply to Community shipowners who have their ships registered in, and flying the flag of, a Member State, provided that these ships comply with all conditions for carrying out cabotage in that Member State.

Vessels that are documented in the first registers of member states are eligible to engage in EU maritime cabotage services. However, vessels documented in off-shore registers and some second registers, cannot engage in EU maritime cabotage services under Council Regulation 3577/92.[19]

---

15 See: Greek Law 3872/2010 on Liberalization of Cruise Ships. Enacted 31 August 2010.
16 See: European Commission, Fifth Report on the implementation of Council Regulation (EEC) No. 3577/92 applying the principle of freedom to provide services to maritime cabotage (2001–2010) (COM(2014) 231 final, European Commission 2014). This legislation was adopted in Greece in the context of an infringement procedure that was closed in 2011 by the European Commission.
17 Spain, Portugal, France and Italy liberalized island cabotage in 1999.
18 See appendix 1 of Council Regulation (EEC) No. 3577/92 for EU member states' adaptation of their national laws to comply with EU maritime cabotage law.
19 The second registers of member states that comply with EU cabotage regulation are the Spanish REC register, Portuguese MAR register, Danish DIS cargo vessels, German ISR vessels on a case-by-case basis and not in regular/year-round cabotage, and Finnish vessels entered on the 'List of merchant vessels in international trade' on a case-by-case basis and not in regular/year-round cabotage. However, ships registered in the Italian second register and passenger ships registered in the Danish second register are prohibited from Community maritime cabotage. Offshore registers prohibited from maritime cabotage activities under Regulation 3577/92 are the

The adoption of Council Regulation 1370/2007[20] appears to have caused some confusion. Article 1(2) of the Regulation provides that it shall apply to the national and international operation of public passenger transport services by road, rail and other track-based modes of transport. However, the concern is that member states may apply Article 1(2) of 1370/2007 to public passenger transport by inland waterways without prejudice to Regulation 3577/92. The problem stems from the fact that the term 'national sea waters' is not expressly defined in any of the EU or international legal instruments. Thus, the application of Regulation 1370/2007 to maritime cabotage within the EU raises serious questions of conflict and compatibility with Regulation 3577/92, which is the authority on EU maritime cabotage. However, the Commission has provided a three-stage response to this concern as follows:

a   Regulation 1370/2007 does not apply automatically to public passenger transport by national seawaters, except where a member state makes it expressly applicable.[21]
b   Regulation 1370/2007 applies only to public transport of passengers by road or rail. However, the bulk of the maritime cabotage transport services covered under Council Regulation 3577/92 are a combination of freight and passengers. Thus, Regulation 1370/2007 cannot apply to a maritime transport service carrying only freight or a combination of passenger and freight.
c   Regulation 1370/2007 may only be applied by member states to the transportation of passengers by national seawaters if it does not conflict with or prejudice the implementation of Regulation 3577/92. Where there is a conflict between the two legislations, Regulation 3577/92 shall take precedence, with Regulation 1370/2007 serving in a supplementary capacity.[22]

Thus, it is evident that elements of protectionist measures remain within the 'liberal' EU maritime cabotage law and policy framework. These protectionist

Kerguelen Register, the French Southern and Antarctic Territories' Register (TAAF Register), the Dutch Antilles' Register, the Isle of Man Register and the Bermuda and Cayman Islands registers.

20  Council Regulation (EC) No. 1370/2007 of the European Parliament and the Council on public passenger transport services by rail and by road, which repeals Council Regulation (EEC) No. 1191/69 and Council Regulation (EEC) No. 1107/70, was adopted on 23 October 2007. See: O.J. L 315. 3 December 2007, p. 1.
21  It has already been established that inland waterways transport services within the EU that is not of a maritime nature does fall within the scope of Council Regulation (EE) No. 3577/92. Instead, such transport services fall under Council Regulation (EEC) No. 3921/91.
22  For a broader discussion on how Regulation (EC) No. 1370/2007 conflicts with Council Regulation (EEC) No. 3577/92 on maritime cabotage, see: European Commission, 'Communication from the Commission: On the interpretation of Council Regulation (EEC) No. 3577/92 applying the principle of freedom to provide services to maritime transport within Member States (maritime cabotage)' European commission COM(2014) 232 final, 22 April 2014).

measures will no doubt be amplified with reports of ongoing discussions to redefine the scope of the EU maritime cabotage legislation. There are propositions to expand the scope of Regulation 3577/92 to include maritime cabotage trade and services 'between' member states. This contrasts with the current framework, which limits the scope of maritime cabotage to 'within' member states of the European Union. The objective of the proposed expansion is to exclude non-European Union persons from providing intra community maritime trade or services.[23]

Thus, there remain several challenges that still hinder the holistic liberal policy provision of maritime services within the European Union. For instance, the fact that territorial waters represent the external borders of the European Union for the purposes of customs control is an impediment. Hence, a ship sailing between two European countries is deemed by law to have left EU customs territory. The effect of this is that the cargo on that vessel is subjected to custom clearance at both its departure and destination ports.[24] This contradicts the notion of free movement of people and goods within the European Union as contemplated by Regulation 3577/92. For the United Kingdom, this is likely to get more complicated when Brexit is eventually triggered. Nevertheless, one argues that a true liberal policy should reflect the freedom to provide maritime transport services that covers the full spectrum of commerce and transportation.[25]

## Judicial decisions arising from Council Regulation 3577/92

### *Alpina and Nicko Tours v. Chioggia Port Authority*[26]

This was a request for a preliminary ruling on the interpretation of Council Regulation 3577/92 and its application to cruise vessels operation within a member state. This request arose from a dispute between the partnership of the Swiss company (Alpina River Cruises GmbH) and the German company (Nicko Tours GmbH), hereinafter known as Alpina and Nicko Tours, as plaintiff. The Senior Ministry for Infrastructure and Transport – Chioggia Port Authority in Italy was the defendant. The issue in contention was the refusal by the Chioggia Port

---

23 For an elaborate read on the proposed expansion of the legal framework on Council Regulation (EEC) No. 3577/92, see: B. Parameswaran, *The Liberalization of Maritime Transport Services* (Springer 2004). See generally: chapters 4 and 5; and particularly: pp. 348–350.
24 There are ongoing discussions to address this issue. See: Report on Motorways of the Sea – State of Play and Consultation, (SEC (2007) 1367). See also: European Commission, 'Blue Belt: A Single Transport Area for Shipping' European Commission COM(2013) 510 final (Brussels, 8 July 2013).
25 See: J. Chuah, 'Short Sea Shipping: The Blue Belt Package' [2013], *Journal of International Maritime Law*, 19(1), 256–258.
26 Case C 17/13 [2014] *Alpina River Cruises GmbH and Nicko Tours GmbH v. Ministero delle infrastrutture e dei trasporti — Capitaneria di Porto di Chioggia*. Judgment of the court (Third Chamber) 27 March 2014.

Authority to permit Alpina and Nicko Tours to sail a Swiss-flagged tourist vessel through the Italian territorial sea.

Alpina GmbH owned the tourist vessel in question (*MS Bellissima*) and Nicko Tours were the intended users of the vessel. Alpina and Nicko Tours had arranged a cruise tour whose itinerary included departing from Venice (Italy), crossing the Venetian lagoon to Chioggia (Italy), crossing territorial sea between Chioggia and Porto Levante (Italy), sailing for about 60 km up the river Po (Italy) to the town of Polesella (Italy), and finally returning to Venice on the reverse itinerary.

Alpina and Nicko Tours' application for authorization to cross the territorial sea between Chioggia and Porto Levante was rejected by the port authority in Chioggia (Capitaneria di Porto di Chioggia). Justification for the rejection was because under Italian law, maritime cabotage is reserved for ships flying the flag of a member state of the European Union.[27] Vessels flying the Swiss flag do not meet that specific requirement.

Alpina and Nicko Tours contested the refusal before the Veneto Regional Administrative Court (Tribunale amministrativo regionale per il Veneto), but the case was dismissed. The plaintiffs proceeded to challenge the refusal before the Italian Council of State (the Consiglio di Stato). They argued that the concept of maritime cabotage applies only to services that involve true sea transport pursuant to Council Regulation 3577/92. Furthermore, they claimed that apart from the short passage through the territorial sea between Chioggia and Porto Levante, the intended cruise did not involve sea transport and was scheduled only to take place in internal waters. It is important to note here that if the *MS Bellissima* was smaller in size, crossing the stretch of Italian territorial sea between the ports of Chioggia and Porto Levante would not have been necessary as cruise vessels can navigate the canal connecting Chioggia with the river Po. Hence, there would have been no need to apply for permission.[28] The Consiglio di Stato asked the Court of Justice of the European Union to determine 'Whether a cruise, which starts and ends, with the same passengers, in the same port of a Member State falls within the scope of Regulation 3577/92'.[29]

We should remember here that the reference to 'cruise liners' in Article 3(1) of Council Regulation 3577/92 and the derogation that was provided for some cruise services under Article 6(1) of the same regulation are clear evidence that the regulation covers cruise transportation.

---

27  See: Article 224 of the Italian Shipping Code (Royal Decree No. 327 of 30 March 1942, as amended) ('the ISC').

28  From the Judgement of the CJEU, the plaintiffs would still have been in breach of EU Regulation 3577/92 had they simply just embarked on their cruise journey without applying for permission from the Chioggia port authority. This is because the court held that other parts of the cruise vessel Itinerary fell within the scope of Regulation 3577/92.

29  It is important to observe that, the reference to 'cruise liners' in Article 3(1) of Council Regulation 3577/92, and the derogation that was provided for some cruise services under Article 6(1) of the same regulation, are clear evidence that the regulation covers cruise transportation.

The CJEU confirmed in its ruling that the EU cabotage regulation only relates to transport services within a member state (cabotage) that are of a maritime nature.[30] Hence, inland waterway transport services in a member state that are not of a maritime nature are not covered under the EU cabotage regulation. Such services are covered under Regulation 3921/91, which provides for the carriage of goods or passengers by inland waterway within member states by non-resident carriers. The CJEU proceeded to hold that, contrary to the claims made by Alpina and Nicko Tours, the cruise at issue did not have a mainly non-maritime nature. The court argued that, apart from the sea area between Chioggia and Porto Levante, the cruise vessel also had to navigate in the Venetian lagoon and the mouth of the river Po, both of which form part of Italy's internal maritime waters.

However, Regulation 3577/92 does not provide an exclusive definition of the 'sea'. Rather, the definition of the 'sea' was accorded a wider scope under the Regulation by the ECJ.[31] One argues that this wider meaning is quite distinct from the usual definition of the sea in public international law, under the United Nations Convention on the Law of the Sea 1982.[32] Hence, under Council Regulation 3577/92 the 'sea' extends beyond the limit of the territorial seas. It includes internal maritime waters, which are on the landward side of the baseline of the territorial sea. The expanded definition of the sea as upheld in this case is significant. This is because, barring such expanded definition, a smaller vessel would perform the schedule without triggering the debate on whether the law of maritime cabotage applied.[33] For smaller vessels, the organizers would have had the option of navigating the canal, which connects Chioggia with the river Po. On this basis, one questions how far a vessel should travel in the territorial sea to confer a maritime nature on the voyage. This question was not considered by the court. Further, the CJEU provided *obiter dictum*, suggesting that because the kind of services envisaged in Article 2(1) is introduced by the term 'in particular', the provisions of that article must not be interpreted as exhaustive. This is because such interpretation would have the effect of excluding transport services that possess all the essential characteristics of maritime cabotage from the scope of Regulation 3577/92.[34]

30  See: Article 1(1) of Council Regulation (EEC) No. 3577/92.
31  *Commission of the European Communities v. Kingdom of Spain* Case C-323/03 [2006] ECR I-2161; EU: C: 2006:159, paragraphs 25 to 27. 9 March 2006.
32  See; Article 3 of UNCLOS 1982 (The Montego Bay Convention), signed on 10 December 1982; in force, 16 November 1994. Approved on behalf of the European Community by Council Decision 98/392/EC of 23 March 1998 (OJ 1998 L 179, p. 1). Also: Article 8 of UNCLOS 1982, specifically defines 'Internal Waters' (bays, estuaries, fjords and inlets), thereby distinguishing it from the territorial sea.
33  This was the basis upon which Alpina and Nicko Tours claimed that, apart from the short passage through the territorial sea between Chioggia and Porto Levante, the cruise was scheduled to occur in internal waters and hence had a mainly non-maritime nature. Hence Regulation 3577/92 should not apply. The CJEU rejected this argument.
34  See: Case C-251/04 *Commission v. Hellenic Republic* [EU: C: 2007:5] for the effect of the phrase 'in particular'.

Hence, the CJEU held that all cruise services provided for remuneration in the maritime waters of a member state are covered under Council Regulation 3577/92. This is irrespective of whether or not the cruise services start and end with the same passengers in the same port.[35] This decision was reached notwithstanding that the relevant provisions of Council Regulation 3577/92 stipulate that carriage by sea must occur between 'two or more ports of the same Member State'.[36]

It is useful to highlight some difficulties that arise from this ruling. The first difficulty relates to the concept of 'port' for the purposes of maritime cabotage. It focuses on the scope of what is properly understood as a single port system instead of a multiple port system. The second difficulty is concerned with the meaning of the sea. By this, we mean the scope of 'sea transport' within the context of the Council Regulation 3577/92.

With regards to the first difficulty, the Regulation does not specifically offer any definition of 'port'. However, it has been defined as any infrastructure whether temporary or small scale that serves as a terminal for the loading and discharging of cargo or passengers for carriage by sea.[37] Moreover, in the context of transport services, Article 2(1) (a) to (c) of Regulation 3577/92 explicitly states that the carriage should have a departure port that is distinct from the arrival port. This is of huge significance because the facts in this case indicate clearly that the vessel was scheduled to start and end in the same port with the same passengers. It is suggested that the decision in the Alpina case is a clear contradiction of the express provisions of Article 2(1) of Regulation 3577/92. A more troubling question is whether any sort of navigation of a vessel away from the port of departure irrespective of the short distance would satisfy the 'different port' proviso of the Regulation. Furthermore, where the vessel carries other types of cargo and not passengers, it is debatable whether arriving at the same port of departure would qualify as the sort of 'carriage by sea' envisaged by the Regulation.

Also, the apparent suggestion by the CJEU that the provisions of Article 2(1) should not be deemed as exhaustive is questionable.[38] This is because, even if it could be argued that the list is not exhaustive, the concept needs to be consistent with the general understanding of maritime cabotage internationally. The CJEU's refusal to be constrained by the wording of the Regulation goes against the

---

35 For a different application of the law of maritime cabotage, see: Article 40 of The Navigation and Maritime Trade Law 'NMTL' of Mexico (Article 40 Ley de Navegación y Comercio Marítimos), which entered into force in 2006.

36 Article 2 provides 'For the purposes of this Regulation: (1) "maritime transport services within a Member State (maritime cabotage)" shall mean services normally provided for remuneration and shall in particular include: (a) mainland cabotage: the carriage of passengers or goods by sea between ports situated on the mainland or the main territory of one and the same Member State without calls at islands.'

37 See: *Commission of the European Communities v. Kingdom of Spain* Case C-323/03 [2006] ECR I-2161; 9 March 2006.

38 For a comparative analysis of the scope of maritime cabotage law in different jurisdictions, see: C. Lopez, 'Mexico: The Legal Treatment of Vessels and Offshore Installations under the Mexican Foreign Investment and Navigation Frameworks' [2013], *Maritime and Transport Law News*, 9(1).

common understanding that to be considered maritime cabotage there should be transportation of cargo between two or more ports of the same member state.[39] This understanding is bolstered by the express wording in Article 2(1) EU Regulation 3577/92. Furthermore, the wording in Article 2(1) raises further issues that require some understanding. First, the word 'between' as used in Article 2(1) cannot be given any other grammatical and logical meaning except that there should always be two or more ports in the same member state. Second, an analogy might be drawn from the carriage of commercial goods. It would not make commercial, maritime or logical sense for endeavours such as the sailing of a commercial vessel from one port and returning to the same port with the same cargo to be considered as carriage of goods by sea. Thus, the objective of sea carriage here is quite different from what is generally understood commercially as maritime cabotage. It is instructive that the CJEU had clearly seen fit to extend the concept.[40]

With this ruling, the Court of Justice of the European Union (CJEU) has injected further controversy into the already contentious subject of maritime cabotage.[41] The effect of this decision is that the carriage by sea occurring even within a 'single port system' will trigger the application of the EU Regulation on maritime cabotage.[42] The ambivalent and uncertain direction in which the CJEU has gone with respect to interpreting the provisions of Regulation 3577/92 raises concern. One wonders whether the CJEU and the national courts will continue to interpret the provisions of Regulation 3577/92 broadly as demonstrated in this case.[43]

### Commission of the European Communities v. France[44]

This case was the result of complaints brought by the European Commission's against France. The Commission argued that France had defaulted in amending a

39  See: Case C-251/04 *Commission v. Hellenic Republic* EU: C: 2007:5, paragraphs 28–32.
40  This ruling is a clear example of the ambivalent nature of maritime cabotage and how it is implemented differently in different jurisdictions. The maritime cabotage law in Mexico permits the operation and management of tourism, sport and leisure vessels in Mexican maritime zones by foreign shipowners or operators with foreign vessels.
41  For an instructive read and broader assessment of the issues in this case and the decision of the CJEU, see the author's earlier work at: A. Akpan, 'A Precarious Judicial Interpretation of the Scope of EU Maritime Cabotage Law' [2014], *Journal of International Maritime Law*, 20(6), 444–447.
42  See: *Shipbuilders Council of America et al. v. United States of America et al.* 868 F. 2d 452 (DC Cir. 1989). Decided 3 March 1989 in the United States Court of Appeals, District of Columbia Circuit; nos 88–5095, 88–5119. In this case, the United States Custom service sanctioned the use of a single port system in the movement of cargo in the coastal waters of the United States as not contravening the relevant provisions of the Merchant Marine Act of 1920. Their decision was because the cargo was loaded and unloaded at the same point.
43  Case C-251/04 *Commission v. Greece* EU: C: 2007:5
44  Case C – 160/99 [2000] *Commission v. France* ECR I-6137.

provision of their 1977 Customs Code within a reasonable period. That provision stated that only vessels flying the French flag were entitled to participate in cabotage activities in France. In response, France explained that it took administrative steps to ensure temporary application of Council Regulation 3577/92. The steps taken by France included publishing a circular setting out the terms of the cabotage regulation, and inserting a footnote into the Customs Code.

It was held by the European Court of Justice (now, CJEU) that the measures taken by France were inadequate to relieve France of their European Commission's Treaty obligation to ensure that their national law complies with Community law. The decision of the ECJ was based on a Community law principle which states that an EC Treaty obligation is breached where a member state fails to amend, within a reasonable time, a national law that is inconsistent with Community law.[45]

It is argued that at best, this was an unfair decision that border on a wrong decision. It is observed that the essence of the EU cabotage law is to facilitate freedom to provide maritime transport services between member states. Therefore, the evaluation of whether that obligation is complied with is tested when a Community shipowner is restricted from providing maritime transport services. It therefore should not matter whether the measure is temporary or permanent, as far as at any point in time, an eligible shipowner from another member state is able to provide maritime transport services without any unnecessary restraint. This position is bolstered further by the fact that Regulation 3577/92 provides for safeguard measures that allow member states to suspend application of the Regulation if there is a serious disturbance of the internal transport market.[46]

### Commission of the European Communities v. Greece [47]

The Commission of the European Communities accused the Hellenic Republic of contravening several sections of Council Regulation 3577/92.[48] The parties

45 Formerly – Articles 10 and 249 of the Treaty on European Union (Maastricht Treaty). Since the Lisbon Treaty came into force in 2009, the principles of the old articles 10 and 249 of the EC Treaty are now captured in Article 4(3) of the Treaty on the Functioning of the European Union (TFEU). The provisions of this article stipulate that member states must take appropriate measures to fulfil the obligations resulting from the acts of the institutions of the Union. Furthermore, member states must refrain from measures which would jeopardize the attainment of the Union's objectives. This principle applies even where a Community measure such as the Cabotage Regulation is directly applicable within the national legal orders of the member states. However, this is different from the principle of 'direct effect' of European Union Law. The principle of direct effect was first established by the European Court of Justice (ECJ) in *Van Gend en Loos v. Nederlandse Administratie der Belastingen* (Case 26/62); [1963] ECR 1; [1970] CMLR 1.

46 See: Article 5 of Council Regulation (EEC) No. 3577/92. Spain used the safeguard measure in 1993 for two consecutive six-months periods.

47 Case C-288/02 [2004] *Commission v. Greece* ECR I-10071, Judgement of the Court (second Chambers), 21 October 2004.

48 OJ 1992 L 364. Adopted 7 December 1992. Regulation applying the principle of freedom to provide services to maritime transport within Member States (maritime cabotage).

attempted unsuccessfully to resolve the issues through a pre-litigation procedure. Hence, the Commission brought this action, alleging that Greece breached articles 1, 3 and 6 of Regulation 3577/92. The Commission complained specifically that Greece failed to comply with her obligations under the Regulation by:

a   Conferring the right to carry passengers between Greek mainland ports solely upon Greek passenger ships. In addition, the right to carry out tours with passenger ships exceeding 650gt between Greek islands was also conferred solely upon Greek vessels.[49]

b   Requiring from Community ships entered in a second or international register a certificate issued by the competent authority of the flag state declaring that the ship is authorised to provide cabotage services in that member state.[50]

c   Considering that the Peloponnese constitutes an island.[51]

d   Applying to Community tankers, freighters, passenger ships and tourist ships, and to Community cruise liners which carry out maritime transport by way of cabotage, its national rules as host state relating to manning conditions.[52] Also, requiring shipowners to apply to the Department for the Supervision of Merchant Ships for measurement of the ship gross tonnage to enable the Greek authorities to calculate the composition of the crew.[53]

The Commission withdrew the second part of the fourth complaint because of additional clarifications provided by Greece during the written proceedings. Furthermore, the first complaint was dropped at the start of the hearing because of the passing of Greek Presidential Decree No. 344/2003.[54] Thus, only the second and third complaints and the first part of the fourth complaint came before the court for determination. The remaining complaints were rooted in Circular No. 1151.65/1/98,[55] whereas the first part of the fourth complaint had its basis in Circular No. 1151.65/2/98.[56]

49  See (prior to its amendment Presidential Decree No. 344/2003); Article 165 of the Greek Code of Public Maritime Law ('the KDND') Decree-Law No. 187/1973 (FEK A 261), as amended by Presidential Decrees Nos 113/97 (FEK A 99) and 84/98 (FEK A 77).

50  See: Article 2.1.2 of Circular No 1151.65/1/98 adopted on 4th August 1998 by the Ypourgeio Emporikis Naftilias (Ministry of the Merchant Marine).

51  See: Article 2.1.1 of Circular No 1151.65/1/98.

52  Article 2.4.1 of Circular, No. 1151.65/2/98 of 18 December 1998.

53  See: Circular No. 2311.10/10/98 of 21 December 1998.

54  FEK 314 A of 31 December 2003. This Decree amended Article 165 of the Greek Code of Public Maritime Law ('the KDND'), which was the architect of the first complaint by the Commission.

55  This Circular, entitled 'Activities of cargo vessels and tankers flying Community flags which carry out maritime cabotage', was adopted on 4 August 1998 by the Ypourgeio Emporikis Naftilias (Ministry of the Merchant Marine). The circular points out in particular that Regulation No. 3577/92 forms an integral part of Greek legislation and prevails over any conflicting provision.

56  Circular, No. 1151.65/2/98 of 18 December 1998 entitled 'Activities of passenger, tourist and cruise ships flying Community flags which operate tours (cruises) in Greek

*The second complaint*

By its second complaint, the Commission claimed that the Greek government impeded the objectives of Regulation 3577/92 by obstructing the freedom to provide maritime transport services. Greece required Community ships entered in a second or international register to present a certificate from the flag state, certifying the ship's eligibility to perform cabotage in that flag state. This complaint is based on Article 1 of Regulation 3577/92, which reserves maritime cabotage to Community ships registered in the first register of a member state.[57] Article 1 also demands that Community ships comply with all the conditions for carrying out cabotage in that member state. This means that a mere registration of a vessel is not in itself sufficient. Rather, the vessel must qualify by her registration to perform maritime cabotage in that member state.

The reason for this is because vessels registered in 'second registers' and 'offshore international registers' of member states do not qualify automatically to perform maritime cabotage under Council Regulation 3577/92.[58] The Commission submitted that the objective of confirming which vessels qualify to perform maritime cabotage could still be achieved through less restrictive measures. Accordingly, it suggested the following alternatives:

a   Placing on Community shipowners, an obligation to submit a copy of the legislation of the member state authorising ships entered in a second register to provide cabotage services.

waters'. Specifically, Article 2.4.1 stipulates as follows: 'In general, Greek legislation (as the legislation of the host state) is to apply to the composition of the crews of Community passenger, tourist and cruise ships authorised to carry out cruises between mainland ports and the islands or between island ports of our country, while the legislation of the flag state is to apply to cruises between ports situated on the mainland'.

57  The express provision of Article 1 of Council Regulation 3577/92 is: 'Freedom to provide maritime transport services within a Member State (maritime cabotage) shall apply to Community shipowners who have their ships registered in, and flying the flag of a member state, provided that these ships comply with all conditions for carrying out cabotage in that Member State, including ships registered in Euros, once that Register is approved by the Council.'

58  See: European Commission, 'Communication from the Commission: on the interpretation of Council Regulation (EEC) No. 3577/92 applying the principle of freedom to provide services to maritime transport within Member States (maritime cabotage)', European Commission COM(2014) 232 final (Brussels, 22 April 2014). The second registers of member states which comply with the European Union cabotage regulation are vessels registered in the Spanish REC register, Portuguese MAR register, Danish DIS cargo vessels, German ISR vessels on a case-by-case basis and not in regular/year round cabotage, and Finnish vessels entered on the 'List of merchant vessels in international trade' on a case-by-case basis and not in regular/year round cabotage. Offshore registers prohibited from maritime cabotage activities under Council Regulation (EEC) No. 3577/92 are the Kerguelen Register, the French Southern and Antarctic Territories' Register (TAAF Register), the Dutch Antilles' Register, the Isle of Man Register, and the Bermuda and Cayman Islands Registers. Also, ships registered in the Italian second register and passenger ships registered in the Danish second register are prohibited from Community maritime cabotage.

b   Establishing exchange of annual communication of information between member states on the development of legislation in the maritime sector.
c   The Greek authorities could also informally put forward any questions to the Commission for clarification in that regard.

The Commission argued that it publishes reports every two years for the attention of member states in accordance with Article 10 of Regulation 3577/92.[59] It claimed that these reports are useful for checking whether Community ships fulfil the legal requirements for carrying out cabotage services in the flag state. In addition, The Commission claimed that pursuant to Article 9 of Regulation 3577/92, it provides information regularly to member states regarding national legislative amendments on second registers.[60] These include amendments occurring between two reports, provided the Commission is notified of the development by the member state.

The Greek government disagreed that the measures proposed by The Commission were less restrictive than the obligation to provide a certificate from the flag state confirming the ship's eligibility to perform cabotage services. For instance, The Commission's suggestion that a copy of the flag state legislation which authorises the ship to perform cabotage in that member state could be submitted to the host state, was described by the Greek government as not proportionate to the objective sought. Instead, it argued that such proposal would complicate matters because the flag state would need to translate the legislation officially so that it can be interpreted by the host state. With regard to the exchange of annual communication between member states, the defendants submitted that at best, this proposal would convey the required information to the host state after a considerable and unacceptable delay. In some instances, such proposal could turn out to be disadvantageous to Community shipowners who may be unaware of amendments that give them rights to perform cabotage.

The Commission suggested that the host state could pose questions to the Commission directly, pursuant to Article 9 of Regulation 3577/92.[61] However, it acknowledged that it relies on member states to notify it of amendments to its legislation on second and international registers. Nevertheless, the defendants argued that this proposition cannot be considered less restrictive than an authorized certificate from the flag state. This is because the Commission cannot

59  The provisions of Article 10 of Council Regulation 3577/92 are as follows: 'The Commission shall submit to the Council, before 1 January 1995, and thereafter every two years, a report on the implementation of this Regulation and, if appropriate, shall also put forward any necessary proposals.'
60  Article 9 of Council Regulation 3577/92 states: 'Before adopting laws, regulations or administrative provisions in implementation of this Regulation, Member States shall consult the Commission. They shall inform the latter of any measures thus adopted.'
61  Furthermore, in the interest of monitoring the cabotage market, member states may request shipowners to supply advance information on the services they intend to provide. The Commission considers that such advance information may help member states to better assess the real transport needs.

guarantee that it will always be able to provide the latest accurate information to the host state.

The Commission also suggested that its biennial report which must be published, pursuant to Article 10 of Council Regulation 3577/92 was a useful alternative. The Greek government responded that there was a considerable delay in the publications of these reports. Therefore, the host state would be relying on outdated reports with no certainty on the status of a Community vessel at the time it sought to perform maritime cabotage services. In contrast, its certificate system allowed the host state to ascertain consistently and unequivocally the status of a Community vessel seeking to perform maritime cabotage services.

FINDINGS OF THE COURT ON THE SECOND COMPLAINT

The ECJ observed that a national requirement which demands Community ships not documented in a first register to produce a certificate from the flag state that confirms its eligibility to provide cabotage services is prima facie discriminatory. On that premise, such requirement would ordinarily constitute a restriction on the freedom to provide maritime transport services.[62] The court observed that Article 1 of Regulation 3577/92 does not stipulate how to certify that a ship complies with all the conditions for carrying out cabotage in the flag state. Therefore, it considered that a state may restrict the freedom to provide services where there are justified overriding reasons in the public interest of the host member state. However, the national measure employed must be proportionate to the objective sought and must not go beyond what is necessary to attain it.[63]

Hence, the Commission's second complaint fell within that context of the proportionality of the national legislation in question. The court opined that the solutions proposed by the Commission would not achieve the objective sought. It also considered that the proposed solutions were more complex and restrictive of the freedom to provide cabotage services than the disputed certificate system. Therefore, the ECJ decided that the Commission could not prove that the Hellenic Republic failed to fulfil its obligations under the Regulation by requiring the presentation of a certificate. Accordingly, the second complaint was dismissed. Therefore, requiring Community ships not documented in the first registers to present a certificate from the flag state which certifies their eligibility to perform cabotage cannot be considered superfluous to the freedom to provide maritime transport services between member states.[64]

62 See the judgement in: *Asociacion Profesional de Emresas Navieras de Lineas Regulares (Analir) and others v. Admninstration General Del Esado* (Case C-205/99) [2001] ECR 1271.

63 See: Joined Cases C-128/10 and C-129/10 *Naftiliaki Etaireia Thasou* [2011] ECR I-1887.

64 See: European Commission, 'Communication from the Commission: on the interpretation of Council Regulation (EEC) No. 3577/92 applying the principle of freedom to provide services to maritime transport within Member States (maritime cabotage)', European Commission COM(2014) 232 final (Brussels, 22 April 2014).

*The third complaint*

By its third complaint, the Commission claimed that the Hellenic Republic was wrong in conferring the status of an island on the Peloponnese. Hence, it accused the Greek government of unlawfully applying Article 6(3) of Regulation 3577/92 to the ports in that region. The Commission also accused Greece of artificially extending the derogation in Article 6(3) to cabotage services between the ports of the Peloponnese and between the ports situated on the mainland and the ports of the Peloponnese.[65] The Commission noted that the Peloponnese cannot be considered an island because, although it is separated from the Greek mainland, it is only so separated by a man-made canal. Furthermore, the Peloponnese and mainland Greece are connected by a railway line and a national road above the Corinth Canal. In contrast, the Greek government contended that the Peloponnese constitutes an actual island since it is entirely surrounded by water, albeit by human action. It referred to *Italy and Sardegna Lines v. Commission* [66] and suggested that according to that case, the decisive criterion for determining what constitutes an island lay in a statistical analysis of trade carried out by sea. However, the court did not express a view on the term 'island' in that case contrary to the defendant's argument. Furthermore, the Greek government observed that the ports of Ceuta and Melilla situated on mainland Africa are treated as island ports by Article 2 (1) (c) of Council Regulation 3577/92. It would therefore be contradictory to regard those ports as island ports while describing the ports located on the Peloponnese that are surrounded entirely by water as mainland ports. Moreover, the Greek government observed that the derogation granted to it under Article 6(3) of Regulation 3577/92 is based on socio-economic cohesion and it would not be inconsistent with that objective to extend the application of that derogation to the Peloponnese, which is a region with a low development index.

The argument put forward by Greece on this point would seem to be weak and provoke a different question. This is because the derogation under Article 6(3) of the Regulation referred to by Greece was temporary and scheduled to end in 2004 at the latest. On that basis, it can be questioned whether the Greek government was arguing for the Peloponnese to be recognized as a temporary island, pursuant to Articles 6(2) and 6(3) of Regulation 3577/92. It is suggested that any derogation arising from the Regulation should be accorded a narrow interpretation.

FINDINGS OF THE COURT ON THE THIRD COMPLAINT

The court observed that the term 'island' is not expressly defined in Council Regulation 3577/92. Nevertheless, the court adopted what it noted as the

---

65  Article 6(3) states: For reasons of socio-economic cohesion, the derogation with respect to island cabotage and cabotage in the archipelagos, as provided for in Article 6(2) shall be extended for Greece until 1 January 2004 (instead of 1 January 1999) for regular passenger and ferry services and services provided by vessels less than 650 gt.

66  Cases C-15/98 and C-105/99 *Sardegna Lines v. Commission* [2000] ECR I-8855.

common meaning of the term 'island' in a maritime context. It described an island as an expanse of land elevated permanently from the sea.[67]

With reference to the ports of Ceuta and Melilla on the one hand and the ports of Peloponnese on the other, the court concluded that Ceuta and Melilla constitute island ports only in the context of Article 2 of the Regulation. Therefore, they remain mainland ports in nature.[68] As the Peloponnese was not constituted as an island by Regulation 3577/92, the Greek government failed to substantiate their argument. Therefore, the Commission's third complaint was upheld.

THE FIRST PART OF THE FOURTH COMPLAINT

The Commission protested against Greece as the host state for applying its national legislation to the manning of Community cruise liners over 650 gt.[69] The Commission claimed that this was inconsistent with Article 3(1) of Regulation 3577/92. That provision directs that for vessels carrying out mainland cabotage and for cruise liners, all matters relating to manning shall be the responsibility of the flag state. The Commission contended that with regard to Community cruise liners, the provisions of Article 3(1) apply regardless of whether they pursue mainland or island cabotage. In contrast, the Greek government posited that under Article 3(1) of the Regulation, the flag state's rules on manning apply only to cruise liners that call at mainland ports. In that regard, it claimed that Article 3(2) of the Regulation must envisage that the law of the host state applies to cruise liners that call at island ports.

FINDINGS OF THE COURT ON THE FIRST PART OF THE FOURTH COMPLAINT

In its decision, the ECJ acknowledged the absence of an express classification of cruise liners in Article 3(1) of Regulation 3577/92. Nevertheless, the court reasoned that if cruise liners performing island cabotage were intended to be covered by Article 3(2), the reference to 'cruise liners' in Article 3(1) would be rendered meaningless. It claimed that 'cruise liners carrying out mainland cabotage' would be already covered by the general phrase, 'vessels carrying out mainland cabotage'. Therefore, there would be no need to specifically mention 'cruise liners' in Article 3(1) of the Regulation but not mention it in Article 3(2).

67  See paragraph 42 of the Judgement. There was no dispute from either the Commission or the court that the Peloponnese remained a peninsular from a geographical perspective despite the man-made alterations made to the surrounding environment.
68  In relation to the African mainland, the ports of Ceuta and Melilla are definitely mainland ports. However, in relation to the European mainland, and in particular to the Iberian Peninsula, they are similar to 'island ports'. This is precisely because they have no land links with Spain. Therefore, it is different from the Peloponnese, which is permanently linked to the rest of Greece by land.
69  The Greek national legislation in question was paragraph 2.4.1 of Circular No 1151.65/2/98.

Hence, the specific mention of 'cruise liners' in Article 3(1) provides it with a validated independent interpretation which vests responsibility in the flag state. It lays down rules on all matters relating to the manning of cruise ships over 650 gt that perform cabotage in island ports. Therefore, the court concluded that the first part of the fourth complaint was well founded and should be upheld. In general, the court declared that Greece failed to fulfil its obligations under Articles 1, 3 and 6 of Council Regulation 3577/92 courtesy of the third and first part of the fourth complaints of the Commission. The remainder of the actions were dismissed.

### Agip Petroli SPA v. Capitaneria di Porto di Siracusa et seq [70]

This case was concerned with crewing requirements that still have some restrictions attached under Council Regulation 3577/92. More specifically, the question before the CJEU was to interpret correctly and to clarify the provisions of Article 3(3) of Council Regulation 3577/92. The wording of Article 3(3) is:

> For cargo vessels over 650 GT carrying out island cabotage, when the voyage concerned follows or precedes a voyage to or from another State, all matters relating to manning shall be the responsibility of the State in which the vessel is registered (flag State).

The facts of this case are that Agip Petroli chartered the Greek-registered tanker *Theodoros IV* to ship a cargo of crude oil from Magnisi to Gela. Both ports of origin and destination are in Sicily. Agip Petroli relied on Article 3(3) of Council Regulation 3577/92 to justify derogating from applying the legislation of Italy the host state. The plaintiff aimed for the laws of the Hellenic Republic, which was the flag state, to apply instead. In its application for permission to carry out this island cabotage, it was stated that the vessel was to subsequently make a voyage directly to a foreign state, albeit without any cargo on board – what is known as a voyage 'in ballast'. The application to execute this voyage was refused by the Italian authorities because the crew of the vessel included sailors who were non-EU nationals from the Philippines. Allowing foreign crew to perform island cabotage was deemed a breach of Article 318 of the Codice delle navigazione (Italian Shipping Code).[71] It was on the back of this refusal by the Italian authorities that Agip Petroli commenced legal proceedings. The question before the court was whether a voyage that follows or precedes the cabotage voyage according to Article 3(3) of Council Regulation 3577/92 refers only to a voyage that is functionally and commercially autonomous – i.e. a voyage with cargo on board destined for or coming from a foreign port. Alternatively, whether a voyage without

---

70  Case C – 456/04 [2006] *Agip Petroli SPA v. Capitaneria di Porto di Siracusa et seq* ECR I – 3395 (Second Chamber).

71  In its decision of 6 December 2001, the Harbour Office justified the application of Italian law, having regard to Circular No. TMA3/CA/0230 of 31 January 2000 of the Ministero dei Trasporti et della Navigazione (Department of Transport and Shipping).

cargo on board – i.e. a voyage in ballast – constitutes a valid voyage as con-templated by Article 3(3) of Council Regulation 3577/92.

The Italian authorities argued that Article 3(3) of Council Regulation 3577/92 only applied where the preceding or follow-up voyage was a voyage by a cargo-laden vessel. Thus, Article 3(3) could not consequently be invoked if 'the ship has already completed or will complete after the voyage of island cabotage, a voyage in ballast or a voyage with a cargo of goods which, in terms of quality and quantity, cannot render the voyage functionally and commercially autonomous. Furthermore, they argued that because the follow up voyage was a ballast voyage, Article 3(2) of the Regulation ought to apply. Article 3(2) of Council Regulation 3577/92 states that 'For vessels carrying out island cabotage, all matters relating to manning shall be the responsibility of the State (host State) in which the vessel is performing a maritime transport service.'

The ECJ ruled that Article 3(3) covers situations where the vessel is on a ballast voyage to another state. We should note that this decision contrasts with the Commission's position in its Interpretative Communication of 2003, where the Commission noted that the host state rules apply where the international voyage that follows or precedes the island cabotage is in ballast. Nevertheless, the court reasoned further that it was common shipping practice for vessels to sail in bal-last.[72] However, the court accepted the possibility of a calculated attempt to cir-cumvent the specific provisions of Article 3(3).[73] Therefore, the court conceded that where it was evident that the preceding or follow up (ballast) voyage to another state was set up to frustrate the rules of the host state on crewing, then the flag state would be prohibited from relying on Article 3(3) of Council Reg-ulation 3577/92. The scope of Community law must in no case be extended to cover abuses by any party. This includes activities aimed at circumventing the rules of Community law and not performed in the context of normal commercial transactions.[74] The burden of proof therefore lies with the host state to show that the said voyage is a legal or commercial hoax.[75] This case confirms that on the one hand EU maritime cabotage law aims to establish freedom to provide maritime

---

72 See however, the decision of the ECJ in *Commission v Hellenic Republic [2007]*, where the court held that towing is an auxiliary service to shipping. It is suggested that a towing service is a common practice in shipping not only reserved for use to assist a broken down or stranded vessel.

73 See: Case 125/76 *Cremer* [1977] ECR 1593, paragraph 21; Case C-8/92 *General Milk Products* [1993] ECR I-779, paragraph 21, and *Halifax*, paragraph 69.

74 It is noted that according to settled case law, Community law cannot be relied on for abusive or fraudulent ends. See: in particular, Case C-367/96 *Kefalas and Others* [1998] ECR I-2843, paragraph 20; Case C-373/97 *Diamantis* [2000] ECR I-1705, paragraph 33, and Case C-255/02 *Halifax and Others* [2006] ECR I-1609, para-graph 68.

75 See: Case C-515/03 *Eichsfelder Schlachtbetrieb* [2005] ECR I-7355, paragraph 40, and *Halifax*, paragraph 76. In accordance with the rules of evidence of national law, the national courts must verify whether action constituting an abusive practice has taken place in the case before it. This verification is subject to the proviso that the effectiveness of Community law is not undermined.

transport services within the European Union. On the other hand it is evident that certain elements of protectionism still exist.[76] Moreover, these subtle protectionist aspects of the EU maritime cabotage law and policy receive tacit judicial endorsement.[77] It may be suggested that where the host state rule applies,[78] Community shipowners can expect to be exposed to different levels of competition. For instance, a shipowner from a member state with an open coast policy (e.g. United Kingdom) providing cabotage services in a state with a closed coast policy (e.g. Italy) under Council Regulation 3577/92 is exposed to less competition. This is because the shipowner only competes with fellow community shipowners. On the other hand, a shipowner from a closed-coast member state providing similar services in a state with an open-coast policy can expect to compete with both community and third-country shipowners.[79]

### Commission of the European Communities v Hellenic Republic [80]

In this case, the European Commission asked the court to declare that a Greek national law which reserved towage services in the open sea within Greek National waters to only vessels flying the Greek flag breached its obligations under Article 1 of Regulation 3577/92 because it was inconsistent with Article 2(1) of that Regulation.[81] Greece did not dispute that the said Greek law was inconsistent with the provisions of Article 2(1) of Regulation 3577/92. However, she argued that a towage service is outside of the scope of Article 2(1) of Regulation 3577/92. Therefore, she was not in breach of the community law.

The question before the ECJ was whether towage services on the open sea came within the scope of Regulation 3577/92. There are three main issues here, namely:

76  The protectionist measures within the European Union maritime cabotage law are most evident in island cabotage – particularly with regard to crewing requirements and fiscal policies (state aid) in the form of public service contracts (PSC) and public service obligations (PSO). See: Articles 2(3), 2(4), 3(2), 4, of Regulation 3577/92.

77  A proposal was submitted by the Commission for a regulation on the generalization of the flag state's responsibility for manning issues 29 April 1998. However, the proposal failed to win the approval of the member states. Thus, The Commission requested for the withdrawal of the proposal on 11 December 2001. The content of that proposal was very similar to the decision of the court in this case. See: COM(1998) 251 final.

78  See: articles 3(2), 5 and 6 of Council Regulation (EEC) No. 3577/92. See also the judicial decisions in *Commission v. Hellenic Republic* [2007] and *Agip Petroli SPA v. Capitaneria di Porto di Siracusa et seq.*

79  In *Agip Petroli SPA v. Capitaneria di Porto di Siracusa et seq* Case C – 456/04 [2006] ECR I – 3395 (Second Chamber), the Italian authorities alluded to this scenario when they referred to the provisions of Article 318 of the Codice delle navigazione (Italian Shipping Code).

80  Case C-251/04 [2007] ECR I – 67 (Second Chamber). Dated 11 January 2007.

81  As a general point, under Article 51(1) EC, freedom to provide services in the field of transport is governed by the provisions of the title of the EC Treaty relating to transport, which include Article 80(2) EC, permitting the Council of the European Union to lay down appropriate provisions for sea transport.

a    whether the list in Article 2(1) of Regulation 3577/92 is exhaustive;
b    the legal nature of towage in Greek law;
c    the needful distinction between towage in the port area and towage outside
     that area for the purposes of determining the scope of Regulation 3577/92 .

On the first point, the Commission conceded that towage service is not mentioned expressly in Article 2(1) of Regulation 3577/92 as a maritime transport
service. However, it argued that the list of services outlined in that disposition is
only 'indicative', since it is introduced by the term 'in particular'.[82] Therefore, all
maritime transport services normally provided for remuneration ought to be described as maritime cabotage. The Commission submitted that towage satisfies all the
elements of that definition. This was rejected by the Greek government who argued
that the term 'in particular', as used in Article 2(1) of Regulation 3577/92 must be
understood as 'more particularly', thus giving the list an 'exhaustive' status. Also,
they submitted that if it was otherwise intended, the draftsman would have
employed words like 'such as' instead of 'Shall in particular'. Furthermore, the
Greek government submitted that the term 'maritime transport service' is also
defined expressly in Article 1(4) of Regulation 4055/86.[83] The Commission conceded that 'maritime transport services' as defined in Regulation 4055/86 includes
towage. Nevertheless, it argued that in any event, that definition should not apply in
this case because that Regulation governs only international maritime transport
services.

On the second point, the Commission submitted that pursuant to Article 3 of
Presidential Decree No 45/83, towage is not always regarded in Greek law as a
service auxiliary to maritime cabotage.[84] It argued that Greece does not view
maritime transport services and the towage services as having distinct features.

---

82  Note that the services listed in Article 2(1) of Council Regulation (EEC) No. 3577/
    92 are: the carriage of passengers and goods in mainland cabotage, island cabotage
    and off-shore supply services.
83  The definition of that term is identical to its definition in Council Regulation (EEC)
    No. 3577/92. It includes the purpose of the transport, namely the carriage of pas-
    sengers or goods, and is, in both cases, exhaustive. Furthermore, the Greek govern-
    ment maintains that maritime assistance services do not constitute a form of transport
    in the usual sense and that vessels which have suffered damage cannot be regarded as
    goods that must be transported. However, See: *Shipbuilders Council of America et al.
    v. United States of America et al.* 868 F. 2d 452 (DC Cir. 1989). Decided 3 March
    1989 in the United States Court of Appeals, District of Columbia Circuit. Nos 88–
    5095, 88–5119 – where it appears that a broken-down vessel is deemed as cargo.
84  Article 3 of Presidential Decree No. 45/83 states that: tugs or other vessels flying the
    flag of a state other than Greece are authorized: '(a) to moor at any Greek port or at
    any point on the Greek coast when they are towing a vessel, an auxiliary boat or other
    floating object the towage of which commenced in a foreign port or at any other point
    on the coast of a foreign State or on open sea; (b) to take over the towage, from any
    Greek port or any place on the Greek coast, of a vessel or any other floating object
    bound for a foreign port or any place on the coast of a foreign State or the open sea;
    (c) to cross Greek territorial waters when, coming from a foreign port or any point on
    the coast of a foreign State or from the open sea, they are towing a vessel, an auxiliary

Hence, Article 3 of Greek Presidential Decree No. 45/83 permits tugs flying the flag of another state to perform towage operations in Greek territorial waters. The Commission pointed out further that Article 3 appears to contradict the provision of Article 1 of the same decree.

The Greek government responded that under Greek law, towage and maritime assistance constitute auxiliary services that support the proper functioning of maritime transport services. Further, it submitted that a vessel without means of self-propulsion being under tow is not sufficient to deprive that service of its auxiliary character or to confer on it the status of maritime transport. Thus, in the absence of a direct link between what is being transported and the tug, services of towage fall outside the ambit of Council Regulation 3577/92.[85] Furthermore, the Greek government submitted that the Commission was wrong in interpreting Article 3 of Presidential Decree No. 45/83 as constituting an exception to Article 1 of the same decree. This suggestion misled the court on the respective scopes of those two provisions. They clarified that Article 1 of Decree No. 45/83 governs professional towage between two points situated in Greek territorial waters. On the other hand, Article 3 of Decree No. 45/83 is restricted to towage services with a foreign component.

On the third point, the Commission pointed out that the Greek authorities failed to distinguish between towage services provided within the port area and those provided outside the port. This failure was contrary to the Commission proposals for a directive on market access to port services. As those proposals do not relate to cabotage outside the port area, the Commission seized the opportunity to argue that Council Regulation 3577/92 should apply in this case. However, the Greek government objected to the Commission's submission and

---

boat or any other floating object and are bound for a foreign port or for any place on the coast of a foreign State or the open sea.'

85 Article 11(1)(b), (aa) and (bb) of Decree Law No. 187/73, which constitutes the Greek Code of public maritime law, reserves towage operations of any kind, specified in Article 188 of the Code, as well as assistance at sea and maritime rescue operations, defined in Article 189 of that code, in national waters to vessels flying the flag of Greece, when they are effected in and between the territorial waters of that member state. In accordance with Article 188(2) of the Code, the port authority is to adopt port regulations setting out the conditions for granting a port towage licence, the regulation of towage, circumstances in which towage services must be provided, towage rights in port and mooring waters and all other necessary details. According to Article 188(3), the extent of the right to tow, occasional or emergency towage by other vessels, related rights of tugs or other vessels flying the flag of a state other than Greece, as well as all other related details, are to be laid down by presidential decree. The granting of such licences is governed by Article 1(1) of Presidential Decree No. 45/83 on the towage of vessels which specifies that 'the carrying out of professional towage between two points within Greek waters as well as the provision of all services directly relating to such an operation are reserved to Greek vessels classed as tugs under the legislation in force, licensed by the competent port authority. Furthermore, Article 4(2)(b) of General Ports Regulations, issued by the Chief of Greek Port Police, requires the vessel owner applying for such a licence to produce to the port authority a certificate of nationality.

questioned what benefit there was in justifying the subjection of towage services to different legislations, based on whether that service is performed within or outside the port area. They submitted that any such distinction made based on the place where towage services are provided is arbitrary and without any legal basis. Furthermore, it was likely to create legal uncertainty in the application of Regulation 3577/92.

In judgement, the ECJ held that towage cannot be regarded as falling within the scope of Article 2(1) of Council Regulation 3577/92. The court submitted that there was no basis for inferring that the term 'in particular' in Article 2(1) of the Regulation should extend to any service that is related, incidental or ancillary to the provision of maritime transport services within the member states. The court insisted that on the facts of this case, it was irrelevant whether the maritime service in question had the essential characteristics of maritime cabotage. In the court's view, to adopt a different position would be contrary to both the purpose and the legal certainty of Council Regulation 3577/92.[86] The court was also concerned of the implications of ruling that ancillary services such as towage fell within the scope of Article 2(1). It feared that this would open the door for ancillary services such as hydrographic and seismic surveys to be considered cabotage services, thereby distorting the purpose of Article 2(1) of Council Regulation 3577/92.[87]

However, given the court's narrow interpretation of the scope of the Regulation, one can argue that towage is generally regarded as a 'service normally provided for remuneration' as contemplated in Article 2(1) of Council Regulation 3577/92. Therefore, the court's narrow legal interpretation of maritime services normally provided for remuneration does not reflect what transpires in commercial practice. The court accepted that towage is a service normally provided for remuneration and the words 'shall in particular include' cannot be interpreted to mean that the list is 'exhaustive'. Nevertheless, it argued that in principle, towage does not entail a 'straightforward' carriage of goods or passengers by sea. Rather, it is directed primarily at assisting in propelling a vessel or similar maritime property. Furthermore, the court argued that towing services are designed to assist the manoeuvre of a stranded vessel by supplementing or substituting that vessel's own propulsive machinery. Therefore, the tug only functions to assist the vessel in which the cargo is carried, it is not itself the transporting vessel.

By 'straightforward carriage' one presumes that the court referred to the process of carriage reasonably contemplated in the minds of both the shipowner when making his vessel available and the shipper when advancing freight for his cargo. Even taking this narrow view, it is suggested that the provisions of the law governing their trade should dictate the workings of the minds of the parties. The first

---

86 *Commission of the European Communities v. Hellenic Republic* – Case C-251/04 [2007] ECR I – 67 (Second Chamber), paragraph 32. Dated 11 January 2007.

87 See the commentary in chapter 9 on the national cabotage laws in the United States, Canada and Nigeria. In those countries, the scope of maritime cabotage law expands to cover the so-called ancillary services such as towage, hydro-graphic surveys and seismic surveys.

problem with the court's reasoning is that carriage by sea as contemplated by the Regulation need not be 'straightforward'. Hence, to construe that only 'straight-forward carriages' fits into the scope of the Regulation is a misdirection that will lead to further controversies. The second problem relates to the method of carriage, where the court seems to suggest that the cargo or passengers must be on-board the carrying vessel for it to be classed as carriage. The effect of this point of view is that the carriage of cargo by sea by either pushing or pulling the cargo is somehow not covered by the Regulation 3577/92. It is suggested that this understanding could not be and does not reflect what the Regulation contemplated. We should note that the carriage of cargo by sea by either pushing or pulling the cargo is sometimes the only feasible method of fulfilling the contract of carriage. Where a vessel cannot execute movement by its own propulsive machinery, it is not unreasonable to argue that such a vessel should be considered cargo. This takes on added significance if the stranded vessel must rely on another vessel to be moved from one point to another. This position should hold, irrespective of how the stranded vessel is being moved (on-board, pulled or pushed), or whether goods or passengers are on-board the stranded or assisting vessel.[88]

The final point of concern is the fact that the ECJ saw fit to accord more weight to phrases such as 'straight forward carriage of goods or passengers by sea' and 'transporting vessel'. There is no doubt that too much importance was conferred on phrases that are not provided for expressly in the Regulation. This invariably devalued the effect of the phrase 'service normally provided for remuneration', which is expressly provided for in Regulation 3577/92.

## Commission of the European Communities v. Kingdom of Spain [89]

This was an action brought by the Commission of the European Communities against the Kingdom of Spain.[90] By its application, the Commission requested the court to declare that by upholding its national legislation, Spain allegedly failed to fulfil its obligations pursuant to both the EC Treaty and articles 1, 4, 7, 9 of Regulation 3577/92. The national legislation in question was Ley 4/1999.[91] The Commission's complaints are that the legislation:

88  For a comparative analysis of judicial reasoning, see: *Shipbuilders Council of America et al. v. United States of America et al.* 868 F. 2d 452 (DC Cir. 1989). Decided 3 March 1989 in the United States Court of Appeals, District of Columbia Circuit. Nos 88–5095, 88–5119. In this case it was argued that a broken-down vessel being taken to a repair yard constitutes cargo, like any other type of cargo.

89  Case 323/03 *Commission of the European Communities v. Kingdom of Spain* [2006]. Judgement of the Court (Second Chambers), 9 March 2006.

90  This action was launched at the behest of several complaints from private parties that the Spanish legislation governing cabotage services in the Vigo estuary was contrary to Regulation No 3577/92.

91  Law 4/1999, de declaración de servicio público de titularidad de la Junta de Galicia del transporte público marítimo de viajeros en la ría de Vig,o BOE No. 118 of 18 May 1999, p. 18552. Adopted on 9 April 1999 by the Autonomous Community of Galicia.

a   Allowed a concession for maritime transport services in the Vigo estuary to be granted to a single operator for a period of 20 years and included experience in transport in the Vigo estuary as a criterion for the concession, thus breaching Article 1 of the Regulation.

b   Allowed the imposition of public service obligations on seasonal transport services with the islands and regular transport services between mainland ports, thus breaching Article 4 of the Regulation.

c   Allowed the introduction of a more restrictive system than that in effect on the date on which Regulation 3577/92 entered into force, thus breaching Article 7 of the Regulation.

d   Was approved without any consultation with the Commission, thus breaching Article 9 of the Regulation.

Ley 4/1999 was adopted by the Autonomous Community of Galicia in 1999, six years after Council Regulation 3577/92 came into force. It declared that maritime passenger transport in the Vigo estuary was a public service belonging to the regional government of Galicia.[92] The relevant parts of Ley 4/1999 are:

a   Articles 2(2) and 2(3) permit the regional authority of Galicia to grant administrative concession for 20 years, renewable for a maximum of ten years in the Vigo estuary.[93]

b   Article 3 provides that the concession is to be awarded by public tender and that account will be taken, inter alia, of experience in operating transport services in the Vigo estuary.

Before addressing the four complaints brought by the Commission, the court considered a preliminary matter raised by the Spanish government. The defendant disputed that Regulation 3577/92 applied to transport services in the Vigo estuary, which is governed by Law 4/1999. The Spanish government argued that maritime cabotage must be understood as the carriage of passengers and goods by sea between ports. On that basis, it described maritime transport in the Vigo estuary as neither carriage by sea nor carriage between ports in the sense given to those terms in the context of Regulation 3577/92.[94] It submitted that 'carriage by sea' should be understood as referring to external sea, not to internal waters.[95]

---

92  It is important to put this in context by giving a brief overview of the Vigo estuary. In the Spanish region of Galicia, there is a deep inlet known as the 'ria de Vigo' (Vigo estuary). On its south bank is situated the city of Vigo and on its north bank the towns of Cangas and Moaña. At the mouth of the estuary lie two islands known as the Cíes Isles.

93  This was the arrangement in force adopted by decision of 11 June 1984 prior to Law 4/1999 The 1984 Arrangement provided that regular maritime passenger and freight services between Vigo and Cangas and between Vigo and Moaña was made subject to the grant of authorization for a renewable period of ten years.

94  See Article 2(1) of Council Regulation 3577/92.

95  External sea corresponds to territorial sea, as defined by international treaties and, more specifically, by Article 8 of the United Nations Convention on the Law of the

Accordingly, it argued that the transport services in the Vigo estuary constitute shipping only within the internal waters. Hence, contrary to Regulation 3577/92, transport in the Vigo estuary could not be considered as an essential component necessary for establishing the internal market.[96] Furthermore, the Spanish government contested that shipping in the Vigo estuary does not constitute shipping between ports. They claimed that pursuant to the applicable national regulation, the estuary is part of the Vigo port services zone. Hence, it submitted that the Cíes Isles do not have a port, but only a quay with limited berthing capacity for the disembarkation of passengers.[97] Finally, the Spanish government referred to Council Directive 98/18/EC and claimed that even the Community rules do not regard the waters of the Vigo estuary as a sea area.[98]

The court ruled that in interpreting a provision of Community law, consideration should not be limited to the wording of the provision. Rather, the context in which the provision is applied and the objects of the rules of which it is part of should also be considered.[99] Therefore, the term 'carriage by sea between ports' should be interpreted according to the objective of Article 2(1) (a) and (c) of Regulation 3577/92, which is to capture the freedom to provide maritime transport services.[100] Hence, equating the term 'sea' within the meaning of Regulation 3577/92 with the term 'territorial sea' within the meaning of the United Nations Convention on the Law of the Sea 1982 (UNCLOS) is likely to undermine that objective. Moreover, there is no indication that Regulation 3577/92 intended to limit its scope to territorial sea within the meaning of UNCLOS 1982. Therefore, it serves no purpose to equate the terms.

With the argument that shipping in the Vigo estuary had little effect on the objective of establishing the internal market, it was held that nothing in Regulation 3577/92 suggests that its scope depends on the economic and social impact that shipping in a specific area would have on establishing the internal market. Therefore, relying on EC Directive 98/18 to claim that maritime transport services in the Vigo estuary do not constitute transport services 'between ports'

---

Sea of 10 December 1982 ('the Montego Bay Convention') which distinguishes it from internal waters which are waters on the landward side of the baseline of the territorial sea.

96 Regulation No 3577/92 is based on the principle that cabotage is both an essential component of the Community transport network and an instrument necessary for establishing the internal market. Unlike external shipping or shipping in territorial sea, shipping entirely within internal waters has a very limited economic and social impact and has little effect on the objective of establishing the internal market in the Community context.

97 See: Ministerial Decree of 23 December 1966 (BOE of 23 January 1967).

98 Article 2 of Council Directive 98/18/EC of 17 March 1998 on Safety Rules and Standards for Passenger Ships (OJ 1998 L 144, p. 1) stipulates that the 'port area' includes all the waters of the Vigo estuary.

99 See: Case C-17/03 *VEMW and Others* [2005] ECR I-4985.

100 See: Case C-205/99 *Analir and Others* [2001] ECR I-1271, paragraph 19.

within the meaning of Regulation 3577/92 is invalid.[101] Moreover, we should note that the scope of the Regulation is not subservient to the laws of any member state.[102] In that connection, the term 'port' in the context of Regulation 3577/92 encompasses infrastructure, albeit small scale, that facilitates the loading and unloading of cargo for carriage by sea.[103] According to settled case law, it follows that the term 'port' must be given an autonomous and uniform interpretation that reflects the context and the purpose of the legislation in which it is used.[104] Hence, the infrastructures that exist in the Cíes Isles, Vigo, Cangas and Moaña must be regarded as ports within the meaning of Regulation 3577/92. Therefore, the court decided that transport services in the Vigo estuary governed by Law 4/1999 fall within the scope of Council Regulation 3577/92.

### The first complaint

The Commission submitted that Law 4/1999 infringed Article 1 of Regulation 3577/92 in two respects. First, it reserved maritime passenger transport services in the Vigo estuary to a single operator for a period of twenty years, renewable for a further ten years through the grant of an administrative concession. The Commission complained that permitting such reservation blocks access to the market for the duration of that concession. Second, Law 4/1999 stated that experience in operating transport services in the Vigo estuary was a criterion for granting the concession. This favoured the existing operator and discriminated against new operators from other member states.

   In its defence, the Spanish government argued that the concession arrangements were justified by overriding reasons in the public interest within the meaning of the case law of the court.[105] First, it contended that maritime transport services to the Cíes Isles is the only possible connection with those islands. As a result, maritime activities in the area must be limited for environmental reasons. Furthermore, it claimed that the limited capacity of the quays on those islands could not support heavy maritime traffic. Hence, the Spanish government argued that the use of a quota system was the only reasonable means of controlling the

---

101 Unlike Article 2(p) of Directive 98/18, which defines/port area as 'an area other than a sea area as defined by the Member States, Regulation 3577/92 does not contain any reference to the law of those states for the purpose of defining the term 'port'.

102 See: Case C-43/04 *Stadt Sundern* [2005] ECR I-4491. Where it was held that because of the need for uniform application of Community law and the principle of equality, the terms for providing Community law which makes no express reference to the law of the member states to determine its meaning and scope must normally be given an autonomous and uniform interpretation throughout the Community, having regard to the context of the provision and the objective pursued by the legislation in question.

103 For a similar argument, see: Case C-205/99 *Analir and Others* [2001].

104 See: Case 327/82 *Ekro* [1984] ECR 107; Case C-287/98 *Linster* [2000] ECR I-6917; Case C-201/02 *Wells* [2004] ECR I-723; Case C-55/02 *Commission v. Portugal* [2004] ECR I-9387; and Case C-188/03 *Junk* [2005] ECR I-885.

105 See: Joined Cases C-128/10 and C-129/10 *Naftiliaki Etaireia Thasou*.

volume of traffic allowed to visit the Cíes Isles on a daily basis. Second, with regard to sea connections between the towns of Vigo, Cangas and Moaña, the Spanish government argued that this was the most direct and most economical means of transport. Therefore, its discontinuation would have a negative impact on the organization of traffic in the Vigo and the Morrazo Peninsula.[106] Third, the defendant argued further that the Vigo estuary is a finite geographical area in which various activities must coexist. These activities include fishing for shellfish from barges or floating craft. Therefore, there was clear need to put limits on shipping traffic. Fourth, the defendant submitted that the duration of the concession could be justified because it was necessary to amortize the investments involved. In this regard they appeared to be applying the economic development rationale and its impact in the area. Finally, with regard to the criterion for experience of carrying out maritime transport in the Vigo estuary, it was claimed that this was not a decisive criterion for the award of the concession, nor did it lead to retaining the existing operator. Also, the Spanish government referred to its rejoinder as evidence that the criterion was withdrawn by Law 9/2003.[107]

THE DECISION OF THE COURT ON THE FIRST COMPLAINT

The court observed that a national measure that reserves maritime transport services in the Vigo estuary to a single operator for a minimum of twenty years is liable to constitute a restriction on freedom to provide services. It rejected the Spanish government's argument that this measure was justified by overriding reasons in the public interest. With regards to monitoring traffic volume to comply with environmental requirements in the Cíes Isles, the court held that there were less restrictive options at the disposal of the defendant compared to the minimum twenty years concession. For example, it could use a system of advance booking and sale of available places for that destination.[108] Moreover, the court posited that the Spanish government could not show how granting a twenty years concession to one operator, was the only way of guaranteeing that a service that caters for more than one million passengers annually across the Vigo estuary remained profitable. On the selection criterion relating to experience in the transport sector in the Vigo estuary. It was held that it was not relevant how much of a deciding

106   It was claimed that it would result in difficulties in terms of excessive use and over-loading of land transport infrastructures. The services relating to those connections were unprofitable and their financial viability was therefore uncertain or poor. Consequently, they argued that the complete liberalization of those services would probably lead to the disappearance of the Vigo-Cangas-Moaña route or to its operation under unsatisfactory conditions as regards safety, frequency of services and prices.
107   Law 9/2003 was enacted 23 December 2003.
108   A state regulation must be justified by the objective of ensuring adequate maritime transport services to areas not otherwise accessible. It must also observe the principle of proportionality, and must therefore not go beyond what 'is necessary and proportionate' to attain that objective. See: Case C-76/90 Sager [1991] ECR I-4221; Case C-19/92 *Kraus* [1993] ECR I-1663; Case C-55/94 *Gebhard* [1995] ECR I-4165; and Case C-272/94 *Guiot* [1996] ECR I-1905.

factor the criterion was in awarding the concession. This is because the finding of a member state's failure to fulfil its obligations is not bound up with a finding as to the damage flowing therefrom.[109] Furthermore, the withdrawal of that criterion by Law 9/2003 was considered irrelevant. Neither was it of relevance that no loss was suffered by any party because of the criterion.[110] It was observed that the question on whether member states fail to fulfil obligations must be determined by reference to the situation prevailing in the member state at the expiration of the reasoned opinion. Therefore, the court did not take account of any subsequent changes.[111] Hence, the first complaint was upheld.

THE SECOND COMPLAINT

By its second complaint, the Commission alleged that Spain infringed Article 4 of Regulation 3577/92. It submitted that Article 4 clearly envisages that member states should conclude public service contracts (PSC) with or impose public service obligations (PSO) on operators that engage only in regular services to, from and between islands. However, the Commission observed that transport services in the Vigo estuary are not regular transport services to or between islands. Firstly, it pointed out that regular services along the Vigo-Cangas and Vigo Moaña routes are not island services. Second, the services to the Cíes Isles are seasonal tourist services. This is contrary to the 'regularity' requirement envisaged by Article 4 of Regulation 3577/92. In response, the Spanish government contended that Article 4 is premised on the assumption that PSC or PSO presents the only means of connecting between the islands or between the islands and the mainland in the area concerned. It argued that the existing land connection was difficult at best. Hence, it was reasonable to apply the principles of Article 4 of Regulation 3577/92 to shipping connections in the Vigo estuary. The Commission conceded that it was possible to extend the application of Article 4 in exceptional cases. This would apply where the alternative to maritime transport services to or between islands present such challenges that effectively, they would cease to constitute real alternatives to the sea connection. However, it categorically rejected that such exceptional situation applied in this case.

THE DECISION OF THE COURT ON THE SECOND COMPLAINT

It was held by the court that the regular maritime transport services between the towns of Vigo, Cangas and Moaña cannot be treated as maritime transport services to or between islands. This was because in addition to the sea connections there is a functional road network connecting the towns directly and affording ready access to them. Furthermore, the Spanish government did not dispute that

---

109 Case C-175/97 *Commission v. France* [1998] ECR I-963.
110 Case C-263/96 *Commission v. Belgium* [1997] ECR I-7453.
111 Case C-209/02 *Commission v. Austria* [2004] ECR I-1211.

maritime transport services to and from the Cíes Isles are not regular services. Therefore, the second complaint was upheld.

### The third complaint

The Commission alleged that the defendant infringed upon Article 7 of Regulation 3577/92 by adopting Law 4/1999. It is observed that Article 7 of the Regulation defers to Article 62 of the EC Treaty.[112] This provision of the EC Treaty prohibits member states from introducing more restrictive measures than those applicable on the date that Regulation 3577/92 came into force. The arrangements that existed under the 1984 Decision of the Autonomous Community of Galicia were less restrictive than those introduced by the adoption of Law 4/1999. It should be noted that Article 62 was repealed by the Treaty of Amsterdam in 1999. This is reflected in Article 6 of Council Regulation 3577/92, which permits member states to uphold existing restrictions in specific cases until 2004 at the latest.

THE DECISION OF THE COURT ON THE THIRD COMPLAINT

It was held that the maritime transport services in the Vigo estuary are not covered by Article 6 of Council Regulation 3577/92. This was because at the expiration period of the reasoned opinion, the adoption of Law 4/1999 could not have infringed on Articles 6 and 7 of Regulation 3577/92. Therefore, the Commission's third complaint was dismissed. The rationale behind the Commission's third complaint is not clear. It is difficult to see how the principle of Article 7 of Regulation 3577/92 could survive the demise of Article 62 of the EC Treaty, which it deferred to.

THE FOURTH COMPLAINT

By its fourth complaint, the Commission submitted that it was not consulted prior to adopting Law 4/1999, thereby breaching Article 9 of Regulation 3577/92.[113] The Spanish government concedes that it failed to inform the Commission before adopting Law 4/1999 pursuant to Article 9 of Regulation 3577/92. Therefore, the fourth complaint was upheld. In summary, it was held that the Kingdom of Spain failed to fulfil its obligations under the Community rules by infringing upon articles 1, 4 and 9 of Council Regulation 3577/92.

112 Article 6 of Council Regulation 3577/92 allows member states to maintain after 1 January 1993 and for a period expiring at the latest on 1 January 2004 existing restrictions in a number of specific cases. It is important to see Article 7 of Council Regulation 3577/92 as complementing Article 6 instead of contradicting it.
113 Article 9 states that before adopting laws, regulations or administrative provisions in implementation of this Regulation, member states shall consult the Commission. They shall inform the latter of any measures thus adopted.

## The United Kingdom and the effect of Brexit

Documented evidence shows that England and then the United Kingdom was the first to enact legislation on a protectionist maritime cabotage law. The chronicle of maritime cabotage legislations in the United Kingdom is as follows. King Richard II enacted a law in 1382 stipulating that 'No person was permitted to import or export merchandise in any port within the realm of England but in ships of the King's liegance'.[114] Adam Smith alluded to the possibility that documented legislation on maritime cabotage existed long before 1382, even though there is no intelligible account of any enactment at so distant an epoch.[115] The protectionist maritime cabotage regime continued under Edward IV, who passed legislation that 'Nobody (except merchant strangers) inhabiting within the realm of England shall transport cargo on a foreign vessel unless there is insufficient freight in the vessels of the denizens of England and Wales'.[116] Furthermore, Henry VII passed a law stipulating that wines and Tholouse woad should be imported into England only on English ships, with only English men as master and crew.[117] This law was sustained under Elizabeth I wherein 'the carriage of goods coastwise by foreigners or in foreign ships was unlawful and thus prohibited'.[118] The protectionist maritime cabotage regime was expanded further under two navigation acts. Hence, the expanded maritime cabotage regime covered international carriage of goods from a foreign port to a port situated in England. First, the Navigation Act of 1651 enacted by Oliver Cromwell stipulated that goods imported from English colonies and Europe into England must only be imported on English ships crewed by English men.[119] Second, after the Restoration Charles II enacted the Navigation Act of 1660. This act was in many ways similar to the Cromwellian act, albeit more stringent.[120] The 1660 act stated that 'All imports and exports from English colonies must be on English ships which were navigated, built and owned by English men'.[121] A separate protectionist Navigation Act was enacted in Scotland in 1661 because until the Act of Union took effect in 1707 Scottish citizens were classed as foreigners in England.[122] It was in 1849 that the protectionist Navigation Act was repealed in the United Kingdom. However, the coastal cabotage trade remained protected for British ships manned by British seamen. It was not

114 [5 Richard II. Stat. i, c. 3.] Richard II's reign was from 1377 to 1399.
115 See Adam's Smith's 1828 treatise – An Inquiry into the Nature and Causes of the Wealth of Nations, vol. IV.
116 [3 Edward IV, c. 1.]
117 [4 Henry VII, c. 10 s i and ii].
118 Statutes of England, 5 Eliz., C. 5, Para VI & VIII. 4 Statutes of the Realm 423 (1547–1624)
119 The Navigational Act, 1651. [Cap. 22] Goods from Foreign Ports by Whom to be Imported.
120 English, Scottish and Irish monarchies were restored under Charles II.
121 [Charles II, c. 18, s i and iii].
122 It is interesting that more than 300 years later, a referendum was held in which Scotland attempted once again to separate and become a foreign country to England.

until 1854 that the protectionist law on coastal cabotage trade in the United Kingdom was finally abolished.[123]

The United Kingdom has been a member state of the European Union (then the European Economic Community) since 1973. Therefore, with respect to the law of maritime cabotage it must abide with the provisions of Council Regulation 3577/92 which applies exclusively. As the United Kingdom had abolished its protectionist maritime cabotage regime in favour of an open coast policy, it did not need to amend its national laws to comply with Council Regulation 3577/92 when it came into force in 1993.[124]

The maritime sector in the United Kingdom has since adopted a different developmental framework. It now pursues policies that promote maritime investment, training of shore and sea-going personnel, and changes in the British shipping registry. These changes have resulted in economic diversity from both direct maritime activities and the resultant maritime cluster activities. The more liberal maritime cabotage regime in the United Kingdom has contributed to its economic development. For instance, during the global financial crisis of 2008, the maritime sector in the United Kingdom contributed a total of £31.7 billion in GDP, supported 634,900 jobs and generated £8.5 billion in tax receipts to the UK Exchequer.[125]

However, the United Kingdom voted in a referendum to leave the European union in 2016 in what is generally termed Brexit. We should remember that this was not Britain's first attempt at exiting the European Union. In 1975, just two years after joining the then EEC, it held a referendum on whether it should remain part of the EEC but voted to continue membership of the Community. It is not clear yet what the ultimate impact of the latest referendum will be. This will depend among many things on the nature of the final agreement between the United Kingdom and the European Commission. In the meantime, the UK has withdrawn from the London Fisheries Convention of 1964. This means the UK will regain full sovereign control of its waters up to 12 nautical miles from her coast. The UK has also signalled that it does not intend to be bound by the EU Common Fisheries Policy at some point after the Brexit transitional period. However, Denmark is already looking to challenge these UK decisions in court because it claims that Danish fishermen have historical rights protected under international law to access the seas around the UK dating back to the 1400s.[126] However, it is possible that the UK may no longer be bound by the CJEU after Brexit. It is not clear yet whether the UK will continue to apply a liberal open

123 House of Commons, 'Coasting Trade Bill', Hansard, 131, 462–466 (London, 7 March 1854).
124 For a broader discussion of England's historical maritime policies, see: T. Fulton, *The Sovereignty of the Sea: An Historical Account of the Claims to England to the Dominion of the British Seas, And of the Evolution of the Territorial Waters: With Special Reference to the Right of Fishing and The Naval Salute* (William Blackwood 1911).
125 Oxford Economics, *The Economic Impact of the UK Maritime Services Sector* (Maritime UK 2013).
126 Article 51 of United Nations Convention on the Law of the Sea 1982.

coast policy or return to a more protectionist maritime cabotage regime. The latter approach would mean that EU states and other countries will require permission to engage in maritime activities in UK coastal waters. Nevertheless, there are three issues that concern us with respect to maritime cabotage law and what authority Council Regulation 3577/92 will have after Britain completes its exit (including the agreed transition period, which may very well go beyond 2019, going by the slow progress in the negotiations between the United Kingdom and the remaining 27 EU member states). They are: single market, customs union, and the Court of Justice of the European Union.

If the United Kingdom decides not to stay in the single market, it means that, prima facie, it will cease to have access to free movement of goods, services, money and people within the European Union and vice versa. The important point here is that under Article 1 of Council Regulation 3577/992, British shipowners will not be able or allowed to provide maritime cabotage services in other member states of the European Union. On the other hand, Community shipowners from member states of the European Union would be able to provide maritime cabotage services in British waters because the United Kingdom implements a liberal open coast policy. Suffice to say that this would be disadvantageous to British shipowners and the domestic maritime sector in the United Kingdom.

The customs union is an arrangement designed to facilitate free trade by ensuring that member states in the EU charge the same import duties on goods that enter the European Union. The goods travelling between countries in the EU are also exempted from tariffs. Hence, member states can trade freely without the unnecessary burden of administrative hindrances. If the United Kingdom decides not to stay in the customs union, it will pose some challenges to cruise vessels and their passengers leaving a UK port with an itinerary to call at countries in the EU. The services sector including maritime transport and coastal services is an important part of the UK economy and would be most affected. For instance, under the liberal EU maritime cabotage framework, the maritime sector in the UK contributed a total of £31.7 billion in GDP. It supported 634,900 jobs and generated £8.5 billion in tax receipts to the Exchequer during the last global financial crisis, which began in 2008.[127] Therefore, it is not clear what the wisdom is in returning to the tried and failed maritime cabotage protectionist approach of the mid-nineteenth century.

The Court of Justice of the European Union (CJEU) is the highest court of law in the European Union. Its duty is to interpret and enforce the rules of the single market on issues including those arising from maritime cabotage services. When the United Kingdom exits the European Union, it is not clear what role, if any, the CJEU will continue to have on issues arising out of UK maritime cabotage. The UK has indicated that there may be some role yet for the EU court, although the UK does not intend to be under the direct jurisdiction of the CJEU after Brexit. This uncertainty is not helpful to what will continue to be Community shipowners and what will now be British shipowners. A new legal mechanism for

---

127 Oxford Economics, *The Economic Impact of the UK Maritime Services Sector* (Maritime UK 2013).

resolving disputes between the United Kingdom and the EU will surely need to be developed and fairly soon.

## South Africa: South African maritime transport policy of 2008

The Republic of South Africa has adopted a strong market-driven shipping policy. It operates a very liberal maritime policy, which permits foreign vessels on international trade to participate in its maritime cabotage services. However, there has been a growing debate on the need to experiment with protectionist maritime cabotage legislation in South Africa. A 1996 government white paper on national transport policy considered maritime cabotage legislation for South Africa. The white paper highlighted the government intention to evaluate the various maritime cabotage options in light of changing international maritime cabotage practices.[128] In 2003, the South African Maritime Black Economic Empowerment Charter was signed into law. The Charter is designed to persuade domestic cargo owners to give preference to South African ships for the carriage of their cargo.[129] It also advocates for the introduction of a maritime cabotage policy where cargo going through South African ports is carried on South African ships.[130] Although South Africa has a large volume of trade, this is not reflected in their ship-owning or ship-operation capacities. Therefore, the South African government has argued that introducing a protectionist maritime cabotage policy would revive the national flag carrier and stimulate the local maritime industry.[131] South Africa's large trade volume would be an important factor when considering what maritime cabotage policy to adopt. However, it should be noted that having a large trade volume is not in itself a sufficient basis to enact maritime cabotage legislation. The draft South African Maritime Transport Policy of 2008 calls for a protectionist maritime cabotage regime to be adopted in South Africa. Section 3.3.4 of the policy states: 'The South African Government shall have a cabotage policy in line with the guidelines established under the auspices of the United Nations Commission on Trade and Development (UNCTAD)'.[132]

Furthermore, the draft maritime policy states that the economic growth and development of South Africa is tied inextricably to the simultaneous growth and development of the African region. Therefore, it was important for South Africa to rethink its domestic maritime policy because regional coastal shipping has become

---

128 Department of Transport, 'White Paper on National Transport Policy' (DOT, 1996). The document emphasized that the introduction of maritime cabotage protection legislation on an African continent or Southern African regional basis was to be seriously considered and investigated.
129 Section 2.3.1 South African Maritime Black Economic Empowerment Charter 2003.
130 Section 2.3.2 South African Maritime Black Economic Empowerment Charter 2003.
131 See: South African Maritime Safety Authority, 'Maritime Sector Skills Development Study', Department of Transport (Pretoria, 21 September 2011).
132 Department of Transport, 'Draft South African Maritime Transport Policy' (DOT, 2008), p. 25.

an important factor in facilitating intra-regional trade and development.[133] The policy categorically states the South African government's intention to:

a    Examine the potential of the regional coastal shipping and to integrate this with the South African Development Community (SADC) cabotage policy.[134]
b    Consider the role that coastal shipping could play in the development of the coastal industry in the region.
c    Engage on all forms of policy (particularly cabotage) that impinge on coastal shipping.[135]

The draft maritime policy has triggered demand from the domestic maritime sector for a policy that introduces maritime cabotage as part of the broad agenda for stimulating the maritime sector in South Africa. However, such agenda must be sequenced appropriately with similar policy developments in other transport sectors. This will help establish a compelling case for the South Africa government to decide on the direction of their maritime cabotage policy.[136] Nevertheless, the conundrum for South Africa is that its maritime cabotage policy must be consistent with both the African Maritime Transport Charter of 1994 and the South African Development Community (SADC) protocol on Transport, Communication and Meteorology of 1996.[137]

The African Maritime Transport Charter advocates for a maritime cabotage policy within the African region similar to that of the European Union. Also, the SADC protocol demands that member nations shall progressively remove restrictions on cabotage by ships registered in a member state.[138] The decision by the SADC is the result of the difficult geographic terrain across the region and other parts of Africa. The poor surface transport network has hindered economic growth and sustainable development in the region.[139]

It is suggested that the success of any maritime cabotage policy in South Africa depends on designing a robust but flexible framework that accommodates the

133   Section 4.2.10.1 of the 2008 Draft South African Maritime Transport Policy.
134   SADC is an inter-governmental organization made up of 15 member nations from the Southern African region.
135   Section 4.2.10.2 of the 2008 Draft South African Maritime Transport Policy, p. 80.
136   Section 3.3 of the revised version of the Draft South African Maritime Transport Policy. Department of Transport, 'Draft South African Maritime Transport Policy' (DOT, 2009), p. 21.
137   See: section 11 of the 1994 African Maritime Transport Charter. This Charter will be replaced by section 15 of the 2010 Charter when it comes into force. This Charter should be juxtaposed with Article 8.2.2 of the South African Development Community (SADC) protocol on Transport, Communication and Meteorology of 1996.
138   South Africa is a signatory to the SADC Protocol and is bound by any decisions of the African Union.
139   Hence, any development in South African maritime cabotage policy is difficult if not sequenced with the policies of other South African Development Community (SADC) nations or the policy under the African Maritime Transport Charter.

objectives of both legal frameworks. Thus, South Africa's inclination to adopt a protectionist maritime cabotage policy may well depend on her ability to convince its South African Development Community (SADC) partners to follow in its footsteps by adopting a similar protectionist maritime cabotage policy.[140] However, this means that South Africa and its SADC partners would not be complying with the objectives and requirements of the African Maritime Transport when it comes into force. It appears that there is now serious consideration of which maritime cabotage approach would benefit the South African economy. However, there is no clear rationale for South Africa to abandon her liberal maritime cabotage policy. Moreover, adopting a protectionist maritime cabotage approach would mean a departure from SADC principles.[141] There has been very little progress on the Draft Transport Policy of 2008. However, it appears that the South African government is determined to finalise the policy framework. This will require a robust legal framework on domestic sea transport and a strategy to trigger economic development from the country's territorial waters.[142]

## New Zealand: Maritime Transport Act 1994

New Zealand is an example of a rapid and far-reaching economic liberalization approach. This has turned New Zealand into one of the most liberal economies in the world.[143] Prior to 1994, maritime cabotage in New Zealand was regulated under the Shipping and Seamen Act 1952. This act reserved maritime cabotage activities in New Zealand to domestic vessels, except in the absence of suitable domestic tonnage. Where foreign vessels were permitted to perform maritime cabotage services because of lack of availability of domestic tonnage, the foreign vessels were subjected to stringent conditions such as limiting them to the carriage of only specified cargo. They were also required to comply with the manning requirements of the flag state and to pay New Zealand wages to the crew working on board such vessels. The requirement on welfare and wages for foreign crew has been retained in New Zealand under the Maritime Labour Convention 2006.

The protectionist maritime regulation was deregulated gradually between 1984 and 1994 during economic reform in New Zealand. That reform witnessed the introduction of the Transport Law Reform Bill 1993, which proposed granting

---

140 For more on this, see: T. Norton, 'Rebuilding the South African Flagged Fleet', The Nautical Institute, 2011.
141 The liberal maritime cabotage policy in South Africa is a relic from both her colonized and apartheid era. The liberal policy allows vessels (particularly vessels affiliated with the United Kingdom) to participate in cabotage activities freely without any restrictions. However, several government policy papers have circulated among relevant stakeholders for consultation on the need to adopt a strict maritime cabotage approach.
142 See: L. Chikunga, 'South Africa Transport Department Budget Vote for 2015–16 Financial Year', Department of Transport (Cape Town, 5 May 2015). Address by the deputy minister of transport on the budget vote.
143 For more discussion, see: S. Goldfinch, 'Economic Reform in New Zealand: Radical Liberalisation in a Small Economy' [2004], *Otemon Journal of Australian Studies*, 30 (1), 75–98.

foreign vessels access to engage in the coastal trade and services of New Zealand without any restrictions.[144] The relevant section of the bill expressly stipulated that

> Cargo loaded, or passengers embarking, at any port in New Zealand intended to be finally unloaded or to finally disembark at any port in New Zealand may be carried by any ship where all appropriate maritime documents are held; in respect of the ship, any maritime products and seafarers on board the ship.[145]

However, the liberal open coast policy proposed in the transport bill failed to get enough support in the legislative house. The proposal for an open coast policy met with stiff opposition, it being argued that such a policy would have a negative impact on indigenous employment, national defence and national economic development.[146] This resulted in the bill being modified substantially. Therefore, rather than a comprehensive deregulation of the policy, it proposed instead that only foreign vessels transiting the New Zealand coast while on international voyage would be allowed to engage in its maritime cabotage services.[147]

Maritime cabotage in New Zealand is now regulated under the Maritime Transport Act of 1994.[148] The Act incorporates the concerns about the negative impact of a total open coast policy but remains largely a liberal maritime cabotage approach. The relevant section of the Act states:

1  No ship shall carry coastal cargo, unless the ship is:

  a  A New Zealand ship; or
  b  A foreign ship on demise charter to a New Zealand based operator who employs or engages a crew to work on board the ship under an employment agreement or contract for services governed by New Zealand law; or
  c  A foreign ship that:

    i  has disembarked at a port in New Zealand, passengers who embarked at a foreign port or unloaded at a port in New Zealand, goods loaded at a foreign port and has not visited a foreign port since that disembarkation or unloading; or
    ii  will, before departing from a port in New Zealand for a foreign port, disembark such passengers or unload such goods; or

---

144 See: A. Bollard, 'New Zealand', in J. Williamson (ed.), *The Political Economy of Policy Reform* (Institute for International Economics 1994), pp. 73–110.
145 Clause 240 of the Transport Law Reform Bill 1993.
146 T. Hazledine, 'New Zealand Trade Patterns and Policy' [1993], *Australian Economic Review*, 26(4), pp. 23–27.
147 For a broader discussion on the subject matter, see: M. Brooks, 'Maritime Cabotage: International Market Issues in the Liberalisation of Domestic Shipping', in A. Chircop et al. (eds), *The Regulation of International Shipping: International and Comparative Perspectives* (Martinus Nijhoff 2012), pp. 293–324,
148 Public Act 1994, No. 104. Assented to on 17 November 1994. The Act came into force in 1995.

   d   A foreign ship that:

       i   has embarked at a port in New Zealand passengers who are to be disembarked at a foreign port or loaded at a port in New Zealand, goods to be unloaded at a foreign port, and has not visited a foreign port since that embarkation or loading; or

      ii   will, before departing from a port in New Zealand for a foreign port, embark such passengers or load such goods.[149]

Section 198 (C and D) of the Act suggests that foreign vessels can have unrestricted access in the coastal waters of New Zealand provided they have discharged cargo from a foreign port or loaded cargo for a foreign port. However, this contrasts with the provisions of the immigration rules in New Zealand which stipulate that, foreign crew are allowed a limited period where they are eligible to work legally.

Schedule 3 of the Immigration (Visa, Entry Permissions and Related Matters) Regulation 2010 of New Zealand stipulates that 'Crews on foreign vessels engaged in coastal trading by virtue of meeting the conditions of section 198 of the Transport Act are limited to only 28 days of work permit for every international voyage'.[150]

It can be argued that the wording about 'crews on foreign vessels', as it appears on Schedule 3 of the Immigration Rule, applies only to the foreign crew and not to the foreign vessel. Thus, it is not clear whether a foreign vessel with indigenous crew would contravene the law. Moreover, section 198(2) of the Maritime Transport Act permits foreign vessels that cannot satisfy the requirements of section 198(1) to engage in maritime cabotage services when there are no suitable domestic-flagged vessels. This waiver has expectedly received strong condemnation from the Labour and Maritime Union of New Zealand. Their opposition to the liberal open coast policy is premised on the fact that foreign shipowners can engage in the New Zealand coastal trade without paying tax.[151] Furthermore, they are concerned about the extra risks to bio-security posed by foreign ships. They argue that foreign bugs from these vessels will settle onshore and threaten key industries and the marine ecology.[152] The 'Rena disaster', which was declared New Zealand's worst-ever maritime environmental disaster, renewed intense debate on the need for New Zealand to return to a protectionist maritime cabotage regime.[153] The labour and

---

149  Part 14, Section 198(1) of the Maritime Transport Act 1994 is as amended by section 9(1) of the Maritime Transport Amendment Act (NO 2) 2005. Public Act 2005, No. 108. Assented to 14 December 2005.

150  See also: E2.95.5 (Ci and Cii) of the Immigration New Zealand Operational Manual. Issued 30 April 2012

151  See: R. May et al., 'Unions and Union Membership in New Zealand: Annual Review for 2000' [2001], *New Zealand Journal of Industrial Relations*, 26(3), 317–329.

152  G. Parsloe, 'Biosecurity Busting Bugs Have an Open Door with International Shipping', Maritime Union of New Zealand, 2010.

153  *The Rena* was a container ship owned by a Greek shipping company with a Filipino crew, which ran aground on the Astrolabe Reef off the coast of Tauranga in New Zealand on Wednesday, 5 October 2011. The ship was carrying 1,368 containers. Eight of the containers contained hazardous materials, as well as 1,700 tonnes of heavy fuel oil and 200 tonnes of marine diesel oil. The disaster threatened wildlife and the area's rich fishing waters.

maritime union has also urged its government to consider Australia's new maritime cabotage approach as an alternative.[154]

The economic reform in New Zealand has culminated in one of the most strictly regulated and controlled economies in the world being replaced by one of the most liberal market-based economies. One of the hallmarks of these reforms was the removal of barriers to international competition in goods and services.[155] The government of New Zealand had argued that the maritime advantages of a deregulated policy to the economy would include reduced domestic transport costs and lower prices of goods. It was further submitted that a liberal maritime cabotage policy would provide a range of shipping benefits to cargo owners, including improved quality of service due to international competition.[156]

On the other hand, there was great concern about the commercial viability of indigenous enterprise in the face of international competition. It was argued that a liberal policy would hamper employment opportunities, national balance of payments, the environment and national defence.[157] The concern about the economic development benefits of a liberal maritime cabotage regime in New Zealand was based on three factors. First, there was the worry that foreign vessels could take advantage of light-handed tax regimes and reduced crewing costs. Furthermore, it was argued that foreign crew are generally not subject to income tax or domestic labour laws on crew welfare and wages and are often entitled to a variety of subsidies from their own governments. This made it more profitable for a shipowner to employ foreign crew over an indigenous crew. Therefore, a deregulated maritime cabotage policy would place domestic vessels and their owners in a difficult position, thereby significantly weakening the economic development of New Zealand's domestic maritime sector. However, many of these concerns – particularly in the areas of crew welfare and wages – have now been tackled as foreign crew must be paid wages that comply with New Zealand labour laws.[158]

154 For more on this, see: J. Fleetwood, 'Complete Overhaul of NZ shipping Required Following Rena Sentencing', Maritime Union of New Zealand, 2012.

155 S. Goldfinch, 'Economic Reform in New Zealand: Radical Liberalisation in a Small Economy' [2004], *Otemon Journal of Australian Studies*, 30(1), 75–98.

156 See: A. Bollard, 'New Zealand', in J. Williamson (ed.), *The Political Economy of Policy Reform* (Institute for International Economics 1994), pp. 73–110.

157 For a broader discussion on related issues, see: M. Brooks, 'Maritime Cabotage: International Market Issues in the Liberalisation of Domestic Shipping', in A. Chircop et al. (eds), *The Regulation of International Shipping: International and Comparative Perspectives* (Martinus Nijhoff 2012), pp. 293–324.

158 See: WJ5.45.15 Minimum Remuneration of WJ5.45 Conditions of Employment for Crew 2012 in *The Immigration New Zealand (INZ) Operational Manual*. See also, Minimum Wage Act 1983. See also: Appendix 9 - Foreign Charter Vessels - Crew Employment Agreements 2012. This is enshrined in the Maritime Labour Convention, which New Zealand is a Signatory.

# 11 The flexible maritime cabotage approach

The general understanding is that for a sovereign state the choice of maritime cabotage approach is limited to either a protectionist or a liberal approach. However, there is a third approach, which we will refer to as the 'flexible maritime cabotage approach'. With this approach a sovereign state can alternate between the protectionist and liberal maritime cabotage approaches as circumstances demand. The countries that adopt a flexible approach are normally those that traditionally have had a protectionist maritime cabotage regime. However, the distinct feature with this approach is the built-in legal mechanism that allows the sovereign state to alternate to a liberal policy when required without the need to go through the typically slow parliamentary process. We will now consider the legal frameworks of maritime cabotage law in some of these countries.

## The Russian Federation: Merchant Shipping Code of 1999

Russia is the largest country in the world, with a geographical area covering one eighth of the earth's inhabited land area.[1] However, a primary challenge with Russia is how to categorize her geographically – in our case particularly with respect to maritime cabotage regulations. The country spans the entirety of northern Asia and much of eastern Europe, sharing both land and maritime borders with several countries in the two continents. Thus, Russia is often identified geographically within Eurasia.[2] Determining a specific jurisdiction for a country is useful from a regional maritime cabotage framework perspective. This is because the confusion about which continent Russia belongs to means that neither Council Regulation 3577/92 which applies in the EU nor maritime cabotage agreements like BIMP – EAGA which apply among some Asian countries can be enforced in Russia.[3] Maritime cabotage in Russia

1 G. Curtis, *Russia: A Country Study* (Library of Congress 1998).
2 From northwest to southeast, Russia shares land borders with Norway, Finland, Estonia, Latvia, Lithuania and Poland, Belarus, Ukraine, Georgia, Azerbaijan, Kazakhstan, China, Mongolia and North Korea. Furthermore, it shares maritime borders with Japan across the Sea of Okhotsk and the U.S. state of Alaska across the Bering Strait.
3 The Brunei-Indonesia-Malaysia-Philippines – East Asia Growth Area was launched in 1994 as a cooperation initiative.

is generally reserved for Russian-flagged vessels, excepta

when a specialized vessel is required and there is no such suitable Russian-flagged vessel; and

b in the event of an urgent need for a vessel for carriage or towage, a foreign vessel may be used if a Russian flagged vessel is not available.[4]

Hence, the ports in which foreign vessels can perform maritime cabotage services such as from Dudinka to Murmansk are published officially in the 'Notifications to Navigators'.[5] Furthermore, the Russian ministry of transport observes a permit system. It is responsible for monitoring and issuing coastal trade permits to foreign vessels in the absence of Russian flagged vessels in their roster. The advantage of adopting this predetermined status relieves foreign-flagged vessels of the burden of proving the unavailability or unsuitability of a Russian-flagged vessel.[6] Also, vessels registered in the Russian International Ship Register seeking entry into Russian maritime cabotage are subjected to the same permit procedures as foreign-flagged vessels.[7]

Nevertheless, vessels that are constructed or procured specifically for national projects such as the exploration of offshore gas-condensate and oil-and-gas fields, may be issued maritime cabotage permits for the validity period of those long-term contracts.[8] The bulk of the foreign vessels engaged in Russian maritime cabotage are offshore marine vessels working in the Sakhalin oil field and other oil and gas projects. This is due to shortage or unavailability of suitable Russian flagged vessels. Maritime cabotage in Russia is regulated by the Merchant Shipping Code 1999 of the Russian Federation. The relevant section is Article 4, which states:

1 Carriage and towage between seaports of the Russian Federation (cabotage) shall be carried out by vessels flying the state flag of the Russian Federation.

2 In compliance with international treaties of the Russian Federation or in cases and in accordance with the procedure established by the Government of the

---

4 See Russian Government Resolution No. 204 dated 8 December 2008 and No. 404 dated 24 May 2000.

5 This is an official publication that is periodically updated by the Russian Federation Ministry of Transport. The publication provides information to the owners of foreign vessels advising them on which Russian ports are open to foreign vessels seeking to engage in the provision of maritime cabotage services.

6 For a more general discussion on permit systems, see: M. Brooks, 'Maritime Cabotage: International Market Issues in the Liberalisation of Domestic Shipping', in A. Chircop et al. (ed.), *The Regulation of International Shipping: International and Comparative Perspectives* (Martinus Nijhoff 2012), pp. 293–324.

7 The Russian International Ship Register (RIR) formed in 2006 with a lower tax regime to lure Russian shipowners back to the Russian flag. Two other registers exist in Russia: the State Register for ocean-going vessels and the Russian River Register for inland river vessels.

8 See clause 8 of Russian Government Resolution No. 204.

Russian Federation, carriage and towage in cabotage may be carried out by vessels flying the flag of a foreign state.[9]

The Merchant Shipping Code is not the first legal instrument designed to regulate Russian maritime cabotage. Prior to enacting the shipping code, a law reserving coasting trade to Russian-flagged vessels that employed Russian crews was passed as early as 1830. However, that law was never implemented. Furthermore, another maritime cabotage law was passed in 1897.[10] The choice of a flexible maritime cabotage approach by Russia is perhaps influenced by its geographical size. However, Russia is also keen to grow her shipping registers. Therefore, the requirement for cabotage vessels to fly the Russian flag is designed to support this agenda. This is in addition to the requirement that such foreign ship-owning companies must establish a commercial presence in the domestic economy.[11]

The flexibility in Russia's maritime cabotage policy is captured when Article 4 (1) and 4(2) of the 1999 Merchant Shipping Code of the Russian Federation are read together. On the one hand Article 4(1) reserves maritime cabotage services for vessels flying the Russian flag. On the other hand, foreign vessels can provide maritime cabotage services under Article 4(2) in accordance with predetermined government policies. The ports, which are published and periodically updated in the 'Notifications to Navigators', are designated specifically as open to foreign vessels providing maritime cabotage services.[12] Furthermore, the Russian national offshore oil and gas projects also benefit from the flexible maritime cabotage approach because it triggers a high demand for foreign offshore vessels.

## The Republic of India: Section 407(1) of the Merchant Shipping Act 1958

India has experimented with different maritime cabotage approaches. For instance, India's Act No. 5 of 1850 was a liberal maritime cabotage statute, which stated that:

> Goods and passengers may be conveyed from one part of the territories under the Government of the East-India Company to another part thereof, in other vessels than British ships, without any restriction, other than is or shall be equally imposed on British ships, for securing payment of duties of customs or otherwise.[13]

---

9 See: Article 4 (Carriage and Towage between Seaports of the Russian Federation) of the Merchant Shipping Code 1999 of the Russian Federation

10 For more on this, see: J. Karel, *The Russian Coasting Trade: United States Consular Report 1897* (Government Printing Office 1897). The 1897 law did not come into force until 1900.

11 See: N. Prisekina, 'Cabotage: Frequent Legal Issues for Contractors on Sakhalin Oil and Gas Projects', Russin & Vecchi (London, 18 November 2003).

12 See: Russian Government Resolution No. 404, Item 2. Dated 24 May 2000.

13 Indian Coasting Trade Act No. 5 of 1850 (An Act for Freedom of the Coasting Trade of India) passed by the governor-general of India in Council on 5 March 1850.

Act No. 5 of 1850 was promulgated when India was a colony within the British Empire and British vessels were accorded the same sovereign national rights as Indian vessels. Soon after the enacting this act, India began to agitate for the right to reserve maritime cabotage services to Indian vessels. However, it took until 1922 to pass a resolution that explored options to develop the Indian merchant marine.[14] This was followed by a legislative bill in 1928 that reserved the Indian maritime cabotage services to Indian vessels and Indian seamen.[15] Section 3 of the draft Indian Merchant Marine Bill 1923 stated: 'No common carrier by water shall engage in the coasting trade of India unless licensed to do so'.[16]

Since its independence from Britain, India's maritime policy has sought to reserve all its maritime cabotage services for national flag vessels. Furthermore, the government of India constituted a 'Reconstruction Policy Sub-Committee on Shipping' in 1945. That committee recommended that maritime cabotage services should be wholly reserved for Indian vessels.[17] Hence, section 407(1) of the Merchant Shipping Act 1958 now regulates maritime cabotage in India. It states:

> No ship other than an Indian ship or a ship chartered by a citizen of India or a company which satisfies the requirements in Clause (b) of Section 21, shall engage in the coasting trade of India except under a licence granted by the Director-General under this section.

Section 21 of the 1958 Act deals with the registration and definition of an Indian ship; clause (b) of section 21 stipulates inter alia that the principal place of business for the company must be in India, and Indian citizens must hold at least 75 per cent of the company's share capital. Nevertheless, section 407(2) of the 1958 Act demonstrates the flexibility in India's maritime cabotage legal and policy framework. It provides that a licence may be granted to permit a foreign vessel to participate in their maritime cabotage services. Moreover, the laws governing Exchange control in India permit Indian citizens to charter foreign vessels to trade in Indian coastal waters. Furthermore, the same regulation also permits 100 per cent foreign investment in Indian shipping companies. Thus, vessels owned by such companies are free from any of the restrictions usually imposed on foreign vessels.[18] We should note that acquiring a licence to perform maritime cabotage services is subject to satisfying stringent conditions, which include the foreign

14 See the resolution moved by Sir P. S. Sivaswamy Aiyer in the Indian National Assembly on 12 January 1922.
15 Mr. Sarabhai N. Haji's bill was introduced in the Legislative Assembly on 9 February 1928 and was accepted by 71 votes to 46 on 28 September 1928.
16 This bill was drafted in 1923/24 but was not introduced to the Legislative Assembly till 1928.
17 See: I-maritime, 'Indian Shipping Industry Report 2000' (Research & information Division, 2000).
18 India's Ministry of Commerce and Industry, 'Investing in India: Foreign Direct Investment-Policy & Procedures', Secretariat for Industrial Assistance (New Delhi, 2008), pp. 6 and 17.

enterprise proving the non-availability of a suitable Indian-flagged vessel. Nevertheless, it is submitted that the liberal policy of the Exchange Regulation is in contrast with the clear provisions of clause (b) of section 21 of the Merchant Shipping Act. It is uncertain how these two opposite positions can be reconciled. Furthermore, where both regulations apply simultaneously, it is not clear which one takes precedence.

The flexible mechanism has been implemented several times by relaxing India's traditionally protectionist maritime cabotage law. The objective of triggering the flexible mechanism is always to facilitate economic development in the domestic maritime sector. For instance, the cabotage law was relaxed in 1991 for five years to attract foreign mainline vessels for container traffic.[19] Ten years later, there was further easing of the restrictions so that APL India Ltd, a foreign company for maritime cabotage purposes, could undertake its own feeder services and trans-ship containers to inland container depots.[20] A similar relaxation was approved in 2005, which allowed foreign carriers to move containers between several Indian ports, including Jawaharlal Nehru and Mumbai, to ease congestion at the Nehru container port.[21] Also, following the completion of the International Container Transhipment Terminal (ICTT) at Vallarpadam in 2012, the Indian government again relaxed the cabotage law for a period of three years.[22]

The decision to further relax the cabotage law was taken despite strong opposition by the Indian shipowners' lobby. It allowed foreign vessels to engage in domestic waters to carry export-import (EXIM) containers that are transported through the Vallarpadam transhipment terminal. This was a strategic policy aimed at encouraging transhipment of Indian cargo from the Vallarpadam terminal. The policy also aims to reduce Indian shippers' dependence on nearby foreign hub ports and in turn attract cargo destined for Indian ports that are transhipped in Colombo and other foreign ports.[23]

Some commentators suggest that the primary reason behind the government's decision to relax cabotage rules for liner vessels is to encourage the aggregation of containers at Indian ports.[24] If so, foreign vessels will be allowed to carry export containers from an Indian port to the Indian port of aggregation. This is subject to the proviso that the containers are then shipped directly to the foreign port of destination without further transhipment. Similarly, import containers can be

19 See: India's Directorate General of Shipping, *Shipping Manual: Liberalization in Shipping* (DGS 2012).
20 For a broader discussion, see: Transport Canada, 'Use of International Marine Containers in Canada' (Government of Canada, 2012).
21 See: N. Vasuki Rao, 'India Relaxes Cabotage Law to Ease Nehru Congestion' [2005], *Journal of Commerce*, 10 January.
22 For more on this issue, see: M. Venunath, 'India Prepares to Ease Cabotage Rules', *IHS Maritime 360* (New Delhi, 7 December 2014).
23 See: P. Ghosh and S. Narayan, 'Maritime Capacity of India: Strengths and Challenges' (Observer Research Foundation, 2012).
24 See: India's Directorate General of Shipping, *Shipping Manual: Liberalization in Shipping* (DGS 2012).

shipped by a foreign vessel from the port of aggregation to an Indian port of destination. Again, this is subject to the proviso that the containers arrive at the Indian port of aggregation directly from the foreign port of origin without any previous transhipment. This fits in with the Economic (Liberalisation) Reform Programme established by the government in 1991.[25] When the liberal market-driven approach is triggered, foreign vessels can be hired when an Indian-flagged vessel is not available. In addition, where the difference in the charter rate between an Indian and foreign vessel is less than 10 per cent, the Indian vessel must match the lower rate to avail itself of any preference in the contract. Furthermore, any vessel converted to the Indian flag, irrespective of ownership, is accorded equal treatment as an Indian ship.[26] There are concerns that the existing Indian maritime cabotage law will undergo further relaxation or even a complete reform. The rationale behind this reasoning is that such reform would stimulate commercial growth in the traffic volume of India's maritime cabotage trade and services.[27] However, India's indigenous shipowners argue that further relaxation of the maritime cabotage law will not encourage the desired growth in the cabotage sector. They also claim that a radical reform or repeal of the existing maritime cabotage law will not increase the volume of traffic at the Vallarpadam transhipment terminal. They propose instead, making the present maritime cabotage law more stringent. Furthermore, they propose extending the law to cover goods carried by sea between India and Sri Lanka, to nullify the advantages that the container hub in Colombo has over the Vallarpadam terminal.[28]

## The Federation of Malaysia: Merchant Shipping Ordinance of 1952

Malaysian maritime cabotage law is enshrined in the Merchant Shipping Ordinance of 1952. The regulation did not cover maritime cabotage initially until its amendment in 1980. At the same time, the Domestic Shipping Licence Board (DSLB) was established.[29] The DSLB is the government agency that regulates maritime cabotage trade, controls the licensing of domestic ships engaged in Malaysian cabotage and issues exemption licences to foreign vessels engaged in the domestic cabotage trade and services.[30] The law stipulates that only domestic

---

25 See: H. Haralambides and R. Behrens, 'Port Restructuring in a Global Economy: An Indian Perspective' [2000], *International Journal of Transport Economics*, 27(1), 19–39.

26 See: G. Schulz, 'Cabotage in the Asia Pacific: A Brief Overview' [2011], *Legalseas*, January.

27 P. Tirschwell, 'Stakeholder Split on Impact of India's Relaxed Cabotage Rule' [2018], *Journal of Commerce*, 4 June.

28 For a broader but more generic discussion on the issue, see: S. Sanyal, 'Cabotage: To Keep or Relax?' [2011], *Business Line* (New Delhi, 20 November).

29 Malaysian cabotage law came into force on 1 January 1980 by amending the Merchant Shipping Ordinance 1952 (MSO, 1952).

30 Three types of licences are issued by the DSLB, namely: unconditional, conditional and temporary licences. Unconditional licence: granted to a person who owns a

vessels flying the Malaysian flag that hold a valid license for domestic shipping are permitted to engage in Malaysian maritime cabotage activities.[31] The relevant sections of the Merchant Shipping Ordinance are:

1   Section 65C, which stipulates the function of the Domestic Shipping Licence Board (DSLB).[32]
2   Section 65KA: Prohibition of non-Malaysian ships to engage in domestic shipping:

    a   No ship other than a Malaysian ship may engage in domestic shipping.
    b   A person not qualified to own a Malaysian ship as provided by Section 11 shall not charter or otherwise engage any Malaysian ship for domestic shipping except under and in accordance with such conditions as the Minister may direct or prescribe.[33]

3   Section 65L: Licence for domestic shipping:
    a   No ship shall engage in domestic shipping without a licence.

Sections 65L 3(a) and 65L 3(b) exempts from the provisions of 65L (1): in relation to the State of Sabah, any vessel licensed under the Merchant Shipping Ordinance 1960 of Sabah, and in relation to the State of Sarawak, any vessel licensed under the Merchant Shipping Ordinance 1960 of Sarawak.[34]

Traditionally, Malaysia has adopted a protectionist maritime cabotage approach. However, the Malaysian government reluctantly implemented some major flexible maritime cabotage policies in 2001 and 2009. These policies were in response to concerns raised by indigenous shippers and manufacturers in east Malaysia about the high cost of transhipment.[35] The states of Sabah and Sarawak were particularly

---

    Malaysian flag vessel on the condition that he has a right to own a Malaysian ship, owns 30% equity in the company and employs 70% of Malaysians on the ship as ratings. Conditional licence: granted where all the requirements of an unconditional licence are not met. Temporary licence: granted to Malaysian companies to operate foreign vessels in cabotage trade in the absence of Malaysian vessels upon the permission of the Minister of Transport.

31  See: P. Eswaran, 'Maritime Sector Study of IMT–GT [the Indonesia-Malaysia-Thailand Growth Triangle]' (Asian Development Bank, 2008). Maritime cabotage activities in Malaysia include services such as cable and pipe laying, hydrographic survey and dredging.
32  See introduction to Malaysian cabotage on page above for the creation and the function of the DSLB.
33  Section 11 of the Merchant Shipping Ordinance of 1952 stipulates the requirements and qualifications for registering a vessel as a Malaysian ship. In the case of corporations owning the vessel, it stipulates inter alia that the majority shareholders of the corporation are Malaysian citizens.
34  Sarawak Ordinance (2/60) of 1960.
35  Malaysian cabotage policy was also relaxed in 1994 between Port Klang and Penang Port; 2003 between Port Klang and Pasir Gudang Port, Port Klang and Port of Tanjung Pelepas (PTP); 2006 between Penang port and Port of Tanjung Pelepas (PTP).

affected and shippers making shipments to and from these states demanded a review of the maritime cabotage policy.

The high cost of transhipment was because foreign ships could not call directly at east Malaysian ports under the protectionist maritime cabotage regime. Therefore, all cargo for east Malaysia were transhipped at a port in the west, usually Port Klang, and carried from there on domestic vessels to their destination in east Malaysia.[36] The demand for the maritime cabotage law to be reformed or abolished has been opposed vehemently by indigenous shipowners who argue that a strict maritime cabotage regime is the last bastion of the Malaysian maritime sector.[37] However, the Malaysian government decided to relax its maritime cabotage laws in 2001, prompted by the view that foreign carriers would be attracted to other Malaysian ports and trigger the development of hubs and cargo transhipment centres.[38] Maritime cabotage law was also substantially relaxed in 2009. This allowed foreign vessels to carry containerized transhipment cargo between ports in the peninsula and east Malaysia. The exemption applied to shipments between the following ports: Sepangar and Klang; Bintulu and Klang; Kuching and Klang; Sepangar and Tanjung Pelepas; Bintulu and Tanjung Pelepas; Kuching and Tanjung Pelepas.[39] The impact of the government's decision to relax maritime cabotage law is that since 2003, Port Klang has become the national load centre and Port Tanjung Pelepas (PTP) the national transhipment centre.[40] This has required non-indigenous vessels to be exempted from the protectionist provisions of sub-section 65KA(I) of the MSO 1952.[41] Therefore, foreign vessels on an international voyage can now call at ports in all parts of the country.[42] The Malaysian Shipowners Association (MASA) has protested this development and suggested that by following this direction the government has failed in its duty to empower local maritime businesses and facilitate the economic development of Malaysia.

36  For more discussion on the issue, see: Oxford Business Group, 'Malaysia: Shipping in Protected Waters', Oxford Business Group (London, 27 September 2010).

37  For a general read, see: P. Nambiar, 'Stop Blaming Cabotage Policy', *Business Times* (Kuala Lumpur, 9 March 2009).

38  See: P. Barnsberg, 'Malaysia Eases Cabotage Law, Adds Incentive' [2001], *Journal of Commerce*, 30 April.

39  See the official letter exempting foreign vessels from the provisions of subsection 65 KA(1) of the Merchant Shipping Ordinance 1952, dated 1 June 2009 and signed by Minister of Transport Dato'sri Ong Tee Keat. This directive came into force 3 June 2009. The power to exempt granted to the minister of transport is provided for in section 65U of the Malaysian Merchant Shipping Act 1952.

40  See: D. Keat, 'The Liberalisation of Cabotage Policy is to Address the Peninsula–East Malaysia Trade Imbalance', *Trade and Logistics Malaysia* (Sarawak, 9 July 2009).

41  For a broader discussion, see: K. Fadzil et al., 'Policy Fiasco: The Sabotage of Cabotage Policy Malaysia' [2013], *International Journal of Social Science and Humanity*, 3 (6), 514–517.

42  See: F. Suffian, A. Rosline and M. Karim, 'The Cabotage Policy: Is It Still Relevant in Malaysia?', in R. Hashim, and A. Majeed (eds), *Proceedings of the Colloquium on Administrative Science and Technology* (Springer 2015), pp. 19–28.

## Australia: Coastal Trading (Revitalising Australian Shipping) Act 2012

Maritime cabotage in Australia dates as far back as 1890, when Australia was still under the colonial rule of the United Kingdom. For much of the nineteenth century coastal trading was largely unregulated and Australia's transport system was dominated by coastal shipping.[43] This continued until developments in the inland rail and road networks began to compete and put pressure on the dominance of coastal shipping.[44] The Australian maritime sector responded to the competition from other transport networks by forming a syndicate to restrict foreign vessels that were in receipt of foreign subsidies and paid their crew working in the coastal trade lower wages than standard Australian wages.[45]

Prior to 2012, maritime cabotage in Australia was regulated by Part VI of Navigational Act 1912. The Navigational Act itself did not originally apply to maritime cabotage until Part VI was added in 1921. This amendment occurred amidst serious concerns as to what effect a maritime cabotage policy would have on Australia's economic development.[46] One significant development caused by the Navigational Act was the Australian government introducing financial incentives for shipowners in the mid-1980s. This was to assist Australian shipowners purchase more efficient vessels. The 1912 Act was liberal as it permitted foreign vessels to engage in the coasting trade of Australia provided they were licensed for a maximum period of three years. Vessels seeking a coasting trade licence had to demonstrate that the crew on that vessel had access to the vessel's library facilities and that while the vessel operated on the Australian coast the crew were paid Australian wages.[47] Furthermore, such licensed vessels were held to be in breach of the Act if while engaged in the Australian coasting trade:

a    they were in receipt of a bonus or subsidy from a foreign government; or
b    they had received any bonus or subsidy within the previous twelve months prior to obtaining the licence; or
c    they had an arrangement in place to receive such bonus or subsidy.[48]

Alternatively, unlicensed vessels could carry cargo and passengers between Australian ports under the permit system if:

a    there was no suitable licensed ship available for the service; or

43  See: Report of the Royal Commission on the Navigation Act, 1924, The Parliament of the Commonwealth of Australia No. 103-F.15346.
44  For more on this, see: M. Ganter, 'Australian Coastal Shipping: The Vital Link' [1997], *Australian Maritime Affairs*, No. 3.
45  For more on this, see: C. Berg and A. Lane, 'Coastal Shipping Reform: Industry Reform or Regulatory Nightmare?' (Institute of Public Affairs, 2013).
46  For a broader discussion, see: R. Webb, 'Coastal Shipping: An Overview', Research Paper No. 12 2003–04 (Canberra, 3 May 2004). Information and Research Services Parliamentary Library.
47  Part VI, section 288 of Navigation Act 1912.
48  Part VI, section 287 of Navigation Act 1912.

b the service rendered by licensed ships is inadequate to the needs of such ports; and

c it is considered desirable in the public interest that an unlicensed ship be allowed to engage in that trade.[49]

Vessels carrying cargo and passengers under such a permit system were considered to be providing emergency services and thus not engaged in the Australian coasting trade.[50] Therefore, vessels on permit were not subject to the same degree of compliance as licensed vessels. For instance, vessels on permit were exempted from the trio of Australian Occupational Health and Safety legislation, Part II of the Navigation Act, and seafarers compensation legislation.[51]

However, the Australian maritime cabotage law and policy has since undergone a rollercoaster of reform. Successive Australian governments have been determined to replace one maritime cabotage approach with another. Through the waves of reform, Australian maritime cabotage has gradually transitioned from a largely unregulated sector to a more regulated one. Prior to these reforms, Australia's maritime cabotage policy focused on ensuring all crew working on vessels in Australia's territorial waters were in receipt of fair treatment. This was in addition to ensuring that no vessels providing maritime services in Australia's coastal waters were in receipt of state aid.

The new Coastal Trading (Revitalising Australian Shipping) Act 2012 now regulates Australian maritime cabotage.[52] One of the objectives of the new Act is to maximize the use of vessels registered in the Australian General Shipping Register in coastal trading.[53] The Act signifies the new, more stringent direction on maritime cabotage in which Australia is moving. It comes on top of the Fair Work Act 2009, which already imposes Australian labour standards on foreign-registered vessels operating with foreign crews in the Australian coastal shipping trade.[54] According to Rio Tinto, under the Fair Work Act 2009, the cost of employing foreign crew on a dry bulk carrier on the coastal trade is just 26 per cent of the

49 Part VI, section 286 of Navigation Act 1912. There were two kinds of permits, namely the Single Voyage Permit (SVP) for the carriage of cargo or passengers in a single voyage between designated ports, and the Continuing Voyage Permit, issued for up to a three-month period to carry cargo and passengers between designated Australian ports.

50 Part VI, section 286(2) of Navigation Act 1912.

51 See: J. Bazakas and R. Springall, 'Australian Shipping Industry Reform: Long Awaited' (Holman Fenwick Willan Briefings, 2011).

52 No. 55, 2012: An Act to Regulate Coastal Trading, and for Related Purposes. Assented to 21 June 2012. Part VI of the Navigation Act 1912 (the former regulatory instrument) is now repealed by the Coastal Trading (Revitalising Australian Shipping) (Consequential Amendments and Transitional Provisions) Act, No. 56, 2012: An Act to Deal With the Consequential and Transitional Matters Arising From the Enactment of the Coastal Trading (Revitalising Australian Shipping) Act, and for Related Purposes. Assented to 21 June 2012.

53 See: section 3(1d) of the Coastal Trading (Revitalising Australian Shipping) Act 2012.

54 For more, see: S. Thompson R. Springall and H. Brewar, *A Guide to the Coastal Trading Reforms in Australia* (Holman Fenwick Willan 2012).

cost of crewing it with Australian seafarers.[55] With the Coastal Trading Act 2012, access to the Australian coasting trade will no longer be possible using permits. Hence, vessels seeking to engage in Australia's coasting trade will be required to hold one of the three types of licence.[56]

This has resulted in demands for the cabotage law under the Coastal Trading Act 2012 to be reformed further. In 2014, the National Commission of Audit recommended that the maritime cabotage law and policy in Australia should be abolished completely.[57] That recommendation was later tempered by the Harper Review. The Review agreed that maritime cabotage restrictions should be abolished unless it could be proven that:

a    the benefits of the restrictions to the community outweigh the costs; and
b    the objectives of the policy can be achieved only by restricting competition.[58]

The Harper Review observed that restrictions increase cost and administrative complexity of providing maritime cabotage services. It noted that the Coastal Trading Act had succeeded in burdening foreign vessels with a threshold of requirements designed to benefit Australian shipowners. The Review claimed that the Coastal Trading Act also affects indigenous shippers of cargo on Australia's coastal waters. Therefore, the Review concluded that:

a    The participation of foreign-flagged ships in the coastal trade has decreased dramatically, meaning less competition for Australian operators.
b    The lack of competition has caused a substantial escalation in shipping costs such that Australian shippers are paying up to double the freight rates that could be offered by foreign-flagged ships in a deregulated coastal trade.
c    High-volume shippers are being deprived of the flexibility required to meet unplanned or urgent coastal shipping requirements due to unforeseen changes to operations or external factors.
d    Many foreign-flagged operators engaged in coastal trading provide specialized services that cannot be provided at all or provided efficiently by Australian operators.[59]

55  See: Rio Tinto, 'Submission to Senate Standing Committees on Economics Inquiry into the Shipping Reform Bills (Supplementary)', Government Office, 2008, p. 5.
56  Part 1, Section 3(2) of the Australian Coastal Trading Act 2012.
57  See the report of the National Commission of Audit, phases I and II, titled: *Towards a Responsible Government*. Published February and March 2014 respectively. The National Commission of Audit was an independent body established by the Abbott Government in October 2013 to review and report on the performance, functions and roles of the Commonwealth government.
58  See: I. Harper et al., *Competition Policy Review: Final Report* (The Harper Review), (Commonwealth of Australia 2015).
59  See: C. Keane, M. Thompson and J. Cockerell, 'Harper Review Recommends Changes to Australia's Cabotage Regime and Liner Shipping Exemption', *Clyde & Co Newsletter* (Melbourne, 2 April 2015).

## General licence

All vessels seeking the general license must be registered and continue to be registered in the Australian General Shipping Register (AGSR).[60] General licence holders have unrestricted access to the Australian coastal trade for a period of up to five years.[61] The operator of a vessel under the general licence scheme must ensure that each seafarer on its vessel is not prohibited from working when the vessel operates in the coastal waters of Australia. This means that the seafarer must be an Australian citizen, a holder of an Australian permanent visa, or a holder of an Australian temporary visa with work entitlements.[62] However, vessels registered in the Australian International Shipping Register (AISR) are not eligible to obtain general licences to engage in the Australian coastal trade. Such vessels can apply only for temporary and emergency licences. However, these other licences have several limitations.

## Temporary licence

The temporary licence allows a vessel to engage in the Australian coasting trade for a period of up to 12 months with a minimum of five voyages.[63] Section 40 (a) of the Coasting Trade Act 2012 stipulates that 'Any vessel used to undertake a voyage authorised by a temporary licence must be registered in the Australian International Shipping Register (AISR) or under a law of a foreign country.'

Once an application for a temporary licence is made, a notification by way of publication must be sent out to:

a    every holder of a general licence;
b    a body or organization that the minister considers would be directly affected, or whose members would be directly affected, if the application were granted.[64]

A general licence holder can give a 'Notice in Response' to the publication stating that they can carry some or all of the goods and passengers and perform some or all of the voyages as contained in the application of the temporary licence applicant.[65] The submission of a 'Notice in Response' requires the applicant to negotiate with every general licence holder who has made the submission.[66] The decision to grant a temporary licence depends on the outcome of the negotiation between the two parties, amongst other things. In addition, the comments of third parties who may be affected by the grant of such a licence are taken into

---

60  Section 13(1)(a) and section 21 (a) of the Australian Coastal Trading Act 2012.
61  Sections 3(2a) and 16(1) of the Australian Coastal Trading Act 2012.
62  See Section 13(2) and section 21(b) of the Australian Coastal Trading Act 2012.
63  See: Sections 28(1) and 28(2) of the Australian Coastal Trading Act 2012.
64  Section 30(b) and section 33 of the Australian Coasting Trade Act 2012.
65  Section 31 of the Coasting Trade Act 2012.
66  Sections 32(a) and 32(3) of the Coasting Trade Act 2012.

consideration.[67] However, a temporary licence operator may apply for a general licence if the foreign vessel intends to transition to Australian registration within five years.

### Emergency licence

A vessel registered under the laws of any country can apply for an emergency licence to carry cargo or passengers in emergencies, such as during natural or human-caused disasters.[68] However, an emergency licence is only granted for a maximum period of 30 days.[69] With the new act, emergency licence holders are subject to the same compulsory reporting requirements that apply to the other licence holders. These include information about the type of cargo, number of passengers on-board, and the loading and discharge ports of the vessel.[70]

However, the Australian government continues to demonstrate a willingness to experiment with its maritime cabotage law. A new Coastal Trading (Revitalising Australian Shipping) Amendment Bill 2017 was introduced into parliament in September 2017 to amend the Coastal Trading Act 2012. The proposed bill is designed to adjust the existing cabotage framework to make it more effective rather than comprehensively overhaul it. The bill is a response to complaints about difficulties with the licensing procedures under the current act. It aims to reduce barriers in the coastal shipping sector by simplifying the temporary license application procedure to encourage the use of shipping for domestic freight.[71]

## Judicial decisions arising from Australian maritime cabotage law

### Re the Maritime Union of Australia & Ors; Ex parte CSL Pacific Shipping Inc[72]

This case was decided under the old permit system and reflects the focus of Australian maritime cabotage law at that time regarding paying foreign crew working on the coastal trade wages that were equal to pay rates received by Australian crew. The *River Torrens* was an Australian-registered vessel licensed under section 288 of the Navigation Act 1912 (Cth) to operate in the coasting trade with Australian crew. The licence obliged the operator, the Australian National Line, to pay

67  Sections 33 and 34(3) of the Coasting Trade Act 2012
68  Sections 64(3a) and 72(a) of the Coasting Trade Act 2012.
69  Section 67 of the Coasting Trade Act 2012.
70  See sections 27, 62 and 75 of the Coasting Trading Act 2012 for reporting requirements for General licence, Temporary licence and Emergency licence respectively.
71  The bill was introduced by the minister for infrastructure and transport on 13 September 2017 and had its second reading on the same day. It will go before the Senate (Upper House) for approval. On 19 October 2017, the Senate moved that the following matters be referred to the Rural and Regional Affairs and Transport Legislation Committee for inquiry and report by 4 December 2017. The fate of the bill remains uncertain.
72  *Re The Maritime Union of Australia & Ors; Ex parte CSL Pacific Shipping Inc* [2003] HCA 43; 214 CLR 397 [7 August 2003].

crew the current Australian rate. The vessel was sold later to the Canadian CSL Group and renamed the *CSL Pacific* and registered in the Bahamas. The vessel returned to work on the Australian coast with an Ukrainian crew that had replaced the Australian crew and was issued a permit to operate in the coasting trade under section 286 of the Navigation Act 1912. The important point to note here is that the Ukrainian crew members were paid at rates that met International Transport Federation (ITF) standards but were lower than Australian pay rates. The permit allowed the operators to avoid, amongst other things, the requirement to pay Australian wage rates. However, the Maritime Union of Australia applied to the Australian Industrial Relations Commission (AIRC) to impose Australian labour standards on *CSL Pacific*, and CSL appealed to the High Court.

The question before the court was whether the jurisdiction of AIRC to vary an award on labour standards (wages) also applied to a foreign company operating a foreign vessel with foreign crew trading in Australian waters under a permit. The general understanding was that the AIRC's jurisdiction was limited to coastal voyages between Australian ports. The court ruled that despite being a foreign vessel, the AIRC was constitutionally within its rights and had jurisdiction to impose Australian pay rates on the Ukrainian crew. The court accepted that the 'internal economy' rule was a valid tenet of international law and valid law for Australia as argued by CLS. Nevertheless, it held that the rule did not operate to displace the explicit jurisdiction granted to the AIRC under section 5(3)(b) of the Workplace Relations Act 1996. Although it was ruled that the AIRC had jurisdiction to impose Australian wage standards over CSL, the Commission opted not to do so. Their reason was that such actions could impact negatively on productivity and performance of work. We should note that this case was decided before the Fair Work Act 2009. Hence, under this act, the Australian labour standards applies compulsorily on all vessels engaged in the Australian coastal trade regardless of their foreign or domestic status. .

## CSL Australia Pty Ltd v. Minister for Infrastructure & Transport and Rio Tinto Pty Ltd[73]

This case was concerned with an application by CSL Australia Pty Limited, a general licence holder that sought judicial review of the Minister's decision to vary the temporary licence granted to Rio Tinto Shipping Pty Ltd under the Coastal Trading Act. The licence was in relation to four voyages that were to be performed for Pacific Aluminium under a previously granted temporary licence. The issues relating to the considerations examined by the Minister's authorized delegate were already the subject of two previous judicial considerations.[74] Hence, the judgment of the full Court of the Federal Court of Australia is the latest in the

---

73 *CSL Australia Pty Limited v. Minister for Infrastructure & Transport and Rio Tinto Pty Ltd* [2014] FCAFC 10 (26 February 2014)
74 The judicial decisions were initially by Justice Robertson, see: [2012] FCA 1261; and then by Justice Katzmann, see: [2013] FCA 152.

sequence of judgements on the issues in this case. This case is instructive because it provides clarity on the operation and scope of the Coastal Trading Act 2012.

The general licence holder CSL Australia Pty Ltd, who claimed to have vessels available and suitable to perform the coastal voyages in question, and Rio Tinto, the temporary licence applicant, both made their submissions. The Minister's delegate granted the application for variation based on commercial matters that included asserted freight rate differentials and the requirement of a proposed liquidated damages clause. Therefore, the court was asked to decide what considerations the Minister ought to have regard for in determining whether to grant an original application or vary a temporary licence, which permits the use a foreign-flagged vessel to carry coastal cargo.

The court disagreed with the earlier ruling of the lower court.[75] It held that the mandatory considerations to which the delegate ought to have considered are limited to the suitability of the ship, the timeliness of carriage, and the reasonable requirements of a shipper of the kind of cargo specified in the application.[76] It ruled that commercial considerations such as freight rates or the implications of a liquidated damages clause fall short of such 'reasonable requirements' as contemplated by section 34(3)(d) of the Coastal Trading Act. Therefore, it should not form part of the mandatory considerations. The reasonable requirements of a shipper as contemplated in section 34(3)(d) of the Coastal Trading Act are specified in:

a    sections 32(3) (suitability and availability of general licence vessels);
b    section 34(3)(b) (suitability of general licence vessels)[77]; and
c    section 34(3)(c) (availability of general licence vessels).[78]

The court held that the Minister's delegate erred in interpreting the relevant section of the Act to mean that commercial matters fell within the scope of the mandatory considerations in the Coastal Trading Act. Nevertheless, the court was keen to emphasize that some reasonable requirements of a shipper, such as commercial considerations including freight rates and the economic position of the shipper that fall outside the ambit of sections 32(3), 34(3)(b) and 34(3)(c), can still be taken into consideration by the delegate under section 34(2)(g). This

---

75  Justice Robertson had ruled earlier that, for the purposes of section 34(3)(d), the reasonable requirements of a shipper could include economic considerations such as freight rates, cost impacts and profitability.

76  It is important to note the importance of the phrase: 'The kind of cargo as specified in the application'. This is because such requirements must be distinguished from reasonable generic requirements of a shipper of cargo.

77  The court also held that the suitability requirements of the shipper are intimately connected with the eventual need for safety to persons across the various stages of loading a vessel.

78  The 'requirements of the shipper' referred to in section 32(4) can only relate to the matters that are the subject of the negotiation– that is, the suitability of the vessel and the timeliness of the carriage and excludes any requirements or desires of the shipper as to freight rates or special clauses in the contract of carriage.

section allows the Minister to exercise discretion in contemplating non-mandatory considerations and any other matters the Minister thinks relevant. However, the exercise of this discretion is subject to the proviso that the consideration is within the object of the legislation, as stipulated in section 3(1) of the Coastal Trading Act. Furthermore, the court observed that the Coastal Trading Act is not a vehicle for shippers to obtain the lowest possible freight rates. It cautioned that the weight attached to freight rates in any particular case was a decision for the Minister. However, the Minister cannot attach so much weight to freight such that it distorts the operation of the Coastal Trading Act. The court also held that the impact of commercial considerations on an industry is a consideration available to the Minister. It argued that it was impossible to exclude freight rates and their impact on industry as legally irrelevant and outside the scope of other matters that the Minister's delegate can consider when deciding an application under section 34(2)(g) of the Coastal Trading Act. The court rejected the proposition that decisions under the Act should adopt an assumed bias towards the holders of general licences, at the expense of temporary licence holders using foreign-flagged vessels.

### CSL Australia Pty Ltd v. Minister for Infrastructure & Transport and Braemar Seascope Pty Ltd[79]

The appellant in this case was a general licence operator and was eligible to engage generally in coastal trading. The second respondent, Braemar Seascope, a shipbroker, applied to the first respondent (Minister) for a temporary licence to undertake 17 specified voyages in August 2012. At the time of completing the application form, Braemar were aware that all 17 voyages that it had specified in the application were fictitious. Furthermore, Braemar made a separate application in March 2013 to add a further 7 voyages to its temporary licence. The details provided for each of the voyages – including the type of cargo, volume, load and discharge ports, dates and vessel details – in this application were fictitious. Braemar also knew that it did not own or charter and was neither an agent of any ship nor the shipper of any of the fictitious cargoes. Rather, it anticipated that before the expiration of the 12-month temporary licence, opportunities would arise for it to fix vessels that were not on the general register to carry cargo. It also hoped to find shippers looking to transport their cargoes at the cheaper rates that such vessels offered in comparison to those with general licences. When those opportunities presented themselves, Braemar intended to, and did, apply to the first respondent to vary one or several of the fictitious voyages authorized in its temporary licence. The varied licence would then authorize the actual voyage or voyages that Braemar was seeking to arrange. This is what happened when Braemar successfully lodged an application to vary its temporary licence in July 2013 for the sixth new voyage, which became voyage 23. Therefore, the previously

---

79 *CSL Australia Pty Limited v. Minister for Infrastructure & Transport and Braemar Seascope Pty Ltd* [2014] FCA 1160 (3 November 2014).

fictitious authorized voyage to carry 20,000 tons of grains from Albany to Melbourne loading on 15 August 2013 was varied to reflect a voyage carrying 45,000 tons of coal from Port Kembla to Whyalla with an expected loading date of 2 August 2013. The temporary licence that was varied in July 2013 authorized 21 voyages. Four of those voyages, including voyage 23, were yet to be performed.

The appellant, CSL asked the court to declare that the decision of a delegate of the Minister to grant the temporary licence to Braemar and to vary it on two occasions in April 2013 and July 2013was invalid because Braemar was not eligible to apply for a temporary licence or for its variation. Furthermore, they asked the court to rule that the variation granted on 9 July 2013 was invalid because the Minister's delegate did not follow the appropriate procedure under the Act. Also, the appellant sought a declaration that Braemar used its temporary licence in a way that circumvented the purpose of the general licence provisions or the object of the Coastal Trading Act as contemplated by section 63 of the Act.

The question before the court was whether an application for a temporary licence based on fictitious voyages was valid under the provisions of the Coastal Trading Act 2012. Furthermore, whether such authorized temporary licence could become valid under the Act when varied subsequently to pursue real or further fictitious voyages. The court was also required to determine whether the Minister was within his authority to grant these applications and the subsequent variations if the applications to obtain and vary the temporary licence were invalid. Braemar accepted that at the time of the original application, there was no one with whom the general licensee could negotiate for any of the voyages. Also, they accepted that at the time of the original application, none of the voyages was genuine. However, they claimed that it was their best guess based on industry knowledge. It was significant that Braemar admitted that none of the original 17 voyages for which it applied and was granted temporary licence was ever performed.

The court held that the second respondent had only one plan and that was to vary the application from the fiction that was authorized to the reality of its clients' actual needs when those clients were found ultimately. Braemar knew that it was not eligible to apply for the temporary licence pursuant to section 28(1) of the Coastal Trading Act 2012. It knew that none of the information about the voyages in the August 2012 and March 2013 applications was true. Braemar obtained and used its temporary licence with the plan of obtaining ad hoc variations when an opportunity to transport coastal cargo presented itself to the disadvantage of general licence holders. Such ad hoc use of the temporary licence violated the provisions of section 3(2b) of the Act which stipulate that a vessel used to engage in coastal trading under a temporary licence has access to Australian waters that is limited in time and to voyages authorized by the licence. Furthermore, the actions of the second respondent circumvented the objective of the general licence provisions and the object of the Coastal Trading Act as contemplated in section 63(1) of the Act. The Coastal Trading Act did not envisage that the rights of general licensees would be impinged upon by applications for temporary licences based on fictitious voyages and subsequent variations of that licence based on a commercial opportunity that may arise.

In summary, the court held as follows:

- The decision of the first respondent to grant the second respondent's application for a temporary licence in 2012 was invalid under Section 35 of the Coastal Trading Act 2012. Furthermore, the first respondent lacked jurisdiction to grant temporary licence to the second respondent because it was not eligible to apply for the licence in question, pursuant to section 28(1) of the Act.
- The decision of the first respondent to grant the second respondent's application of April 2013 for a variation of the licence under section 55 of the Act was invalid because the first respondent was without jurisdiction since the licence was incapable of variation because the original 2012 application was invalid under section 35 of the Act as it was based on fictitious facts.
- The decision of the first respondent to grant the second respondent's application of July 2013 for a variation of the licence for voyage 23 from a fictitious voyage to an actual voyage under section 47 of the Act was invalid because the first respondent was without jurisdiction since the licence was incapable of variation because the original 2012 application was invalid under section 35 of the Act as it was based on fictitious facts. Also, as the variation was not based on a matter authorised by the licence, it could not be granted under section 47 of the Act.
- The court decided that the ad hoc use of the temporary licence by the second respondent was clever but designed to undermine the objective of the general licence provisions and the object of the Act as envisaged under section 63(1) of the Act.

## Analysis of Australia's new maritime cabotage regime

The new Australian Coastal Trading Act with its simplified three-tier licensing system shares some characteristics with the Canadian cabotage framework.[80] The new legislation provides a regulatory framework for coastal trading in Australia that improves its overall maritime capability. It promotes a viable shipping industry that contributes to the broader Australian economy. Furthermore, it maximizes the use of Australian-registered vessels by giving them access to proposed Australian taxation incentives, particularly under the new Australian International Shipping Register (AISR).

It is debatable whether the tax exemptions under the new legislation are sufficient to persuade maritime businesses to invest in the Australian maritime sector. One argues that if the tax incentives are not accompanied by significant cost savings, they are unlikely to attract vessels to the Australian international shipping register. Furthermore, the failure to permit vessels on the AISR to obtain general

---

80 See the section above on Canadian maritime cabotage law.

coastal trading licences undermines the success of the new maritime cabotage legislation which depends largely on how attractive the AISR is to both the indigenous and international shipping community.[81] Thus, coastal shipping in Australia has undergone two separate but interacting changes that have increased substantially the regulatory burden on foreign vessels while protecting Australian-registered vessels. First, the Fair Work Act of 2009 imposed Australian labour standards on foreign vessels and their crew operating in the Australian coastal trade. Previously, the Workplace Relations Act 1996 exempted foreign vessels operating on permit from implementing Australia's labour standards.[82] Australia's Maritime Union described the lower foreign labour standards as unfair competition. Second, switching from the old system of licences and permits to the three-tier licence system has redefined the process of engaging in the Australian coasting trade in favour of Australian-registered vessels.

In defence of the new Coastal Trade Act, the Australian Department of Transport released statistical information to show how foreign competition in the coastal waters is forcing Australian vessels out of business at an alarming rate.[83] Following the enactment of the latest legislation, protectionist tax concessions for Australian shipping companies operating in the coastal trade have been introduced through the Shipping Reform (Tax Incentive) Regulation 2012 and the Tax Law Amendment (Shipping Reform) Regulation 2012.

The Shipping Reform (Tax Incentive) Regulation makes it mandatory for shipping companies to employ a minimum of three trainees (deck, engineer and steward) on vessels engaged in the Australian coastal trade. This requirement applies regardless of the company's constraints and operational requirements.[84] Furthermore, the same regulation provides that the shipping company must conduct its crew management within Australia. This is in addition to conducting either its commercial management, its strategic management or its technical management within Australia.[85] The Coastal Trading Act 2012 and

---

81  For more on this, see: D. Maybury and M. Tang, 'Australian Shipping Industry Reform: Coastal Trading Bill' [2012], *Legalseas*, February.

82  However, it is important to see the High Court judgement in: *Re The Maritime Union of Australia & Ors; Ex parte CSL Pacific Shipping Inc* [2003] HCA 43, where it was held that notwithstanding that a vessel used in the Australian coastal trade was a foreign vessel, the AIRC was constitutionally within its rights and had jurisdiction to apply Australian awards to the Ukrainian crew.

83  Department of Infrastructure and Transport, 'Submission to House of Representatives Standing Committee on Infrastructure and Communications in relation to Coastal Trading (Revitalising Australian Shipping) Bill 2012 and Related Bills' (Canberra, 4 October 2012), p, 3. Statistical information from the Australian department of transport shows that in 1996, only four out of 42 vessels engaged in coastal shipping were foreign-registered vessels. By 2006, 11 out of 44 coastal trading vessels were foreign-registered. However, in 2011, 22 Australian-registered licensed vessels were competing on the coast with over 400 foreign-flagged ships operating under permit.

84  See: Part 2, section 4 of Shipping Reform (Tax Incentive) Regulation 2012.

85  Part 2, section 5 of Shipping Reform (Tax Incentive) Regulation 2012.

all the preliminary reports explain why the Australian coasting trade should be improved and expanded through a more stringent regulatory framework. Nevertheless, it is not clear why any such improvement and expansion should mainly comprise Australian-registered vessels. Australia is struggling with a combination of an ageing maritime workforce and high labour costs. Perhaps there is a need to reconsider the benefits of competition from foreign vessels that provide services at lower costs to Australian commodity producers. The Australian Dry Bulk Shipping Users (ADBSU), which depends on domestic sea freight to transport their products, argue that the Act promotes protectionism of Australian shipping without concern for the impact it has on Australian industry and its manufacturing sector. It claimed that data from the Australian cement industry showed that the costs of transporting a cargo of cement from China to Australia was the same as carrying the same cargo between two Australian ports.[86] Several judicial decisions that have gone against temporary licence holders have prompted a new debate on whether the Coastal Trading Act 2012 should undergo a comprehensive reform or be abolished.[87] Perhaps the new Coastal Trading (Revitalising Australian Shipping) Amendment Bill 2017 will address some of the concerns.

## Republic of Chile: Decreto Ley 2222 of 1978

Traditionally, Chile has adopted a protectionist maritime cabotage law approach. The legal framework of maritime cabotage in Chile is formed of several legislations. However, the legal cabotage framework is designed to be robust but flexible to accommodate the fluctuations in Chile's domestic maritime transport services. Maritime cabotage in Chile is normally reserved for Chilean vessels. This was captured in Article 1 of Law 6415 of 1939 that reserved cabotage services to Chilean vessels.[88] A Chilean ship is defined in Article 1 of the Sailing Law 1836 as one 'which is built in shipyards of Chilean Republic or those of other nations and has come to be owned by Chilean natural or legal person by lawful contract'.[89]

The reservation of maritime cabotage trade and services in Chilean waters to its vessels was further preserved in Article 3 of Law 466 of 1974 to promote domestic shipbuilding and indigenous ship-owning capacity.[90] Maritime cabotage law in Chile is regulated currently under Decreto Ley 2222 of 1978.

---

86 Australian Dry Bulk Shipping Users (ADBSU), 'Submission to Senate Standing Committees on Economics Inquiry into the Shipping Reform Bills' (Canberra, 19 April 2012), pp. 1–5.
87 See: A. Shepherd et al., *Towards Responsible Government: The Report of the National Commission of Audit, Phase II* (Commonwealth of Australia 2014). See also: L. Kennedy and J. Leslie, 'Options Paper: Approaches to Regulating Coastal Shipping in Australia', Commonwealth of Australia, 2014.
88 Article 1 of Law 6415 of 1939: Reserva El Comercio De Cabotaje A Las Naves Chilenas. In force 15 September 1939.
89 Article 1 of the Sailing Law (Ley de Navegación) of 1836. Passed by Chilean congress on the 28 July 1836.
90 Article 3 of Law 466 of 1974: Decreto Ley 466 of 1974. Promulgated 21 May 1974.

Article 11 of Decreto Ley 2222 provides that: 'A vessel may only be registered in Chile by a citizen of Chile or a legal person who is registered in Chile'. A foreign person may qualify to register a vessel if they are domiciled in Chile and their principal place of business is in Chile. However, the principal and the majority of the directors of such a company must be Chilean nationals. In addition, more than half the capital must belong to a Chilean natural or legal person. Furthermore, vessels flying the Chilean flag must ensure that the captain, officers and crew are citizens of Chile.[91]

Article 3 of DL 3059/79 continues the tradition that maritime cabotage services in Chilean territorial waters is reserved for Chilean vessels. However, under this regulation, foreign vessels can trade in Chilean waters by participating in a public bidding if the shipper advertises for international tender for the carriage of cargoes above 900 tons.[92] In addition, in the absence of suitable Chilean-flagged vessels, foreign vessels may be granted waivers by the National Maritime Authority to carry cargo less than 900 tons in maritime cabotage trade.[93] Also, empty containers between two or more domestic ports may be carried by foreign vessels based on reciprocity.[94] Foreign vessels engaged in Chilean maritime cabotage services must employ only Chilean crew, and such foreign vessels are charged tax at a higher rate than Chilean companies. The Chilean government has unveiled plans to modify Article 3 of DL 3059/79 by extending maritime cabotage traffic to foreign vessels, subject to the following conditions:

a    vessels must be foreign merchant shipping vessels under regular service;
b    vessels must transport containerised cargo; and
c    vessels must sail between two or more Chilean ports, with such ports registered as the vessels' regular calls.

The government's proposed plan is aimed at reducing the costs of domestic sea transport of cargo to encourage a preference for sea transport over other transport modes. This would optimize fair and productive competition in Chilean maritime cabotage trade and services.[95] However, the indigenous shipping companies oppose the proposed changes because they will open Chilean cabotage services to neighbouring countries without reciprocation. This would hamper the

91   Article 14 of Decreto Ley 2222 of 1978: Law In Lieu of Navigation. Promulgated 2 May 1978.
92   Section 3(ii) of Decree Law No. 3,059 of the Act promoting National Merchant Marine 1979.
93   Section 3(iii) of Decree Law No. 3.059 of the Act promoting National Merchant Marine 1979.
94   However, see Article 47 of Law No. 18899 of 1989, which does not classify carriage of such empty containers as cabotage.
95   For instance, in 2001 there were only two indigenous companies offering regular services for general cargo on the centre-north route, while three companies operated a service to the south. In contrast, a total of 23 independent carriers offered international containerized services, the clear majority of which call at more than one Chilean port.

economic development of the country and might lead to loss of domestic labour.[96] Furthermore, the Chilean mariners have long maintained that a liberal proposal represents a threat to their seafarers' jobs and the survival of Chile's shipping industry.[97] Moreover, they argue that neighbouring countries implement a protectionist maritime cabotage approach without any provision to reciprocate Chile's planned open coast policy.[98] The trade unions have asked the government to consider other options that will not undermine the growth of the domestic maritime sector and the economic development of the country.[99] Furthermore, the Chilean trade unions argue that Chilean legislation on maritime cabotage is already flexible enough as foreign vessels are allowed to engage in Chile's maritime cabotage trade under certain circumstances.[100] Therefore, liberalizing the sector further would be detrimental to the domestic maritime sector and would open the door to foreign vessels and organizations to compete with domestic companies and its labour force. However, the decision to reserve maritime cabotage trade and services to Chilean-flagged vessels has forced the implementation of a state subsidy in the south of Chile for most of the regular shipping trades. The subsidy is to forestall high operating costs that would otherwise be borne by indigenous maritime companies serving these routes.[101]

Chile's maritime cabotage approach has in the past been referred to as the model to be adopted in other countries.[102] However, it is observed that Chile's traditional protectionist maritime cabotage policy contrasts with the liberal economic reform agenda pursued by recent governments in Chile. If the government's open coast proposal is successful, Chile will be the first Latin American country to adopt a liberal maritime cabotage approach.

---

96 The Chilean government's proposal has drawn fierce criticism and led to cross-sectorial strikes by Chilean mariners across Chile's major ports. The strike action demonstrates support for Chile's protectionist maritime cabotage policy.

97 For a more general discussion on the long-standing issues mentioned here, see: J. Hoffmann, 'Maritime Cabotage Services: Prospects and Challenges' [2001], *Bulletin on Trade Facilitation and Transport in Latin America and the Caribbean*, 183(11), 1–7.

98 For general reading, see: R. Rozas, 'Shipping and Transport: Chile: Potential Regulatory Changes in the Cabotage Trade', International Law Office (London, 22 June 2011).

99 See: ITF, 'ITF Backs Union Action to Defend Chilean Shipping Industry' (ITF 2012).

100 See: sections 3(ii) and 3(iii) of Decree Law No. 3,059 of the Act promoting the National Merchant Marine 1979.

101 State aid is normally viewed as a protectionist mechanism. However, the provision of a state subsidy in Chile's case is to prevent the Malaysian experience where the Malaysian indigenous shipowners incurred high operating cost in the maritime cabotage trade and subsequently passed that high cost to domestic shippers and consumers.

102 India referred to the Chilean cabotage approach in their argument to adopt a strict cabotage regime. See: S. Haji, 'Indian Commercial Opinions on the Bill for the Reservation of the Coastal Traffic of India: Introduced in the Indian Legislative Assembly' (Indian Shipping Series no. 9, 1928), p. 13.

## Maritime cabotage law in *sui generis* regions

The book has so far focused on maritime cabotage law in the national and regional domains. This section will focus on the application of maritime cabotage law in geographical areas where several nations claim sovereign rights to explore the resources in the area. This is important because as we may recall from the last three chapters, the right to enact a maritime cabotage law over an area starts with the state having sovereignty over that geographical area. However, this section deals with maritime cabotage law in areas where states have no such sovereignty.

The Gulf of Guinea and the Arctic region are both examples of areas where no one state can claim sovereignty, which is the reason we have classed them as *sui generis* regions. However, this section will focus on the latter because of its importance to many nations and the suggested policy framework proposals for regulating maritime transport in the area. The depleting maritime resources in accessible regions means that the focus has turned to remote regions with challenging geological formations that are difficult to access.[103] These regions tend to hold huge reserves of resources and are now viewed as the future gateway for transporting products from production areas to consumers. Hence, it is useful to develop an effective legal framework that provides for legal certainty if there is a dispute. Such a framework would accommodate the interests of all parties and determine their rights and obligations.

### Maritime cabotage in the Arctic region

This section assesses the rights and interests of coastal states in the Arctic region. The Arctic is a circumpolar region in the north of the Arctic Circle and is regulated by the Arctic Council. This is a high-level inter-governmental forum that addresses issues faced by the Arctic governments and the indigenous people of the Arctic.[104] It was established by the 1996 Ottawa Declaration.[105] The Arctic Council serves as a forum for promoting cooperation, coordination and interaction among the Arctic States.[106] The Arctic Council consists of the eight Arctic states: Canada, the Kingdom of Denmark (including Greenland and the Faroe Islands), Finland, Iceland, Norway, Russia, Sweden and the United States. However, Iceland, Finland and Sweden do not have a coastal frontage in the Arctic Ocean and hence cannot claim maritime zones in the Arctic. The Arctic Indigenous Communities (AIC) are represented by six international organizations with

---

103 For an excellent discourse on the issue, see: D. Toomey, 'Global Scarcity: Scramble for Dwindling Natural Resources', *Yale Environment 360* (California, 23 May 2012).
104 For a broader discussion, see: J. Carman, 'Economic and Strategic Implications of Ice-Free Arctic Seas', in S. Tangredi (ed.), *Globalization and Maritime Power* (National Defence University 2009), pp. 171–188.
105 See: Declaration on the Establishment of the Arctic Council – Joint Communiqué of the Governments of the Arctic Countries on the Establishment of the Arctic Council. Ottawa, Canada, 19 September 1996.
106 Greenland is part of the Kingdom of Denmark, but unlike metropolitan Denmark it is not part of the EU. Iceland has coastal frontage on the Norwegian Sea, while Finland and Sweden have their coastal frontage in the Baltic Sea.

permanent participant status. They join with other inhabitants of the region in contributing to discussions on issues such as Arctic shipping.[107]

The large reserves of natural resources such as oil, gas and minerals in the Arctic Sea has triggered disputes among the Arctic member states. International law allows a country to extend its Exclusive Economic Zone (EEZ) for resource exploitation, where it is proven that its continental shelf extends beyond the 200-mile limit.[108] In Canada, Arctic sovereignty is a top foreign policy priority. Hence, it has made concerted efforts to assert full sovereignty over the Beaufort Sea in the dispute with the United States.[109] This includes claiming the Northwest Passage as an internal Canadian waterway. The controversial straight baselines that Canada has drawn around its Arctic archipelago is disputed by both the United States and EU member states with Arctic coasts. They have protested the baselines, arguing that Canada's representation of the baseline is inconsistent with international law.[110] However, other northern countries maintain that the Passage is an international waterway to be used as a commercial trans-Arctic shipping route.[111] If Canada's view on straight baselines is upheld, then the Northwest Passage would lie within Canada's internal waters and they would have full sovereignty over it.[112] Canada may attempt to justify ownership of the claimed internal waters based on historic rights in those waters. However, the decision of the international court in *The Philippines v. China*[113] suggests that line of argument will likely fail .

107 See: Arctic States, 'Declaration on the Establishment of the Arctic Council', Arctic Council, 1996.
108 Article 76 of the United Nations Convention on the Law of the Sea (UNCLOS) 1982.
109 J. Kraska, *Arctic Security in an Age of Climate Change* (Cambridge University Press 2011). The United States is seeking to reach a compromise over the disputed area. Perhaps the resolution of the long territorial dispute between Russia and Norway in the Barents Sea opens the door for more enhanced cooperation between member nations in the maritime Arctic region.
110 With respect to maritime zones in the Arctic, we note that the Treaty of Spitsbergen 1920 recognized Norway's territorial sovereignty over the Spitsbergen (Svalbard) Archipelago subject to the equal rights of fishing and hunting of the other parties, as well as equal liberty of access to waters, fjords and ports. Norway's right to take non-discriminatory conservation measures regarding flora and fauna in its 'territorial waters' was also recognized. Following the entry into force of the LOS Convention, the question arose on whether or not Norway would be entitled to the usual sovereign rights and jurisdiction seaward of the territorial sea and, if so, whether the regime of the Treaty of Spitsbergen would apply. However, Norway is yet to designate an EEZ off Svalbard and also has not otherwise claimed jurisdiction over vessel-source pollution with regard to foreign vessels seaward of Svalbard's territorial sea.
111 For a more general read, see: M. Byers, 'The Northwest Passage Dispute Invites Russian Mischief', *National Post* (Washington, 28 April 2015).
112 The LOS Convention permits archipelagic states to draw straight baselines around their respective island groups, thereby enclosing archipelagic waters. This does not extend to islands situated off a mainland. Therefore, Canada does not qualify as an archipelagic state.
113 [2016] PCA Case No. 2013–19.

Every coastal state has the right to a territorial sea up to a limit of 12 nautical miles from the baseline. However, coastal states have less sovereign control over straits used for international navigation. In the Arctic region, Canada and Russia argue that this principle does not apply to the Northwest Passage and the Northern Sea Route (NSR) respectively because they are used rarely. However, the United States and other countries take the opposite view. If the Canadian and Russian views are upheld, they would in principle be entitled to absolute coastal state authority in their internal waters and territorial seas. This would be in addition to the powers of coastal states enshrined in Article 234 of the Law of the Sea Convention of 1982 with respect to navigation and the prevention, reduction and control of marine pollution from vessels.

The Northern Sea Route (NSR) is classified as a national asset in Russia and legislations has been developed for navigation through its Arctic waters. Thus, strict policies with respect to passage along the NSR are already in operation and there is likely to be further regulation if the legislation on the NSR is adopted. Furthermore, in 2010, Russia and Norway finally signed a treaty that ended 40 years of boundary dispute in the Barents Sea.[114] The agreement divides the disputed area into two equal parts. Crucially, it stipulates that all oil and gas deposits found along its border can only be explored and developed jointly by both nations. The resolution of this complex dispute suggests that perhaps Canada can resolve its own drawn-out territorial disputes with Denmark over the tiny Hans Island and the United States in the Beaufort Sea, respectively.

There have been several important developments in Arctic governance over the years, with a suite of complex international and national legal regimes establishing the standards for engaging in maritime activities in the Arctic region. Nevertheless, gaps remain in the regulatory framework in the areas of eligibility and rules of engagement in Arctic maritime cabotage activities.[115] For instance, the principles of UNCLOS do a reasonable job of serving as the overarching framework for Arctic governance. However, the Convention does not provide for important and contentious issues such as:

a   The delimitation of boundaries between adjacent or opposite Arctic states.
b   The scope and usage of waters classed as high seas within the Arctic region.
c   Regulatory guidelines on the precise criteria for evaluating claims from Arctic coastal states jurisdiction over the continental shelves that are beyond their EEZ limits.[116]

---

114 The Delimitation agreement was signed on 15 September 2010 in Murmansk and the treaty entered into force on 7 July 2011. In Russia, the law was titled Federal Law on Ratification of the Treaty between the Russian Federation and the Kingdom of Norway on Maritime Delimitation and Cooperation in the Barents Sea and the Arctic Ocean.
115 See: M. Humpert, 'The Future of Arctic Shipping: A New Silk Road for China?' (The Arctic Institute, Center for Circumpolar Security Studies, 2013).
116 For a broader read on these issues, see: M. Byers, *International Law and the Arctic* (Cambridge University Press 2013).

Furthermore, Article 234 of UNCLOS gives coastal states the right to enforce non-discriminatory laws to prevent, reduce and control of marine pollution from vessels in ice-covered areas within the limits of the EEZ. This provision is referred to often inaccurately as sovereign authority for a coastal state to establish a maritime cabotage regime in the Arctic region. However, Article 234 is silent on the rights of coastal states on such sovereign authority. More accurately, Article 234 seeks to regulate and prevent oil pollution in the Arctic region.[117] Commercial ship traffic in the Arctic falls into four categories. These are: destinational transport, intra-arctic transport, trans-arctic transport and maritime cabotage.[118] There are suggestions for a fifth group, the cross-arctic transport category.[119]

We shall focus on maritime cabotage activities that include the transport of cargo or persons and other maritime activities between two points within the same geographical entity. These fall into the intra-arctic transport and the arctic maritime cabotage categories. Intra-Arctic transport involves shipping activities between two or more Arctic states within the Arctic region. On the other hand, Arctic maritime cabotage is the transport of cargo in coastal waters between ports within an Arctic state or group of states within the Arctic region.[120] There has been a significant increase in maritime activities along the Northern Sea Route (NSR), which flows a considerable distance along the northern coast of Russia through the Kara, Laptev, east Siberian and Chukchi seas.[121] The bulk of maritime activities in this part of the Arctic falls within maritime cabotage and is carried out in support of the Norilsk Nickel mining operations on the Taimyr Peninsula near the Kara Sea. As most of the natural resources in the Arctic region are located offshore, it is intrinsic that exploration, production and shipping of the products to world markets would be required.[122] Maritime activities such as exploration, drilling

---

117 Section 8 – Article 234 of the United Nations Convention on the Law of the Sea, 1982.

118 Arctic Council, Arctic Marine Shipping Assessment 2009 Report, p. 12. Destinational transport refers to shipping into or out of the Arctic in support of commercial activities like carriage of Arctic hydrocarbons to world markets. Intra-Arctic transport involves shipping activities between two or more Arctic states within the Arctic region. Trans-Arctic transport refers to using the Arctic as a route between two destinations outside of the Arctic. The two trans-Arctic routes connecting Europe and Eastern Asia are the Northwest Passage (NWP) over the North American continent and the Northern Sea Route (NSR) over Eurasia. Cross-Arctic transport would refer to maritime activities between the Bering Strait and Northern Europe and would lead to increased maritime activity in the Arctic region.

119 For more on this, see: A. Raspotnik and B. Rudloff, 'The EU as a Shipping Actor in the Arctic: Characteristics, Interests and Perspectives', Working Paper FG 2, 2012/ Nr. 04 (Stiftung Wissenschaft und Politik, 2012).

120 This is like the EU maritime cabotage framework. For a broader discussion, see: P. Soles and C. Wilson, 'The Changing Arctic: Increasing Marine Risk and Evolving Governance' (PIANC World Congress, 2014).

121 American Bureau of Shipping, 'Navigating the Northern Sea Route: Status and Guidance' (ABS, 2013).

122 See: O. Young, 'Arctic Governance: Pathways to the Future' [2010], *Arctic Review on Law and Politics*, 1(2), 164–185.

and the development of natural resources in the Arctic have increasingly become an attractive venture to international oil companies. However, this supposedly newfound opportunity also presents a tremendous problem because any incident such as an oil spill, in either the exploration or transportation process, would be disastrous for the Arctic ecosystem.[123] Furthermore, such an incident could stall the continuous commercial development of the Arctic region. This would be particularly difficult if an incident were to occur in the Arctic region in winter, when the Arctic Ocean is frozen with ice. Hence, there must be a robust contingency plan to deal effectively with the possibility of oil spills and related incidents. All indications are that it would be more difficult to contend with an oil spill in the Arctic than in the Gulf of Mexico. For instance, it would be difficult if not impossible at present to move equipment there to build a relief drill, as was the case in the Deep-water Horizon spill in 2010. The direct effect of the Gulf of Mexico disaster was, like many others, minimized because help was readily available and access to the spill site was relatively easy. The challenges with accessing this region was evident in 2013 with the predicament encountered by rescuers who tried to rescue 52 researchers who were stranded in Antarctica. In 2012, the dangers of traversing the Arctic seas were accentuated when a drilling rig with a crew of 67 capsized and sank off Russia's far eastern island of Sakhalin in a storm. This resulted in 53 members of crew losing their lives.[124] It is suggested that even an oil spill of less magnitude than the Gulf of Mexico disaster could be devastating in the frozen seas of the Arctic region. This would effectively halt any plans of Arctic transformation in their tracks. Hence, coastal states in the Arctic region must take precautionary measures under international law to avoid such disaster pursuant to Article 234 of UNCLOS 1982.

As a communal region among its eight member nations, the concept of a maritime cabotage regulatory framework in the Arctic region presents new and difficult challenges to the Arctic Council. Some of the challenges are: who can engage in maritime cabotage activities in the Arctic region? Who would be responsible, and to what degree, if a maritime incident occurs? Would the normal international rules on flag states and coastal states continue to apply? If they did, would those rules be effective in addressing the unique characteristics of the Arctic region?

As the Arctic region is an area with vital strategic and political significance, there is a wide range of factors that must be considered when establishing a regulatory mechanism. One such factor is the degree of liaison between the Arctic Council and other stakeholders such as shipowners, flag states, insurers and port authorities. Furthermore, there is the continued controversy surrounding the jurisdictional status of 'internal water' within the Arctic Ocean.[125] It is suggested that

123 For more on this, see: European Commission, 'Legal Aspects of Arctic Shipping: Summary Report' (European Commission, 2010).
124 See: D. Toomey, 'Global Scarcity: Scramble for Dwindling Natural Resources', *Yale Environment 360* (California, 23 May 2012).
125 See: International Chambers of Shipping, 'Arctic Shipping: Positional Paper' (ICS, 2014).

such uncertainty could result in future disputes over who has national jurisdiction to regulate navigation matters in those waters. This could frustrate efforts aimed at developing the resources in the Arctic region in a manner that recognizes the need for both environmental and economic sustainability.[126]

To manage the present and future conflicts in the Arctic region, the International Chambers of Shipping (ICS) has advocated for a mandatory uniform regulatory framework on Arctic shipping.[127] Achieving this will require harmonizing all national maritime regulations that apply within the 200-nautical mile EEZ of the Arctic waters. This should occur without discriminating against foreign flag vessels by imposing specific build, crew, ownership and flag requirements.[128] Furthermore, the Arctic Council and all concerned stakeholders should refrain from developing alternative legal instruments that may conflict with an agreed harmonized regulatory regime.[129] Also, clear answers should be provided to political questions regarding the extent of the continental shelf of Arctic nations because this has a direct impact on maritime cabotage activities. The longer these legal uncertainties remain, the more difficult it is to get a harmonised framework that regulates and monitors maritime cabotage activities in the Arctic region.[130] The sovereign rights of the Arctic coastal nations should not be used as a bargaining tool in disputes about the right to exploit natural resources or the right to participate in the maritime activities in the Arctic region. The Arctic sea routes are expected to provide a commercially viable alternative to the Suez Canal or the trans-Pacific sea routes. This should facilitate the provision of reliable international maritime services between ports in member states of the Arctic region. However, this will require providing maritime services that are competitive and cost efficient.

Maritime cabotage in the Arctic region can be said to occur particularly along the Alaskan and Greenlandic coasts, in the Canadian Arctic and along the Russian Arctic coast. Therefore, to maximize the economic potential of the Arctic region, it is imperative that the region does not become an area of conflict and political strife. Hence, it is important to set up an independent efficient mechanism to monitor the maritime cabotage regulations of current

---

126 See: Arctic Council, 'Arctic Marine Shipping: Assessment 2009 Report' (Arctic Council, 2009).

127 The idea is to host this under the auspices of the International Maritime Organization (IMO) as the body possesses the necessary legal and technical expertise to facilitate maritime activities in the Arctic region between flag states and coastal states in accordance with the Common Principles of Shipping Policy (CPSP) adopted in 2000 by the Organization for Economic Co-operation and Development (OECD).

128 For more general discussion on this, see: OECD, 'Recommendation of the Council: Concerning Common Principles of Shipping Policy for Member Countries', C(2000) 124/Final (OECD, 2000). The Principle was originally agreed in 1987 and updated in 2000.

129 See: B. Marten, *Port State Jurisdiction and the Regulation of International Merchant Shipping* (Springer 2014).

130 See: International Chambers of Shipping, 'Arctic Shipping: Positional Paper' (ICS, 2014).

and future Arctic coastal states.[131] This is in addition to having a periodic assessment of regulations aimed at preventing or minimizing possible maritime disasters in the Arctic region.[132]

131 See: E. Molenaar, 'Options for Regional Regulation of Merchant Shipping Outside IMO, with Particular Reference to the Arctic Region' [2014], *Ocean Development and International Law*, 45(3), 272–298.
132 See: Arctic Council, 'Arctic Marine Shipping Assessment: 2009 Report', Arctic Council.

# 12 The features of maritime cabotage law

This chapter will assess the features of maritime cabotage law as seen in the regulatory framework of countries with a maritime cabotage regime. The objective is to demonstrate how the law informs the Understanding of a cabotage-controlled concept in the national and regional domains. We will look at how the various features of maritime cabotage law affect the commercial behaviour of shipowners and how the application of the law impacts on the economic development of a country. The principal features of maritime cabotage are that the ship: must be built in the cabotage country; it must be owned by a national of the cabotage country; it must employ only or mainly indigenous crew; and it must be registered and documented in the cabotage country. Some commentators refer to the above features as pillars of maritime cabotage.[1] However, this may be considered a fundamental misconception because the above characteristics cannot be the basis for any country to enact a maritime cabotage law. It is suggested instead that the pillars upon which the maritime cabotage law of a country is premised are sovereignty, economic development and national security. These are the reasons why countries enact maritime cabotage laws. As we have given sufficient coverage to these pillars throughout this book, we will now focus on the features of maritime cabotage law.

Each cabotage country attaches its own priorities to the different features of maritime cabotage law. Many factors can be involved in this but in general it is based on the purpose for which the law is established and the circumstances of the cabotage country. The sovereign right of a country to determine what features to incorporate into its maritime cabotage legislation and how much importance is attached to those features contributes to the lack of a common understanding of the concept of maritime cabotage. Hence, under a regional maritime cabotage regime where a group of countries agree to a single regulatory framework, the concept of maritime cabotage is better understood. It is the degree of importance

---

1 See: M. Igbokwe, 'Advocacy Paper for the Promulgation of a Nigerian Maritime Cabotage Law: Draft Modalities for Implementation of Coastal and Inland Shipping (cabotage) Act' (Nigerian Maritime Authority, 2001); V. Okeke and E. Aniche, 'An Evaluation of the Effectiveness of the Cabotage Act 2003 on Nigerian Maritime Administration' [2012], *Sacha Journal of Policy and Strategic Studies*, 2(1), 12–28.

attached to the different features of maritime cabotage law that determines whether a cabotage country is classified as adopting a protectionist, liberal or flexible maritime cabotage regime. Generally, the concept of maritime cabotage law is held up by four primary requirements that should be satisfied by those who wish to engage in the maritime cabotage trade and services of a country. These requirements are:

a   Vessels must be built and all substantial repair work must be done in the cabotage country.
b   Vessels must be registered in and documented by and fly the flag of the cabotage country.
c   Vessels must be wholly or substantially owned by nationals of the cabotage country.
d   Vessels must employ a crew that is wholly or mainly nationals of the cabotage country.

However, we will consider other features not normally stipulated in the various national maritime cabotage legislations but that satisfy the same objectives as the four features above. These new features are:

• cabotage vessels should be classed by a domestic ship classification society; and
• cabotage vessels should be recycled in a domestic ship recycling facility.

We will refer to these as 'the future features' of maritime cabotage law. Each of these features will be assessed to show how the influence a protectionist or liberal maritime cabotage regime. A snapshot of all the features of maritime cabotage law and its requirements is illustrated below.

## The building and repairing of vessels requirement

The capacity to construct and repair vessels usually indicates that a country has a vibrant domestic and seagoing fleet.[2] Shipbuilding and repair in domestic shipyards is a prominent requirement in many protectionist maritime cabotage regimes. This means that all vessels that provide maritime services in the territorial waters of that country must be built in a shipyard in that country. Furthermore, any substantial repair, conversion or alteration work on such vessels must also be carried out in a shipyard in that country.[3] The United States and Nigeria are

2   See: J. Gabriel, 'Revitalisation of the Shipbuilding Industry' [2009], *Petrobas Magazine*, 58(1), 5–10. See also: T. Rhodes and G. McDonald, 'Brazilian Shipyards: Industry in Crisis or Growing Pains?' (CMS Cameron McKenna, 2014). See also: J. Leahy and S. Pearson, 'Rousseff's Dream of Brazilian Shipbuilding Titan in Deep Water', *Financial Times* (Rio de Janeiro, 25 January 2015).
3   See for instance, the maritime cabotage legislations in the United States and the Federal Republic of Nigeria respectively.

*Table 12.1* Features of maritime law and requirements

| Current features of maritime cabotage law | Requirements |
|---|---|
| Shipbuilding and ship repair | All vessels engaged in maritime cabotage must be built or repaired in a domestic shipyard in the cabotage country. |
| Ship registration and documentation | All vessels engaged in maritime cabotage must be registered in and fly the flag of the maritime cabotage country or that of a member state (where applicable). |
| Ship ownership | All vessels engaged in maritime cabotage must be owned wholly or substantially by nationals of the cabotage country. |
| Crewing | All vessels engaged in maritime cabotage must employ a crew that is wholly or mainly nationals of the cabotage country. |
| Future features of maritime cabotage law | Requirements |
| Ship classification society | All vessels engaged in maritime cabotage should be classified by a domestic ship classification society in the cabotage country. |
| Ship recycling | All vessels engaged in maritime cabotage, should be recycled in a domestic ship recycling yard in the cabotage country when they have reached the end of their economic life. |

examples of countries that apply this stringent feature to their maritime cabotage law[4] – although in the case of Nigeria, because of the lax regulatory framework, this requirement is an exercise in theory. Where the shipbuilding requirement is applied in its most stringent form, it is suggested that the term 'domestic' could cause some confusion. This is because it may be argued that a vessel built or repaired in a domestic shipyard may not necessarily satisfy that requirement if that shipyard is wholly or substantially owned by a foreign entity. Stipulating for ships to be built and repaired in the national maritime cabotage legislation is credited with creating domestic employment opportunities and contributing significantly to the economic development of a country.[5] This can be seen in countries where ship construction and repair form part of their manufacturing sector. Hence, domestic shipbuilding ensures that the domestic shipyards can continue to generate business and contribute to economic development. According to a study by the United

---

4 See: 46 U.S.C. App. § 833, 46 U.S.C. 50101 and 46 U.S.C. 55102; and section 3 of the Coastal and Inland Shipping (Cabotage) Act No. 5 of 2003 of the Laws of the Federation of Nigeria, respectively.
5 See: National Shipbuilding and Procurement Strategy, 'Results of the National Shipbuilding and Procurement Strategy' (Government of Canada, 2011).

States Department of Commerce, the shipbuilding industry in the United States is a strategic asset.[6] Therefore, the United States Merchant Marine Act of 1920 is vital for the survival of their domestic shipbuilding sector.[7] The shipbuilding industry also has a huge economic impact in South Korea, Japan and China.[8] It contributes to their respective national economies on the back of building and repairing ships for use by foreign nations or for use in their ocean-going and domestic maritime trade and services. It is remarkable that none of these three countries have specifically incorporated the shipbuilding and ship repair requirement into their respective maritime cabotage legislation. The effectiveness of the ship building and repair feature depends on whether the cabotage country possesses the fundamental prerequisites. These include functional structural infrastructures like shipyards and dry-docks and competent technical expertise like naval architects and structural engineers. This is where Nigeria, with the shipbuilding and repair requirement in its maritime cabotage law, struggles. On the other hand, China is thriving as a result of its shipbuilding and repair development programme because it possess the above prerequisites.

As of 2014, Chinese shipyards were looking to take about $10 billion in orders for new liquefied natural gas tankers in the next decade.[9] The objective was to restructure and safeguard China's shipbuilding sector by enabling domestic shipyards to secure a quarter of the global market for high-tech ships, thereby increasing its capability in high-tech shipbuilding. More than 20 per cent of liquefied natural gas (LNG) vessels projected to be added worldwide in the future are expected to be built in China to deliver gas to its ports. This would allow China to challenge South Korean and Japanese shipyards, traditionally the main suppliers of large gas tankers. Currently, more than 70 per cent of LNG carriers and storage vessels on order go to South Korean shipyards. China hopes that its own output on these highly sophisticated vessels will soon outstrip that of Korea and Japan. However, there is the general perception that Chinese shipyards may continue to struggle to win orders for sophisticated ship projects from international buyers, regardless of their commitment to investing in the sector.[10] It is not clear what the basis for this perception is. Nevertheless, judging by China's strategic development programme, it is likely to cement its position as a major player in the international shipbuilding sector sooner rather than later.

6 See: BXA, 'U.S. Shipbuilding and Repair: National Security Assessment of the U.S. Shipbuilding and Repair Industry' (BXA, 2001).
7 For a general discussion on this, see: C. Papavizas and B. Gardner, 'Coast Guard Rejects Industry Petition to Change Jones Act Vessel Rebuilding Regulations' (Winston & Strawn LLP, 2012).
8 For a broader read, see: M. Brooks, 'Maritime Cabotage: International Market Issues in the Liberalisation of Domestic Shipping', in A. Chircop et al. (eds), *The Regulation of International Shipping: International and Comparative Perspectives* (Martinus Nijhoff, 2012), pp. 293–324.
9 World Maritime News, 'Chinese Shipyards Vying to Enter LNG Market', *World Maritime News* (Shanghai, 5 August 2014).
10 For a general read on this, see: 'China Pushes to Build its Own Ships to Deliver Gas', *New York Times* (New York, 5 August 2014).

However, in incorporating the shipbuilding and ship repair 'feature' into the maritime cabotage law of a country, consideration should be given to whether ships can be built and repaired in the cabotage country at a cost-effective price even when the country possesses technical expertise and the other prerequisites. For instance, it cost approximately $209 million to build a 3,600 TEU vessel in the United States in 2013. In contrast, a comparably sized vessel was built for less than a fifth of that price in Asia.[11] On the other hand, where a country lacks the prerequisites to enforce compliance with the shipbuilding and repair requirement, the only viable option is to resort to the use of waivers, as in the case of Nigeria. This results in the abuse of the waiver provision in particular and circumventing the maritime cabotage law in general. This is because operators both foreign and domestic can expect to get an automatic waiver on the shipbuilding requirement. Therefore, the waiver provision where applicable is used as a first option rather than on the basis of exception for which it is designed.

The difficulties that the shipbuilding requirement presents mean many maritime cabotage countries have opted to exclude this complex requirement from their maritime cabotage law.[12] There are growing demands in both Nigeria and the United States for a reconsideration of the shipbuilding requirement in their respective maritime cabotage legislations.[13] It is observed that in aviation and land cabotage, there are no requirements for the transport vehicle to be built or repaired in the cabotage country. Developing a national shipbuilding and repair capacity is clearly important. However, it may be suggested that this is an onerous and perhaps detrimental requirement to impose through a country's maritime cabotage legislation. This is because only a few countries can implement it in such a way that it is cost effective and beneficial to the domestic economy of the country.

## The ship registration 'feature' in the country

Ship registration is a long-standing tradition that began as a means of controlling ships entitled to carry cargoes within the seaborne empires of Europe. The

---

11 See: Drewry Maritime Research, 'US Cabotage Protection gets more Expensive', *Drew Maritime Research* (London, 17 November 2013).

12 Canada, Japan, China, Brazil, Indonesia and the Philippines are some of the other maritime nations that have adopted a protectionist maritime cabotage policy but do not specifically stipulate for compulsory in-country shipbuilding and ship repair requirement in their maritime cabotage law.

13 For an in-depth examination of the issue, see: C. Papavizas and B. Gardner, 'Coast Guard Rejects Industry Petition to Change Jones Act Vessel Rebuilding Regulations' (Winston & Strawn LLP, 2012); W. Gray, 'Performance of Major US Shipyards in 20th/21st Century' [2008], *Journal of Ship Production*, 24(4), 202–213; W. Yost, 'Jonesing For a Taste of Competition: Why an Antiquated Maritime Law Needs Reform' [2013], *Roger Williams University Law Review*, 18(1), 52–77. See also: V. Okeke and E. Aniche, 'An Evaluation of the Effectiveness of the Cabotage Act 2003 on Nigerian Maritime Administration' [2012], *Sacha Journal of Policy and Strategic Studies*, 2(1), 12–28; S. Ajiye, 'Nigerian Cabotage: Its Policy, Prospects and Challenges' [2013], *Journal of Economics and Sustainable Development*, 4(14), 11–1.

granting of nationality to vessels was originally conceived to help with identifying vessels that traversed the often lawless seas of the eighteen and nineteenth centuries. In particular, it offered protection to the owners of those vessels and her crew.[14] Assigning nationality to a vessel became mandatory under the 1958 Geneva Convention on the High Seas.[15] From then on, every newly built or newly purchased vessel was required to be documented and granted the nationality of a country.[16] However, ship registration has become a convenient means of establishing title to the property in a vessel. With respect to all relevant legal, administrative and social matters, registration confers nationality on a ship and brings it within the jurisdiction of the law of its country of registration.[17] This includes all responsibilities and liabilities such as safety of the ship, ship mortgages and the health and welfare of the crew.

For many centuries there was a simple and straightforward process for registering a vessel for both domestic and international purposes. The shipowner was required to register his vessel in his country of residence, which was invariably his country of nationality. The vessel consequently acquired the owner's nationality.[18] This is no longer the case as shipowners are increasing inclined to register their vessels in ship registries stipulating the bare minimum of legal requirements. In these registries the 'concept of the genuine link' remains just that – a concept, which is circumvented at ease.[19] Although there is no express definition of 'the genuine link' concept, its meaning and the scope of its application can be accurately enough deduced from the 1958 Convention of the High Seas.[20] A combination of low taxes and poorly enforced safety, labour and environmental

14  See: K. Li and J. Wonham, 'New Developments in Ship Registration' [1999], *International Journal of Marine and Coastal Law*, 14(1), 137–146.
15  See: Article 5(1) of The Convention on the High Seas, 1958. However, there are reports that ship registration may date back to the early 1800s where the idea of ships as legal residents first appeared in some bilateral treaties between countries that agreed to recognize the nationality of each other's vessels.
16  For a broader read, see: R. Coles and E. Watt, *Ship Registration: Law and Practice* (2nd edn, Taylor & Francis 2013).
17  Article 94 (1), (2), (3) of United Nations Convention on the Law of the Sea (UNCLOS 1982).
18  For a broader discussion on the issue, see: B. Baker, 'Flags of Convenience and the Gulf Oil Spill: Problems and Proposed Solutions' [2012], *Houston Journal of International Law*, 34(3), 697–715.
19  One of the treaties that allude to the 'Genuine Link' Concept is the United Nations Convention on the Law of the Sea. See: Article 91(1) of UNCLOS 1982.
20  Article 5(1) of The Convention on the High Seas 1958: Each state shall fix the conditions for the grant of its nationality to ships, for the registration of ships in its territory, and for the right to fly its flag. Ships have the nationality of the state whose flag they are entitled to fly. A genuine link between the state and the ship must exist; in particular, the state must effectively exercise its jurisdiction and control in administrative, technical and social matters over ships flying its flag. One argues that the words 'in particular' set up a threshold for the relationship between the flag state and the ship. It is suggested that anything below that threshold will be a derogation of the standard every flag state should be held to. See also: Article 91(1) of UNCLOS 1982.

regulatory standards lures shipowners to overseas ship registries where they can benefit from a competitive advantage through lower operating costs.[21]

This second 'feature' of maritime cabotage law stipulates that all vessels seeking to engage in the maritime cabotage activities of a country must be registered in the appropriate ship registry of that country and fly its flag making that country what is commonly termed the 'flag state'.[22] Therefore, a cabotage country can set the threshold of requirements that a ship operator in the cabotage trade should satisfy for registration without fear of breaching international law. This would remain the case even if such domestic threshold of requirement falls below international standards.

There are four categories of registries open to shipowners to register their ships. They are: traditional (home) registries, open registries, offshore registries and international registries. However, only the traditional registry would satisfy this second feature of maritime cabotage law. This is because a traditional registry would normally only accept vessels that are owned by persons who are citizens and residents of that country.[23] Furthermore, such vessels would normally be required to employ crew who are nationals of the country of registration. This establishes the 'genuine link' between the vessel and the country of registration.[24] Also, although international (second) registries provide the shipowner with some of the benefits of the traditional register, there remain some limitations. Hence, vessels registered in offshore and some international registries may not necessarily be eligible to provide maritime cabotage services in some jurisdiction. This is demonstrated under the EU maritime cabotage law framework where such registered vessels cannot provide maritime cabotage services pursuant to Article 1 of the EU Regulation 3577/92.

Ship registration undertaken to satisfy international legislations would not necessarily qualify such vessels to participate in a country's maritime cabotage activities. In Nigeria for instance, vessels seeking to participate in maritime cabotage activities must register in a 'special register' in addition to fulfilling all the other prerequisites.[25] In Brazil, foreign vessels that have suspended their original flag to fly the Brazilian flag because the vessel was built in Brazil must register in the Special Brazilian Registry (REB) for maritime cabotage purposes.[26] Even in the European Union, where a liberal maritime cabotage policy exists among

---

21 For more on this, see: J. Mansell, *Flag State Responsibility: Historical Development and Contemporary Issues* (Springer 2009).

22 See: S. Sucharitkul, 'Liability and Responsibility of the State of Registration or the Flag State in Respect of Sea-Going Vessels, Aircraft and Spacecraft Registered by National Registration Authorities' [2006], *American Journal of Comparative Law*, vol. 54, American Law in the 21st Century: U.S. National Reports to the XVII International Congress of Comparative Law (Fall), 409–442.

23 Traditional registries include Japan, Germany, France, United Kingdom and the USA.

24 For a related discussion, see: J. Perkins, 'Ship Registers: An International Update' [1997], *Tulane Maritime Law Journal*, 22(1), 197–199.

25 Article 22(1) and Article 29(1) of the Coastal and Inland Shipping (Cabotage) Act 2003 of Nigeria.

26 Decree No. 2256/97 in pursuant of Article 10(III) of Law No. 9432/97.

member states, freedom to engage in maritime cabotage activities requires community shipowners to have their ships registered in, and flying the flag of, a member state.[27] Moreover, offshore registers as well as some second registers of member states are prohibited from engaging in maritime cabotage activities within the European Union under Council Regulation 3577/92.[28] This is where open registries differ from those registries set up for maritime cabotage purposes. International and offshore registries generally relax crewing requirements, whereas countries that set up a special register for maritime cabotage purposes are more stringent in this area. These registries generally stipulate that shipowners should satisfy the indigenous crew requirement as an integral and important condition.

Generally, vessels registered in traditional registries must have a 'genuine link'. The United Nations Conference on Trade and Development (UNCTAD) shows the connection between registration under maritime cabotage law, and the 'genuine link' concept. It states that to satisfy the 'genuine link' condition:

a   a vessel must contribute to the national economy and be reflected in national accounting;
b   indigenous crew must be employed on board the vessel;
c   the ownership of the vessel must be beneficial to the country of registration.[29]

This point is central to the principles of modern maritime cabotage law, which aims to promote the economic development of the cabotage country. It achieves this by ensuring that there is a genuine link between where the vessel is built, the shipowner, where the vessel is registered and the nationality of the crew on the one hand and the maritime cabotage country on the other hand.[30] Shipowners would generally seek to register their vessels where there are incentives and multiple benefits such as low taxes, cheap labour and a favourable regulatory environment. However, these benefits are not necessarily available when registering a vessel for maritime cabotage purposes. Indeed, registering a vessel in a maritime cabotage register can be more expensive for the shipowner.[31] This has become a highly vexed issue in Australia Where the revised maritime cabotage regulation has

---

27   Article 1 of European Union Regulation 3577/92.
28   The European Union have in the past considered plans of setting up a European Union-wide international ship registry. See: S. Moloney, 'Euros flag drive stepped up: EU presidency will draw up legislation with commission', *Lloyd's List* (London, 3 February 1994).
29   UNCTAD, 'Economic Consequences of the Existence of Lack of a Genuine Link between Vessel and Flag of Registry', TD/B/c.4/168 (UNCTAD Trade and Development Board, 1997), pp. 20–21.
30   For similar argument on the issue, see: J. Zheng, Q. Meng and Z. Sun, 'Impact Analysis of Maritime Cabotage Legislations on Liner Hub-and-Spoke Shipping Network Design' [2014], *European Journal of Operational Research*, 234(3), 874–884.
31   Shipowners who register their vessels in the United States to comply with the Merchant Shipping Act of 1920 accrue higher costs from building vessels, repairing vessels and crew wages.

established the Australian International Shipping Register (AISR) as a second national register to revive Australia's maritime cabotage services.[32]

## The ownership requirement

The word shipowner comes with a lot of confusion and there have been difficulties in ascertaining who a shipowner really is. The coming into force of the Maritime Labour Convention of 2006 has further exacerbated the confusion.[33] The convention's definition of a shipowner is expansive and includes: ship managers (who indeed may only be service providers), agents and charterers. This definition contrasts with the traditional definition of a shipowner.[34] Guidance from the International Association of Classification Societies (IACS) suggests that the MLC shipowner should be the entity that holds the International Safety Management Document (ISMD) of Compliance.[35] This can cause legal uncertainty, with an 'owner' and a 'shipowner' considered as two distinct entities, i.e. the 'ship operator' and the 'cash buyer' respectively.

The ownership 'feature' requirement demands that maritime cabotage vessels must be wholly or substantially under the beneficial ownership of nationals of that country.[36] Where a company owns the vessel, there is usually the requirement that citizens of that country must hold all or most of the shares in the vessel free from any encumbrance to any foreigner.[37] What makes matters doubly difficult is that in many countries the ownership requirement is often accompanied by another onerous requirement demanding that any such persons or company engaged in maritime cabotage must establish and have their principal place of business in that country.[38] Where there is a waiver of the comprehensive ownership structure by the citizens of a country, there is usually a less friendly substitute requiring

---

32  For a deeper analysis of the legal and economic implications of the new reforms in Australia's coastal shipping and the new AISR, see: J. Porter, 'Australian Coastal Shipping: Navigating Regulatory Reform' [2015], *Australian and New Zealand Maritime Law Journal*, 29(1), 8–17.

33  The Maritime Labour Convention of 2006 came into force internationally on 20 August 2013 for the 30 countries with registered ratifications on 20 August 2012. For all other countries that have ratified, it will enter in force 12 months after their ratifications were registered. The Convention came into force on 7 August 2014 in the United Kingdom.

34  See Article II(j) of Maritime Labour Convention, 2006.

35  For a general read, see: L. McMahon, 'MLC 2006: Who is the Shipowner and Why Does It Matter?', *Lloyds List* (London, 22 August 2013).

36  See the maritime cabotage legislations of the United States, Nigeria, India, Indonesia, Japan and Indonesia.

37  See the maritime cabotage legislations of the Philippines and China. See also; M. Brooks, 'Maritime Cabotage: International Market Issues in the Liberalisation of Domestic Shipping', in A. Chircop et al. (eds), *The Regulation of International Shipping: International and Comparative Perspectives* (Martinus Nijhoff 2012), pp. 293–324.

38  See the maritime cabotage legislations of Chile, Brazil, Nigeria, and Japan. See also; C. Liu, *Maritime Transport Services in the Law of the Sea and the World Trade Organization* (Peter Lang 2009).

anything between 40 per cent and 75 per cent beneficial ownership in favour of nationals of that country.[39]

In the United States, the stringent Merchant Marine Act of 1920 requires that all merchandise transported between points in the United States by water shall be carried only on vessels owned by American citizens.[40]

The legislative text of the Nigerian Cabotage Act of 2003 stipulates for a vessel that is owned wholly and beneficially by Nigerian citizens or a Nigerian company. In addition, all the shares in the vessel must be held by Nigerian citizens free from encumbrance to any foreigner.[41] Other maritime countries that stipulate indigenous vessel ownership requirements in their maritime cabotage regulations include Indonesia.[42] In China, wholly foreign capital enterprises and Sino-foreign joint ventures are excluded from the operation and management of maritime transport in Chinese waters without the permission of the competent authority.[43] In the Philippines, vessels engaged in the coastal trade must have at least 75 per cent of their capital stock vested in citizens of the Philippines. In the case of corporations engaged in maritime cabotage trade, the president or managing directors shall be citizens of the Philippines.[44] Vessels engaged in the Japanese coastal trade must satisfy even more onerous ownership requirements. Such vessels must be owned by a state organ, a Japanese national, a company established under Japanese law if its representatives and more than two-thirds of its officers are Japanese, or a foreign company if its representatives are Japanese nationals.[45] Despite the acclaimed liberal approach, the EU Regulation on maritime cabotage restricts ownership eligibility to:

a    Nationals of a member state or a maritime company established in a member state in accordance with the legislation of that member state and pursuing shipping activities.
b    Shipping companies established in accordance with the legislation of a member state, and whose principal place of business is situated, and effective control exercised, in a member state.
c    Nationals of a member state or shipping companies established outside the Community and controlled by nationals of a member state, if their ships are registered in and fly the flag of a member state in accordance with its legislation.[46]

39  See the chapters on protectionist, liberal and flexible maritime cabotage approaches. See the sections on; Nigeria, China, Brazil and Indonesia.
40  See: 46 U.S.C. App. § 833, 46 U.S.C. 50101 and 46 U.S.C. 55102.
41  Section 3 of the Coastal and Inland Shipping (Cabotage) Act No. 5 of 2003 of the Laws of the Federation of Nigeria.
42  See: Article 158 of Law 17 of 2008. It stipulates that vessels used for maritime cabotage must be owned by Indonesian citizens or business entity domiciled in Indonesia
43  Article 7 of The 1987 Regulation on Waterway Transport Administration of the People's Republic of China.
44  Section 806 of the Tariff and Custom Code of the Philippines (RA 1937) of 1957.
45  Article 1 of the 1899 Ship Law of Japan.
46  Article 2(2) of Council Regulation (EEC) No. 3577/92.

The second and third categories of shipowner, as stipulated in Articles 2(2b) and 2(2c) of Council Regulation 3577/92 respectively, raise serious questions as to where the 'effective control' of the vessel lies in the event of an emergency, pursuant to the EU law on maritime cabotage.[47] A maritime cabotage regime that stipulates indigenous ownership of vessels may empower and build indigenous capacity. However, it is not uncommon for such provision to empower only a very small percentage of indigenous persons. Hence, a stipulation of indigenous ship ownership 'feature' may turn out to hamper growth, economic development and investment.[48]

### The shipowner in the context of maritime cabotage law

The section above on the ship ownership requirement began by examining two separate but identical issues. It queried the definition of a shipowner and identified the conflicts between the various conceptions surrounding the definition of shipowner. This was followed by a discussion on the various dimensions in which the ownership feature has been enacted and implemented in the maritime cabotage law of several countries. However, it is useful to revisit the identity of the shipowner in the context of maritime cabotage law. This is important because shipowners are increasingly wary of exposing their identity and are generally keen to benefit from a 'one-ship company' structure.[49] In the United Kingdom, they are able to take advantage of the legal protection under the corporate veil principle, first espoused in the landmark case of *Salomon v. A. Salomon & Co. Ltd.* [50] Therefore, the short answer to the question of who the shipowner is in the context of maritime cabotage law is that it could be any one of the following:

a   the financial purchaser of the vessel in the capacity of a beneficial owner (who bears the risks, enjoys the profits and suffers the loss);
b   an agent (acting either for the shipowner or charterer);
c   the ship management company;
d   the charterer;
e   the financial lender (such as a bank);
f   the entity that holds the International Safety Management Document (ISMD) of Compliance (MLC 2016);
g   a lien holder; or
h   a combination of any two or more of these persons.

---

47   For a more detailed reading, see: the Commission Consolidated Jurisdictional Notice under Council Regulation (EC) No. 139/2004 on the control of concentrations between undertakings (2008/C 95/01), OJ C 95, 16 April 2008, p. 1.
48   See, for instance, the impact that such requirement has had in the Nigerian maritime sector, and to a large extent, its impact on the coastal trade of the United States.
49   *Adams v. Cape Industries* [1991] 1 All ER 929.
50   [1897] AC 22 (HL).

Therefore, to answer the question it is important to understand the rationale behind the ship ownership requirement in various maritime cabotage legislations. Let us assume that the aim of a maritime cabotage law is to stimulate the economic development of a country via its maritime sector. It is suggested that the rationale behind the ship ownership requirement is based on the economic argument espoused to justify a protectionist maritime cabotage approach. It could be argued that a vibrant domestic fleet can be pivotal in attracting further investment into the domestic maritime sector. This would include opening up opportunities to the related areas of ship finance, ship classification and ship broking. On this basis it is suggested that the most appropriate definition of a shipowner for the purposes of maritime cabotage law should be 'a person or group of persons that truly own and control the equity in both the vessel and the ship-owning company. This would be the beneficial owner and not necessarily the registered or legal owner'.[51] This definition of the shipowner is the most consistent with the ideology behind the law of maritime cabotage. It is argued that to find otherwise would require a total disregard for the principles and objectives of the law of maritime cabotage, which have been captured in this book under the theory of developmental sovereignty.

## The crew 'feature' requirement

The crew requirement is a contentious issue that goes well beyond the scope of maritime cabotage. This requirement attracts international attention from both the domestic and international domains.[52] For the purposes of maritime cabotage, the crewing requirement generally demands that vessels should have a crew that wholly or substantially satisfies the citizenship requirement of the cabotage country. In countries where waivers are granted on the wholly indigenous crew prerequisite, the alternative is usually not exactly simple. The waiver often requires the shipowner to ensure that the crew consist of a minimum of 75 per cent citizens of the cabotage country. For instance, a key objective for the Brazilian maritime cabotage law is the creation of employment within the domestic maritime sector. Therefore, foreign crew on board ships engaged in Brazilian maritime cabotage are permitted to work for 30 days only.[53] The crew of a foreign vessel operating for longer than 90 days continuously in Brazil's coastal waters must comprise at least one-fifth Brazilian employees aboard the vessel on a permanent basis. For vessels in maritime cabotage operations lasting more than 180 days,

---

51  See: the Obiters of Lords Neuberger (Paras 75–80) and Sumption (Para 27) in *Petrodel Resources Ltd v. Prest* [2013] UKSC 34. It should be noted that in this case the veil was not pierced as there was no need to. The court reached its decision using another criterion: the beneficial ownership link. Although, S. 24(1)(a) of the Matrimonial Causes Act, 1973 may have influenced the minds of the judges; Lady Hale and Lord Wilson alluded to that in their judgement.

52  See ITF's support for Indigenous Manning of Vessels, in: ITF, 'ITF Backs Union Action to Defend Chilean Shipping Industry' (ITF, 2012).

53  Article 2(2) of the Brazilian National Immigration Council Normative Resolution (NR.) 72/06.

one-third of the crew must comprise Brazilians working permanently.[54] Furthermore, the captain, the chief engineer and two-thirds of the crew of vessels flying the Brazilian flag must be Brazilian nationals.[55] In addition, foreign vessels that suspend their original flag to fly the Brazilian flag must register in the Special Brazilian Registry (REB).[56] For such vessels, the Brazilian maritime cabotage legislation stipulates that the captain and the chief engineer must be citizens of Brazil.[57]

The United States Merchant Marine Act of 1920 states that all the officers and at least 75 per cent of the crew on board coastwise vessels must be citizens of the United States.[58] The immediate impact of this provision is that it increases the operational cost of the vessel. This is because of the high labour cost associated with employing American seamen compared to the lower labour cost of employing qualified seamen from developing maritime nations.[59] In Indonesia, all domestic activities of sea transportation must be performed by Indonesian vessels with a full complement of Indonesian crew. The exception to this requirement is where there is evidence that there are no qualified Indonesian seafarers to fill the vacant positions.[60] Japanese maritime cabotage law stipulates that an eligible vessel engaged in the Japanese coastal trade must ensure that more than two-thirds of the vessel's officers are Japanese nationals.[61] Nigerian maritime cabotage legislation imposes a strict requirement that cabotage vessels must have 100 per cent Nigerian crew members.[62] However, this requirement does not manifest in reality as there are still foreign seafarers working in Nigerian territorial waters. This is notwithstanding the fact that many unemployed Nigerian seafarers have the appropriate mandatory qualifications. The maritime cabotage policy in the European Union is often viewed as evidence of an effective liberal maritime cabotage approach. However, it should be re-emphasized that this liberal approach only applies to member states within the European Union. Moreover, the liberal provisions do not necessarily extend to crewing requirements. There are two scenarios where an element of protectionism is imported into Council Regulation 3577/92.

---

54 Article 3(3a & 3b) of the Brazilian National Immigration Council Normative Resolution (NR) 72 of 10 October 2006.
55 Chapter IV, Article 4 of Law No. 9432/97
56 See Decree No. 2256/97 in pursuant of Article 10(III) of Law No. 9432/97.
57 Chapter VII, Article 11(6) of Law No. 9432/97.
58 46 U.S. Code § 8103.
59 For a broader read, see: H. Sampson, 'Maritime Futures: Jobs and Training for UK Ratings', (Seafarers International Research Centre, 2015). See also: T. Kvinge and A. Odegard, 'Protectionism or Legitimate Protection? On Public Regulation of Pay and working Conditions in Norwegian Maritime Cabotage', Report 2010:30 (FAFO, 2010).
60 Article 8(1) of Law 17 of 2008 on shipping. This requirement extends to the oil and gas sector, which is normally exempted from the Indonesian maritime cabotage legislation.
61 Article 1 of the 1899 Ship Law of Japan.
62 Section 3 of the Coastal and Inland Shipping (Cabotage) Act No. 5 of 2003 of the Laws of the Federation of Nigeria.

The first scenario is where the cruise ship or vessel carrying out mainland cabotage is smaller than 650 gt.[63] The second scenario arises where vessels are only engaged in island cabotage.[64] In both scenarios, all matters relating to crewing are the responsibility of the host cabotage state, which typically stipulates for a full complement of crew that are nationals of the host cabotage state.[65]

The creation of domestic employment is central to the economic development argument used by many countries to justify their choice of maritime cabotage approach. This argument gains traction when used by maritime countries with a large population and high unemployment index. Perhaps, there should be no surprises that maritime nations like China, United States, Brazil, Nigeria, Japan and India all stipulate for the crewing requirement in their respective maritime cabotage legislations. In conclusion, the application of all four traditional features of maritime cabotage law embraces the 'genuine link' concept rather than what we may now term the 'missing link' concept as witnessed in some of the open registries.

## Future features of the law of maritime cabotage

We have covered the four features of the law of maritime cabotage in some detail. The general justification for applying these requirements centres on the economic development argument. This raises the question of why there are only four of these requirements and whether there is scope for expanding the list of requirements. There are two other requirements that would fit the concept of maritime cabotage. The first is the requirement to certify all maritime cabotage vessels by a classification society that is wholly or substantially indigenous and domestic. The second requirement is stipulating for the recycling of all maritime cabotage vessels at the end of their working life in the maritime cabotage country. Both requirements satisfy the economic and development arguments often relied upon in choosing a maritime cabotage approach.

### The ship classification society requirement

Ship classification arose out of the need for shipowners to present acceptable evidence to their insurers and charterers concerning the build quality of their vessel. The dual role of a ship classification society means that the organization often works for both the shipowner and the flag state.[66] The classification society is obliged to assess whether the vessels in the registry satisfy the safety requirements as laid down by relevant legislations of the flag state. This includes conducting certain periodic statutory surveys, mainly relating to the construction quality of the

---

63　See: Articles 3(1) of Council Regulation (EEC) No. 3577/92.
64　See: Articles 3(2) of Council Regulation (EEC) No. 3577/92.
65　See: *Agip Petroli SPA v. Capitaneria di Porto di Siracusa et seq.* Case C – 456/04 [2006] ECR I – 3395 (Second Chamber).
66　See: N. Lagoni, *The Liability of Classification Societies* (Springer 2007).

vessel. On the other hand, the shipowner instructs a classification society to carry out mandatory surveys on their vessels and provide regular certification of the ongoing standard of their vessel. The fact that classification societies are privately contracted and paid by shipowners to perform a public service has led to suggestions that such relationships amount to a conflict of interest.[67] The last century has witnessed a huge surge in the number of classification societies.[68] However, many of them lack the expertise to survey and certify vessels to the recognized international standard. Many vessels sent to ship recycling yards following detention in various ports either had no class or got their certification from class societies that are not members of the International Association of Classification Societies (IACS).[69]

Many of the maritime cabotage countries assessed in this book have their own indigenous classification society, with several of them attaining membership status of the IACS.[70] Other maritime cabotage countries compensate for their lack of an indigenous class society by appointing established classification societies to perform surveys and certifications on vessels registered in their registries.[71] For instance, although there are several IACS-member classification societies operating in the Philippines, the focus mainly on surveying and certifying foreign-going vessels. This is because most of the domestic vessels fail to meet the international safety standards.[72] Hence, many Philippine-flag vessels engaged in maritime

67  For a broader read on the issue, see: J. Mansell, *Flag State Responsibility: Historical Development and Contemporary Issues* (Springer 2009). For an analysis on conflict of interest with shipowners, albeit from a slightly different perspective, see: *Marc Rich Co AG and Others v. Bishop Rock Marine Co Ltd and Others* [1995] UKHL 4.
68  See IMO Document FSI 13/10/2 of 23 December 2004, which identifies about 65 ship classification societies.
69  R. Des Bois, 'Ship-Breaking', *Bulletin of Information and Analysis on Ship Demolition*, No. 33 (Paris, 26 November 2013). Statistics indicate that between the second and part of the third quarter of 2013, 23 per cent of vessels detained for being sub-standard and consequently sent to recycling yards either had no class or were certified by non-IACS members. Members of the IACS are deemed to have the required expertise and experience to survey and certify vessels on behalf of the flag states and shipowners. IACS members are: LR, DNV-GL, CCC, KR, ABS, RINA, BV, NK, RS, IRS, CRS and PRS.
70  KR – Korea Register of Shipping (Korea, 1960); CCS – China Classification Society (China, 1956); NKK – Nippon Kaiji Kyokai (Japan, 1899); PRS – Philippine Register of Shipping (Philippines, 1989); VR – Vietnam Register (Vietnam, 1964); ABS – American Bureau of Shipping (USA, 1862); RBNA – Registro Brasileiro de Navios (Brazil, 1982); LR – Lloyd's Register (United Kingdom, 1760); RINA – Registro Italiano Navale (Italy, 1861); BV – Bureau Veritas (France, 1828); RS – Russian Maritime Register of Shipping (Russia, 1913); IRS – Indian Register of Shipping (India, 1975); DNV-GL (Det Norske Veritas-Germanischer Lloyd) (Norway and Germany, 2013); SCM – Ships Classification Malaysia (Malaysia, 1994); BKI – Biro Klasifikasi Indonesia (Indonesia, 1964).
71  Out of the 18 countries reviewed in this book, only Canada, Nigeria, Australia, South Africa, Chile and New Zealand are yet to own an 'indigenous' ship classicisation society.
72  G. Llanto and A. Navarro, 'Relaxing the Cabotage Restrictions in Maritime Transport' (Senate Committee on Trade, Commerce and Entrepreneurship, 2014).

cabotage services in the Philippines face either having no class at all or being surveyed and certified by the indigenous Philippine Register of Shipping (PRS).[73] The Russian Maritime Register of Shipping (RS) leverages its home advantage to focus on strengthening its Arctic position via its extensive ice-class expertise.[74] Russia's classification society uses its extensive experience to maximize its advantage in the face of growing competition in Arctic maritime cabotage transport and services.[75] The Arctic has huge potential and is becoming increasingly attractive to providers of maritime transport services in the region.

In Indonesia, all national-flagged vessels weighing 100gt and above are required to get class and certification under the rules of the Indonesian Classification Bureau (Biro Klasifikasi Indonesia).[76] However, this requirement triggers a different problem – namely, finding an underwriter to insure the ships and its cargo. As the Biro Klasifikasi Indonesia is not a member of the IACS, international marine underwriters are averse to insuring Indonesian-flagged vessels certified by the domestic classification society.[77] Moreover, domestic marine underwriters lack the capacity to provide adequate insurance cover for these vessels.[78] To mitigate this problem, the Indonesian government has opted to permit the dual classification of Indonesian-flagged vessels used in cabotage trade by members of IACS.[79] This effectively nullifies any benefit that could have arisen from Communication No. 20 of 2006 that mandated Indonesian vessels to be certified by the Indonesian Classification Bureau. In a related development, the Chinese Classification Society (CCS) has benefited immensely from the huge growth in the Chinese maritime cabotage fleet.[80]

We have established that many countries that have a maritime cabotage regime also have a national classification society. Thus, apart from the flaccid attempts by Indonesia and China, it is remarkable that more cabotage countries have not legislated compulsorily that 'Class and Certification' obtained from indigenous ship classification societies are acceptable for vessels involved in cabotage trade and services. This is particularly so given the economic and development arguments often relied upon to justify the choice of maritime cabotage approach. This is in addition to the pivotal role that a classification society plays during the shipbuilding and insurance life of a vessel.

---

73 G. Knowler, 'Scrap Cabotage Law to Cut Congestion and Costs, Philippine Agency Says' [2015], *Journal of Commerce*, 4 February.
74 See: B. Liversedge, 'What RINA can learn from Russia', *Superyacht News* (Milan, 13 June 2013).
75 For a general read, see: G. Fedoroff, 'Activities in the Arctic Maritime Region: The Russian View' (National Oceanic and Atmospheric Administration, 2011).
76 Decree of the Minister of Communications No. 20 of 2006: Regarding the Obligation of Indonesian Flagged Vessels to be Classified under Biro Klasifikasi Indonesia.
77 For a general read, see: S. Woods et al., 'Cabotage Regime: Implications for Foreign Owners, Operators and Financiers' (Marine Money offshore, 2012).
78 See: T. Mafira, 'Shipping Transportation in Indonesia' (Makarim & Taira, 2013).
79 Indonesian Decree KM 20 of 2006.
80 See: Lloyd's List, 'Top 10 Classification Societies: A New Class of Class is Emerging' (London, 13 December 2013).

*The ship recycling requirement*

Ship recycling is the process of dismantling decommissioned vessels that have reached the end of their economic life span. The age of the vessel, the freight market and the sale and purchase markets are major determinants of the ship recycling market. Furthermore, the economics of demand for scrap steel, weak labour markets and lax health and safety regulations create a relatively bullish ship recycling market in many Asian countries.[81] The steel and other materials used in the construction of ships are often of the highest quality. e wood and steel from ship recycling was instrumental in resourcing the industrial revolution.[82] The steel industry is a reliable indicator of economic progress because of the important role it plays in the global economy through the construction sector.[83] The economic boom in China and India has caused a massive increase in the demand for steel in those countries in recent years.[84] About 98 per cent of all the tonnage that is recycled in the world occurs in ship recycling yards in Bangladesh, China, India, Pakistan and Turkey.[85] These economies share the same underlying factor of having a huge market for scrap steel. This statistic has ignited serious debate on the corporate social responsibility that shipowners have by choosing to recycle their vessels in poor countries with lax safety regulations.[86] In many of these countries, the ship recycling industry supplies more than 60 per cent of the raw materials for the local steel industry.[87]

It is argued that local manufacturing and shipbuilding sectors can develop on the back of a strong domestic ship recycling industry because of the transferable skillset in both industries. However, while the industrialized countries construct the bulk of the world shipping fleet, vessels that have reached the end of their economic life are recycled mainly in developing countries. China is the exception as they have an extensive shipbuilding and ship recycling programme. In 2013, China climbed in the rankings as one of the major ship recycling countries. With two thirds of the ships demolished in China belonging to Chinese shipowners, this should not come as any surprise.[88]

---

81 For a comprehensive read on ship recycling, see the author's earlier work: A. Akpan, 'The Ship Recycling Industry: Hope or Despair?' (John Moores University, 2005).

82 For example, the famous department store, Liberty, which opened in 1875, is constructed from the timbers of the fighting ships *HMS Impregnable* and *HMS Hindustan*.

83 For a related read, see: C. Broadbent, 'Life Cycle Assessment in the Global Steel Industry' (World Steel Association, 2013).

84 For more discussion on the issue, see: Z. Changfu, 'The Role of the Iron & Steel Industry in China's Future Economic Development' (World Steel Association, 2012).

85 See: A. Akpan, 'The Ship Recycling Industry: Hope or Despair? (John Moores University, 2005). See also: N. Mikelis, 'Ship Recycling Markets and the Impact of the Hong Kong Convention' (International Maritime Organization, 2013).

86 See: N. Mikelis, 'Responsible Recycling of Ships', *Cleaner Seas* (London, 6 June 2014).

87 For more on this, see: U. Engels, *European Ship Recycling Regulation: Entry-Into-Force Implications of the Hong Kong Convention* (Springer 2013).

88 See: R. Des Bois, 'Ship-Breaking', *Bulletin of Information and Analysis on Ship Demolition,* No. 33 (Paris, 26 November 2013).

In addition to the Hong Kong Convention, the Basel Convention has also been instrumental in tackling poor practice of ship recycling from a trans-boundary movement of hazardous waste perspective.[89] Ships sent to the recycling yards in Asia typically contain a high percentage of hazardous waste, which is dangerous to lives and the environment.[90] Furthermore, the European Commission (EC) moved in 2013 to facilitate the process of greener ship recycling by introducing a new regulation.[91] This regulation is designed to reduce the negative impacts associated with recycling EU-flagged vessels in Asian countries without creating unnecessary economic burdens on EU shipowners.[92] It will compel ship recycling yards to improve the standard and technical capabilities of their operations before they are named in the approved facility list for recycling vessels registered in any of the EU member states. Perhaps one area that should be given more attention and resources is the design and build of vessels with end-of-life solutions in mind.[93] The Hong Kong Convention has received heavy criticism for not banning the beaching method of ship recycling used exclusively in South Asia.[94] However, it may be argued that the Convention's goal is to promote safety and not to eliminate the ship recycling industry that is a major source of revenue generation for government in these countries and provides employment to many people who would otherwise have no job. This is in addition to encouraging the growth of domestic manufacturing industries.[95] In Bangladesh, the government generates more than 130 million dollars yearly through a variety of taxes on the ship recycling industry. In addition, more than 50,000 people are employed directly and another 100,000 are involved indirectly in the ship recycling industry.[96] According to the Gujarat Maritime Board of India, the first vessel scrapped at Alang (India) was *MV Kota Tenjung* in 1983. Six years later, the ship-scrapping industry in India had provided 40,000 people with employment.[97] These benefits must be

---

89 The Basel Convention on the Control of Trans-boundary Movements of Hazardous Wastes and their Disposal. The Convention. Entered into force on 5 May 1992.

90 For a comprehensive discourse on the hazardous waste carried on vessels sent to the recycling yards in Asian countries with poor regulatory standards, see: A. Akpan, 'The Ship Recycling Industry: Hope or Despair?' (John Moores University, 2005).

91 Regulation (EU) 1257/2013 of the European Parliament and of the Council of 20 November 2013 on Ship Recycling.

92 For more on this see: N. Mikelis, 'The Recycling of Ships' (GMS, 2018).

93 Lloyd's Register is working on a design for recycling using futuristic technologies and scenarios as they apply to shipping, with the belief that new approaches to ship design will lead to safer ship recycling.

94 For more on this, see: K. Jain, J. Pruyn and J. Hopman, 'Critical Analysis of the Hong Kong International Convention on Ship Recycling' [2013], *World Academy of Science, Engineering and Technology International Journal of Environmental, Chemical, Ecological, Geological and Geophysical Engineering*, 7(10), 438–446.

95 A. Akpan, 'The Ship Recycling Industry: Hope or Despair?' (John Moores University, 2005).

96 For a general read on this subject, see: Young Power in Social Action, *Benefits from Ship Breaking* (YPSA, 2012).

97 Lloyd's Register, 'Ship Recycling: Practice and Regulation Today', *Lloyd's Register* (London, June 2011).

recognized as influential factors which indicate that the ship recycling industry can drive an economically viable and environmentally proactive growth strategy. Furthermore, the current evolution in the ship recycling industry towards a safer and more sustainable system demonstrates that the industry can shade its bad reputation while facilitating further economic benefits in the countries that have a ship recycling programme.[98] Considering the economic benefits of this industry, one wonders why countries stipulate for an indigenous shipbuilding requirement but refuse to consider ship recycling as a feature of their maritime cabotage regime. This is more astonishing given that the skills and expertise required for building and demolishing vessels are transferable. Moreover, it can be argued that the number of vessels built and demolished balance out over time. Therefore, the economic development arguments used to support the domestic shipbuilding programme should apply to the ship recycling programme.

Perhaps the dangers that ship demolition poses to the safety of people and the environment is responsible for the reluctance to incorporate this feature into some of the national maritime cabotage regimes. If so, it should be noted that shipbuilding is not free from danger either. The shipbuilding industry was once a very dangerous place to work, until stricter safety regulations and newer technologies were introduced. A similar evolution is now occurring within the ship recycling industry, with many of the recycling facilities already implementing better safety standards than was previously the case.[99] The correlation between the new shipbuilding and ship demolition markets is such that a country could have a stronger economy and a more vibrant maritime sector if ship recycling was pursued responsibly as a requirement of maritime cabotage law in the various national domains. It appears China is already ahead of the race with their combined shipbuilding and ship demolition programme.

---

98 See the impact of the Hong Kong International Convention for the Safe and Environmentally Sound Recycling of Ships 2009. Furthermore, see the impact of: Regulation (EU) 1257/2013 of the European Parliament and of the Council of 20 November 2013 on Ship Recycling.

99 See: Lloyd's Register, 'Ship Recycling: Practice and Regulation Today', *Lloyd's Register* (London, 2011).

# 13 Future directions of maritime cabotage law

Our assessment of maritime cabotage law reveals on the one hand the growing expansion of the concept of maritime cabotage and on the other its increasing legal uncertainty. We have also observed that sovereignty, economic development and national security are the basis for adopting a maritime cabotage law in many countries. We must now consider what the future direction of maritime cabotage law will be. It is suggested that the ambit of maritime cabotage law will continue to expand, particularly in the international domain. This will require developing a comprehensive framework that addresses the various concerns that cause uncertainty and make the concept of maritime cabotage a complex matter. Any success will depend on whether we can find an appropriate balance between a national sovereignty-directed system and a harmonized international agenda.

## A harmonized international maritime cabotage concept

It is acknowledged that an international framework of maritime cabotage law is fraught with several challenges. This is because many nations refuse to accept that the concept of maritime cabotage is more than a domestic policy agenda. For instance, Japan, USA and China have been reluctant to consider any reform that may challenge their domestic maritime cabotage regime. We submit that a harmonized international framework would provide the required leverage to address some of the concerns expressed by these countries. A harmonized international system would have the necessary support to resolve some of the critical issues that arise from providing maritime cabotage services in territorial waters.[1] Such a framework would be better equipped to identify and tackle the pockets of resistance that have hindered previous attempts to develop a harmonized international concept. It is further argued that the trend on matters such as world economics, commerce and national security indicates that an inclusive approach is now a strength rather than a weakness.[2] One of the

---

1 See: S. Chapelski, 'CETA: Opening up Canadian Waterways to Foreign Vessels' (Bull Housser, 2014).
2 For a related argument, see: B. Roermund, 'The Coalition of the Willing: Or Can Sovereignty Be Shared?' [2005], *Journal of the European Ethics Network*, 12(4), 443–464.

advantages of an international framework is economy of scale, with rules and standards tailored to fit the agenda of the different maritime cabotage nations.[3] The EU maritime cabotage framework demonstrates that it is possible to deal successfully with the concept of maritime cabotage outside the domestic sovereignty system. However, we recognise that other regional blocs have attempted unsuccessfully to replicate the EU cabotage framework. These include North America under the NAFTA (now USMCA Trade Agreement) framework, Africa under the African Maritime Transport Charter framework and parts of Asia under the ASEAN Free Trade Agreement. It is suggested that a harmonized international maritime cabotage regime can be pursued under either a mega-regional regime platform or an international relay framework.

### International agenda-based on a mega-regional maritime cabotage regime

There are many regional agreements based on countries having a common objective. Some result from loose cooperation agreements, others are based on an integrated common market with a centralized maritime transport policy. The success of a mega-regional framework agreement will depend on finding common ground regarding the important issues that affect the short and long-term economic development of member nations in the region. Furthermore, national security and geopolitical issues must also be considered so that a robust but flexible legal and policy framework that accommodates the economic and commercial considerations of member nations can be developed.[4] For instance, the European single market was developed based on the geopolitical considerations of member states. However, economic considerations have become an important factor driving the continued existence and proper functioning of the European Union. Similarly, NAFTA (now USMCA) may have been negotiated on the basis of geopolitical concerns, but the focus shifted swiftly towards economic and commercial considerations.[5] Also, regional trade agreements (RTAs) have become more common and exist alongside the World Trade Organization (WTO). Hence, NAFTA (now USMCA), the European Union and the major regional economies in Asia now have some form of functional mega-regional agreements.[6] The Trans-Pacific Partnership (TPP) and the Trans-Atlantic Trade and Investment Partnership (TTIP) further demonstrate that regional

---

3 For a broader read, see: H. Yoshizaki et al., 'Integration of International and Cabotage Container Shipping in Brazil', in J. Bookbinder (ed.), *Handbook of Global Logistics: Transportation in International Supply Chain* (Springer Science & Business Media 2013), pp. 117–138.
4 For a related discussion, see: E. Molenaar, 'Options for Regional Regulation of Merchant Shipping Outside IMO, with Particular Reference to the Arctic Region' [2014], *Ocean Development and International Law*, 45(3), 272–298.
5 The United States has in recent times called for NAFTA to be renegotiated based on current economic and commercial considerations.
6 By the end of 2013, 432 Regional Trade Agreements (RTA) had been notified to the World Trade Organization, of which 238 were in force.

partnerships are better accepted now.[7] With modern mega-regional frameworks there is scope for them to be better equipped legally, geopolitically, commercially and economically to address modern challenges than the WTO.[8] This is because they can be specifically developed to address the twenty-first century concerns in maritime cabotage.[9] The TPP and TTIP aim to achieve extensive liberalization of both goods and services, involving comprehensive coverage of trade in services, non-tariff measures and regulatory compatibility.[10] It has been suggested that the more significant gains from the TPP and TTIP will come from eliminating non-tariff measures that constitute barriers to trade and services.[11] Maritime cabotage is arguably the biggest non-tariff barrier to trade and services in the maritime sector and beyond. Hence, it is surprising that the latest mega-regional agreements exclude negotiations on reform policies for maritime cabotage. We accept that a mega-regional agreement is not without its challenges, such as distorting the world trade system. However, it is argued that the benefits of a mega-regional partnership outweigh the challenges that it poses. Therefore, an international maritime cabotage law framework has a better chance of success if it is premised on a stable mega-regional maritime cabotage regime. This will require member nations to sacrifice some sovereignty in return for regional and international economic development.[12] However, a harmonized international maritime cabotage regulation based on a regional maritime cabotage regime will require some provisions to be considered. They include:

7  The TPP is a stepping-stone to the creation of a Free Trade Agreement among all Asia-Pacific Economic Cooperation (APEC) members. Originally a four-way FTA between Brunei, Chile, New Zealand and Singapore, the TPP now encompasses seven additional countries: Australia, Canada, Japan, Malaysia, Mexico, Peru and Vietnam. The United States withdrew its membership in 2017. On the other hand, the TTIP aims for a far-reaching trade agreement between the US and the EU, focusing on trade liberalization and other non-tariff barriers. It also seeks a high standards approach to alignment, compatibility and possible harmonization of regulations and standards governing the goods and services.

8  For more, see: A. González, 'Mega-regional Trade Agreements: Game-Changers or Costly Distractions for the World Trading System?', Global Agenda Council on Global Trade and FDI: World Economic Forum (Geneva, 9 July 2014).

9  For a general discussion, see: R. Baldwin, 'Multilateralising 21st-Century Regionalism', OECD Global Forum on Trade: Reconciling Regionalism and Multilateralism in a Post-Bali World (Paris, 11–12 February 2014).

10  See the very informative monograph by: P. Draper, S. Lacey and Y. Ramkolowan, 'Mega-Regional Trade Agreements: Implications for The African, Caribbean, and Pacific Countries', Occasional Paper No. 2/2014 (European Centre for International Political Economy, 2014).

11  See: A. Stoler, 'Will the WTO have Functional Value in the Mega-Regional World of FTAs?', in R. Meléndez-Ortiz (ed.), 'Strengthening the Multinational Trading System: Regional Trade Agreements Group; Proposals and Analysis' (International Centre for Trade and Sustainable Development, 2013), pp. 43–48.

12  B. Roermund, 'The Coalition of the Willing: Or Can Sovereignty Be Shared?' [2005], *Journal of the European Ethics Network*, 12(4), 443–464.

- An appropriate international regulatory institution should be established with the responsibility of monitoring and regulating maritime cabotage under the harmonized international maritime cabotage law framework.[13] It is debatable whether the WTO would be fit for purpose given past inconsistencies and failures.[14]
- Existing international judicial forum like the ICJ should be incorporated or an effective new one established to resolve disputes between member nations.[15] One accepts that multi-national disputes will test even the most specialized and robust judicial framework.
- Establish a robust financial institution in the form of an international maritime cabotage bank (IMCB). As member nations are likely to use different national currencies, a common currency or types of currencies will be required for commercial purposes. The Regional Maritime Development Bank (RMDB) for Africa is a useful example.

The relative success of the European Union Council Regulation 3577/92 triggers the important question of why attempts to replicate similar regional maritime cabotage frameworks have been unsuccessful elsewhere.[16] It is submitted that a logical reason for this scenario is the structural setup for membership. The regions that have attempted unsuccessfully to establish a regional maritime cabotage framework place the geographical proximity of the different countries as the most important criterion for membership. Hence, they form an entity made up of a coalition of both willing and unwilling member nations. Thus, the different members may be at diverging levels of economic development with different priorities. It is therefore difficult to design a successful regional framework that satisfies the needs and aligns with the priorities of the different member nations. Perhaps this explains why these regions have not succeeded in establishing a harmonized regional maritime cabotage framework. On the other hand, the relative success in implementing the regional maritime cabotage law within the European Union is indicative of the prerequisites required to achieve success. The EU is not an entity comprised solely of member states connected by geographical proximity. Joining the European Union requires prospective members to satisfy stringent conditions on issues such as economic development, stable financial markets, commitment towards protecting the environment and human rights legislation.

---

13 See the strategic regulatory and monitoring framework adopted by the European Commission to assess the impact of Council Regulation (EEC) No. 3577/92.
14 See WTO's handling of maritime cabotage matters at the Uruguay, post-Uruguay and Doha Rounds.
15 See for instance the relevance of the Court of Justice of the European Union (CJEU) and how it contributes to the success of the Council Regulation (EEC) No. 3577/92 by ascertaining the position of the law as it concerns maritime cabotage within the EU, even though it has not always been successful in doing so.
16 Regional maritime cabotage frameworks in North America (the so-called NAFTA cabotage), as well as the ASEAN framework, Central America framework and Africa transport policy framework, are yet to succeed.

This ensures that the member states of the European Union are not at opposite ends in thelevel of development and their priorities. Hence, it was relatively easy to find common ground to design a workable, harmonized regional maritime cabotage framework that is suitably robust and flexible to deal with the complex nature of maritime cabotage in the European Union. This means that a harmonized international maritime cabotage framework must acknowledge the distinctive economic, political and environmental features of different member nations.

### International maritime cabotage relay

The concept of international maritime cabotage relay is based on the notion that a foreign vessel may be permitted to load and discharge cargo in more than one port in a country. This is contrary to the traditional maritime cabotage position in which the operations of foreign vessels are restricted to only one port in the host cabotage country.

The framework for international maritime cabotage relay compromises between the outright protectionist and liberal maritime cabotage approaches. It is, however, reflective of the flexible maritime cabotage approach concept. The international relay approach is driven by the commercial impact it has on the domestic shipping sector of a country. For instance, the operation of the protectionist maritime cabotage law in the United States means that the alternative to an international maritime cabotage relay is to complete the transport cycle of the cargo on land.[17] There are strong indications that road and rail transportation contributes to congestion and pollution, in addition to being substantially less efficient than sea transport. More than 500,000 international containers that could have qualified under the international relay scheme were moved by road and rail services in 2012. It has been argued that, if these international containers had completed their transportation cycle via the international relay scheme, the economic benefit to the maritime sector of the United States would be more than US$200 million.[18] The maritime cabotage regulation in China is as stringent as the Merchant Shipping Act of the United States, albeit with the obvious absence of the domestic shipbuilding requirement.[19] Implementing the international relay scheme in China would open up opportunity for about ten million containers to be transhipped through Chinese ports. The international relay scheme can generate revenue in excess of US$321 million for the Chinese coastal shipping sector. In addition, it could save Chinese shippers around US$700 million annually through better efficiency in the shipping networks, lower inventory costs, and reduction in port charges.[20] This would be more effective than the current practice of transhipping

17 For a related discussion, see: S. Beason et al., 'Myth and Conjecture? The "Cost" of the Jones Act' [2015], *Journal of Maritime Law & Commerce*, 46(1), 23–50.
18 World Economic Forum, 'Enabling Trade: Valuing Growth Opportunities' (Bain & Company and the World Bank, 2013).
19 See: Article 4 of the Maritime Code of the People's Republic of China.
20 World Economic Forum, 'Enabling Trade: Valuing Growth Opportunities' (Bain & Company and the World Bank, 2013).

international cargoes at several neighbouring hub ports in the south-east and east Asia regions.[21]

Other maritime cabotage countries with growth markets such as Indonesia, India and Brazil have also considered introducing the international relay scheme into their maritime cabotage law. In India, about 70 per cent of exports and imports are transhipped in the ports of neighbouring countries. The first step was taken in 2012, when India relaxed their maritime cabotage law for three years. Furthermore, the international maritime relay scheme was introduced to facilitate the transhipment of cargo through the Vallarpadam international container terminal. The Vallarpadam terminal has been slow to reach the targets that were expected. To mitigate this shortcoming, the Tuticorin Port Trust has proposed constructing another transhipment hub in India. The expectation is that a second hub port will provide more alternatives and further strengthen India's position as the most suitable transhipment hub in the region. This will allow foreign flag vessels to carry export-import (EXIM) containers in domestic waters, provided the same cargoes have been shipped through the Vallarpadam and Tuticorin transhipment terminals. In Australia, the international relay scheme is in practice in the form of 'triangular trades'. This allows foreign vessels to load and discharge foreign cargo in more than one Australian port. Therefore, if a foreign ship is discharging foreign cargo in one Australian port and loading foreign-going cargo in another Australian port, the foreign vessel can carry cargo between the discharging and loading ports in Australia under the 'triangular trade' arrangement.[22] The European Commission has urged member states to consider adopting an international maritime cabotage relay scheme to take advantage of the substantial cost savings that can be derived from its implementation.[23]

The adoption of the international relay scheme by some nations is because of the economic impact of adopting a maritime cabotage law approach where the economic cost outweighs the intended economic benefits.[24] The World Economic Forum report has called for maritime nations to consider adopting triangular trades or international relay schemes. The report suggests that this would mitigate the impact of cabotage policies on supply chain costs and the complexities of transport logistics.[25] Therefore, an international relay scheme is not as objectionable as it once was.

The advantages that are associated with the international maritime cabotage relay scheme have been discussed comprehensively. However, it is argued that for

21 V. Wee, 'China Cabotage Rules Benefit Hong Kong: HIT', *Seatrade Global* (Asia, Port and Logistics) (Victoria, 10 October 2013).
22 For more on this, see: C. Berg and A. Lane, 'Coastal Shipping Reform: Industrial Reform or Regulatory Nightmare?' (Institute of Public Affairs, 2013).
23 See European Commission Report: COM (2003) 595 final; December 2003.
24 For a related argument, see: K. Magee, 'U.S. Cabotage Laws: Protective or Damaging? A Strategy to Improve Cruise Vessel Competitiveness and Traffic to U.S. Ports' (Monterey Institute of International Studies, 2002).
25 World Economic Forum, 'Enabling Trade: Valuing Growth Opportunities' (Bain & Company and the World Bank, 2013).

all those advantages, the concept does have two major drawbacks. The first issue is traditional and is as old as the law of maritime cabotage itself. This is concerned with the prevalent argument that allowing an intermediary carriage of cargo by foreign carriers deprives indigenous shipowners the opportunity to carry those cargoes. The second problem is more unconventional and stems from the nature of the concept of international maritime cabotage relay. The issue here is that international maritime cabotage relay schemes may only resolve issues relating to domestic freight rates and consumer prices, neglecting the many other issues that arise from adopting any maritime cabotage approach. The international maritime cabotage relay scheme may not be the absolute abolition of protectionist maritime cabotage laws that liberal advocates seek. On the other hand, advocates of a protectionist maritime cabotage regime may it as a derogation from the protectionist maritime cabotage approach. Nevertheless, we are convinced that the concept of an international maritime cabotage relay represents an important step in developing a harmonized international maritime cabotage law framework.

Finally, it is submitted that contentious issues surrounding maritime cabotage do not need to be tackled as an unbroken aggregate in one fell swoop. Rather, these issues can be separated into different categories that allow the parties to find common ground for reaching a satisfactory compromise, be it in the national, regional or international domain. If this happens, we would have succeeded in proving that the theory of developmental sovereignty provides a platform where the inconsistencies of maritime cabotage law can be either reconciled or accommodated.

# Bibliography

Adams, S., 'DNV GL to Class Two Pipe Laying Vessels at New Vard Promar Yard in Brazil' (2013), DNV.GL.

Adelman, I., 'Fallacies in Development Theory and Their Implications for Policy' (1999), Working Paper No. 887, California Agricultural Experiment Station, Giannini Foundation of Agricultural Economics.

Adler, N., Yazhemsky, E., and Tarverdyan, R., 'A Framework to Measure the Relative Socio-Economic Performance of Developing Countries' (2010), *Socio-Economic Planning Sciences*, 44(3), 73–88.

Ajiye, S., 'Nigerian Cabotage: Its Policy, Prospects and Challenges' (2013), *Journal of Economics and Sustainable Development*, 4(14), 11–19.

Akabogu, E., 'Nigeria: Aggrieved Ship Owners Can Bring Action to Enforce Cabotage Claims' (2015), Akabogu & Associates.

Akpan, A., 'The Ship Recycling Industry: Hope or Despair?' (2005), John Moores University.

Akpan, A., 'A Precarious Judicial Interpretation of the Scope of EU Maritime Cabotage Law' (2014), *Journal of International Maritime Law*, 20(6), 444–447.

Alexandrowicz, C., *An Introduction to the History of the Law of Nations in the East Indies: 16th, 17th and 18th Centuries* (Clarendon Press 1967).

American Bureau of Shipping (ABS), 'Navigating the Northern Sea Route: Status and Guidance' (2013), ABS.

American Maritime Partnership (AMP), 'Why We Need the Jones Act' (2011), AMP.

Anand, R., *Development of Modern International Law and India* (Nomos 2005).

Anderson, S. et al., *Field Guide to the Global Economy* (The New Press 2000).

Antrim, C. and Galdorisi, G., 'Creeping Jurisdiction Must Stop' (2011), *U.S. Naval Institute Proceedings*, 137(4), 66–71.

Aoki, M. et al., 'Beyond The East Asian Miracle: Introducing the Market Enhancing View. The Role of Government in East Asian Economic Development' (1997), *Comparative Institutional Analysis*, 1(1), 1–37.

Arctic Council, 'Arctic Marine Shipping Assessment 2009 Report' (2009), Arctic Council.

Armitage, D., *The Ideological Origins of the British Empire* (Cambridge University Press 2000).

Arnsdorf, I., 'U.S. Shipbuilding Is Highest in Almost 20 Years on Shale Energy' (2013), *Bloomberg Newsletter*, 18 September.

Arthur, T., 'Competition Law and Development: Lessons from the U.S. Experience', in D. Sokol, T. Cheng and L. Ioannis (eds), *Competition Law and Development* (Stanford University Press 2013).

Asrofi, M., 'Cabotage Full Implementation vs Cabotage Relaxation' (2011), Frost & Sullivan Market Insight.

Australian Dry Bulk Shipping Users (ADBSU), 'Submission to Senate Standing Committees on Economics Inquiry into the Shipping Reform Bills' (2012), ADBSU.

Australian Shipowners Association (ASS), 'Options Paper: Approaches to Regulating Coastal Shipping in Australia' (2014), ASS.

Auty, R., 'Aid and Rent-driven Growth: Mauritania, Kenya, and Mozambique Compared', in G. Mavrotas (ed.), *Foreign Aid for Development Issues, Challenges, and the New Agenda* (Oxford University Press2010).

Badenhop, M., 'Economic Growth and Structure by Simon Kuznets' (1966), *Journal of Farm Economics*, 48(1), 148–150.

Bajpai, N. and Shastri, V., 'Port Development in Tamil Nadu: Lessons from Chinese Provinces' (1999), Development Discussion Paper No. 731, Harvard Institute for International Development, Harvard University.

Baker, B., 'Flags of Convenience and the Gulf Oil Spill: Problems and Proposed Solutions' (2012), *Houston Journal of International Law*, 34(3), 697–715.

Balassa, B., *The Newly Industrializing Countries in the World Economy* (Pergamon Press1981).

Baldwin, R., 'Multilateralising 21st Century Regionalism' (2014), OECD Global Forum on Trade: Reconciling Regionalism and Multilateralism in a Post-Bali World, 11/12 February.

Barnsberg, P., 'Malaysia Eases Cabotage Law, Adds Incentive' (2001) *Journal of Commerce*, n.d.

Bartik, T., 'The Market Failure Approach to Regional Economic Development Policy' (1990) *Economic Development Quarterly*, 40(4), 361–370.

Bauer, P. and Yamey, B., *The Economics of Under-developed Countries* (Cambridge University Press1957).

Bazakas, J. and Springall, R., 'Australian Shipping Industry Reform: Long Awaited' (2011), Holman Fenwick Willan Briefings.

Beason, S. et al., 'Myth and Conjecture? The "Cost" of the Jones Act' (2015), *Journal of Maritime Law & Commerce*, 46(1), 23–50.

Beckman, R., 'International Law, UNCLOS and the South China Sea', in C. Schofield et al. (eds), *Beyond Territorial Disputes in the South China Sea: Legal Frameworks for the Joint Development of Hydrocarbon Resources* (Edward Elgar Publishing2013).

Bellamy, V., 'The Implementation of Cabotage Principle in Indonesia' (2010), HG. Org Legal Resources.

Bentham, J., *Introduction to the Principles of Morals and Legislation* (London, 1780).

Berg, C. and Lane, A., 'Coastal Shipping Reform: Industrial Reform or Regulatory Nightmare?' (2013), Institute of Public Affairs.

Bhattacharjea, A., 'Who Needs Antitrust? Or, Is Developing-Country Antitrust Different? A Historical Comparative Analysis', in D. Sokol, T. Cheng and L. Ioannis (eds), *Competition Law and Development* (Stanford University Press2013).

Blanco, L., *Shipping Conferences under EC Antitrust Law: Criticism of a Legal Paradox* (Hart Publishing2007).

Bliss, F., 'Rethinking Restrictions on Cabotage: Moving to Free Trade in Passenger Aviation' (1994), *Suffolk Transnational Law Review*, 17(2), 382–407.

Bodin, J., *Six Livres de la Republique* (Paris, 1576).

Bollard, A., 'New Zealand', in J. Williamson (ed.), *The Political Economy of Policy Reform* (Institute for International Economics1994).

Bonanno, G. and Haworth, B., 'Intensity of Competition and the Choice between Product and Process Innovation' (1998), *International Journal of Industrial Organization*, 16 (4), 495–510.

Bonefeld, W., 'Freedom and the Strong State: On German Ordoliberalism' (2012), *New Political Economy*, 17(5), 633–656.

Bossche, P., *The Law and Policy of the World Trade Organization: Text, Cases and Materials* (2nd edn, Cambridge University Press2008).

Brigham, L., 'Arctic Marine Shipping Assessment 2009 Report' (Arctic Council, 2014).

Broadbent, C., 'Life Cycle Assessment in the Global Steel Industry' (2013), World Steel Association.

Brooks, M., 'Fleet Development and the Control of Shipping in Southeast Asia' (1985), Institute of Southeast Asian Studies.

Brooks, M., 'NAFTA and Short Sea Shipping Corridors' (2005), Australia Institute of Market Studies.

Brooks, M., 'The Jones Act Under NAFTA and Its Effects on the Canadian Shipbuilding Industry' (2006), Atlantic Institute for Market Studies.

Brooks, M., 'Liberalization in Maritime Transport' (2009), International Transport Forum OECD/ITF Forum Paper 2009–2002.

Brooks, M., 'Maritime Cabotage: International Market Issues in the Liberalisation of Domestic Shipping', in A. Chircop et al. (eds), *The Regulation of International Shipping: International and Comparative Perspectives* (Martinus Nijhoff2012).

Brouwer, E., van Dalen, H., Roelandt, T., Ruiter, M. and van der Wiel, H., 'Market Structure, Innovation and Productivity: A Marriage with Chemistry', in G. Gelauff et al. (eds), *Fostering Productivity: Patterns, Determinants and Policy Implications* (Elsevier 2004), pp. 199–212.

Burtless, G. et al., 'Globaphobia: Confronting Fears about Open Trade', in R. Broad (ed.), *Global Backlash: Citizen Initiatives for a Just World Economy* (Rowman & Littlefield 2002).

Butcher, L., 'Shipping: EU Policy' (2010), House of Common Library Report, SN/BT/55.

Butler, E., *Public Choice: A Primer* (Institute of Economic Affairs2012).

BXA, 'U.S. Shipbuilding and Repair: National Security Assessment of the U.S. Shipbuilding and Repair Industry' (2001), BXA.

Byers, M., *International Law and the Arctic* (Cambridge University Press2013).

Byers, M., 'The Northwest Passage Dispute Invites Russian Mischief' (2015), *National Post*, 28 April.

Cafruny, A., 'Flags of Convenience', in R. Jones (ed.), *Routledge Encyclopaedia of International Political Economy* (Routledge2002).

Campos, C., 'PROMEF: The Brazilian Shipbuilding Market is Booming' (2014), *Petrobas Magazine*, 11 February.

Carlisle, R., *Sovereignty for Sale: The Origins and Evolution of the Panamanian and Liberian Flags of Convenience* (MD Naval Institute Press1981).

Carman, J., 'Economic and Strategic Implications of Ice-Free Arctic Seas', in S. Tangredi (ed.), *Globalization and Maritime Power* (Institute for National Strategic Studies, National Defence University 2009).

Casey, L. and Rivkin, D., 'Making Law: The United Nations' Role in Formulating and Enforcing International Law', in B. Schaefer (ed.), *Conundrum: The Limits of the United Nations and the Search for Alternatives* (Rowman & Littlefield2009).

Cass, R., 'Competition in Antitrust Regulation: Law beyond Limits' (2009), *Journal of Competition Law & Economics*, 6(1), 119–152.

Cefali, M., 'Oil and Gas Industry: An Exception in Newly Effective Indonesian Cabotage Regulation' (2011), MA Law Firm.

Cervantes, M. and Guellec, D., 'The Brain Drain: Old Myths, New Realities' (2002), *OECD Observer*, no. 230, January.

Changfu, Z., 'The Role of the Iron & Steel Industry in China's Future Economic Development' (2012), World Steel Association.

Chapelski, S. and Bromley, J., 'CETA: Opening up Canadian Waterways to Foreign Vessels' (2014), Bull Housser.

Charusheela, S., *Structuralism and Individualism in Economic Analysis: The 'Contractionary Devaluation Debate' in Development Economics* (Routledge2013).

Chen, M., 'China Will Not Open its Cabotage to Foreign Vessels' (2010), *China Shipping Gazette*, no. 844.

Chenery, H., *Structural Change and Development Policy* (Johns Hopkins University Press1979).

Chester, S., 'Grotius, Selden and 400 Years of Controversy' (2009), *Slaw Legal Magazine*, 1 November.

Chida, T. and Davies, P., *The Japanese Shipping and Shipbuilding Industries: A History of their Modern Growth* (2nd edn, Bloomsbury2012).

Chikunga, L., 'South Africa Transport Department Budget Vote for 2015–16 Financial Year' (2015), Department of Transport.

Chirathivat, S., 'Ten Years after the Asian Crisis: Toward Economic Sustainability in Southeast Asia' (2007), Cambodia Foundation for Cooperation and Peace.

Chuah, J., 'Short Sea Shipping: The Blue Belt Package' (2013), *Journal of International Maritime Law*, 19(1), 256–258.

Coles, R. and Watt, E., *Ship Registration: Law and Practice* (2nd edn, Taylor & Francis2013).

Commission of the European Communities, 'Towards a future Maritime Policy for the Union: A European Vision for the Oceans and Seas' (2006), Green Paper, Volume II – Annex, Com (2006) 275 final, {SEC (2006) 689}.

Commonwealth of Australia, *Report of the Royal Commission on the Navigation Act 1924*, No. 103-F.15346 (Parliament of the Commonwealth of Australia1924).

Cooper, J., 'Aviation Cabotage and Territory', (1952), *US and Canadian Aviation Reports*, 1(1) 256–272.

Coulter, D., 'Globalization of Maritime Commerce: The Rise of Hub Ports', in S. Tangredi (ed.), *Globalization and Maritime Power* (Institute for National Strategic Studies, National Defence University2009).

CPMR Islands Commission (CPMR), 'Consultation on the 5th Maritime Cabotage Report' (2009), CPMR.

Crawford, G., 'The World Bank and Good Governance: Rethinking the State or Consolidating Neo-liberalism?', in A. Paloni and M. Zanardi (eds), *The IMF, World Bank and Policy Reform* (Routledge2006).

Crotty, J., 'The Neoliberal Paradox: The Impact of Destructive Product Market Competition and Modern Financial Markets on Non-financial Corporation Performance in the Neoliberal Era', in G. Epstein (ed.), *Financialization and the World Economy* (Edward Elgar2005).

Cseres, K., 'Competition Law and Consumer Protection' (2005), Kluwer Law International.

Curtis, G., *Russia: A Country Study* (Library of Congress1998).

Cypher, M., *The Process of Economic Development* (4th edn, Routledge2014).

Darling, J., 'Report of Inquiry on the Coasting Trade of Canada and Related Marine Activity' (1970), Canadian Transport Commission.

de Vattel, E., *The Law of Nations* (Book 1, Article 288, T. & J. Y. Johnson1758).

Delacroix, J. and Bornon, J., 'Can Protectionism Ever Be Respectable?: A Skeptic's Case for the Cultural Exception, with Special Reference to French Movies' (2005), *Independent Review*, 9(3), 353–374.

Department for International Development, 'Competition Policy, Law and Developing Countries' (2001), Trade Matters Series, 1–6.

Department of Transport (DOT), 'Draft South African Maritime Transport Policy' (2008), DOT.

Department of Transport (DOT), 'Draft South African Maritime Transport Policy' (2009), DOT.

Department of Transport (DOT), 'White Paper on National Transport Policy' (1996), DOT.

des Bois, R., 'Ship-Breaking' (2013), *Bulletin of Information and Analysis on Ship Demolition*, No. 33, 26 November.

Desierto, D., 'Postcolonial International Law Discourses on Regional Developments in South and Southeast Asia' (2008), *International Journal of Legal Information*, 36(3), 387–431.

Dewar, A., 'The Freedom of The Seas' (1930), *Journal of the Royal Institute of International Affairs*, 9(1), 63–67.

Dhall, V., 'Competition Law and Consumer Protection: Insights into Their Interrelationship', in H. Qaqaya and G. Lipimile (eds), *The Effects of Anti-Competitive Business Practices on Developing Countries and Their Development Prospects* (UNCTAD2008).

Dicken, P., *Global Shift: Mapping the Changing Contours of the World Economy* (6th edn, SAGE Publications2011).

Dixon, C., 'The Pacific Asian Challenge to Neoliberalism', in D. Simon and A. Narman (eds), *Development as Theory and Practice* (Prentice Hall1999).

Dixon, M., *International Law* (5th edn, Oxford University Press2005).

Draper, P., Lacey, S. and Ramkolowan, Y., 'Mega-Regional Trade Agreements: Implications for The African, Caribbean, and Pacific Countries' (2014), Occasional Paper No. 2/2014, European Centre for International Political Economy.

Drewry Maritime Research, 'Shanghai's New Cabotage Laws a Disappointment' (2013), *Drewry Maritime Research Insight*, wk. 47.

Drewry Maritime Research, 'US Cabotage Protection gets more Expensive' (2013), *Drew Maritime Research*, wk. 47.

Drexhage, J. and Murphy, D., *Sustainable Development: From Brundtland to Rio 2012* (2010), International Institute for Sustainable Development.

Eckstein, A., *China's Economic Revolution* (Cambridge University Press1977).

Edmond, G., 'The Freedom of Histories: Reassessing Grotius on the Sea' (1995), *University of Wollongong Australia Law Text Culture*, 2(9), 179–217.

Edmonson, B., 'Navy Official Calls for a Fleet of Dual-Use Marine Highway Ships' (2011), *Journal of Commerce*, 13 July.

Elhauge, E. and Geradin, D., *Global Antitrust Law and Economics* (2nd edn, Thomson Reuters2011).

Elkan, W., *An Introduction to Development Economics* (Penguin Books1978).

Elstrodt, H. et al., 'Connecting Brazil to The World: A Part to Inclusive Growth' (2014), McKinsey Global Institute.

Engels, U., *European Ship Recycling Regulation: Entry-Into-Force Implications of the Hong Kong Convention* (Springer2013).

Environmental Hansard, 'MPs Resumed Discussion about the Government's Fisheries Investment Fund Commitment to Newfoundland and Labrador' (2015), House of Commons Debates, 41st Parliament, 2nd Session, No. 167, 2 February.

Eswaran, P., 'Maritime Sector Study of IMT-GT [the Indonesia-Malaysia-Thailand Growth Triangle]' (2008), Asian Development Bank.

European Commission, 'Blue Belt: A Single Transport Area for Shipping' (2013), European Commission, COM(2013) 510 Final.

European Commission, 'Communication from the Commission: On the interpretation of Council Regulation (EEC) No. 3577/92 applying the principle of freedom to provide services to maritime transport within Member States (maritime cabotage)' (2014), European Commission, COM(2014) 232 Final.

European Commission, 'Report on Motorways of the Sea: State of Play and Consultation' (2007), European Commission, SEC(2007) 1367.

European Commission, 'Europe 2020: A Strategy for Smart, Sustainable and Inclusive Growth' (2010), European Commission, COM(2010) 2020 Final.

European Commission, *Legal Aspects of Arctic Shipping: Summary Report* (2010), European Commission (Publications Office of the European Union 2010).

Evans, M., 'The Law of the Sea', in M. Evans (ed.), *International Law* (2nd edn, Oxford University Press2006).

Evenett, S., 'What is the Relationship between Competition Law and Policy and Economic Development?' (2005), University of Oxford.

Fadzil, K. et al., 'Policy Fiasco: The Sabotage of Cabotage Policy Malaysia' (2013), *International Journal of Social Science and Humanity*, 3(6), 514–517.

Fairplay 24, 'China's Domestic Fleet Grows Slower' (2012), *Fairplay 24*, 27 July.

Falk, R., 'The New States and the International Legal Order' (1966), *Recueil de Cours*, 118(1) 34–43.

Fassbender, B. and Peters, A., 'Introduction: Towards A Global History of International Law', in B. Fassbender and A. Peters (eds), *The Oxford Handbook of the History of International Law* (Oxford University Press2012).

Federal Reserve Bank of New York (FRBNY), 'Report on the Competitiveness of Puerto Rico's Economy' (2012), FRBNY.

Fedoroff, G., 'Activities in the Arctic Maritime Region: The Russian View' (2011), National Oceanic and Atmospheric Administration.

Fei, J. and Ranis, G., *Development of the Labor Surplus Economy: Theory and Policy* (Irwin1964).

Fels, A. and Ng, W., 'Rethinking Competition Advocacy in Developing Countries', in D. Sokol, T. Cheng and L. Ioannis (eds), *Competition Law and Development* (Stanford University Press2013).

Ferraro, V., 'Dependency Theory: An Introduction', in G. Secondi (ed.), *The Development Economics Reader* (Routledge2008).

Fforde, A., *Understanding Development Economics: Its Challenge to Development Studies* (Routledge2013).

Flanders, S., 'Moody's cuts Italy, Spain and Portugal's Credit Ratings' (2014), *BBC News*, 14 February.

Fleetwood, J., *Complete Overhaul of NZ shipping Required Following Rena Sentencing* (Maritime Union of New Zealand 2012).

Fox, E., 'Competition, Development and Regional Integration: In Search of a Competition Law Fit for Developing Countries' (2012), New York University Law and Economics Research Paper No. 11-04.

Francois, J., Arce, H., Reinert, K. and Flynn, J., 'Commercial Policy and the Domestic Carrying Trade' (1996), *Canadian Journal of Economics*, 29(1), 181–198.

Fraser, A., Mason, R. and Mitchell, P., *Japan's Early Parliaments, 1890–1905: Structures, Issues and Trends* (Routledge1995).

French, H., 'China's Dangerous Game' (2014), *The Atlantic* (November), 96–109.

Freudmann, A., 'WTO Urged to Avoid Cabotage Controversy' (1999), *Journal of Commerce*, 9 February.

Frittelli, J., 'Federal Freight Policy: An Overview' (2012), Congressional Research Service Report for Congress, 2 October.

Fulton, T., *The Sovereignty of the Sea: An Historical Account of the Claims to England to the Dominion of the British Seas, And of the Evolution of the Territorial Waters: With Special Reference to the Right of Fishing And The Naval Salute* (William Blackwood 1911).

Furse, M., *Competition Law of the EC and UK* (6th edn, Oxford University Press2008).

Gabriel, J., 'Revitalisation of the Shipbuilding Industry' (2009), *Petrobas Magazine*, 58(1), 5–10.

Gal, M., 'The Ecology of Antitrust: Preconditions for Competition Law Enforcement in Developing Countries', in P. Brunsick et al. (eds) *Competition, Competitiveness and Development: Lessons From Developing Countries* (UNCTAD2004).

Galbraith, S., 'Thinking Outside the Box on Coastal Shipping and Cabotage' (2014), *Maritime Trade Intelligence*, 1 December.

Ganter, M., 'Australian Coastal Shipping: The Vital Link' (1997), *Australian Maritime Affairs*, No. 3.

GATT, 'The Marrakech Agreement: Agreement Establishing the World Trade Organization' (1994), United Nations.

Gehring, M., 'Sustainable Competition Law' (2003), Fifth Session of the Ministerial Conference of the World Trade Organization, Cancún, 10–14 September.

Gerber, D., 'Economic Development and Global Competition Law Convergence', in D. Sokol, T. Cheng and L. Ioannis (eds) ,*Competition Law and Development* (Stanford University Press2013).

Ghosal, V., 'Resource Constraints and Competition Law Enforcement: Theoretical Considerations and Observations from Selected Cross-Country Data', inD. Sokol, T. Cheng and L. Ioannis (eds), *Competition Law and Development* (Stanford University Press2013).

Ghosh, P. and Narayan, S., 'Maritime Capacity of India: Strengths and Challenges' (2012), Observer Research Foundation (ORF).

Gilbert, R. and Steven, S., 'Incorporating Dynamic Efficiency Concerns in Merger Analysis: The Use of Innovation Markets' (1995), *Antitrust Law Journal*, 63(2), 569–601.

Gilbert, R., 'Competition and Innovation' (2006), *Journal of Industrial Organization Education*, 1(1), 1–30.

Global Business Guide Indonesia (GBG), 'Going Local: Understanding Indonesia's Local Content Requirement' (2014), GBG, 5 May.

Gold, E., *Maritime Transport: The Evolution of International Marine Policy and Shipping Law* (D. C. Heath & Co. 1981).

Goldfinch, S., 'Economic Reform in New Zealand: Radical Liberalisation in a Small Economy' (2004), *Otemon Journal of Australian Studies*, 30(1), 75–98.

Goldstein, M., 'Debt Sustainability, Brazil, and the IMF' (2003), Institute Of International Economics, WP 03–01.

González, A., 'Mega-regional Trade Agreements: Game-Changers or Costly Distractions for the World Trading System?' (2014), Global Agenda Council on Global Trade and FDI: World Economic Forum, 9 July.

Gootiiz, B. and Mattoo, A., 'Services in Doha: What's on the Table?' (2009), World Bank Policy Research Working Paper No. 4903.

Goulet, D., *The Cruel Choice: A New Concept on the Theory of Development.* (Atheneum1971).

Government of Canada, *Report of the Royal Commission on Coasting Trade: The Spence Commission* (Queen's Printer1957).

Government of Canada, *Report on the Royal Commission on Transportation: The Macpherson Commission 1959* (Queen's Printer1961).

Government of Canada, 'Government of Canada Announces New Tariff Measures for Ships for a More Competitive Canadian Economy' (2010), Department of Finance.

C. Grabow, 'U.S. Maritime Sector Among the Jones Act's Biggest Victims', CATO Institute (Washington, 28 June 2018).

Granville, B. and Mallick, S., 'Integrating Poverty Reduction in IMF-World Bank Models', in A. Paloni and M. Zanardi (eds), *The IMF, World Bank and Policy Reform* (Routledge2006).

Gray, J. and Dawn, F., *The Delusions of Global Capitalism* (New Press2000).

Gray, W., 'Performance of Major US Shipyards in 20th/21st Century' (2008), *Journal of Ship Production*, 24(4), 202–213.

Greaves, R., *EC Transport Law* (Pearson Education2010).

Grey, V., 'Freedom of the Seas' (1930), *Foreign Affairs*, 8(3), 325–335.

Grosso, M. et al., 'Services Trade Restrictiveness Index (STRI): Transport and Courier Services' (2014), OECD Trade Policy Paper No. 176.

Grotius, H., 'Mare Liberum: The Freedom of the Seas OR The Right Which Belongs To The Dutch To Take Part in the East Indian Trade', translated by R. Magoffin, in J. Scott (ed.), *Classics of International Law* (Oxford University Press1916).

Grotius, H., 'The Freedom of the Seas' (1608), translated by R. Magoffin, in J. Scott (ed.) *Classics of International Law* (Oxford University Press1916).

Gurtner, B., 'The Financial and Economic Crisis and Developing Countries' (2010), *International Development Policy.* 1(1), 189–213.

Hackston, D., English, G., Taylor, R. and MacDonald, J., 'Research Study on the Coasting Trade Act' (2005), Research and Traffic Group, Association of Canadian Port Authorities.

Haji, S., 'Indian Commercial Opinions on the Bill for the Reservation of the Coastal Traffic of India: Introduced in the Indian Legislative Assembly' (1928), Indian Shipping Series, No. 9.

Haji, S., *Economics of Shipping: A Study in Applied Economics* (Tata1924).

Hamilton, D. and Schwartz, P., 'A Transatlantic Free Trade Area: A Boost to Economic Growth?' (2012), Center for Transatlantic Relations and New Direction – The Foundation for European Reform, January.

Hannum, H., *Autonomy, Sovereignty and Self-determination: The Accommodation of Conflicting Rights*' (2nd edn, Pennsylvania University Press1996).

Haralambides, H. and Behrens, R., 'Port Restructuring in a Global Economy: An Indian Perspective' (2000), *International Journal of Transport Economics*, 27(1), 19–39.

Harmes, A., *The Return of the State: Protestors, Power-Brokers and the New Global Compromise* (Douglas & McIntyre 2004).

Harper, I. et al., *Competition Policy Review: Final Report* (The Harper Review), (Commonwealth of Australia2015).

Harris, D., *Cases and Materials on International Law* (7th edn, Thomson Reuters2010).

Harvey, D., *The New Imperialism* (Oxford University Press2005).

Hayton, B., *The South China Sea: The Struggle for Power in Asia* (Yale University Press 2014).

Hazledine, T., 'New Zealand Trade Patterns and Policy' (1993), *Australian Economic Review*, 26(4), 23–27.

Hendrickson, M., 'Trade Liberalisation, Trade Performance and Competitiveness in the Caribbean', in N. Duncan et al. (eds), *Caribbean Development Report* (2007) 1(1), 222–254.

Hesse, N., 'International Air Law: Some Questions on Aviation Cabotage' (1953), *McGill Law Journal*, 1(1), 129–140.

Hodgson, J. and Brooks, M., 'Towards a North American Cabotage Regime: A Canadian Perspective' (2007), *Canadian Journal of Transportation*, 1(1), 19–35.

Hodgson, J. and Brooks, M., 'Canada's Maritime Cabotage Policy: A Report for Transport Canada' (2004), Marine Affairs Program, Dalhousie University.

Hoff, K. and Stiglitz, J., 'Modern Economic Theory and Development', in G. Meier and J. Stiglitz (eds), *Frontiers of Development Economics: The Future in Perspective* (World Bank and Oxford University Press2000).

Hoffmann, J., 'Maritime Cabotage Services: Prospects and Challenges' (2001), *Bulletin on Trade Facilitation and Transport in Latin America and the Caribbean*, 183(11), 1–7.

Hoselitz, B., 'Economic Policy and Economic Development', in H. Aitken (ed.), *The State and Economic Growth* (Social Science Research Council1959).

House of Commons, 'Coasting Trade Bill' (1854), *Hansard*, 131, 462–466, 7 March.

House of Commons, 'Japanese Ships Coasting Trade' (1912), *Hansard*, 39, 1838–1839, 20 June.

Howard, D., 'The 2008Shipping Law: Deregulation or Re-regulation?' (2008), *Bulletin of Indonesian Economic Studies*, 44(3) 383–406.

Howell, T. et al., 'China's New Anti-Monopoly Law: A Perspective from the United States' (2009), *Pacific Rim Law & Policy Journal*, 18(1), 53–95.

Hubner, W., 'Regulatory Issues in International Maritime Transport' (2001), Organisation for Economic Cooperation and Development.

Humpert, M., 'The Future of Arctic Shipping: A New Silk Road for China?' (2013), The Arctic Institute Center for Circumpolar Security Studies.

Hung, R. and Li, R., 'Rostow's Stages of Growth Model, "Urban Bias" and Sustainable Development in India' (2013), *Journal of Contemporary Issues in Business Research*, 2(5), 170–188.

Hussain, A. et al., 'Effective Demand, Enterprise Reforms and Public Finance in China' (1991), *Economic Policy*, 6(12), 141–186.

Igbokwe, M., 'Advocacy Paper for the Promulgation of a Nigerian Maritime Cabotage Law: Draft Modalities for Implementation of Coastal and Inland Shipping (cabotage) Act' (2001), Nigerian Maritime Authority.

I-maritime, 'Indian Shipping Industry Report 2000' (2000), Research & Information Division.

Independent Consumer & Competition Commission, 'Final Report: Review of the PNG Coastal Shipping Industry' (2007), 16 February.

Indian Mercantile Marine Committee, 'Indian Mercantile Marine Committee 1923–24: Report' (Delhi, 1924). Held by the British Library (Asian and African Studies).

International Energy Agency, 'Energy Supply Security: Emergency Response of Partner Countries 2014 – Indonesia' (OECD/IEA Publications, 2014).

India's Directorate General of Shipping (DGS), '*Shipping Manual: Liberalization in Shipping* (DGS 2012).

India's Ministry of Commerce & Industry, 'Investing in India: Foreign Direct Investment – Policy & Procedures' (2008), Secretariat for Industrial Assistance.

Indonesian National Shipowners Association (INSA), 'The Development of Container Traffic Carried by Domestic Vessels' (2013), INSA.

International Chambers of Shipping (ICS), 'Arctic Shipping: Positional Paper' (2014), ICS.

International Competition Network (ICN), 'ICN Factsheet and Key Messages' (2009), ICN.

Ioannis, L., Mateus, A. and Raslan, A., 'Is There Tension Between Development Economics and Competition?', in D. Sokol, T. Cheng and L. Ioannis (eds), *Competition Law and Development* (Stanford University Press2013).

Isham, D., 'The Neo-Colonial Dependence Model and the Diverging Economic Paths of Chile and Argentina' (2012), *Indian Journal of Economics & Business*, 11(2), 303–321.

Itagaki, Y., 'Criticism of Rostow's Stage Approach: The Concepts of Stage, System and Type' (2007), *Developing Economies*, 1(1), 1–17.

International Trade Centre (ITC), 'Economic Effect of Significant U.S. Import Restraints Report' (2007), ITC.

International Transport Workers' Federation (ITF), 'Transport: The WTO's Problem Industry' (2003), *Transport International Magazine*, 11 April.

International Transport Workers' Federation (ITF), 'ITF Backs Union Action to Defend Chilean Shipping Industry' (2012), ITF, 11 December.

Ito, T., 'Growth Crisis and the Future of Economic Recovery in East Asia', in J. Stiglitz and S. Yusuf (eds), *Rethinking the East Asian Miracle* (Oxford University Press2001).

Jackson, J., 'Sovereignty – Modern: A New Approach to an Outdated Concept' (2003), *American Journal of International Law*, 97(1), 782–802.

Jain, K., Pruyn, J. and Hopman, J., 'Critical Analysis of the Hong Kong International Convention on Ship Recycling' (2013), *World Academy of Science, Engineering and Technology International Journal of Environmental, Chemical, Ecological, Geological and Geophysical Engineering*, 7(10), 438–446.

Japan Federation of Coastal Shipping Associations (JFCSA), 'Coastal Shipping Cargo Transportation' (2011). JFCSA .

Japan Federation of Coastal Shipping Associations (JFCSA), 'Adherence to the Cabotage System' (2011), JFCSA.

Jati, D., 'Liberalised but Protected: Shipping Law Introduces New Cabotage Rules and Welcomes Private Sector Participation' (2011), Oxford Business Group.

Jin, C., 'Maritime Policy in China After WTO: Legal and Economic Approach' (2006), Hong Kong Polytechnic University.

Johnson, C., 'Advances in Marine Spatial Planning: Zoning Earth's Last Frontier' (2014), *Journal of Environmental Law and Litigation*, 29(1), 191–246.

Johnston, D., *The International Law of Fisheries: A Framework for Policy-Oriented Inquiries* (New Haven Press1987).

Jomo, K., 'Rethinking the Role of Government Policy in Southeast Asia', in J. Stiglitz and S. Yusuf (eds), *Rethinking the East Asian Miracle* (Oxford University Press2001).

Jong-Il, K. and Lau, L., 'The Sources of Economic Growth of the East Asian Newly Industrialized Countries' (1994), *Journal of the Japanese and International Economies*, 8 (1), 235–271.

Joshi, R., 'WTO Review Fears Derail Proposed Jones Act Amendment' (2009), *Lloyd's List*, 28 October.

Kaczorowska, A., *Public International Law* (3rd edn, Routledge Cavendish2005).

Kalen, S., 'Cruise Control and Speed Bumps: Energy Policy and Limits for Outer Continental Shelf Leasing' (2013), *Environmental & Energy Law & Policy Journal*, 7(2), 155–189.

Kanbur, R., 'Economic Policy, Distribution and Poverty: The Nature of Disagreements' (2001), *World Development*, 29(6), 1083–1094.

Kant, I., *Perpetual Peace: A Philosophical Sketch*, translated by W. Hastie 1891 (Clark1795).

Kanuk, L., 'UNCTAD Code of Conduct for Liner Conferences: Trade Milestone or Millstone – Time Will Soon Tell, The Perspectives' (1984), *Northwestern Journal of International Law & Business*, 6(2), 357–372.

Karel, J., 'Consular Report: Reports from the Consuls of the United States on the Commerce, Manufactures, etc., of Their Consular Districts' (1897), vol. LV, no. 204.

Karel, J., *The Russian Coasting Trade: United States Consular Report 1897* (Government Printing Office1897).

Karunaratne, N., 'The Asian Miracle and Crisis: Rival Theories, the IMF Bailout and Policy Lessons' (1999), *Intereconomics*, January/February, 19–26.

Keane, C., Thompson, M. and Cockerell, J., '*Harper Review* Recommends Changes to Australia's Cabotage Regime and Liner Shipping Exemption' (2015), *Clyde & Co Newsletter*, 2 April.

Keat, D., 'The Liberalisation of Cabotage Policy is to Address the Peninsula–East Malaysia Trade Imbalance' (2009), *Trade and Logistics Malaysia*, 9 July.

Kennedy, K., 'GATT 1994', in P. Macrory, A. Appleton and M. Plummer (eds), *The World Trade Organization: Legal, Economic and Political Analysis* (vol. 1, Springer2007).

Kennedy, L. and Leslie, J., 'Options Paper: Approaches to Regulating Coastal Shipping in Australia' (Commonwealth of Australia, 2014).

Kevin, C. et al., 'Maritime Policy in China after WTO: Impacts and Implications for Foreign Investment' (2005), *Journal of Maritime Law & Commerce*, 36(1), 77–139.

Kilgour, J., 'The Energy Transportation Security Act of 1974' (1975), *Journal of Maritime Law and Commerce*, 7(4), 557–572.

Kissinger, H., 'The Congress of Vienna: A Reappraisal' (1956), *World Politics*, 8(2), 264–280.

Knight, W., *A Changing United Nations: Multilateral Evolution and the Quest for Global Governance* (Macmillan2000).

Knowler, G., 'Philippine Ports Ready for Rising Volumes After Cabotage Law Change' (2015), *Journal of Commerce*, 12 August.

Knowler, G., 'Scrap Cabotage Law to Cut Congestion and Costs, Philippine Agency Says' (2015), *Journal of Commerce*, 4 February.

Knowles, S. and Garces, A., 'Measuring Government Intervention and Estimating its Effect on Output: With Reference to the High Performing Asian Economies' (2000), CREDIT Research Paper 00/14, Centre for Research in Economic Development and International Trade, University of Nottingham.

Knowles, S. and Garces-Ozanne, A., 'Government Intervention and Economic Performance in East Asia' (2003), *Economic Development and Cultural Change*, 51(2), 451–477.

Koh, H., 'Why Do Nations Obey International Law?' (1997), Yale Law School Legal Scholarship Repository Faculty Scholarship Series, Paper 2101.

Koskenniemi, M., 'The Politics of International Law' (1990), *European Journal of International Law*, 1(1), 4–32.

Kraska, J., 'Grasping the Influence of Law On Sea Power' (2009), *Naval War College Review*, 62(3), 113–135.

Kraska, J., *Arctic Security in an Age of Climate Change* (Cambridge University Press2011).

Krugman, P., 'The Myth of Asia's Miracle' (1994), *Foreign Affairs*, 73(1), 62–78.

Kumar, S. and Hoffmann, J., 'Globalization: The Maritime Nexus', in C. Grammenos (ed.), *Handbook of Maritime Economics and Business* (Informa2002).

Kurniasari, N., 'Connecting Indonesia's Maritime Cabotage and the 1982 United Nations Convention on the Law of the Sea' (2011), *Indonesian Journal of International Law*, 8(4), 716–734.

Kvinge, T. and Odegard, A., 'Protectionism or Legitimate Protection? On Public Regulation of Pay and Working Conditions in Norwegian Maritime Cabotage' (2010), FAFO, Report 2010:30.

Lagoni, N., *The Liability of Classification Societies* (Springer2007).

Lalor, J., 'Coasting Trade', in *Cyclopaedia of Political Science, Political Economy, and of the Political History of the United States* (Maynard, Merrill & Co. 1881).

Lawrence, R. and Weinstein, D., 'Trade and Growth Import Led or Export Led? Evidence from Japan and Korea', in J. Stiglitz and S. Yusuf (eds), *Rethinking the East Asian Miracle* (Oxford University Press2001).

Leahy, J. and Pearson, S., 'Rousseff's Dream of Brazilian Shipbuilding Titan in Deep Water' (2015), *Financial Times*, 25 January.

Lee, G., 'Inter-Island Shipping Development in the ASEAN and the Pacific Region' (2012), Korean Maritime Institute, Seminar on the Development of an Integrated Transport and Logistics System in ASEAN Countries and Pacific Sub Region, 21–23 November, Bangkok.

Leeson, P., 'The Lewis Model and Development Theory' (1979), *The Manchester School*, 47(3), 196–210.

Lekakou, M. and Vitsounis, T., 'Market Concentration in Coastal Shipping and Limitations to Island's Accessibility' (2011), *Research in Transportation Business & Management*, 2(1), 74–82.

Lewis, J., 'Veiled Waters: Examining the Jones Act's Consumer Welfare Effect' (2013), *Issues in Political Economy*, 22(1), 77–107.

Lewis, W., 'Economic Development with Unlimited Supplies of Labour' (1954), Manchester School of Economics and Social Studies.

Li, K. and Wonham, J., 'New Developments in Ship Registration' (1999), *International Journal of Marine and Coastal Law*, 14(1), 137–146.

Li, X., 'Policy and Administrative Implications of the China Maritime Code 1992' (1996), *Logistics and Transportation Review*, 32(3), 301–318.

Li, X., Cullinane, K. and ChengJin, 'The Application of WTO Rules in China and the Implications for Foreign Direct Investment' (2003), *Journal of World Investment and Trade*, 4(2), 343–364.

Lianos, I., Mateus, A. and Raslan, A., 'Development Economics and Competition: A Parallel Intellectual History' (2012), Centre for Law, Economics and Society (CLES) Working Paper Series, 1/2012.

Lin, J. and Yao, Y., 'Chinese Rural Industrialization in the Context of the East Asian Miracle', in J. Stiglitz and S. Yusuf (eds), *Rethinking the East Asian Miracle* (Oxford University Press 2001).

List, F., *The National System of Political Economy*, translated by G. Matile, notes by H. Richelot and S. Colwell (1841 edn, J. B. Lippincott & Co. 1856).

Liu, C., *Maritime Transport Services in the Law of the Sea and the World Trade Organization* (Peter Lang2009)

Liversedge, B., 'What RINA Can Learn from Russia' (2013), *Superyacht News*, 13 June.

Llanto, G. and Navarro, A., 'The Impact of Trade Liberalization and Economic Integration on the Logistics Industry: Maritime Transport and Freight Forwarders' (2012), *Philippine Journal of Development*, 71(1/2), 95–117.

Llanto, G. and Navarro, A., 'Relaxing the Cabotage Restrictions in Maritime Transport' (2014), Senate Committee on Trade Commerce and Entrepreneurship.

Llanto, G., Basilio, E., and Basilio, L., 'Competition Policy and Regulation in Ports and Shipping' (2007), Philippine Institute for Development Studies, Research Paper Series No. 2007-04.

Lloyd's Register, 'Ship Recycling: Practice and Regulation Today' (2011), *Lloyd's Register*, June.

Lopes, V., 'Brazilian Cabotage Shipping Project' (2011), *Log-in*, n.d.

Lorca, A., 'Eurocentrism in the History of International Law', in B. Fassbender and A. Peters (eds), *The Oxford Handbook of the History of International Law* (Oxford University Press 2012).

Lorenzo, M., 'The Domestic Shipping Industry of the Philippines: A Situation Report' (1997), Maritime Industry Authority.

Lucas, R., 'On the Mechanics of Economic Development' (1988), *Journal of Monetary Economics*, 22(1), 3–42.

Lucas, R., 'On the Mechanics of Economic Development' (1988), *Journal of Monetary Economics*, 22(1), 3–42.

Luttrell, D., Atkinson, T. and Rosenblum, H., 'Assessing the Costs and Consequences of the 2007–09 Financial Crisis and Its Aftermath' (2013), *Economic Letter*, 8(7), 1–4.

Mafira, T., 'Shipping Transportation in Indonesia' (2013), Makarim & Taira, World Services Group, February.

Magee, K., 'U.S. Cabotage Laws: Protective or Damaging? A Strategy to Improve Cruise Vessel Competitiveness and Traffic to U.S. Ports' (2002), Monterey Institute of International Studies.

Mailer, G., 'Europe, the American Crisis, and Scottish Evangelism: The Primacy of Foreign Policy in the Kirk?', in W. Mulligan and B. Simms (eds), *The Primacy of Foreign Policy in British History, 1660–2000: How Strategic Concerns Shaped Modern Britain* (Palgrave Macmillan2010).

Mansell, J., *Flag State Responsibility: Historical Development and Contemporary Issues* (Springer2009).

Marcos, F., 'Do Developing Countries Need Competition Law and Policy?' (2006), Instituto de Empresa, Madrid.

MariNova Consulting Ltd, 'Ontario Marine Transportation Study: Phase II Final Report – Market Issues, Competitiveness, Opportunities and Recommendations' (2009), prepared for Ontario Ministry of Transportation and Ontario Marine Transportation Forum.

Maritime Administration, 'The Maritime Administration's Ready Reserve Force', (2014), *MARAD* (U.S. Department of Transportation).

Maritime Administration, 'United States Flag Privately-Owned Merchant Fleet: 2000–2014' (2014), *MARAD* (U.S. Department of Transportation).

Mark, J., 'The Battle of Kadesh and the First Peace Treaty' (2012), *Ancient History Encyclopedia* (online), 18 January.

Marle, G., 'Africa Presses for Cabotage Laws Despite Davos Warning' (2013), *The Loadstar*, 2 June.

Marten, B., *Port State Jurisdiction and the Regulation of International Merchant Shipping* (Springer2014).

Marvin, W., *The American Merchant Marine: Its History and Romance from 1620 to 1902* (Charles Scribner's Sons1902).

Matison, R., 'Economic Growths False Paradigm' (2014), *Market Oracle*, 27 January.

Mattos, J. and Acosta, M., *Maritime Transport Liberalization and the Challenges to Further its Implementation in Chile*, CEPAL, Serie Comercio International 43 (United Nations Publications2003).

May, R. et al., 'Unions and Union Membership in New Zealand: Annual Review for 2000' (2001), *New Zealand Journal of Industrial Relations*, 26(3), 317–329.

Maybury, D. and Tang, M., 'Australian Shipping Industry Reform: Coastal Trading Bill' (2012), *Shipping Legalseas*, February.

McGeorge, R., 'United States Coastwise Trading Restrictions: A Comparison of Recent Customs Service Rulings with the Legislative Purpose of the Jones Act and the Demands of a Global Economy' (1990), *Northwestern Journal of International Law & Business*, 11(1), 62–86.

McKeever, K., 'Researching Public International Law (2006), Columbia University, Arthur W. Diamond Law Library Research Guides (online).

McMahon, L., 'MLC 2006: Who is the Shipowner and Why Does It Matter?' (2013), *Lloyds List*, 22 August.

McNally, D., 'Turbulence in the World Economy' (1999), *Monthly Review*, 51(2), 38–52.

Medury, U., 'Effective Governance: The New Public Management Perspective', in P. Sahni and U. Medury (eds), *Governance for Development: Issues and Strategies* (Prentice-Hall2003).

Mehta, P. et al., 'Competition Policy and Consumer Policy: Complementarities and Conflicts in the Promotion of Consumer Welfare', in H. Qaqaya and G. Lipimile (eds), 'The Effects of Anti-Competitive Business Practices on Developing Countries and Their Development Prospects' (2008), UNCTAD, Geneva.

Melitz, M., 'When and How Should Infant Industries be Protected?' (2005), *Journal of International Economics*, 66(1), 177–196.

Mendes, P., *Cabotage in Air Transport Regulation* (Martinus Nijhoff1992).

Merk, O. and Li, J., 'The Competitiveness of Global Port-Cities: The Case of Hong Kong – China' (2013), OECD Regional Development Working Papers, 2013/16.

Mikelis, N., 'Ship Recycling Markets and the Impact of the Hong Kong Convention' (2013), International Maritime Organization'sInternational Conference on Ship Recycling, World Maritime University, Malmo, 7–9 April.

Mikelis, N., 'Responsible Recycling of Ships' (2014), *Cleaner Seas*, 6 June.

Mikelis, N., 'The Recycling of Ships' (2018), GMS.

Mikroulea, A., 'Competition and Public Service in Greek Cabotage', in A. Antapassis, L. Athanassiou and E. Rosaeg (eds) ,*Competition and Regulation in Shipping and Shipping Related Industries* (Martinus Nijhoff2009).

Molenaar, E., 'Options for Regional Regulation of Merchant Shipping Outside IMO, with Particular Reference to the Arctic Region' (2014), *Ocean Development and International Law*, 45(3), 272–298.

Moloney, S., 'Euros flag drive stepped up: EU presidency will draw up legislation with commission' (1994), *Lloyd's List*, 3 February.

Moore, J., 'UNCLOS Key to Increasing Navigational Freedom' (2008), *Texas Review of Law & Politics*, 12(2), 459–467.

Moran, C., 'The Legal Treatment of Vessels and Offshore Installations under the Mexican Foreign Investment and Navigation Frameworks' (2013), *Newsletter of the Maritime and Transport Law Committee of the International Bar Association*, 9(1).

Morano-Foadi, S., 'Citizen Migration within the European Research Area: The Italian Example', in A. Arranz et al. (eds), *New Europe, New World? The European Union, Europe, and the Challenges of the 21st Century* (Peter Lang2010).

Nafziger, E., *Economic Development* (5th edn, Cambridge University Press2012).

Nagle, G., *Development and Underdevelopment* (Thomas Nelson1998).

Nambiar, P., 'Stop Blaming Cabotage Policy' (2009), *Business Times*, n.d.

National Shipbuilding and Procurement Strategy Secretariat, 'Results of the National Shipbuilding and Procurement Strategy' (Government of Canada 19 October 2011)

Ncube, M., 'The Impact of Quantitative Easing in the US, Japan, the UK and Europe' (2014), African Development Bank, 12 February.

Neff, S., *War and the Law of Nations: A General History* (Cambridge University Press2005).

Norton, T., 'Rebuilding the South African Flagged Fleet' (2011), *Nautical Institute Online*, 8 September.

Nurkse, R., *Problems of Capital Formation in Underdeveloped Countries* (Oxford University Press1953).

O'Brien, J., *International Law* (Cavendish Publishing2001).

Oduntan, G., 'International Laws and the Discontented: Westernisation, the Development and the Underdevelopment of International Laws', in A. Dhanda and A. Parashar (eds), *Decolonisation of Legal Knowledge* (Taylor & Francis2009).

Organization for Economic Cooperation and Development (OECD), 'Understanding on Common Shipping Principles' (1993), OECD/LEGAL/5012.

Organization for Economic Cooperation and Development (OECD), 'Recommendation of the Council: Concerning Common Principles of Shipping Policy for Member Countries' (2000), C(2000)124/Final.

Organization for Economic Cooperation and Development (OECD), 'Regulatory Issues in International Maritime Transport' (2001). Available at www.oecd.org/sti/transport/ma ritimetransport/2065436.pdf.

Organization for Economic Cooperation and Development (OECD), 'Foreign Direct Investment for Development: Maximising Benefits, Minimising Costs' (2002), OECD Publications.

Organization for Economic Cooperation and Development (OECD), 'Ownership and Control of Ships' (2003), Maritime Transport Committee, Directorate for Science, Technology and Industry, March.

Oi, J., 'The Role of the Local State in China's Transitional Economy' (1995), *China Quarterly*, 144 (Special Issue: China's Transitional Economy), 1132–1149.

Okazaki, T., 'The Government-Firm Relationship in Postwar Japan: The Success and Failure of Bureau Pluralism', in J. Stiglitz and S. Yusuf (eds), *Rethinking the East Asian Miracle* (Oxford University Press2001).

Okeke, V. and Aniche, E., 'An Evaluation of the Effectiveness of the Cabotage Act 2003 on Nigerian Maritime Administration' (2012), *Sacha Journal of Policy and Strategic Studies*, 2(1), 12–28.

Okonjo-Iweala, N., 'Maritime Safety: Harnessing the Potential of Nigeria's Maritime Sector for Sustainable Economic Development' (2012), Presidential Retreat, Abuja.

Onis, Z., 'The Limits of Neoliberalism: Toward A Reformulation of Development Theory' (1995), *Journal of Economic*, 29(1), 97–119.

Oppenheim, L., 'The Meaning of Coasting-Trade in Commercial Treaties' (1908), *Law Quarterly Review*, 24(1), 328–330.

Oppenheim, L., 'The Subjects of the Law of Nations', in R. Roxburgh (ed.), *International Law: A Treatise* (vol. 1, 3rd edn, The Lawbook Exchange2005).

Oppenheim, L., *International Law: A Treatise* (vol. 1, Longmans Green & Co. 1905).

O'Rourke, R., 'DOD Leases of Foreign-Built Ships: Background for Congress' (2010), Congressional Research Service Report for Congress, 7-5700, 28 May.

Oxford Business Group, 'Malaysia: Shipping in Protected Waters' (2010), Oxford Business Group.

Oxford Economics, 'The Economic Impact of the UK Maritime Services Sector' (2013), Maritime UK.

Oxford Economics, 'The Economic Impact of the UK Maritime Services Sector' (2015), Maritime UK.

Oyedemi, W., 'Cabotage Regulations and the Challenges of Outer Continental Shelf Development in the United States' (2012), *Houston Journal of International Law*, 34(3), 607–651.

Paasman, B., *Multilateral Rules on Competition Policy: An Overview of the Debate*, CEPAL/ECLAC, Serie Comercio International 2 (United Nations Publications1999).

Pack, H., 'Technological Change and Growth in East Asia Macro versus Micro Perspectives', in J. Stiglitz and S. Yusuf (eds), *Rethinking the East Asian Miracle* (Oxford University Press2001).

Papastavridis, E., *The Interception of Vessels on the High Seas: Contemporary Challenges to the Legal Order of the Oceans* (Hart Publishing2013).

Papavizas, C. and Gardner, B., 'Coast Guard Rejects Industry Petition to Change Jones Act Vessel Rebuilding Regulations' (2012), Winston & Strawn LLP.

Parameswaran, B., *The Liberalization of Maritime Transport Services* (Springer2004).

Parr, J., 'On the Regional Dimensions of Rostow's Theory of Growth' (2001), *Review of Urban & Regional Development Studies*, 13(1), 2–19.

Parsloe, G., 'Biosecurity Busting Bugs have an Open Door with International Shipping' (2010), Maritime Union of New Zealand.

Pasinetti, L., *Structural Change and Economic Growth: A Theoretical Essay on the Dynamics of the Wealth of Nations* (Cambridge University Press1983).

Pastor, R., 'The Great Powers in an Age of Global Governance: Are They Still Great?', in J. Clarke and G. Edwards (eds), *Global Governance in the Twenty-first Century* (Palgrave Macmillan2004).

PaulJ., *Easing the Law on Container Transhipments Will Reduce Freight Rates and Boost Shipping* (2012), *Economic Times*, 6 September.

PDP Australia Pty Ltd and Meyrick & Associates, 'Promoting Efficient and Competitive Intra-ASEAN Shipping Services: Cambodia Country Report' (2005), REPSF Project 04/001, Final Report, March.

Pepa, R., 'How U.S. Neocolonial Development Failed the Philippines' (2013), *News Junkie Post*, 7 November.

Pera, A., 'Deregulation and Privatisation in an Economy-wide Context' (1989), *OECD Economic Studies*, 12(2), 159–204.

Perkins, J., 'Ship Registers: An International Update' (1997), *Tulane Maritime Law Journal*, 22(1), 197–199.

Petrova, R., 'Cabotage and the European Community Common Maritime Policy: Moving towards Free provision of Services in Maritime Transport' (1997), *Fordham International Law Journal*, 21(3), 1–76.

PF Collins, 'Temporary Importation of Vessels into Canada's Coasting Trade: Information for Contractors and Vessel Operators' (2014), PF Collins.

Phang, S., 'Competition Law and the International Transport Sectors' (2009), *Competition Law Review*, 5(2), 193–213.

Pieterse, J., *Development Theory* (2nd edn, SAGE Publications2010).

Podolny, J., 'A Status-Based Model of Market Competition' (1993), *American Journal of Sociology*, 98(4), 829–872.

Pontanus, J., *Discussiones Historicae de Mari Libero: Adversus Johannem Seldenum* (Harderwyck1637).

Porter, J., 'Australian Coastal Shipping: Navigating Regulatory Reform' (2015), *Australian and New Zealand Maritime Law Journal*, 29(1), 8–17.

Porter, M., *The Competitive Advantage of Nations* (Free Press1990).

Portes, A., 'Neoliberalism and the Sociology of Development: Emerging Trends and Unanticipated Facts' (1997), *Population and Development Review*, 23(2), 229–259.

Potter, P., *The Freedom of the Seas in History, Law and Politics* (Longmans1924).

Pouch, R., 'The U.S. Merchant Marine and Maritime Industry in Review' (1999), *Naval Institute Proceedings*, May, 104–111.

Powell, J., 'Protectionist Paradise?', in E. Hudgins (ed.), *Freedom to Trade: Refuting the New Protectionism* (Cato Institute1997).

Power, V., *EU Shipping Law* (3rd edn, Informa2015).

Preiser, W., 'History of The Law of Nations: Ancient Times to 1648', in R. Bernhardt (ed.), *Encyclopedia of Public International Law*, (7(1) (Elsevier1984).

Prisekina, N., 'Cabotage: Frequent Legal Issues for Contractors on Sakhalin Oil and Gas Projects' (2003), Russin & Vecchi LLP.

Qian, Y., 'Government Control in Corporate Governance as a Transitional Institution Lessons from China', in J. Stiglitz and S. Yusuf (eds), *Rethinking the East Asian Miracle* (Oxford University Press2001).

R. Churchill and A. Lowe, *The Law of the Sea* (2nd edn, Manchester University Press1988).

Rasmussen, W. et al., 'Evaluation of State Economic Development Incentives from a Firm's Perspective' (1982), *Business Economics*, 17(3), 23–29.

Raspotnik, A. and Rudloff, B., 'The EU as a Shipping Actor in the Arctic: Characteristics, Interests and Perspectives' (2012), Working Paper FG 2, 2012/Nr (Stiftung Wissenschaft und Politik), 4 December.

Rayfuse, R., *Non-Flag State Enforcement in High Seas Fisheries* (Martinus Nijhoff2004).

Reddie, J., *Researches, Historical and Critical, in Maritime International Law* (Thomas Clark1844).

Rees, G. and Smith, C., *Economic Development* (2nd edn, Macmillan Press1998).

Reuters, 'China Pushes to Build Its Own Ships to Deliver Gas' (2014), *New York Times*, 5 August.

Rhodes, T. and McDonald, G., 'Brazilian Shipyards: Industry in Crisis or Growing Pains?' (2014), CMS Cameron McKenna.

Rhodes, T. and McDonald, G., 'Brazilian Shipyards: Industry in Crisis or Growing Pains?' (2014), CMS Cameron McKenna Nabarro Olswang LLP, *Lexology*.

Robinson, S. et al., *Industrialization and Growth: A Comparative Study* (Oxford University Press1986).

Rodger, B. and MacCulloch, A., *Competition Law and Policy in the EC and UK* (4th edn, Routledge-Cavendish2009).

Rodrigue, J. et al., *The Geography of Transport Systems* (3rd edn, Routledge2013).

Rodríguez, A., 'The Role of Merger Policy in Recently Liberalized Economies' (1996), Monterey Institute of Advanced Technological Studies.

Rodrik, D., 'King Kong Meets Godzilla: The World Bank and the East Asian Miracle', inA. Fishlow et al. (eds), *Miracle or Design? Lessons from the East Asian Experience* (Overseas Development Council 1994).

Rodrik, D., *The Developing Countries' Hazardous Obsession with Global Integration* (Harvard University Press2001).

Roermund, B., 'The Coalition of the Willing: Or Can Sovereignty Be Shared?' (2005) *Journal of the European Ethics Network*, 12(4), 443–464.

Ross, M., 'The Political Economy of the Resource Curse' (1999), *World Politics*, 51(2), 297–322.

Rostow, W., 'The Take-off to self-Sustained Growth' (1956), *Economic Journal*, 66(1), 25–48.

Rostow, W., *The Stages of Economic Growth: A Non-Communist Manifesto* (3rd edn, Cambridge University Press1990).

Rothwell, D. and Stephens, T., *The International Law of the Sea* (Hart Publishing2010).

Rowbotham, M,. *Introduction to Marine Cargo Management* (2nd edn, Routledge2014).

Rozas, R., 'Shipping and Transport – Chile: Potential Regulatory Changes in the Cabotage Trade' (2011), *International Law Office*.

Rudder, G., 'China Revamps Cabotage for Empties' (2003), *Journal of Commerce*, 6 July.

Sampson, H., 'Maritime Futures: Jobs and Training for UK Ratings' (2015), Seafarers International Research Centre, January.

Samuelson, A., *Foundations of Economic Analysis* (Harvard University Press1947).

Sanyal, S., 'Cabotage: To Keep or Relax?' (2011), *The Hindu Business Line*, 20 November.

Sarel, M., 'Growth in East Asia: What We Can and What We Cannot Infer' (1997), *Economic Issues*, 1(1), 1–22.

Schilirò, D., 'Structural Change and Models of Structural Analysis: Theories, Principles and Methods' (2012), Munich Personal RePEc Archive, MPRA Paper No. 41817.

Schmidt, K., 'Managerial Incentives and Product Market Competition' (1997), *Review of Economic Studies*, 64(2), 191–213.

Schneiderman, D., 'Globalisation, Governance, and Investment Rules', in J. Clarke and G. Edwards (eds), *Global Governance in the Twenty-first Century* (Palgrave Macmillan2004).

Schulz, G., 'Cabotage in the Asia Pacific: A Brief Overview' (2011), *Shipping Legalseas*, January.

Sefara, A., 'Achieving Access to the Maritime Transport Services Market in the European Union: A Critical Discussion of Cabotage Services' (2014), *Australian Journal of Maritime & Ocean Affairs*, 6(2), 106–110.

Shafaeddin, M., 'Trade Liberalization and Economic Reform in Developing Countries: Structural Change or De-industrialization?', in A. Paloni and M. Zanardi (eds), *The IMF, World Bank and Policy Reform* (Routledge2006).

Sharma, K. and Herath, G., 'Trade Orientation, Growth and Poverty: What have We Learned From the Asia Experience', inK. Sharma (ed.), *Trade Policy, Growth and Poverty in Asian Developing Countries* (Routledge2003).

Shekhar, V. and Liow, J., *Indonesia as a Maritime Power: Jokowi's Vision, Strategies, and Obstacles Ahead* (Brookings Institution Press2014).

Shepherd, A. et al., *Towards Responsible Government: The Report of the National Commission of Audit, Phase II* (Commonwealth of Australia2014).

Singer, H., 'Dualism Revisited: A New Approach to the Problems of Dual Societies in Developing Countries' (1970), *Journal of Development Studies*, 7(1): 60–61.

Singh, A., '"The Market-Friendly Approach to Development" vs. an "Industrialised Policy": A Critique of the World Development Report 1991 and an Alternative Policy Perspective' (1993), Instituto Nacional de Educación Física (INEF) Report 4/1993.

Skinner, G., 'The Neoclassical Counterrevolution and Developing Economies: A Case Study of Political and Economic Changes in the Philippines' (2007), *Social Sciences Journal*, 7(1), 51–58.

Slattery, B., Riley, B., and Loris, N., 'Sink the Jones Act: Restoring America's Competitive Advantage in Maritime-Related Industries' (2014), Heritage Foundation Backgrounder, No. 2886.

Slow, R., 'A Contribution to the Theory of Economic Growth' (1956), *Quarterly Journal of Economics*, 1(70), 65–94.

Smith, A., 'An Inquiry into the Nature and Causes of the Wealth of Nations', in J. McCulloch (ed.), *With a Life of the Author: An Introductory Discourse, Notes, and Supplemental Dissertations* (vol. IV, Longman1828), 378.

Smith, F., 'Sustainable Development: A Free Market Perspective' (1994), *Boston College Environmental Affairs Law Review*, 28(2), 297–308.

Sokol, D. and Stephan, A., 'Prioritizing Cartel Enforcement in Developing World Competition Agencies', in D. Sokol, T. Cheng and L. Ioannis (eds), *Competition Law and Development* (Stanford University Press2013).

Soles, P. and Wilson, C., 'The Changing Arctic: Increasing Marine Risk and Evolving Governance' (2014), 33rd PIANC International Navigation Congress: Navigating the New Millenium, San Francisco, 1–5 June.

Solow, M., 'A Contribution to the Theory of Economic Growth' (1956), *Quarterly Journal of Economics*, 1(70), 65–94.

Sornarajah, M., 'The Asian Perspective to International Law in the Age of Globalization' (2001), *Singapore Journal of International & Corporative Law*, 5(1), 284–313.

South African Maritime Safety Authority, 'Maritime Sector Skills Development Study' (2011), Department of Transport.

Staker, C., 'Jurisdiction: The Individual and the International Legal System', in M. Evans (ed.), *International Law* (4th edn, Oxford University Press2014).

Stiglitz, J., 'From Miracle to Crisis to Recovery: Lessons from Four Decades of East Asian Experience', in J. Stiglitz and S. Yusuf (eds), *Rethinking the East Asian Miracle* (Oxford University Press2001).

Stiglitz, J., 'Trade and the Developing World: A New Agenda' (1999), *Current History Magazine*, November, 387–393.

Stoler, A., 'The Current State of the WTO' (2003), Workshop on the EU, the US and the WTO, Stanford University, 28 February–1 March.

Stoler, A., 'Will the WTO have Functional Value in the Mega-Regional World of FTAs?', in R. Meléndez-Ortiz (ed.), 'Strengthening the Multinational Trading System: Regional Trade Agreements Group; Proposals and Analysis' (2013), International Centre for Trade and Sustainable Development (ICTSD), December.

Stucke, M., 'Is competition always good?' (2013), *Journal of Antitrust Enforcement*, 1(1), 162–197.

Sucharitkul, S., 'Liability and Responsibility of the State of Registration or the Flag State in Respect of Sea-going Vessels, Aircraft and Spacecraft Registered by National Registration Authorities' (2006), *American Journal of Comparative Law*, 54, American Law in the 21st Century: U.S. National Reports to the XVII International Congress of Comparative Law (Fall), 409–442.

Suffian, F., Rosline, A. and Karim, M., 'The Cabotage Policy: Is It Still Relevant in Malaysia?', in R. Hashim and A. Majeed (eds), *Proceedings of the Colloquium on Administrative Science and Technology* (Springer2015).

Sun, G., and Zhang, S., 'Chinese Shipping Policy and the Impact of its Development', in T. Lee et al. (eds), *Shipping in China* (Ashgate Publishing2002).

Syrquin, M. and Chenery, H., *Patterns of Development, 1950–70* (Oxford University Press 1975).

Syrquin, M., 'Patterns of Structural Change', in H. Chenery and T. Srinivasan (eds), *Handbook of Development Economics* (vol. 1, Elsevier1989).

Tapia, J., 'From the Oil Crisis to the Great Recession: Five Crisis of the World Economy' (2013), University of Michigan.

Taylor, L., 'The Revival of the Liberal creed: The IMF and the World Bank in a Globalized Economy' (1997), *World Development*, 25(2), 145–152.

Taylor, M., *International Competition Law: A New Dimension for the WTO?* (2nd edn, Cambridge University Press2006).

Teo, C., 'Competition Policy and Economic Growth' (2003), ASEAN Conference on Fair Competition Law and Policy in the ASEAN Free Trade Area, Bali, 4–8 March.

The Maritime Executive (MarEX), 'Shanghai's New Cabotage Laws: A Disappointment' (2013), MarEX, 18 December.

The Ministry of Communication of the People's Republic of China, *China Shipping Development Report 1999* (Renmin Jiaotong Press2000).

The World Bank, *The East Asian Miracle: Economic Growth and Public Policy* (Oxford University Press1993).

The World Bank, *World Development Report 1983* (Oxford University Press1983).

The World Bank, *World Development Report 1991: The Challenge of Development* (Oxford University Press1991).

Thirlwall, A., *Economics of Development* (9th edn, Palgrave Macmillan2011).

Thompson, S., Springall, R. and Brewar, H., *A Guide to the Coastal Trading Reforms in Australia* (Holman Fenwick Willan2012).

Thornton, H., 'John Selden's Response to Hugo Grotius: The Argument for Closed Seas' (2006), *International Journal of Maritime History*, 18(2), 105–128.

Tibbetts, G., 'Arab Navigation in the Archipelago', in T. Hellwig and E. Tagliacozzo (eds), *The Indonesia Reader: History, Culture, Politics* (Duke University Press2009).

Tirschwell, P., 'Stakeholder Split on Impact of India's Relaxed Cabotage Rule' (2018), *Journal of Commerce*, 4 June.

Todaro, M. and Smith, S., *Economic Development* (12th edn, Pearson Education Limited 2015).

Toomey, D., 'Global Scarcity: Scramble for Dwindling Natural Resources' (2012), *Yale Environment 360*, 23 May.

Toye, J., *Dilemmas of Development: Reflections on the Counter-Revolution in Development Theory and Policy* (Blackwell1987).

Transport Canada, *Use of International Marine Containers in Canada* (Government of Canada2012).

Transportation Institute, *Jones Act/Domestic Shipping* (Transportation Institute2009).

UNCTAD, 'Guidelines towards the Application of the Convention on a Code of Conduct for Liner Conferences' (1986), UNCTAD.

UNCTAD, 'Economic Consequences of the Existence of Lack of a Genuine Link between Vessel and Flag of Registry' (1997), TD/B/c.4/168, UNCTAD.

UNCTAD, 'The Role of Competition Policy in Promoting Economic Development: The Appropriate Design and Effectiveness of Competition Law and Policy' (2010), TD/RBP/CONF.7/3, UNCTAD.

Underhill, G., 'Global Governance and Political Economy: Public, Private and Political Authority in the Twenty-first Century', in J. Clarke and G. Edwards (eds), *Global Governance in the Twenty-first Century* (Palgrave Macmillan2004).

UNEP, ITC and ICTSD, 'Trade and Environment Briefings: International Transport; ICTSD Programme on Global Economic Policy and Institutions' (2012), Policy Brief No. 5, International Centre for Trade and Sustainable Development.

Union of Brazilian Shipowners, 'The Brazilian Coastwise Traffic' (2010), Syndarma.

Urata, S., 'Emergence of an FDI Trade Nexus and Economic Growth in East Asia', in J. Stiglitz and S. Yusuf (eds), *Rethinking the East Asian Miracle* (Oxford University Press 2001).

U.S. Department of Justice, 'Final Report of the International Competition Policy Advisory Committee to the Attorney General and Assistant Attorney General for Antitrust' (2000).

Van Cayseele, P., 'Market Structure and Innovation: A Survey of the Last Twenty Years' (1998), *De Economist*, 146(3), 391–417.

VanGrasstek, C., 'The History and Future of the World Trade Organization' (2013), World Trade Organization.

Vasuki-Rao, N., 'India Relaxes Cabotage Law to Ease Nehru Congestion' (2005), *Journal of Commerce*, n.d.

Venunath, M., 'India Prepares to Ease Cabotage Rules' (2014), *IHS Maritime 360*, 7 December.

Veon, J., *The United Nations Global Straightjacket* (Hearthstone1999).

Vianna, G., 'Cabotage Industry Faces Major Challenges to Growth' (2007), Shipping & Transport, Brazil, *International Law Office*, 22 August.

Wade, R., *Governing the Market: Economic Theory and the Role of Government in East Asian Industrialization* (Princeton University Press1990).

Wallace, R. and Martin-Ortega, O., *International Law* (7th edn, Sweet & Maxwell2013).

Wang, K., 'Foreign Trade Policy and Apparatus of the People's Republic of China' (1973), *Law and Contemporary Problems*, 38(2), 182–200.

Warr, P., 'Poverty Reduction and Sectoral Growth in South-East Asia', in K. Sharma (ed.), *Trade Policy, Growth and Poverty in Asian Developing Countries* (Routledge 2003).

Webb, R., 'Coastal Shipping: An Overview' (2004), Information and Research Services Parliamentary Library Research Paper No. 12 2003–04, 3 May.

Wee, V., 'China Cabotage Rules benefit Hong Kong: HIT' (2013), *Seatrade Maritime News*, 10 October.

Wee, V., 'INSA Sees Local Owners Dominating Offshore by 2015' (2014), *Seatrade Maritime News*, 14 April.

Weil, D., *Economic Growth* (3rd edn, Prentice Hall2013).

Weisbrot, M., 'Globalism on the Ropes', in R. Broad (ed.), *Global Backlash: Citizen Initiatives for a Just World Economy* (Rowman & Littlefield2002).

Weiss, L., 'Global Governance, National Strategies: How Industrialized States Make Room to Move Under the WTO' (2005), *Review of International Political Economy* 12(5), 723–749.

Whitehurst, C., *American Domestic Shipping in Domestic Ships: Jones Act Costs, Benefits and Options* (American Enterprise Institute Press 1985).

Williamson, J., 'The Progress of Policy Reform in Latin America' (1990), *Policy Analyses in International Economics*, 28(J1), 1–83.

Woods, S. et al., 'Cabotage Regime: Implications for Foreign Owners, Operators and Financiers' (2012), *Marine Money*, 25 March.

World Bank, 'New Directions in Development Thinking', in G. Secondi (ed.), *The Development Economics Reader* (Routledge2008).

World Bank, *World Development Report 1991: The Challenge of Development* (Oxford University Press 1991).

World Commission on Environment and Development, *Our Common Future* (The Brundtland Report) (Oxford University Press1987).

World Economic Forum, *Enabling Trade: Valuing Growth Opportunities* (Bain & Company and the World Bank2013).

World Maritime News, 'Chinese Shipyards Vying to Enter LNG Market' (2014), *World Maritime News*, 5 August.

World Trade Organization (WTO), 'Communication from the European Communities and its Member States' (2005). TN/S/O/EEC/Rev.1. 05–2792.

World Trade Organization (WTO), 'How Can the WTO Help Harness Globalization?' (2007), World Trade Organization Forum, Geneva, 4–5 October.

World Trade Organization (WTO), 'Synthesis Paper on the Relationship of Trade and Competition Policy to Development and Economic Growth' (1998), WT/WGTCP/W/80.

World Trade Organization (WTO), 'The Fundamental Principles of Competition Policy' (1999), WT/WGTCP/W/127.

Yataro, I., 'Patriotic Duty and Business Success: Letter to Mitsubishi Employees' (1876), Mitsubishi.

Yoshizaki, H.. et al., 'Integration of International and Cabotage Container Shipping in Brazil', in J. Bookbinder (ed.), *Handbook of Global Logistics: Transportation in International Supply Chain* (Springer Science & Business Media2013).

Yost, W., 'Jonesing For a Taste of Competition: Why an Antiquated Maritime Law Needs Reform' (2013), *Roger Williams University Law Review*, 18(1), 52–77.

Young, A., 'Lessons from the East Asian NICs: A Contrarian View' (1994), *European Economic Review*, 38(3–4), 964–973.

Young, O., 'Arctic Governance: Pathways to the Future' (2010), *Arctic Review on Law and Politics*, 1(2), 164–185.

Young Power in Social Action (YPSA), 'Benefits from Ship Breaking' (2012), *Ship Breaking in Bangladesh*, YPSA.

Yusuf, S., 'The East Asian Miracle at the Millennium', in J. Stiglitz and S. Yusuf (eds), *Rethinking the East Asian Miracle* (Oxford University Press2001).

Zhang, K. et al., 'China (Shanghai) Pilot Free Trade Zone (SH PFTZ)' (2014), PwC Group, February.

Zheng, J., Meng, Q. and Sun, Z., 'Impact Analysis of Maritime Cabotage Legislations on Liner Hub-and-Spoke Shipping Network Design' (2014), *European Journal of Operational Research*, 234(3), 874–884.

# Index

Printed in the United States
by Baker & Taylor Publisher Services